Counseling the Contemporary Woman

Counseling the Contemporary Woman

Strategies and Interventions Across the Lifespan

edited by
Suzanne Degges-White
Marcela Kepic
Wendy Killam

ROWMAN & LITTLEFIELD
Lanham • Boulder • New York • London

Executive Editor: Mark Kerr
Assistant Editor: Courtney Packard
Production Editor: Kellie Hagan
Cover Designer: Sally Rinehart

Published by Rowman & Littlefield
An imprint of The Rowman & Littlefield Publishing Group, Inc.
4501 Forbes Boulevard, Suite 200, Lanham, Maryland 20706
www.rowman.com

6 Tinworth Street, London SE11 5AL

British Library Cataloguing in Publication Information Available

Library of Congress Cataloging-in-Publication Data

Names: Degges-White, Suzanne, author. | Kepic, Marcela, 1976–, author. | Killam, Wendy K., author.
Title: Counseling the contemporary woman : strategies and interventions across the lifespan / Suzanne Degges-White, Marcela Kepic, Wendy Killam.
Description: Lanham : Rowman & Littlefield Publishing Group, 2020. | Includes bibliographical references and index. | Summary: "This book provides a unique perspective on the development, challenges, and needs of women as they navigate through life. It includes culturally diverse case studies, interventions, and best practices for counselors working with women across the lifespan. Topics include normative developmental issues, relationships, self-esteem, body image, addictions, parenting, caregiving, and loss"—Provided by publisher.
Identifiers: LCCN 2019050782 (print) | LCCN 2019050783 (ebook) | ISBN 9781538123607 (cloth) | ISBN 9781538123614 (paperback) | ISBN 9781538123621 (epub)
Subjects: LCSH: Women—Counseling of. | Women—Psychology. | Teenage girls—Counseling of. | Counseling psychology.
Classification: LCC HQ1206 .D3584 2020 (print) | LCC HQ1206 (ebook) | DDC 155.3/33—dc23
LC record available at https://lccn.loc.gov/2019050782
LC ebook record available at https://lccn.loc.gov/2019050783

Contents

Acknowledgments

This project is the culmination of the efforts of many individuals who are dedicated to doing what they can to better the lives of others. We celebrate the investment of energy and time by all of the clinicians who work with women, as well as the energy and time invested by their clients who work on themselves. We are grateful to everyone who advocates for the needs of women and to those who strive to provide the best care they can. We hope this book provides helpful information as well as validation of the work that is done to enhance the lives of others. We also would like to acknowledge the support of our editorial team at Rowman & Littlefield, including Courtney Packard and Mark Kerr.

Acknowledgments

Part I

Foundational Perspectives and Theory

Chapter One

Reenvisioning the Feminine Ideal

Women Are the Sum of Many Diverse Parts

Adrienne N. Erby

Throughout the lifespan, women and girls receive explicit and implicit messages about the value and roles they hold in society. These messages are heavily shaped by cultural values; however, it is also important to recognize that many of these cultural values are steeped in systems of oppression, including sexism, genderism, patriarchy, and androcentrism (Singh & Mingo, 2018). These intertwined systems of oppression directly and indirectly affect people of all genders, setting standards, rules, and norms about gender identity, expression, and behavior. Gender typing begins early in development as children are socialized into a gender binary that gives differential value to boys and girls while overlooking nonbinary and gender-variant identities entirely. Children quickly associate behaviors with gender and assign value based on the gendered norms and ideals that pervade all aspects of society, from preschool teachers to mass media (Comstock, 2005). The "feminine ideal" typically refers to a narrow, culturally laden visage of valued womanhood, encompassing both appearance and behavior. An online search for stock photos using the phrase "all-American girl" yielded results of mostly white, thin, young, able-bodied, feminine women with flowing blond hair. This image is often set as the standard for women, creating a restrictive lens through which all women are evaluated and most often found wanting. These images belie the breadth of women's diversity and communicate clear cultural messages about American womanhood.

Given this context, it is not surprising that women and girls as well as transgender and gender nonconforming individuals in the United States face unique physical and mental health risks connected to gender-specific issues such as gender conformity, role overload, and body image (American

Psychological Association [APA], 2018; Crissman, Stroumsa, Kobernik, & Berger, 2019; Glynn, Maclean, Forte, & Cohen, 2009). These and other issues of health information, health-care access, and health risks are identified for women and girls around the globe. Women are disproportionately impacted by sexual violence and intimate partner violence, as well as health and income disparities (APA, 2018; James et al., 2016; Planty, Langston, Krebs, Berzofsky, & Smiley-McDonald, 2013; Singh & Mingo, 2018; Vardeman-Winter, 2017). Even within these issues, there is considerable intragroup (i.e., within-group) variation that is not strictly dichotomous. To provide effective counseling, counselors must understand women's experience and issues through a multifaceted lens that fully embraces cultural diversity and complexity.

Sue and Sue's (2013) tripartite model addressing individual, cultural, and universal factors provides the most comprehensive frame of personal identity, in which all individuals, in many respects, are (a) like no other individual, (b) like some individuals, or (c) like all other individuals (p. 41). First, individual uniqueness entails factors specific to the individual, such as genetic specificity, convergence of multiple social identity groups, and lived experience. As each woman's experience differs from all other women's experiences, understanding the individual is fundamental to ethical counseling practice. But individual experience does not occur in a vacuum; rather, experience is influenced and shaped by a cultural and sociopolitical context that all people are affected by and contribute to. Cultural identity reflects the most complex element of identity, including areas of shared identities and experiences, such as being Southeast Asian or being a woman. Within these cultural groupings, there is still wide variation and overlap that cannot be conceptualized in an additive form. As Bowleg (2008) stated, "Black + lesbian + woman ≠ Black lesbian woman," suggesting that shared membership in each group does not result in a uniform experience. Lastly, universal dimensions of identity include factors common to all people, such as the ability to use symbols and experience emotions. It is at this universal level that counselors initiate the professional relationship, demonstrating respect and value for each person on a human level. From this point, counselors build knowledge and understanding of cultural and individual identity. The challenge for counselors is attending to all domains of identity and recognizing that each is influenced by regional, national, and global contexts that socially locate identity and experience. In this chapter, the cultural domain will be emphasized, specifically examining cultural complexity, identity salience, identity convergence, and sociopolitical context in counseling women.

MULTICULTURAL AND SOCIAL JUSTICE COUNSELING FOUNDATIONS

Historically, the mental health professions emphasized an individual or universal approach to understanding personal development and mental health issues, prevention, and treatment, largely ignoring culture and context. In the 1960s and 1970s, the mental health professions experienced a radical shift led by counselors and psychologists of color from focusing solely on individual and universal approaches to multicultural counseling approaches that encompassed individual, cultural, and universal factors (Jackson, 1995). Their critical examination identified culturally laden, Eurocentric assumptions in the "neutral" universal-and-individual-focused counseling approaches (Katz, 1985; Sue & Sue, 1977). The multicultural approach specifically focused on racial cultural values and norms in counseling as well as the impact of privilege and oppression with four racially minoritized populations in the United States, including African Americans, Asian Americans, Native Americans, and Latinx populations.

Within-group diversity and other identities, such as gender and affectional/sexual orientation, were nominally addressed, but the emphasis was predominantly racial (Ratts, Singh, Nassar-McMillan, Butler, & McCullough, 2016). This was in large part due to the noticeable absence of race and culture in counseling theory and practice. While a narrow focus was necessary at the time, continued development in multicultural and social justice indicated a need to more fully examine cultural complexity, both to understand individual experience and the interconnected nature of oppressive systems. In the 1990s and 2000s, the multicultural movement expanded to cultural identities outside of race, commonly including gender and sexual orientation. However, there were still considerable limitations in the practice of multicultural counseling. Identifying salient cultural factors easily allowed for between-group comparisons (e.g., white people and people of color); however, client experiences in counseling indicated that counselors often overlook the sociopolitical realities of their experiences, multiple identities, and within-group variation (Hunt, Matthews, Milsom, & Lammel, 2006; McCullough et al., 2017). Solely addressing dichotomous categories of identity can result in cultural stereotyping, rather than multicultural counseling, ignoring the caution of early scholars (Sue & Sue, 1977) against overgeneralization and oversimplification.

To address these issues, the Multicultural Counseling Competencies (Arredondo et al., 1996; Sue, Arredondo, & McDavis, 1992) were revised in 2015. The Multicultural and Social Justice Counseling Competencies (MSJCC; Ratts, Singh, Nassar-McMillan, Butler, & McCullough, 2015) shifted the counseling profession toward a more comprehensive framework of multicultural counseling, operationalizing the definition set forth by the

American Counseling Association (ACA) (2014) as "counseling that recognizes diversity and embraces approaches that support the worth, dignity, potential, and uniqueness of individuals within their historical, cultural, economic, political, and psychosocial contexts" (p. 20). The MSJCC embraced the complexity of cultural identity and multilayered sociopolitical contexts, emphasizing intersectionality as a meaningful framework for counselors because of its complexity and flexibility.

INTERSECTIONALITY: A CRITICAL LENS FOR WOMEN'S ISSUES

Intersectionality is rooted in a critical black feminist tradition that can be traced back to freedwoman and activist Sojourner Truth, whose 1851 speech "Ain't I a Woman" radically challenged homogenous images of women's experience. In illuminating racialized gender experiences, Truth called for women's rights leaders to address the marginalization of all women and acknowledge the erasure of black women in women's rights political movements. Even Truth's speech can only be understood through two drastically different versions that were provided as transcriptions by two white women (Siebler, 2010). In 1977, the Combahee River Collective, a black feminist group in Boston, Massachusetts, issued a powerful positionality statement addressing racism, sexism, classism, and heterosexism from their unique experiences as black women. In opposition to the narrow, culturally laden, and oppressive gender molds promulgated by white women and black men, they stated, "We reject pedestals, queenhood, and walking ten paces behind. To be recognized as human, levelly human is enough" (Combahee River Collective, 1977, p. 4). Their statement gave voice to many women of color, often sidelined by the single-issue politics of the black liberation and women's rights movements. Women existing outside of the white, middle-class, able-bodied, heterosexual Christian feminine ideal were frequently othered, relegated to the status of outsider. It is from this "outsider within" social location that Collins's (2000) black feminist thought and intersectionality (Collins & Bilge, 2016) emerge.

Women of color have actively deconstructed white, Western ideals of womanhood and shaped critical discourse on gender through an intersectionality lens that addresses race, gender, and other cultural identities as multifaceted, interactive, and sociopolitically situated. From this philosophical grounding, Crenshaw (1988, 1989, 1991) coined the term "intersectionality" as a conceptual tool through which to examine the ways multiple systems of oppression interact and influence one another. Intersectionality theorists (Collins, 2000; Collins & Bilge, 2016; Crenshaw, 1989, 1991) challenge dominant views of social inequality along a single axis (e.g., gender) that only conceptualize between-group issues (e.g., men and women). Instead, intersectionality is used to examine social issues via the interactions within categories (e.g., race and gender) across multiple systems (e.g., individual and institutional racism and sexism). Collins and Bilge (2016) state, "Rather than seeing people as a homogenous, undifferentiated mass, intersectionality provides a framework for explaining how social divisions of race, gender, age, and citizenship status, among others, positions people differently in the world, especially in relation to global inequality" (p. 15).

Intersectionality adopts a multidimensional perspective to interwoven cultural identities through a prism of systemic privilege and oppression (Bowleg, 2008, 2013; Watts-Jones, 2010). The six core features of intersectionality include social inequality, power, relationality, social context, complexity, and social justice, which are typically present in application of an intersectionality framework (Collins & Bilge, 2016). Intersectionality has been used to interrogate problems of *social inequality* through recognition of multifaceted domains of *power*, which can include structural, disciplinary, cultural, and interpersonal domains. *Relationality* refers to the interconnectedness of different forms of oppression; that is, understanding how multiple oppressive systems relate to one another in different and interactive ways (e.g., racism, genderism, and sexism as complementary) in shaping experience. Thus, instead of focusing on how race and gender may differ, intersectionality emphasizes their commonalities and the implications of these intersections (Bowleg, 2012; Bowleg, Huang, Brooks, Black, & Burkholder, 2003). Further, contributing factors, interactions, and consequences of interrelated systems of social inequality must be understood within a given *social context* to have meaning. Therefore, it is important to contextualize power, relationality, and inequality in a social context (e.g., counseling practice in the United States). These interconnections result in a *complexity* that exceeds the reach of single-issue (e.g., race or gender) perspectives. Lastly, *social justice* speaks to the purpose of intersectionality; Collins and Bilge (2016) maintain that social justice is not a requirement of intersectionality but recognize that social justice action is often the purpose of its use. Thus, intersectionality serves as a practical lens through which to examine privilege and oppression as experienced by women from their different social locations.

ADDRESSING THE COMPLEXITY OF WOMEN'S DIVERSITY

Hays (1996, 2016) developed the ADDRESSING model to outline several dimensions of cultural diversity for conceptualizing client issues and experiences. The ADDRESSING model includes **a**ge and generational influences, **d**evelopmental or other **d**isability, **r**eligion and spiritual orientation, **e**thnic and racial identity, **s**ocioeconomic status, **s**exual orientation, **i**ndigenous heritage, **n**ational origin, and **g**ender. Within these cultural dimensions, there are a variety of issues and experiences that must be considered in conjunction with gender. It is helpful to understand some contextual issues specific to women across multiple aspects of cultural diversity, while highlighting relationality and overlap across cultural domains. While each domain of the model could be its own chapter, this chapter introduces intersectionality from a gendered framework using the ADDRESSING model as a guide. Instead of addressing gender separately, gender will be interwoven throughout each dimension of the model.

Age and Generational Influences

Generational influences heavily affect how women and girls understand gender roles, career possibilities, competence, attractiveness, and body image. Downing and Roush's (1985) conceptual model of feminist identity development outlined the process of moving from passive acceptance of sexism and patriarchy to active commitment to dismantling sexism from a position of identity achievement, described as the often-unachieved apex of feminist identity. While not the final stage, the preceding stage of synthesis was described as the highest stage typically achieved. Each wave of feminism had its own distinct emphasis and societal perception, which strongly connects to women's alignment with a feminist label. Research found that both feminist and nonfeminist women endorsed items corresponding to strength, independence, and identity as a woman, with younger women rarely identifying previous inconsistent views (Erchull et al., 2009). Erchull et al. (2009) concluded that the gains of the feminist movements may have shifted younger women's perceptions of womanhood, suggesting that Downing and Roush's (1985) synthesis stage may be a starting point, in contrast to previous generations. In addition to these generational influences, ageism, adultism, ableism, and sexism intertwine in a youth-oriented society that negatively frames women's aging, while simultaneously dismissing the self-determination and agency of younger women. By connecting much of women's value to their appearance and ability, negativity toward aging can engender dissatisfaction and feelings of inadequacy in women of all ages (Comstock, 2005; Dougherty, Dorr, & Pulice, 2016).

Developmental or Other Disability

Disabilities are typically conceptualized through two frameworks. The first, the biological or medical model, focuses primarily on "fixing" or managing medical aspects of disability. In this model, professionals primarily emphasize medical interventions and symptom management. Despite the medicalization of disability, women with disabilities show significant disparities in health-care access, reporting less access compared to women without disabilities and men with disabilities, according to the 2006 National Health Interview Survey (Smith, 2008). The second model, termed the social or sociopolitical model, frames disability from a minoritized group perspective and recognizes the societal barriers and challenges for people with disabilities. Without negating medical, physical, mental, psychological, developmental, or other factors in disability, the social model largely focuses on access and equitable treatment regarding attitudinal, physical, and communication barriers (Berens & Erford, 2018). The social model strongly aligns with a multicultural counseling approach in conceptualizing minoritized identities, oppression, and attitudinal and institutional barriers. Women with visible disabilities are often viewed as less attractive and less capable, perpetuating a "weaker sex" sexist narrative. This intertwined ableism and sexism exacerbates sexist stereotypes of women's intelligence and competence and can create barriers in multiple life domains, particularly in vocational and career development (Noonan et al., 2004).

Religion and Spiritual Orientation

Religion and spirituality play an important role in culture and identity. A national survey (Pew Research Center, 2015a) indicates that 77 percent of participants identified religion as somewhat to very important in their lives. This is particularly relevant as gender roles and expectations are often shaped by religious doctrine and mores. This can include restricted gendered roles in religious service (e.g., nuns and priests) or day-to-day norms regarding male-dominated household structures and expectations of women's modesty, sexuality, and reproductive decision making. Frame (2003) suggests that spirituality encompasses "values, beliefs, mission, awareness, subjectivity, experience, sense of purpose and direction, and a kind of striving toward something greater than oneself. It may or may not include a deity" (p. 3). In contrast, religion is more closely aligned with a more structured experience of spirituality, dogma, rituals, and communal expectations. Although frequently merged into a single category, religion and spirituality are distinct components of identity, which may or may not be congruent for different individuals. In a sample of low-income, rural women, Gill, Barrio Minton, and Myers (2010) found high correlations between spirituality and religiosity; combined, spirituality and religiosity accounted for nearly 40 percent of total variance in wellness. While some women may experience frustration with religion-based gender roles and expectations, others find a sense of purpose in them.

Ethnic and Racial Identity

Race and ethnicity heavily influence gender socialization, norms, and experiences (Collins, 2000; Crenshaw, 1989, 1991). The invisibility of racial privilege for white women often results in limited recognition of the racialized experience of gender, reflecting a common critique of white feminism. It is from this position of white womanhood that McIntosh (1988) identified her privileged racial reality as a white woman with her simultaneous oppression as a woman. Gender roles and expectations can be influenced by multiple cultural factors, including interconnected race, ethnicity, and religion. For example, *Marianismo*, a Latinx cultural construct rooted in the Christian figure of the Virgin Mary, exemplifies cultural expectations associated with virtue, religiosity, self-sacrifice, and silencing the self (Caplan & Whittemore, 2013; Lara-Cinisomo, Wood, & Fujimoto, 2018). These cultural gender roles may be rigidly binary and androcentric in nature, which can also marginalize women within their own racial cultural community. These gender roles often set extremely high expectations for women of color to show strength, manage multiple roles through self-sacrifice, and serve as the nucleus of their families and communities (Abrams, Javier, Maxwell, Belgrave, & Nguyen, 2016; Abrams, Maxwell, Pope, & Belgrave, 2014). Similarly, Jones and Shorter-Gooden (2003) found that 40 percent of black/African American women downplayed their strengths and skills to accommodate black/African American men. A recent study identified gendered racial themes in Asian American women's experience that differed from perceptions experienced by all Asians (Mukkamala, & Suyemoto, 2018). Abrams et al. (2016) argued that even with similarities among women of color, there is a need for culture-specific understanding of women's experiences.

Socioeconomic Status

Social class and socioeconomic status are closely connected to gender in a variety of ways. Regardless of life choice across single, married/partnered, or divorced status, women navigate education, employment outside of the home, and caretaking differently than men. Women and children are significantly overrepresented in poverty statistics, with 31.6 percent of women-headed households below federal poverty level compared with 15.8 percent of male-headed households (U.S. Census Bureau, 2014). Women are also disproportionately impacted by divorce, contributing to the "feminization of poverty" as women are most frequently custodial parents, bearing the brunt of the caretaking and financial responsibility for children. Even for those in heterosexual, two-parent households, discrepancies appear in parent perspectives of responsibilities. A national survey found that fathers are more likely to view parenting responsibilities as equally shared, while mothers say they take on a larger role (Pew Research Center, 2015b). Women who choose to be mothers may experience challenges negotiating career advancement and gendered caretaking expectations of children and older relatives. In addition, women are frequently socialized into lower-paying occupations (e.g., nurses instead of physicians, teachers instead of administrators), despite surpassing men's rates of bachelor's degree completion by age 31 (Bureau of Labor Statistics, 2018). Further, the absence of equal pay contributes to lower overall earnings for women compared to men. This is further complicated by racial disparities in which black and Hispanic women's median earnings in 2018 were between $163 and $200 lower than white women's median earnings, while Asian women's earnings were higher than all groups, due to educational attainment (Hegewisch & Hartmann, 2019). Thus, examining inequity through a single lens of race or gender fails to encompass the complexity of wage discrepancies.

Sexual Orientation

Previous views of same-gender attractions and relationships as sexually deviant and inherently pathological have been superseded by a more liberal view, emphasizing personal relationships (e.g., "love is love") and biological determination (e.g., "born this way"). Neither approach fully encompasses the breadth and fluidity of affectional/sexual orientation, which includes sexual attraction, sexual behavior, sexual fantasies, emotional preference, social preference, same-gender or other-gender lifestyle, and self-identity (American Institute of Bisexuality, 2014). To this, there is also a political dynamic that had largely been ignored, particularly in the context of women's experience. Rich (1980) argued compulsory heterosexuality for women is rooted in a deeply political system of sexism and patriarchy that assumes heterosexuality for women and focuses on the function that women serve to men. Diamond (2005) suggested that media representations of same-gender affectional or sexual behavior are depoliticized, exoticized for the male gaze, and complicit in erasing women's bisexuality. Many models of sexual orientation identity development focus on individual awareness and experiences in self-labeling. In contrast, McCarn and Fassinger's (1996) lesbian identity development model emphasizes relational factors that parallel and influence individual identity, addressing individual, relational, and political factors of a lesbian identity. Because the language of affectional/sexual orientation is gender based (e.g., *lesbian* used for women whose dominant attractions are to other women), trans and gender-variant women commonly experience marginalization and exclusionary practices from cisgender individuals in queer communities (Chang & Singh, 2016; Farmer & Byrd, 2015).

Indigenous Heritage

Indigenous heritage reflects a variety of cultural elements, including race, ethnicity, national origin, as well as migration and colonization histories. Issues of law, sovereignty, and land uniquely affect indigenous women, particularly with sexual violence. The Centers for Disease Control and Prevention (CDC; Smith et al., 2018) reports that nearly one in three women has experienced sexual violence involving some form of physical contact. In this already high number, the National Congress of American Indians (NCAI) Policy Research Center (2013) reported that native women have the highest rates of sexual assault among all U.S. groups, with women on tribal lands most vulnerable. Further, perpetrators of sexual violence against native women are more likely to be nonnative, which is unique to this population as most sexual violence crimes are intraracial. This is further complicated by tribes' lack of authority to prosecute nonnative people who commit crimes on tribal land, with U.S. attorneys declining to prosecute many violent cases (NCAI Policy Research Center, 2013). Thus, positionality as a native woman is impacted by the privilege of many nonnative perpetuators, limiting their recourse in the criminal justice system.

National Origin

National origin is often overlooked as a critical diversity factor in women's experience. Immigrants can occupy different statuses, including naturalized citizens, permanent residents, refugees, asylees, temporary visa holders, and undocumented immigrants. The reasons people immigrate vary considerably, and the sociopolitical context of host countries and possible premigration trauma (e.g., witnessing violence, unexpected death of a loved one) pose significant mental health risks for refugees and immigrants with different racial cultural identities from different areas of the world (Sangalang et al., 2018; Shishehgar, Gholizadeh, Digiacomo, Green, & Davidson, 2017). Immigrant and refugee women often face differential risks of violence and trauma. In a study of refugee and undocumented immigrant women, Goodman, Vesely, Letiecq, and Cleaveland (2017) identified three trauma types among participants, including sociopolitical context surrounding immigration, trauma related to their political and citizens status, and postmigration trauma, some of these gender based in nature, including rape and witnessing sexual assault. Common stressors include family separation, language barriers, employment, and economic and situational stressors (Goodman et al., 2017; Shishehgar et al., 2017). The multitude of separations and disruptions in relationships can have deleterious effects; however, the importance of familial relationships, connection with similar others, and social service agencies were identified as contributing to resilience (Goodman et al., 2017).

IMPLICATIONS FOR COUNSELING AND ADVOCACY

Intersectionality has been used in a variety of ways, conceptualizing individual experiences (Bowleg, 2013; Purdie-Vaughns & Eibach, 2008) but also large-scale issues such as disparities in public health (Bowleg, 2012). Intersectionality goes beyond simply identifying interactions of oppressive systems and identities; rather, it is designed as a tool to conceptualize complex issues. Clearly, women are differentially affected by systems of social inequality at the individual, group, and community levels. Thus, it is important to recognize how counselors can best intervene in their professional roles. An important addition to the MSJCC is balancing individual counseling interventions and advocacy interventions (Ratts et al., 2016). Counselors are well trained for individual and group counseling; however, training often fails to prepare counselors for advocacy at multiple levels. The ACA Advocacy Competencies (Lewis, Arnold, House, & Toporek, 2003) laid the groundwork for counseling advocacy with and for marginalized groups. Bridging the Multicultural Counseling Competencies (Arredondo et al., 1996; Sue et al., 1992) and the Advocacy Competencies, the MSJCC delineate counseling and advocacy interventions using a socioecological model that addresses intrapersonal, interpersonal, institutional, community, public policy, and international and global affairs (Ratts et al., 2015).

Individual counseling primarily focuses on the unique, individual characteristics of the client; however, an intersectionality perspective takes this a step further by contextualizing these experiences in a socioecological context. Culturally relevant counseling strategies can include the use of empowerment theories that fully integrate cultural perspectives and context. Counseling approaches, including feminist therapy, narrative therapy, and relational cultural therapy (Comstock, 2005; Crethar, Torres Rivera, & Nash, 2008; Jordan, 2010; White & Epston, 1990), intentionally focus on social construction of knowledge and experience, highlighting issues of power, agency, relationships, and the sociopolitical nature of experience. These strategies can be woven into counseling practice with all women, addressing each client's interactions of privileged and marginalized identities. Counselors should also assist clients in recognizing power structures and controlling images, as these can impact views of self and create psychosocial barriers in mental health treatment (Abrams et al., 2016; Caplan & Whittemore, 2013; Dougherty et al., 2016; Lara-Cinisomo et al., 2018).

Counselors too need to be aware of the multiple, layered cultural factors they identify with and how they are affected. To this, counselors must add an understanding of their clients' cultural identities and the interactions in the counseling relationship (Ratts et al., 2016; Watts-Jones, 2010). Further, counselors must be able to recognize culturally laden and gender-biased influences in counseling assessment and diagnosis (Katz, 1985; Marecek &

Garvey, 2013). Counselors are encouraged to initiate these conversations through broaching behaviors using multicultural and social justice counseling competencies as a foundation (Day-Vines et al., 2007). Counselors can then assist clients in deconstructing internalized oppression, rejecting cultural stereotypes, and developing their own, culturally relevant meaning of womanhood.

There is a long history of advocacy for clients in the mental health professions (Kiselica & Robinson, 2001), but there is also a history of marginalization and discrimination against people of color, women, and other minoritized groups (Jackson, 1995; Marecek & Garvey, 2013; Sue & Sue, 1977). To fully shift the profession, counselors must understand minority stress, the impact of social conditions on wellness, and client access to social and economic resources. Instead of adopting an individual advocacy lens for individual clients in a single setting, there is growing momentum with counselors focusing on larger systemic issues, such as the impact of oppression on mental health and the impact of public policy on mental health access and services (Lewis et al., 2003; Ratts et al., 2016). Counselors can develop or utilize existing community resources to create change. While large-scale research may seem out of reach for many, research using smaller-scale designs, such as single-subject design, participatory action research, and qualitative research, can promote deeper understanding of groups often overlooked in research. It is also imperative that counselors stay abreast of and engaged in local, state, national, and global affairs as these issues engulf client and counselor experiences. Counselors may underestimate their role as advocates and leaders, but as counselors work to empower women in their communities, it is also critical that they too become empowered as social justice advocates, adding mental health issues of women to the social and political agendas of policy and decision makers.

CONCLUSION

Clearly, women are not a homogenous group and are differentially affected by issues based on membership in other social identity groups. Additional cultural factors interact with gender in women's experience, complicating the reductionist "women's issues" label that often solely focused on the experiences of white, cisgender, heterosexual, able-bodied women. Using intersectionality as a conceptual framework for understanding women's social location and positionality allows for more comprehensive understanding of cultural identity and lived experience. Application of intersectionality lays the foundation for appropriate individual counseling and counseling advocacy that can be precisely designed for each client's unique experience.

REFERENCES

Abrams, J. A., Javier, S. J., Maxwell, M. L., Belgrave, F. Z., & Nguyen, A. B. (2016). Distant but relative: Similarities and differences in gender role beliefs among African American and Vietnamese American women. *Cultural Diversity and Ethnic Minority Psychology, 22*, 256–67. doi:10.1037/cdp0000038

Abrams, J., Maxwell, M., Pope, M., & Belgrave, F. (2014). Carrying the world with the grace of a lady and the grit of a warrior: Deepening our understanding of the "strong black woman" schema. *Psychology of Women Quarterly, 38*, 503–18. doi:10.1177/0361684314541418

American Counseling Association. (2014). *ACA code of ethics*. Alexandria, VA: Author.

American Institute of Bisexuality. (2014). *The Klein sexual orientation grid*. Retrieved from http://www.americaninstituteofbisexuality.org/thekleingrid

American Psychological Association. (2018). *APA guidelines for psychological practice with girls and women*. Retrieved from http://www.apa.org/about/policy/psychological-practice-girls-women.pdf

Arredondo, P., Toporek, R. L., Brown, S. P., Jones, J., Locke, D., Sanchez, J., & Stadler, H. (1996). Operationalization of the multicultural counseling competencies. *Journal of Multicultural Counseling and Development, 24*, 42–78. doi:10.1002/j.2161-1912.1996.tb00288.x

Berens, S., & Erford, B. T. (2018). Disability, ableism, and ageism. In D. G. Hays & B. T. Erford (Eds.), *Developing multicultural counseling competence: A systems approach* (pp. 224–54). New York, NY: Pearson.

Bowleg, L. (2008). When black + lesbian + woman ≠ black lesbian woman: The methodological challenges of qualitative and quantitative intersectionality research. *Sex Roles, 59*(5–6), 312–25. doi:10.1007/s11199-008-9400-z

Bowleg, L. (2012). The problem with the phrase women and minorities: Intersectionality—an important theoretical framework for public health. *American Journal of Public Health, 102*(7), 1267–73. doi:10.2105/AJPH.2012.300750

Bowleg, L. (2013). "Once you've blended the cake, you can't take the parts back to the main ingredients": Black gay and bisexual men's descriptions and experiences of intersectionality. *Sex Roles, 68*(11–12), 754–67. doi:10.1007/s11199-012-0152-4

Bowleg, L., Huang, J., Brooks, K., Black, A., & Burkholder, G. (2003). Triple jeopardy and beyond: Multiple minority stress and resilience among black lesbians. *Journal of Lesbian Studies, 7*, 87–108. doi:10.1300/J155v07n04_06

Bureau of Labor Statistics. (2018). Women more likely than men to have earned a bachelor's degree by age 31. Retrieved from https://www.bls.gov/opub/ted/2018/women-more-likely-than-men-to-have-earned-a-bachelors-degree-by-age-31.htm

Caplan, S., & Whittemore, R. (2013). Barriers to treatment engagement for depression among Latinas. *Issues Mental Health Nursing, 34*, 412–24. doi:10.3109/01612840.2012.762958

Chang, S. C., & Singh, A. A. (2016). Affirming psychological practice with transgender and gender nonconforming people of color. *Psychology of Sexual Orientation and Gender Diversity, 3*, 140–47. doi:10.1037/sgd0000153

Collins, P. H. (2000). *Black feminist thought: Knowledge, consciousness, and the politics of empowerment* (2nd ed.). New York, NY: Routledge.

Collins, P. H., & Bilge, S. (2016). *Intersectionality*. Malden, MA: Polity Press.

Combahee River Collective. (1977). The Combahee River Collective statement. Retrieved from https://americanstudies.yale.edu/sites/default/files/files/Keyword%20Coalition_Readings.pdf

Comstock, D. L. (2005). Women's development. In D. Comstock (Ed.), *Diversity and development: Critical contexts that shape our lives and relationships* (pp. 111–32). Belmont, CA: Thomson Brooks/Cole.

Crenshaw, K. (1988). Race, reform, and retrenchment: Transformation and legitimation in antidiscrimination law. *Harvard Law Review, 101*(7), 1331–87. Retrieved from http://www.jstor.org/stable/pdf/1341398.pdf

Crenshaw, K. (1989). Demarginalizing the intersection of race and sex: A black feminist critique of antidiscrimination doctrine, feminist theory and antiracist politics. *University of Chicago Legal Forum, 1989*(1), 139–67.

Crenshaw, K. (1991). Mapping the margins: Intersectionality, identity politics, and violence against women of color. *Stanford Law Review, 43*(6), 1241–99. doi:10.2307/1229039

Crethar, H. C., Torres Rivera, E., & Nash, S. (2008). In search of common threads: Linking multicultural, feminist, and social justice counseling paradigm. *Journal of Counseling & Development, 86*, 269–78. doi:10.1002/j.1556-6678.2008.tb00509.x

Crissman, H. P., Stroumsa, D., Kobernik, E. K., & Berger, M. B. (2019). Gender and frequent mental distress: Comparing transgender and non-transgender individuals' self-rated mental health. *Journal of Women's Health, 28*, 143–51. doi:10.1089/jwh.2018.7411

Day-Vines, N. L., Wood, S. M., Grothaus, T., Craigen, L., Holman, A., Dotson-Blake, K., & Douglass, M. J. (2007). Broaching the subjects of race, ethnicity, and culture during the counseling process. *Journal of Counseling & Development, 85*, 401–9. doi:10.1002/j.1556-6678.2007.tb00608.x

Diamond, L. M. (2005). "I'm straight, but I kissed a girl": The trouble with American media representations of female–female sexuality. *Feminism & Psychology, 15*, 104–10. doi:10.1177/0959353505049712

Dougherty, E. N., Dorr, N., & Pulice, R. T. (2016). Assisting older women in combatting ageist stereotypes and improving attitudes toward aging. *Women & Therapy, 39*(1–2), 12–34. doi:10.1080/02703149.2016.1116308

Downing, N. E., & Roush, K. L. (1985). From passive acceptance to active commitment: A model of feminist identity development for women. *Counseling Psychologist, 13*, 695–709. doi:10.1177/0011000085134013

Erchull, M. J., Liss, M., Wilson, K. A., Bateman, L., Peterson, A., & Sanchez, C. E. (2009). The feminist identity development model: Relevant for young women today? *Sex Roles, 60*(11–12), 832–42. doi:10.1007/s11199-009-9588-6

Farmer, L. B., & Byrd, R. (2015). Genderism in the LGBTQQIA community: An interpretative phenomenological analysis. *Journal of LGBT Issues in Counseling, 9*, 288–310, doi:10.1080/15538605.2015.1103679

Frame, M. W. (2003). *Integrating religion and spirituality into counseling: A comprehensive approach*. Pacific Grove, CA: Brooks/Cole-Thomson.

Gill, C. S., Barrio Minton, C. A., & Myers, J. E. (2010). Spirituality and religiosity: Factors affecting wellness among low-income, rural women. *Journal of Counseling & Development, 88*, 293–302. doi:10.1002/j.1556-6678.2010.tb00025.x

Glynn, K., Maclean, H., Forte, T., & Cohen, M. (2009). The association between role overload and women's mental health. *Journal of Women's Health, 8*, 217–23. doi:10.1089/jwh.2007.0783

Goodman, R. D., Vesely, C. K., Letiecq, B., & Cleaveland, C. L. (2017). Trauma and resilience among refugee and undocumented immigrant women. *Journal of Counseling & Development, 95*, 310–21. doi:10.1002/jcad.12145

Hays, P. A. (1996). Addressing the complexities of culture and gender in counseling. *Journal of Counseling & Development, 74*, 332–38. doi:10.1002/j.1556-6676.1996.tb01876.x

Hays, P. A. (2016). *Addressing cultural complexities in practice: Assessment, diagnosis, and therapy* (3rd ed.). Washington, DC: American Psychological Association.

Hegewisch, A., & Hartmann, H. (2019). The gender wage gap: 2018 earnings differences by race and ethnicity. Retrieved from https://iwpr.org/publications/gender-wage-gap-2018/

Hunt, B., Matthews, C., Milsom, A., & Lammel, J. A. (2006). Lesbians with physical disabilities: A qualitative study of their experiences with counseling. *Journal of Counseling & Development, 84*, 163–73. doi:10.1002/j.1556-6678.2006.tb00392.x

Jackson, M. L. (1995). Multicultural counseling: Historical perspectives. In J. G. Ponterotto, J. M. Casas, L. A. Suzuki, & C. M. Alexander (Eds.), *Handbook of multicultural counseling* (pp. 3–16). Thousand Oaks, CA: Sage.

James, S. E., Herman, J. L., Rankin, S., Keisling, M., Mottet, L., & Anafi, M. (2016). *The report of the 2015 U.S. transgender survey*. Washington, DC: National Center for Transgender Equality.

Jones, C., & Shorter-Gooden, K. (2003). *Shifting: The double lives of black women in America.* New York, NY: HarperCollins.
Jordan, J. V. (2010). *Relational-cultural therapy.* Washington, DC: American Psychological Association.
Katz, J. H. (1985). The sociopolitical nature of counseling. *Counseling Psychologist, 13*, 615–24. doi:10.1177/0011000085134005
Kiselica, M. S., & Robinson, M. (2001). Bringing advocacy counseling to life: The history, issues, and human dramas of social justice work in counseling. *Journal of Counseling & Development, 79*, 387–97. doi:10.1002/j.1556-6676.2001.tb01985.x
Lara-Cinisomo, S., Wood, J., & Fujimoto, E. M. (2018). A systematic review of cultural orientation and perinatal depression in Latina women: Are acculturation, marianismo, and religiosity risks of protective factors? *Archives of Women's Mental Health, 22*(5), 557–67. doi:10.1007/s00737-018-0920-4
Lewis, J. A., Arnold, M.S., House, R., & Toporek, R. L. (2003). Advocacy competencies. Retrieved from https://www.counseling.org/docs/default-source/competencies/aca-2018-advocacy-competencies.pdf?sfvrsn=1dca552c_6
Marecek, J, & Garvey, N. (2013). DSM-5 and beyond: A critical feminist engagement with psychodiagnosis. *Feminism and Psychology, 23*(1), 3–9. doi:10.1177/0959353512467962
McCarn, S. R., & Fassinger, R. E. (1996). Revisioning sexual minority identity formation: A new model of lesbian identity and its implications. *Counseling Psychologist, 24*, 508–34. doi:10.1177/0011000096243011
McCullough, R., Dispenza, F., Parker, L. K., Viehl, C. J., Chang, C. Y., & Murphy, T. M. (2017). The counseling experiences of transgender and gender nonconforming clients. *Journal of Counseling & Development, 95*, 423–34. doi:10.1002/jcad.12157
McIntosh, P. (1988). White privilege and male privilege: A personal account of coming to see correspondence through work in women's studies. In M. Anderson & P. Hill Collins (Eds.), *Race, class, and gender: An anthology* (pp. 94–105). Belmont, CA: Wadsworth.
Mukkamala, S., & Suyemoto, K. L. (2018). Racialized sexism/sexualized racism: A multimethod study of intersectional experiences of discrimination for Asian American women. *Asian American Journal of Psychology, 9*(1), 32–46. doi:10.1037/aap0000104
National Congress of American Indians, Policy Research Center. (2013). Policy insights brief: Statistics on violence against Native women. Retrieved from http://www.ncai.org/resources/ncai_publications/policy-insights-brief-statistics-on-violence-against-native-women
National Congress of American Indians, Policy Research Center. (2015). A spotlight on native women & girls. Retrieved from http://www.ncai.org/policy-research-center/research-data/prc-publications/A_Spotlight_on_Native_Women_-_Girls.pdf
Noonan, B. M., Gallor, S. M., Hensler-McGinnis, N. F., Fassinger, R. E., Wang, S., & Goodman, J. (2004). Challenge and success: A qualitative study of the career development of highly achieving women with physical and sensory disabilities. *Journal of Counseling Psychology, 51*, 68–80. doi:10.1037/0022-0167.51.1.68
Pew Research Center. (2015a). America's changing religious landscape. Retrieved from https://www.pewforum.org/2015/05/12/americas-changing-religious-landscape/
Pew Research Center. (2015b). How American parents balance work and family life when both work. Retrieved from https://www.pewresearch.org/fact-tank/2015/11/04/how-american-parents-balance-work-and-family-life-when-both-work/
Planty, M., Langston, L., Krebs, C., Berzofsky, M., & Smiley-McDonald, H. (2013). Female victims of sexual violence, 1994–2010. Retrieved from https://www.bjs.gov/content/pub/pdf/fvsv9410.pdf
Purdie-Vaughns, V., & Eibach, R. P. (2008). Intersectional invisibility: The advantages and disadvantages of multiple subordinate-group identities. *Sex Roles, 59*, 377–91. doi:10.1007/s11199-008-9424-4
Ratts, M. J., Singh, A. A., Nassar-McMillan, S., Butler, S. K., & McCullough, J. R. (2015). Multicultural and social justice counseling competencies. Retrieved from https://www.counseling.org/knowledge-center/competencies
Ratts, M. J., Singh, A. A., Nassar-McMillan, S., Butler, S. K., & McCullough, J. R. (2016). Multicultural and social justice counseling competencies: Guidelines for the counseling

profession. *Journal of Multicultural Counseling and Development, 44*, 28–48. doi:10.1002/jmcd.12035

Rich, A. (1980). Compulsory heterosexuality and lesbian existence. *Signs, 5*, 631–60.

Sangalang, C. C., Becerra, D., Mitchell, F. M., Lechuga-Peña, S., Lopez, K., & Kim, I. (2018). Trauma, post-migration stress, and mental health: A comparative analysis of refugees and immigrants in the United States. *Journal of Immigrant and Minority Health, 21*(5), 909–19. doi:10.1007/s10903-018-0826-2

Shishehgar, S., Gholizadeh, L., Digiacomo, M., Green, A., & Davidson, P. M. (2017). Health and socio-cultural experiences of refugee women: An integrative review. *Journal of Immigrant and Minority Health, 19*, 959–73. doi:10.1007/s10903-016-0379-1

Siebler, K. (2010). Far from the truth: Teaching the politics of Sojourner Truth's "Ain't I a woman?" *Pedagogy: Critical Approaches to Teaching Literature, Language, Composition and Culture, 10*, 511–33. doi:10.1215/15314200-2010-005

Singh, A. A., & Mingo, T. (2018). Gender and sexism. In D. G. Hays & B. T. Erford (Eds.), *Developing multicultural counseling competence: A systems approach* (pp. 127–53). New York, NY: Pearson.

Smith, D. L. (2008). Disparities in health care access for women with disabilities in the United States from the 2006 National Health Interview Survey. *Disability and Health Journal, 1*, 79–88. doi:10.1016/j.dhjo.2008.01.001

Smith, S. G., Zhang, X., Basile, K. C., Merrick, M. T., Wang, J., Kresnow, M., & Chen, J. (2018). *The National Intimate Partner and Sexual Violence Survey (NISVS): 2015 data brief—updated release*. Atlanta, GA: National Center for Injury Prevention and Control, Centers for Disease Control and Prevention

Sue, D., Arredondo, P., & McDavis, R. J. (1992). Multicultural counseling competencies and standards: A call to the profession. *Journal of Counseling and Development, 70,* 477–86. doi:10.1002/j.1556-6676.1992.tb01642.x

Sue, D. W., & Sue, D. (1977). Barriers to effective cross-cultural counseling. *Journal of Counseling Psychology, 24*, 420–29. doi:10.1037/0022-0167.24.5.420

Sue, D. W., & Sue D. (2013). *Counseling the culturally diverse: Theory and practice* (6th ed.). Hoboken, NJ: John Wiley & Sons.

U.S. Census Bureau. (2014). *Current population survey: 1961 to 2018 annual social and economic supplements*. Retrieved from https://www.census.gov/content/dam/Census/library/visualizations/2018/demo/p60-263/figure2.pdf

Vardeman-Winter, J. (2017). The framing of women and health disparities: A critical look at race, gender, and class from the perspectives of grassroots health communicators. *Health Communication, 32*, 629–38. doi:10.1080/10410236.2016.1160318

Watts-Jones, T. (2010). Location of self: Opening the door to dialogue on intersectionality in the therapy process. *Family Process, 49*, 405–20. doi:10.1111/j.1545-5300.2010.01330.x

White, M., & Epston, D. (1990). *Narrative means to therapeutic ends*. New York, NY: W. W. Norton.

Chapter Two

Integrating Feminist Therapy into Counseling Practice

Suzanne Degges-White

The history of feminist theory stretches back to the late 1800s, when women first began organizing and staging protests as they fought for the right to vote (Hannam, 2012). In fact, it might surprise some readers to realize that women in the United States have only held the right to vote since 1920. Feminism, like most social movements, rolled through on "waves," and the first wave was tied to women's fight for the right to vote. The next wave arrived in the 1960s, when women, as a group, began to recognize that the circumscription of their lives (which defined their life roles and options primarily as wives and mothers) was due, in part, to traditional gender role expectations and the limits imposed by their gender in a patriarchal society.

This dawning awareness of the structurally embedded inequities between genders led women to engage in grassroots efforts to communicate and confront these gender-enforced limitations. Thus, the "Women's Movement," as most of us know it, was born. Women began to organize and participate in consciousness-raising groups that provided participants opportunities to develop a sense of sisterhood and connection with other like-minded women. These groups uncovered feelings of unrest and distress that women previously had no place to acknowledge or express. A collective sense of shared identity developed, and groups coalesced to address and pursue equality between the genders, appropriate medical and psychological care for women, and safe spaces for women who were victims of male aggression or control.

In essence, feminist theory was developed as a response to the culturally accepted gender roles and gender rules that unfairly privileged men (Israeli & Santor, 2000). A patriarchal society possesses power to limit the aspirations, not just the achievements, of women. Feminists recognized that these rules and roles were actually forms of oppression and that women were disempowered and silenced by the fact of their gender. The most elemental goal that drove feminist activities in the second wave was the empowerment of all women through raised awareness and advocacy.

Today, the third wave of feminism is described as one that maintains a focus on gender role socialization but encompasses a widened lens that addresses the presence of *multiple* oppressions that are faced by diverse women and other marginalized groups. The lens also includes the roles of power and privilege and the fight for social justice (Enns & Byars-Winston, 2010). Feminist therapists aim to empower their clients and facilitate client movement toward self-differentiation and the self-determination of their goals and, ultimately, their lives (Wooley, 1995) regardless of the roadblocks they face from a patriarchal society. Feminist therapists also work to demystify the therapeutic process to allow their clients to understand and collaborate in facilitation of their healing journeys.

FEMINIST THOUGHT MEETS FEMINIST THERAPY

Therapy informed by feminist theory is shaped and enacted from the perspective of the clinician rather than by a set of specific techniques that are applied (Brown, 2018). Feminist therapists firmly believe that gender role socialization is a primary force that negatively affects the healthy development of women. Feminist therapists recognize that a client's truth is undeniably the client's "truth." Feminist therapists also recognize that it is the patriarchal culture and its unjust practices that give rise to the issues that bring clients into their offices. For instance, Israeli and Santor (2000) noted that a woman's depressed mood may be a very normal reaction to a world in which patriarchy favors men in such a way that women feel helpless and hopeless and doubt their self-worth. Thus, feminist-oriented therapists recognized the need for a theory that creates a therapeutic environment in which the client can be empowered and actively participate in their own care. The basic definition of feminist therapy embraces this idea. Laura S. Brown (1994, pp. 21–22) defined feminist therapy in the following way:

> The practice of therapy informed by feminist political philosophies and analysis, grounded in multicultural feminist scholarship on the psychology of women and gender, which leads both therapist and client toward strategies and solutions advancing feminist resistance, transformation and social change in daily personal life, and in relationships with the social, emotional and political environments.

This specific definition was developed approximately a quarter of a century ago, but the heart of the definition is still relevant for clients today. While third-wave feminism has broadened the construct by including specific focus on inclusion and intersectionality, the basic belief that "the personal is political" is still very much at the core of feminist philosophy. This underscores the belief that what are traditionally considered to be "women's issues" are broader and more culturally embedded and external than they may first appear. In fact, feminist theory has often been used with marginalized groups and minority groups in addition to women due to the collaborative nature of the theory.

Feminist counseling theory has been developed to more fully invite the collaboration and expertness of clients into the counseling process (Worell & Remer, 2003). Lenore E. A. Walker (1990) described feminist therapy as being supported by six basic tenets; over time, these tenets have been fleshed out and expanded by additional feminist writers (Corey, 2015). Following is a synopsis of the current status of these six beliefs:

1. The personal is political, and those things that happen "out there" in society that limit women's opportunities, well-being, or survival are also happening "in her(e)" as well. A woman's individual experience is a glimpse into the experiences of all women facing the same monolithic cultural obstacle.
2. Social action is necessary to promote social change, which is seen as the surest route to ensuring that women's lives also change. Feminist therapists move beyond their offices to engage in advocacy for their clients in order to enhance the climate of their communities and the globe. Therapists facilitate their clients' understandings of the privileges that they may possess and the oppressions they may experience. Without awareness and advocacy, change cannot be realized.
3. The voices of the marginalized and the oppressed are valued and the ways of "knowing" that are different from the standard, androcentric scientific method are also valued and heard. The experiences of all people are to be honored rather than viewed as deviant or suspect. A person's truth is her truth.
4. Relationships between therapists and clients must be egalitarian. This relationship serves as a model in which women take personal responsibility and exhibit assertiveness in getting their needs met. There exists authenticity, mutuality, and respect between counselor and client. When clients present for care, an inherent power difference exists between the helpee and the helper. Feminist practitioners acknowledge the power differential, explore it with the client, and seek ways to minimize it.
5. Feminist therapy eschews the medical model of diagnosis and treatment as feminist practitioners believe that women's problems are described as coping mechanisms that are activated by a society that can

be inhospitable to women. Thus, the understanding of psychological distress is shifted, and those symptoms that might be seen as "disruptive problems" in one lens may be viewed as "survival mechanisms" through the feminist lens.

6. Regardless of their basis, oppression of any type is acknowledged and recognized and the connections and interrelationships between them are explored and addressed in therapy.

Feminist Therapy: Not for Women Only

Although feminist therapy arose out of the movements to forward women's equality, this form of therapy is also useful when working with virtually all clients, as each of us bring with us an intersectional identity (Wolf, Williams, Darby, Herald, & Schultz, 2018). In 2000, Root introduced the construct of *intersectional identities*; this construct expanded the notion that gender alone could account for different experiences in a patriarchal society.

In essence, the benefits of this clinical orientation are found in the way clients are viewed in context and in relation to other entities in their world—not just as isolated individuals with stand-alone, idiosyncratic problems. Additionally, the therapy process is described as gender fair, meaning that language chosen is gender fair and all genders are treated with the same level of respect (Worell & Remer, 2003). Feminist therapy is flexible and multicultural, making it applicable to all individuals, regardless of their unique, diverse identities. It focuses on interaction between the individual and the environment. It also takes a lifespan perspective that honors the development and change that humans exhibit as they grow, learn, and mature. The thread that runs through all aspects of feminist thought and feminist therapy is the drive toward client empowerment.

What Does Empowerment Look Like?

Feminist clinicians desire to empower clients to discover and articulate their therapeutic goals as well as empower clients to work toward these goals. While most of us would say that we "know empowerment when we see it," Worell (1993) developed a model that identified ten specific behaviors that would be present as evidence of empowerment as a woman took control of her own well-being. These included the following: self-evaluation; comfort–distress ratio (comfort would increase while feelings of distress would decrease); gender- and culture-role awareness; personal control/self-efficacy; self-nurturance; problem-solving skills; assertiveness; resource access; gender and cultural flexibility; and social activism. Brown (2018) further specified that empowerment is, in essence, liberating clients from their own internalized forms of oppression in order for them to gain power to intentionally confront their external obstacles.

Taken together, these ten behaviors inform a model in which an individual is able to perceive both the influences of the external culture on her beliefs and behaviors while acknowledging her own role in choosing to reject harmful cultural expectations and in practicing appropriate self-care. Each of the ten areas of assessment affirms the belief that all clients are capable of being responsible for their own well-being, which can be likened to the perspective of Carl Rogers and client-centered therapy (Proctor & Napier, 2004; Wolter-Gustafson, 2004). Client-centered therapy focuses on helping clients become more congruent; congruency exists when one's experiencing of the world matches one's sense of self. Feminist therapy has a similar focus in helping clients reach empowerment as a way to feel in control of their own lives within a cultural paradigm over which they hold little control. Power is not perceived of as an "all or nothing" construct within feminist thought. Power exists on a continuum and even when a client feels that they possess no power, clinicians help clients to understand ways they do hold power, even if its magnitude is not yet as significant as the client may wish (Brown, 2018).

The Four Realms of Personal Power

Brown (2018, p. 41) described four realms in which individuals function and hold power: (1) somatic, (2) intrapersonal/intrapsychic, (3) interpersonal/social-contextual, and (4) spiritual/existential. Somatic power is related to the body and is marked by feelings of being "safe" within one's own skin; satisfied with the body's size and shape; appreciative of the body in whatever form it takes, regardless of abilities; and experiencing compassion toward one's physical form. Intrapersonal/intrapsychic power is marked by knowing what one thinks and the presence of flexibility, rather than rigidity, in thoughts and feelings; being able to trust one's own intuition and to believe in the messages sent by one's feelings; and being able to be present in the moment, experience powerful emotions, and not fall into "numbness" as a way to cope. Interpersonal and social-contextual power is effected by being able to establish and maintain healthy relationships with others and being able to maintain a healthy balance between independence and dependence. Spiritual and existential power includes the ability to make meaning of life, understand the way one fits into the larger scheme of things, feel that one's life has purpose, and be able to engage in creativity and fantasy while maintaining a strong grounding in reality.

Feminist therapists are able to facilitate clients' awareness of these various realms while helping them to recognize the ways they hold and can enact power in each realm. Most clients seek counseling as a "last resort" when they have exhausted all other possible solutions to their concerns. Clients often feel powerless at this point, and rather than being cast as the "source" of a client's solution, feminist counselors help their clients recognize the ways they can use their own power to find their solutions. It is important to consider not just empowerment but other practices common to the theory.

Feminist Therapy in Practice

Empowerment is the most essential goal for clients, but Worell and Remer (2003) outlined eight additional related goals of feminist therapy:

- Become aware of your own experience of gender role socialization.
- Recognize the internalized messages you've been taught and replace these with self-enhancing, positive messages.
- Gain awareness of the ways sexist and oppressive societal beliefs and practices negatively influence you.
- Develop a set of skills that will allow you to make changes to the environment in which you function.
- Restructure existing institutions to eliminate any discriminatory practices they support.
- Acknowledge and evaluate the impact that social factors have on your life.
- Establish a sense of personal and social power.
- Acknowledge and value the power of relationships and connection to others.
- Trust your own experience and intuition.

As you reflect on these practices, it is clear that they are as applicable to men as they are to women. In fact, these may be especially relevant for men who are employed in positions that are strongly associated with masculinity, such as law enforcement or the armed forces (Carr & McKernan, 2015). When forced to abide by stringent gender role expectations, some men may suffer psychological distress brought on by the hyper-masculine environment. Feminist-oriented clinicians can provide a space where men can explore contradictory or ambiguous feelings about their actions. Examples of populations that might benefit from feminist-centered work include veterans dealing with PTSD (Carr & McKernan, 2015) or men who feel constrained or overwhelmed by the culturally enforced gender role expectations (Silver, Levant, & Gonzalez, 2018). The use of this theory has more applications than counselors may realize, and depending on the client, the therapist selects appropriate techniques that may be pulled from a variety of other therapeutic orientations.

Feminist Therapy Techniques

With the focus that feminist clinicians place on individuals and the client's unique needs, it is likely not a surprise that there is not a standard catalog of techniques and interventions from which a feminist therapist draws a treatment plan. In fact, it is the *relationship* between therapist and client that is likely the most predictable aspect of feminist therapy. According to Brown (2018), the feminist therapist engages with the client in an egalitarian and liberatory relationship. While the structure of the practice of counseling is one in which the helper holds a different type of power than the client, it is essential for the client to be accorded the relevant power that is due. The client's expert stance on her own experiences and life is valued, as is the clinical expertise of the therapist. This creates a robust working alliance in which the client feels heard, understood, and validated.

The client's voice, way of knowing, and individual experiences are consciously valued and privileged by the therapist rather than privileging only the voice of those who deliver the therapy (Brown, 2018). Feminist practitioners also enter each new alliance with a willingness to explore and reexplore her own biases as she works with her clients. Brown (2018) noted the potential presence of *aversive* biases held by the therapist. These are the kind of biases that are seldom acknowledged or owned due to the self-criticism or shame that they may bring up for the counselor herself. An example would be a lesbian therapist who carries a bias against bisexual clients of which she, herself, is still unaware. She may acknowledge challenges she feels in relating to a female client who identifies as bisexual, but she may not appreciate the covert depth of her own bias unless she takes time to self-assess and evaluate her own feelings. Aversive biases may be the product of our own cultural upbringings or beliefs that we have accepted or developed independently. Feminist therapists must be able to openly explore their own privilege and covert attitudes in order to engage in an egalitarian and liberatory relationship with their clients.

In addition to the self-exploration that the therapist is doing outside her practice, she is also likely to incorporate self-disclosure into her work with clients (Brown, 2018). This willingness to be open, authentic, and vulnerable in the therapeutic relationship is another hallmark of feminist practice. Brown also noted that self-disclosure is not always explicit but can be accomplished through less obvious, but equally transparent, means. Therapists also bear in mind the power that they hold in having choice in what they disclose in contrast with the lack of power that clients have in terms of expected disclosure. Self-disclosure, as a technique, sets the stage for the work of therapy to be conducted.

Within the feminist paradigm, it is possible for creative clinicians to shape many interventions to fit within the feminist paradigm. Following are additional techniques that are frequently used within this framework.

Assertiveness Training

While assertiveness training may be viewed as "old school" due to its arrival on the self-help scene in the 1970s (Speed, Goldstein, & Goldfried, 2017), it still holds significant value as a tool to help clients gain mastery over their cognitions and behaviors. The goal of assertiveness training is to facilitate a client's ability to stand up for herself and express her thoughts and feelings with confidence while recognizing that her own behavior should not restrict the rights or freedoms of another (Alberti & Emmons, 1970). The implementation of this technique may include skills such as behavior rehearsal, learning to avoid manipulative exchanges with others by consistently staying on topic, and learning to acknowledge shortcomings without feeling guilt or shame.

Behavior rehearsal occurs when a counselor asks a client to practice, in session, the statements or questions that the client wants to use outside of session. For instance, if a client feels that her work supervisor is unfairly assigning work tasks based on gender, her counselor can ask her to state, in session, what she would like to express to her supervisor. She might try out statements such as, "Mr. Jackson, I feel that you assign me more of the background research on projects than you do the men in our department. I'd like the opportunity to meet with potential clients, not just do the fact-finding on their businesses." The counselor can invite her to practice the statement several times in session as well as play out the potential conversation through role play by having the client and counselor take turns playing out the roles of employee and supervisor. This allows the counselor the opportunity to try and manipulate the conversation in ways that will give the client practice in keeping to the facts and refusing to allow herself to be "derailed" in her advocacy for her rights on the job. The counselor may also encourage the client to practice the statement in front of a mirror to help her practice assertive, strong posture and facial expressions.

Learning to be accepting of one's shortcomings can be especially challenging when a client has been taught that her identity has little value and is an impediment to success. Counselors can provide clients with the space to discuss the negative messages they receive about their gender, appearance, identity, and so on. Following the discussion, the counselor can help the client to tease out any "truths" in the message and help the client to "own" her weaknesses without any sense of shame. For instance, if a client acknowledges that she is stronger in "street smarts" than "book smarts," she can discuss ways her "weakness" has strengths and become less defensive about her lack of formal education.

Assertiveness training can be especially appropriate for clients who are able to recognize instances in which they are being "shut down" or disregarded. Women experiencing marginalization in any sector of life, including home, school, work, institutional organizations, and so on, can gain significantly from learning how to communicate assertively and effectively. It is not unusual for women who have been reared in environments that fostered gender-based power imbalances to have difficulty developing assertive communication skills. They may experience cognitive dissonance in their early attempts to practice assertiveness as the mastery of the new skills may be in conflict with the values and gendered behavioral expectations with which they were raised. Counselors may choose to incorporate consciousness-raising discussions and gentle challenges to hesitant clients to encourage movement toward change and increased confidence in practice of new skills.

Relabeling and Reframing

These two related techniques are common to many cognitive-behavioral therapeutic orientations and are used to provide clients with the power to alter, or renegotiate, their perceptions of situations or circumstances that they have allowed to negatively affect them.

Relabeling is the practice of replacing a negative description of a characteristic with a more positive word. For instance, if a woman has been called "mannish" due to a more muscular or stereotypically masculine physique, the therapist might suggest that the client brainstorm alternative adjectives to describe herself. She could be encouraged to replace the negative or hurtful word with a substitute such as "healthy" or "strong." Language is filled with gendered adjectives that can create covert obstacles for clients owning aspects of their identities that do not fit these gendered expectations. Encouraging clients to be creative in how they express themselves and their identities returns to them the power to own their choices and embrace all aspects of their identities.

Reframing is similar but typically is used to translate a potentially negative circumstance or event into a more positive experience. For instance, reframing could be used when a client is not hired for a specific position or is not accepted into a specific training program. She can be encouraged to see the perceived roadblock as an opportunity to seek out a better fitting position or career. Clients often get mired in negative thinking and feel overwhelmed by external circumstances. Helping clients to reframe disappointing or distressing experiences and to shift their perspective to a more empowered stance may help them become "unstuck" and develop new goals. Reframing an experience returns power to clients to take ownership in their interpretation and reaction to events over which they may feel little control.

Social Identity and Gender Role Analysis

The goal of this exercise is to allow a client to explore the ways culturally messaged beliefs about gender and broader social issues have influenced her life, choices, and behaviors. There are four steps involved in this intervention:

1. Invite your client to reflect on the overt and covert gender role expectations that she recalls having received over her life.
2. Ask your client to explore both the positive and negative results that these messages have had on her life. Work with her to brainstorm how she has internalized these messages.
3. Next, explore these messages with your client and help her decide which of these internalized messages she would like to change.
4. Lastly, work with your client to co-construct a plan that will move her forward to make the changes she feels necessary for her well-being.

For women who have grown up in homes in which women were expected to forgo careers in order to care for their families, imagining a different life can create both excitement and anxiety. By helping a client break down her own gender/family-instilled psychological limitations, therapists can help her begin to imagine a life path of her own choosing. It is also important for counselors to validate a client's fears related to breaking new ground as well as the courage exhibited in her desire to do so.

Related to the gender role analysis is the *gender role intervention* (Brown, 2018; Worell & Remer, 2003). This involves a more general, less personal exploration of the ways gender role or social identity expectations play out. The goal is to help clients recognize the strengths and abilities they possess that can be used to confront or contradict the negative stereotypes they might face. This type of analysis may be especially useful for clients who are currently experiencing a sense of failure or shame related to past decisions that were made based on societal gender role expectations. For example, a midlife client longing for a career in engineering after a life spent caring for others may feel ashamed of her earlier decision to drop out of college when she chose to get married before the end of her senior year. By inviting the client to reflect on the ways society downplays or disregards women's scientific expertise, she can discuss the variety of ways gender informs cultural norms. Counselors can help clients recognize their lives are microcosms of the greater cultural macrocosm. This intervention allows a client to externalize problems they have experienced, which moves the "problem" outside of themselves and frees them up to begin to develop a workable solution to their problematic situation.

Power Analysis

The purpose of this intervention is to raise a client's awareness of the ways access to power and resources can vary according to gender and identity and to explore how the client's own reality is affected by this circumstance. Facilitating a client's identification of the power differentials that influence her goals, lived experience, and well-being provides the opportunity for her to develop plans for overcoming and maneuvering around these obstacles. This intervention is similar to the gender role analysis, but it moves beyond gender to include multiple factors that determine to *whom* and under *what circumstances* power is conferred.

Bibliotherapy

Bibliotherapy is the integration of books, stories, and other printed matter into therapy. It can be extremely helpful in normalizing the issues a woman is facing as well as educating her on ways to overcome challenges or understand the reasons she might feel as she does. In addition to printed materials, relevant documentaries or movies are potential resources that might be recommended to clients. Many clients feel that they are the only ones who have feelings like they do, and some may struggle to imagine how to conquer the challenges they are confronting. Reading about or in the case of films seeing another person face and overcome similar obstacles can often empower clients to tackle their own hurdles or misconceptions. Bibliotherapy frequently provides illustrations of ways women successfully integrate the practice of other interventions. For instance, viewing a film about a successful and assertive woman (e.g., *Norma Rae* and *Erin Brockovich*) offers a model of the ways assertiveness skills can positively influence greater change.

CONCLUSION

Although times have changed immeasurably since the birth of the feminist movement, women and other marginalized populations continue to face the institutionalized barriers that feminism aimed to diminish. With an emphasis on the individual experiences of the client as a product of the cultural landscape that surrounds her, feminist therapy is a vehicle that can lead to change at multiple levels. Feminist therapists support and engage in active involvement in advocacy for their clients, self-examination to address their own potential shortcomings, and awareness of the power they wield in their roles as helpers. Integrating the core beliefs of feminist therapy can be effective with diverse clients, including men and boys. To be a feminist practitioner is to be aware of the multiple realities in which people must function and to be committed to the client's ability to effect personal change and development even in a world in which unfair boundaries have been created that limit the available opportunities based on gender, race, sexual orientation, birthplace, and numerous other factors over which individuals have no control.

REFERENCES

Alberti, R., & Emmons, M. (1970). *Your perfect right: A guide to assertive behavior.* San Luis Obispo, CA: Impact Press.

Brown, L. S. (1994). *Subversive dialogues: Theory in feminist therapy.* New York: Basic Books.

Brown, L. S. (2018). *Feminist therapy* (2nd ed.). Washington, DC: American Psychological Association.

Carr, E. R., & McKernan, L. C. (2015). "Keep your chin up": Treating male veterans with posttraumatic stress disorder from an integrative feminist theoretical perspective. *Journal of Psychotherapy Integration, 25*(4), 253–66.

Corey, G. (2015). *Theory and practice of counseling and psychotherapy* (10th ed.). Boston, MA: Cengage Learning.

Enns, C. Z., & Byars-Winston, A. (2010). Multicultural feminist therapy. In H. Landrine & N. F. Russo (Eds.), *Handbook of diversity in feminist psychology* (pp. 367–88). New York, NY: Springer.

Hannam, J. (2012). *Feminism.* New York, NY: Routledge.

Israeli, A. L., & Santor, D. A. (2000). Reviewing effective components of feminist therapy. *Counseling Psychology Quarterly, 13*(3), 233–47.

Proctor, G., & Napier, M. (2004). *Encountering feminism: Intersections between feminism and the person-centered approach.* Ross-on-Wye, UK: PCCS Books.

Root, M. P. P. (2000). Rethinking racial identity development: An ecological framework. In P. Spickard & J. Burroughs (Eds.), *We are a people: Narrative in the construction and deconstruction of ethnic identity* (pp. 237–47). Philadelphia, PA: Temple University Press.

Silver, K. E., Levant, R. F., & Gonzalez, A. (2018). What does the psychology of men and masculinities offer the practitioner? Practical guidance for the feminist, culturally sensitive treatment of traditional men. *Practice Innovations, 3*(2), 94–106.

Speed, B. C., Goldstein, B. L., & Goldfried, M. R. (2017). Assertiveness training: A forgotten evidence-based treatment. *Clinical Psychological Science Practice, 25*, 1–20.

Walker, Lenore E. A. (1990). A feminist therapist views the case. In Dorothy W. Cantor (Ed.), *Women as therapists* (pp. 78–79). New York, NY: Springer.

Wolf, J., Williams, E. N., Darby, M., Herald, J., & Schultz, C. (2018). Just for women? Feminist multicultural therapy with male clients. *Sex Roles, 78*(5–6), 439–50. doi:10.1007/s11199-017-0819-y

Wolter-Gustafson, C. (2004). Towards convergence: Client-centered and feminist assumptions about epistemology and power. In G. Proctor & M. B. Napier (Eds.), *Encountering feminism: Intersections between feminism and the person-centered approach* (pp. 97–115). Ross-on-Wye, UK: PCCS Books.

Wooley, S. G. (1995). Feminist influences on the treatment of eating disorders. In K. D. Brownell & C. G. Fairburn (Eds.), *Eating disorders and obesity: A comprehensive handbook* (pp. 294–98). New York, NY: Guilford Press.

Worell, J. (1993, November). What do we really know about feminist therapies: Approaches to research on process and outcome. Invited presentation to the Texas Psychological Association, Austin, Texas.

Worell, J., & Remer, P. (2003). *Feminist perspectives in therapy: Empowering diverse women* (2nd ed.). Hoboken, NJ: Wiley.

Chapter Three

Integrating Relational-Cultural Therapy into Counseling Practice

Katherine M. Hermann-Turner

> "Intimate relationships are the conduit to the development of the sense of self." (Frey, 2013, p. 178)

In 1976, Jean Baker Miller published *Toward a New Psychology of Women*, which elaborated on feminist principles and set the foundation for what would eventually become relational-cultural therapy (RCT). Fueled by these writings and the pathologization of typical female characteristics (i.e., empathy and the desire for connection to others being considered needy, dependent, or overly emotional), Miller along with Irene Stiver, head of the Department of Psychology at McLean Hospital, and Janet Surrey and Judith Jordan, psychologists at McLean, began having bimonthly meetings (Jordan, 2017). During these Monday meetings, the women discussed deficiencies they observed in traditional clinical theories, reflected on their female clients' unique concerns, and explored the effects of patriarchal influences. Through this dialogue, Miller, Stiver, Surrey, and Jordan recognized the value of traditional female characteristics and identified relationships as a source of connection and growth for their clients, beliefs disregarded by traditional theories.

The meetings of these four women eventually led to the creation of the Jean Baker Miller Training Institute at Wellesley College, hundreds of working documents on RCT, a biennial conference, and most importantly energy around and interest in the importance of relationships (Jordan, 2017). They challenged the egocentric foundation of many existing theories. Relationship, connection, and collective growth were embraced, and practitioners and theorist alike began to acknowledge that humans may not grow in isolation.

These women and their writings opened the doors for the exploration of growth through connections. These writings have continued to welcome and integrate the voices of people of color and all sexual orientations (Duffey & Somody, 2011; Frey, 2013). The ideas of RCT are not static but rather continue to flex to adapt to different cultures and individual perspectives.

A RELATIONAL-CULTURAL THERAPY UNDERSTANDING

RCT is considered a feminist therapeutic approach in that it values individual clients' lived experiences, assumes a strength-based attitude, incorporates an egalitarian clinical relationship, integrates a multicultural perspective, focuses on change rather than acceptance, and conceptualizes an individual within the larger social, economic, and political context (Frey, 2013). The implication of traditional psychological models is twofold: (1) one must have power over others to have power, and (2) connection and relationship are a source of weakness rather than openness and strength (Jordan, 2018). Unlike these traditional models, where the individual is primary and the relationship is secondary, this theory looks at individuals within the context of their relationships—both personal and clinical (Jordan, 2017, 2018). A person's level of development or actualization is not assessed by their achievement of individualization and autonomy or the strength of their boundaries (Comstock et al., 2008; Duffey & Somody, 2011; Frey, 2013). According to RCT, boundaries may be erected to protect against outside dangers, to insulate, or to gain power and ascend the prevertebral hierarchical ladder alone, untouched, and unaffected by others. Isolation, according to RCT, is not a source of strength; rather, it restrains individuals and maintains oppression.

RCT believes that one does not have to be alone to be strong. One does not need power over another to be powerful. Rather, individuals grow through and in connection to others. We do not enter, exist, or exit a relationship, whether minor or significant, without being affected. Every person we come into contact with regardless of the depth of the interaction affects us, and we in turn impact them. There is no limit to our need for or the benefit of connection (Jordan, 2017). We change and grow through relationships. Therefore, relationship are a source of strength, learning, and development for everyone involved. Our own vulnerability fuels change, and we need others to grow!

According to the theorists at the Stone Center, RCT is built on the following eight principles (Jordan, 2000, 2018):

1. Relational growth is ongoing throughout the lifespan.
2. Maturity is demonstrated by mutuality and engagement with others, not independence.

3. More complex and diverse relationships demonstrate growth.
4. Growth-fostering relationships (GFRs) are founded on mutual empathy and empowerment.
5. In a GFR, both people are affected, and both people grow.
6. A therapeutic alliance is built on a unique kind of mutuality.
7. Mutual empathy is the tool for change in counseling.
8. Authenticity and honest engagement are essential for mutual empathy to occur.

These RCT principles provided a revolutionized way of viewing individuals' development that values relational competencies.

Culture is intentionally placed at the center of RCT (Jordan, 2018). In order to understand an individual, one must understand them within the context of their culture. This context often includes "experiences of isolation, shame, humiliation, oppression, marginalization, and macroaggressions [which] are relational violations and traumas" (Comstock et al., 2008, p. 280). These experiences often lead to internalized pain, which affects one's ability to engage in relationships on both a micro (individual relationships) and a macro (connection to society) level. The fear and unease caused by historical and ongoing oppression motivates one to find safety through seclusion and separation, which translates to guarded, unauthentic personal relationships and a truncated potential for growth. Similarly, on a macro level, past traumatization encourages isolation from one's community. Therefore, RCT "integrates multiculturalism, intersectionality, resilience, and strength-based foci into counseling practice" (Singh & Moss, 2016, p. 398). The goal of every counseling relationship is to increase the visibility of one's multiple spheres of influence (i.e., friends, family, community, workplace, media, etc.) to see a person as their whole self (Jordan, 2017). Therefore, RCT uses multicultural and social-justice-informed practices to address difficult issues and promote authenticity.

While RCT emphasizes the need and value of relationships, the theory acknowledges that not all relationships are healthy. Unhealthy relationships are described with the term "power-over" (Jordan, 2017). These relationships do not exemplify mutual growth and development but rather an inequality of power where one person dominates over another. This power-over may be evidenced in extreme cases such as physical or emotional abuse but also in less extreme cases like when an individual loses their voice, does not act authentically, or cannot be vulnerable. A relationship where someone fears being rejected for their thoughts, beliefs, or appearance is an example of a power-over relationship that does not facilitate connection and growth.

CORE COMPONENTS OF RCT

In addition to the eight principles summarized above, RCT has unique components that are integrated throughout the theory's philosophical perspective and clinical applications. Each of these components will be presented and discussed below.

Mutuality

Mutuality is a way of relating where all individuals are open to being affected and affecting another (Frey, 2013; Jordan, 2018; Miller, 1986; Miller & Stiver, 1997). This acknowledgment of the reciprocal nature of a relationship creates openness and shared understanding. Mutuality means shared growth rather than sameness. For instance, in a counseling relationship, both the client and the counselor grow, yet the counselor is still responsible and focused on the client's development (Jordan, 2018).

Mutual Empathy

In 1981, the concept of mutual empathy was added to the RCT model to emphasize the reciprocal nature of connection and the empathy necessary for therapeutic growth (Jordan, 2018). In relationships, including the counseling relationship, each person has an impact on another (Singh & Moss, 2016). As such, an RCT counselor acknowledges and openly expresses that they empathize with a client and are affected by the client's experience (i.e., "when you talk about losing your best friend to cancer, I am deeply saddened"). As a result, the client understands their impact, grows in connection, and reduces feelings of isolation (Duffey & Somody, 2011). This understanding of mutual connection through cocreated, mutual empathy is the foundation of a growth-fostering relationship (GFR) and a start to repairing past relationships and experiences of disconnection.

Authenticity

Authenticity is the capability to represent oneself fully, honestly, and truthfully within a relationship (Duffey & Somody, 2011; Jordan, 2018; Miller, 1986; Miller & Stiver, 1997). Authenticity serves to deepen a relationship if paired with self-awareness of one's impact on others (Frey, 2013; Jordan, 2018)—statements should be made in a way that is honest, not hurtful or judgmental. Authentic statements are not based on impulse but rather on thoughtfulness. Two people in a relationship can have different opinions and views, yet both persons should be empowered to express themselves without fear of how it could affect their connection and relationship. For instance, two friends who have different opinions on cohabitation and marriage express their opinions openly without judging their friends' beliefs or choices. Their friendship is bigger than one topic, and having different opinions is an opportunity for both friends to learn about a different outlook.

Nevertheless, it is difficult for individuals who have experienced a history of oppression, rejection, and marginalization to garner the trust to function authentically within a relationship (Duffey & Somody, 2011). Self-empathy facilitates authenticity; as individual's develop self-compassion, they are empowered to accept themselves and present themselves vulnerably (i.e., authentically) without shame (Duffey & Somody, 2011). Therefore, the first step to being authentic with others is accepting oneself.

Growth-Fostering Relationships

A growth-fostering relationship (GFR) is an authentic, genuine relationship facilitated by mutuality, mutual empathy, and authenticity (Jordan, 2018). In these relationships, both individuals express themselves openly without fear of rejection. Conflicts arise, but instead of being a source of tension, disagreements enable a positive exploration of diversity and differences that promotes growth and deeper connection (Frey, 2013).

The Five Good Things

RCT theorist describe the positive outcomes of a GFR and being engaged in relational connection by the "five good things": (1) zest, evidenced by increased energy and vitality; (2) an increased sense of worth and personal value; (3) clarity of self and other, understanding one's role accurately in a relationship; (4) increased productivity, which is linked to the experience of being empowered; and (5) a desire for more and deeper connections (Comstock et al., 2008; Duffey, Haberstroh, & Trepal, 2009; Jordan, 2008, 2018; Miller, 1986; Miller & Stiver, 1997). These outcomes, which can look a little like a "love bubble" in a new relationship, are very different in their ability to sustain themselves and fuel a more authentic relationship.

Relational Images/Expectations

Relational images are an individual's preconceived understanding or schema of current relationships based on previous experiences (Duffey & Somody, 2011). For instance, someone who has been bullied in the past expects people to treat them with this same kind of disrespect and enters a new relationship guarded. Relational images from chronic and ongoing abuse and rejection can be difficult to re-create; nevertheless, a GFR, the development of self-empathy, and ongoing authentic engagement can empower clients to revisit and re-create these images (Duffey & Somody, 2011).

Central Relational Paradox

RCT describes individual's paradoxical reaction to seek isolation when they desire connection as the "central relational paradox." This reaction can be learned behavior after experiencing chronic disconnections in meaningful relationships (Frey, 2013), or it may be driven by fear and a desire for safety (Comstock et al., 2008). If you have a client say, "I just need a weekend home alone," you may ask them to consider if this is for rejuvenation or to avoid potential relational connection.

Condemned Isolation

Condemned isolation is the experience of feeling completely alone, excluded, and prevented from building connections. It is caused by "relational disconnections, power differentials, gender role socialization, racism, cultural oppression, health disparities, heterosexism, and other social injustice" (Comstock et al., 2008, p. 282). The experience can be societal after feeling like an outsider as a result of being a member of a minority or marginalized population, or it can be social such as being rejected by family because of sexual orientation (Singh & Moss, 2016). This feeling is reinforced through ongoing marginalization and inauthentic, nonmutual relationships and can produce long-term feelings of shame and inferiority.

Disconnection

Disconnections are inevitable in relationships (Jordan, 2017). They may be the result of arguments or withdrawing after feeling disregarded, misunderstood, or unappreciated and can also be paired with feelings of shame and humiliation (Comstock et al., 2008). A disconnection can lead to emotional injury and isolation or provide an opportunity for relational growth. When individuals in a relationship, social or clinical, address a disconnection and work through the hurt, a closer, more authentic relationship is formed, which then advances individual and relational development and maturity. While disconnections are uncomfortable, addressing them openly is imperative for the ongoing, lifelong development presented by RCT.

RELATIONAL-CULTURAL THERAPY IN PRACTICE

The goal of RCT therapy is movement away from isolation (Duffey & Somody, 2011) into relational competence and growth (Frey, 3013; Singh & Moss, 2016). This is all done through the strength of connection and the therapeutic relationship. Within the confines of this relationship, a "quality of presence" (Jordan, 2000, p. 1014) is formed, and together a counselor and client can explore the presenting concern, evaluate past relationships, and experience disconnection and connection.

While the therapeutic relationship appears to begin with an imbalance of power due to a counselor's expertise, RCT contends that both individuals in the counseling relationship bring their own competence and knowledge. Each person contributes to the sessions and the relationship. The counselor may be the expert clinically, but she is not the expert on the client's life, and both individuals will grow through the connection developed in their therapeutic alliance. The counselor is responsible for acknowledging social discrimination, prejudice, and contextual factors that contribute to stress (Comstock et al., 2008) and then helping clients conceptualize themselves within their cultural context (Duffey & Somody, 2011).

The therapy process begins with an assessment phase (Jordan, 2018). While building the relationship, the counselor integrates some psychoanalytic components, gathering background information and learning the client's early relational experiences (Frey, 2013; Jordan, 2018). Understanding the client's history and looking at ongoing patterns of connection can be valuable in learning current ways of relating. The counselor also explores the client's strengths, similar to other feminist therapies, and seeks to discover the client's resiliencies, how they resolve conflicts, and what strategies they use for disconnection (e.g., fighting, instigating arguments, or withdrawing). The counselor discovers ineffective relational dynamics and explores how these have been reinforced by social influences (Comstock et al., 2008).

RCT describes the following six components as part of the therapeutic process (Jordan, 2018):

1. Working though relational connections and disconnections both in the therapeutic relationship and elsewhere. During counseling, clients are challenged to objectively evaluate their relationships. How do they relate to others? When do they feel connected? What influences their willingness to be vulnerable? What past experiences may affect this vulnerability? How do disconnections arise? When do they feel threatened? By exploring the answers to these and other related questions and working through the counselor–client relationship, clients begin to understand their feelings around relationships and their role in making them genuine or inauthentic.

2. Development of mutual empathy to include empathy for oneself. As described above, RCT is unique in the inclusion of two-way or mutual empathy as a counseling technique. During the therapy process, empathy is not a one-sided experience where the counselor expresses empathy for the client. Rather, they engage in the mutual empathy process, where it is apparent both people are affected empathetically. The counselor does not stop with a statement such as, "It must have been very difficult to have experienced that kind of ongoing abuse." Rather, they extend the connection by not only expressing empathy but also describing that they are affected, such as, "It must have been very difficult to have experienced that kind of ongoing abuse. Hearing your story really affects me." Through this powerful model of connection, clients feel valued and empowered and begin to learn self-empathy.

3. Processing and re-creating negative relational images. During counseling, clients explore their relational expectations, and through the example of the therapeutic relationship and counselor's support, they are challenged to begin to dispute these images. A counselor may ask for discrepant relationships that contest ingrained expectations (i.e., discovering a relative or teacher who treated them with respect and compassion). The counselor also works to nurture new expectations of new relationships as a way to prevent the reoccurrence of past patterns, as many people are drawn to relationship patterns that are familiar even if they are unhealthy or abusive. By recognizing and re-creating relational images and planning for healthy relationships within the context of a relationship based on mutual empathy, clients feel valued and empowered to make changes.

4. Counselor responsiveness and willingness to be affected by a client. To be an RCT counselor, one must be open to being vulnerable. Because RCT is grounded in cooperative relationship, the counselor must be open to change; nevertheless, the counselor must remain in their occupational role. The clinician is there for the client, conscious of their ethical responsibilities and attentive to their clinical judgment and intuition. Being affected does not mean shifting the focus from helping to being helped or distracting a client from their emotional experience by the counselor sharing their reactions. Rather, it means opening oneself to an authentic experience where the client truly feels in connection.

5. Integration and acceptance of the client's unique culture. As mentioned, a counselor acknowledges a client's culture and the many positive and negative experiences that may be the result (e.g., marginalization, prejudice, heterosexism). By drawing attention to multiculturalism and intersectionality, the counselor fully accepts the client and attempts to learn from the client's unique experiences. Differences between the client and counselor are broached, as working through these differences openly can provide another layer of healing and connection. A counselor does not need to have a similar past to the client, but they do need to be open to addressing and empathetically working to understand the client's history.

6. Development of relational "resilience." Resilience alone is not an element of RCT therapy as it denotes a potential movement toward isolation rather than learning to reach out and connect to others. Rather than seeking seclusion, relational resilience demonstrates movement toward comfort with vulnerability, confidence, empowerment, and evolution as a relational being. Bouncing back from hurt and continuing to attempt connection to others is difficult but also an opportunity for deeper connection and better understanding of oneself.

The co-occurrence of these six elements during counseling can help a client learn a new style of relating authentically where unproductive patterns of connecting can vulnerably be addressed and sustainable healthy strategies for relationship be created (Duffey & Somody, 2011). Through this process, individuals develop emotional strength and decrease distress (Frey, 2013).

RELATIONAL-CULTURAL THERAPY TECHNIQUES

As described throughout this chapter, RCT is a paradigm shift from an individualistic perspective to therapy founded on connections and diverse meaningful relationships as a basis for developmental growth. Change is not believed to be the result of specific therapeutic techniques; rather, a high quality of engagement between the client and counselor provides the foundation for the counseling process (Frey, 2013; Haskins & Appling, 2017). Counselors are encouraged "to think beyond symptom reduction and remedial helping interventions" (Comstock et al., 2008, p. 280), and presenting concerns and movement toward growth are conceptualized from a strength-based and relational perspective (Frey, 2013). While the theory is grounded in more of a perspective shift, some specific practices can help facilitate the growth process.

A GFR is an essential part of the therapeutic process. While creating this relationship is not a technique in and of itself, the development of this connection requires the use of the principles of mutuality, mutual empathy, and therapeutic authenticity (Duffey & Somody, 2011). To build the deep trust of a GFR, the counselor must practice mutuality and mutual empathy, letting the client know that they have truly affected the counselor. This movement into mutuality is prompted by the counselor's authenticity and openness to being changed. Using these techniques is essential to building a GFR and the RCT therapeutic process.

The RCT therapeutic process also utilizes a psychoanalytic component (Frey, 2013; Jordan, 2018), employing a retrospective perspective to evaluate ongoing relational patterns and explore their origin before making plans to re-create patterns of relating (Duffey & Somody, 2011). The technique of carefully exploring the past is an essential part of the assessment phase as a counselor gathers information to understand the client and finds discrepancies from current relational images. A counselor may explore a turbulent mother–daughter relationship where a client felt rejected by their mother and then seek exceptions to this way of relating. For instance, have there been other motherlike figures or mentors in the client's life who were accepting? If so, the counselor would explore these exceptions to help the client re-create their expectation of a motherlike figure from rejection to acceptance. The process of exploring, evaluating, and rationally using past experiences to make changes can help clients move from "shame-based and mistrustful interpersonal impasses and disconnections and back into transformative connections" (Comstock et al., 2008, p. 283). Asking about and processing the past provides opportunities for healing for a client and information to re-create new relational plans.

Developing a client's relational awareness involves discussions in counseling and practice outside of sessions. A client must better understand their past and also be aware in the present to avoid the re-creation of past ineffective patterns and make long-term, sustained changes. Gaining this skill "is the first step in developing more sophisticated relational capacities that enable one to identify, deconstruct, and resist disconnections and obstacles to mutual empathy in counseling relationships and in the broader culture" (Comstock et al., 2008, p. 202).

Working through disconnections (Duffey & Somody, 2011), which are an unavoidable part of all relationships, including the client–counselor relationship (Comstock et al., 2008), is another essential technique. Counselors must develop a strong awareness of the onset of disconnections in sessions and be comfortable with addressing these uncomfortable rifts. Through honest confrontation of uncomfortable experiences, within the context of a GFR, clients are able to learn the skills necessary to work through disconnections in their own life and build the stronger connections that result.

Lastly, the RCT therapy process can often benefit from creative interventions (Duffey & Somody, 2011). Creative techniques in and of themselves can provide clients with a different way of viewing the world (Gladding, 2016). The use of creative arts can stimulate a client, provide memorable experiences, and also engage a different part of the brain than typically used in talk therapy. This movement toward a holistic counseling experience can facilitate a vulnerable experience for clients and provide a viable platform for clients and counselors to work together toward an end goal.

While RCT is not a technique-driven theory, the conscious use of specific skills can facilitate the development of a GFR, focus a counselor's attention, and assist client growth. Throughout the therapeutic process, a counselor must remain grounded in the RCT belief in growth through relationship and be attentive to past wounds from marginalization and discrimination. Focusing on the client and the relationship first, and then using techniques to build upon these central elements, can facilitate a positive, long-lasting therapeutic outcome.

CROSS-CULTURAL APPLICATION OF RELATIONAL-CULTURAL THERAPY

Although RCT was developed by women with the goal of understanding and addressing the unique needs of women, it has been applied to various populations (Jordan, 2018). Currently, RCT is applied to the "psychology of men and women, those at the margin and those at the center of society" (Jordan, 2017, p. 232). Some specific topics of research and application include couples counseling (Jordan & Carlson, 2014), new mothers' experience of isolation (Paris & Dubus, 2005), eating disorders (Trepal, Boie, & Kress, 2012), self-injurious behavior (Trepal, 2010), adolescents (Cannon, Hammer, Reicherzer, & Gilliam, 2012; Tucker, Smith-Adcock, & Trepal, 2011), body image (Sanftner, Ryan, & Pierce, 2009), professional mentoring (Fletcher & Ragins, 2007), and LGBTQQ clients (Singh & Moss, 2016). RCT has also been integrated with other theoretical orientations and counseling practices such as reality therapy (Haskins & Applng, 2017) and play therapy (Vicario, Tucker, Smith Adcock, & Hudgins-Mitchell, 2013). Through ongoing research, the applicability of RCT to an extensive range of populations has been validated.

CONCLUSION

The RCT approach to counseling and view of development provides a paradigm shift in understanding individuals and human development. The transition from the disregard and downgrading of relational principles to viewing connection as a strength and essential component of developmental growth has transformed our understating of relationships. With this framework, "mental health professionals can explore how issues related to sex role socialization, power, dominance, marginalization, and subordination affect the mental health and relational development of all people" (Comstock et al., 2008, p. 279). Culture, past experiences, and connections can now be used constructively to help clients develop relational skills and improve long-term prognosis.

REFERENCES

Cannon, K. B., Hammer, T. R., Reicherzer, S., & Gilliam, B. J. (2012). Relational-cultural theory: A framework for relational competencies and movement in group work with female adolescents. *Journal of Creativity in Mental Health, 7*(1), 2–16.

Comstock, D., Daniels, J., & D'Andrea, M. (2006). Building unity and vision: A relational-cultural approach. *Counseling Today , 49*(2), 38.

Comstock, D., Hammer, T. R., Strentzsch, J., Cannon, K., Parsons, J., & Salazar, G., II. (2008). Relational-cultural theory: A framework for bridging relational, multicultural, and social justice competencies. *Journal of Counseling & Development , 86*(3), 279–87.

Duffey, T. (2006). Promoting relational competencies in counselor education through creativity and relational-cultural theory. *Journal of Creativity in Mental Health* , *2*(1), 47–59.

Duffey, T., Haberstroh, S., & Trepal, H. (2009). A grounded theory of relational competencies and creativity in counseling: Beginning the dialogue. *Journal of Creativity in Mental Health* , *4*(2), 89–112.

Duffey, T., & Somody, C. (2011). The role of relational-cultural theory in mental health counseling. *Journal of Mental Health Counseling, 33*(3), 223–42.

Fletcher, J. K., & Ragins, B. R. (2007). Stone Center relational cultural theory. In B. R. Ragins & K. E. Kram (Eds.), *The handbook of mentoring at work: Theory, research, and practice* (pp. 373–99). Thousand Oaks, CA: Sage.

Frey, L. L. (2013). Relational-cultural therapy: Theory, research, and application to counseling competencies. *Professional Psychology: Research and Practice, 44*(3), 177–85.

Gladding, S. T. (2016). *The creative arts in counseling* (5th ed.). Alexandria, VA: American Counseling Association.

Haskins, N. H., & Appling, B. (2017). Relational-cultural theory and reality therapy: A culturally responsive integrative framework. *Journal of Counseling & Development, 95*(1), 87–99.

Jordan, J. V. (2000). The role of mutual empathy in relational/cultural therapy. *Journal of Clinical Psychology, 56*(8), 1005–16.

Jordan, J. V. (2008). *The power of connection: Recent developments in relational-cultural theory*. Philadelphia, PA: Haworth Press.

Jordan, J. V. (2017). Relational-cultural theory: The power of connection to transform our lives. *Journal of Humanistic Counseling, 56*(3), 228–43.

Jordan, J. V. (2018). *Relational-cultural therapy*. Washington, DC: American Psychological Association.

Jordan, J. V., & Carlson, J. (2014). *Creating connection: A relational-cultural approach with couples*. New York, NY: Routledge.

Miller, J. B. (1986). What do we mean by relationships? Work in progress no. 22. Stone Center, Wellesley College.

Miller, J. B., & Stiver, I. (1997). *The healing connection: How women form relationship in therapy and in life*. Boston, MA: Beacon Press.

Paris, R., & Dubus, N. (2005). Staying connected while nurturing an infant: A challenge of new motherhood. *Family Relations, 54*(1), 72–83.

Ruiz, E. (2005). Hispanic culture and relational cultural theory. *Journal of Creativity in Mental Health, 1*(1), 33–55.

Sanftner, J. L., Ryan, W. J., & Pierce, P. (2009). Application of a relational model to understanding body image in college women and men. *Journal of College Student Psychotherapy, 23*(4), 262–80.

Singh, A. A., & Moss, L. (2016). Using relational-cultural theory in LGBTQQ counseling: Addressing heterosexism and enhancing relational competencies. *Journal of Counseling & Development, 94*(4), 398–404.

Trepal, H. C. (2010). Exploring self-injury through a relational cultural lens. *Journal of Counseling & Development, 88*(4), 492–99.

Trepal, H. C., Boie, I., & Kress, V. E. (2012). A relational cultural approach to working with clients with eating disorders. *Journal of Counseling & Development, 90*(3), 346–56.

Tucker, C., Smith-Adcock, S., & Trepal, H. (2011). Relational-cultural theory for middle school counselors. *Professional School Counseling, 14*(5), 310–16.

Vicario, M., Tucker, C., Smith Adcock, S., & Hudgins-Mitchell, C. (2013). Relational-cultural play therapy: Reestablishing healthy connections with children exposed to trauma in relationships. *International Journal of Play Therapy, 22*(2), 103–17.

Vogel, J. (2006). Using relational-cultural theory to conceptualize couple interventions in the treatment of sex addiction. *Journal of Creativity in Mental Health* , 2(4), 3–17.

Part II

Development from Adolescence through Older Adulthood

Chapter Four

Counseling Adolescent Girls

Marcela Kepic

CASE VIGNETTE: SOFIA

Sofia has recently celebrated her sixteenth birthday. She has one younger brother, but she considers herself homeless. Her mother and younger brother have been moving from shelter to shelter since shortly after Sofia's father was deported back to Mexico due to charges of domestic violence and child abuse. Sofia and her mother have a rather distant relationship that has been getting worse in recent months. Sofia attends school but struggles academically. She enjoys the arts, especially painting. Sofia does not have a lot of friends but, on occasion, speaks with one girl from her art class. She hangs out with other teens on her block but is not close to any of them due to frequent relocations. Last weekend, she got home very late and was drunk. This sparked a heated argument between Sofia and her mother. Her mother is forcing Sofia to get a job so they can afford to find their own place to live. Her mother's employment is very inconsistent as she is undocumented and has difficulty locating a long-term, stable job. Sofia's school counselor referred her to an independent living program for teenage girls, where Sofia met her clinical mental health counselor, Anna, who specializes in counseling teenage girls.

* * *

Adolescence is a period of significant development across multiple domains due, in part, to pubertal changes that occur as girls move from childhood into emerging adulthood. Significant development occurs in the areas of physical, cognitive, emotional, behavioral, and sexual development as many milestones are reached. Growth spurts, menarche, the development of secondary sexual characteristics, and other tangible signs of development are accompanied by inner changes that mark the passage from childhood into adulthood. These are visible in the areas of emotional, behavioral, and cognitive functioning.

Emotional, Behavioral, and Cognitive Changes

Due to hormonal changes that occur during puberty, emotional stability can be challenged and this can yield notable behavioral changes, as well. Increased levels of androgens and estrogens are produced, as these spur the development of primary and secondary sexual characteristics, and changes in the levels of serotonin and dopamine also occur, which yield heightened sensitivity to stress during adolescence (Walker, 2002). Moodiness, or extreme and rapid shifts in emotions, seem to be more characteristic of adolescence than any other developmental period. Hormonal changes are more likely to affect a young woman's mood if they are combined with negative life circumstances (e.g., parental separation, academic problems). Moreover, moodiness seems to be associated with peer relationships, parental expectations, and an adolescent's self-concept. Gutman, Peck, Malanchuk, Sameroff, and Eccles (2017) found that self-esteem levels tend to vary more for females than males during the adolescent years. Gutman et al. also found ethnicity was a key factor for self-esteems; African American adolescent females are less likely to show the decline that is typical of this period for European Americans. They also found that self-esteem tended to increase in early adolescence, from ages 12 to 15, but began dropping at age 16 and continued its decline until age 20 was reached. A combination of factors likely affect adolescent females' self-esteem levels including gender-based discrimination, body image issues, lower expectations for success, not feeling supported by others, and an early onset of puberty. As adolescent females face these and other stressors, there is a greater risk for experiencing depressive symptoms during this period, as well. Hormonal changes may play a role in depressive symptomology, but studies have suggested that exposure to social media and screen time engagement may also account for the rise in depressive symptoms that are seen in contemporary adolescents (Twenge, Joiner, Rogers, & Martin, 2018). Girls might experience more depressive symptoms not only due to the number of stressors faced but also because of their tendency to adopt a co-ruminating coping style. Rumination is the practice of focusing attention internally toward negative thoughts and feelings, which increases in frequency throughout adolescence (Mazzer, Boersma, & Linton, 2019), and co-rumination is the practice of focusing on negative feelings and distressing events in conversations with friends. Adolescence is a period in which social status and social connections play a significant role in a young woman's identity; building alliances based on mutual empathy and support can be efficacious, but when co-rumination is the primary focus of engagement, the end result may be compromised, not fortified, psychological well-being (Mazzer et al., 2019). While puberty alone does not necessarily cause a rise in depressive symptoms, the interactions between physiological changes and the role of social acceptance and fear of social rejection may cause the rise in depressive symptoms for older adolescent females (McGuire, McCormick, Koch, & Mendle, 2019).

One benefit of the changes going on in the adolescent brain is the increased cognitive potential through acquisition and integration of new information. This allows adolescents to gradually reach the formal operations stage, Piaget's last stage of cognitive development (Piaget, 1965). The gradual improvement in abstract reasoning skills is evident in adolescents' advanced information processing skills, which yield greater processing speed and extended capacity of their working memory. The capacity for abstract thought in adolescent years can influence many aspects of teenage life, such as perspectives they take on sociopolitical climate, religion, relationships with parents and peers, and, finally, self-evaluation and self-identity.

Identity Development

Identity formation is a central task for adolescents to achieve. In fact, Erikson (1968) termed the central conflict during this period as "*identity versus identity confusion*." This period is shaped by an individual's ability to successfully overcome challenges that relate to solidification of a young woman's identity. As adolescents seek to define their identities, they may face challenges in terms of acceptance by their families, peers, or significant others as they "try on" behaviors they feel congruent to the identity they are trying to portray. For instance, if a young woman is seeking to be accepted by a particular social clique, she may emulate behaviors and attitudes endemic to these peers. If these behaviors are not congruent with how the young woman sees herself or how close friends see her, and her efforts do not win her acceptance into the desired group, she may drop these behaviors from her repertoire.

Using Erikson's theory as a framework, James Marcia and his associates (1980) identitfied and labeled four discrete statuses that may be achieved during the identity formation process. These are moratorium, diffusion, foreclosure, and achievement. Identity moratorium occurs when the adolescent is exploring various identities to find the one that is most congruent with her true self, but is not yet committed to a final choice. Diffusion is marked by a lack of awareness that identity options are available for exploration. Foreclosure represents a status in which a young woman has not faced any type of identity crisis or has felt the need to explore identities beyond the one she currently possesses, which may likely conform to the expectations of others. Identity achievement is the result of having explored possible identities and having chosen the one that best fits how the young woman sees herself. Despite the fact that identity formation begins during adolescent years, as young people make visible strides in developing who they will be as adults, the formation of identity does not end in adolescence. Through ongoing growth and development, self-representation might change several times over the lifespan, and life stories may be revised by life circumstances.

Even though Erikson's developmental theory has been widely accepted, it faces some criticism that it is primarily centered on emphasizing separateness or autonomy, a significant feature of masculinity, and fails to emphasize connectedness as a healthy personality development, especially for women (Gilligan, 1982). Regardless of gender, having a sense of social belonging plays a key role in healthy identity development (Medina, Rivas-Drake, Jagers, & Rowley, 2019). Research suggests that relational issues are much more important for women's development than they are for men; further, adolescent girls tend to have closer friendships than boys, which leaves them more vulnerable to distress when friendships end (Collins & Steinberg, 2006). In addition, females tend to value interpersonal, communal aspects of their identities more highly than males. As for whether identity development pathways are different for women and men, the question remains complex and lacks any definite answer at this point. Research suggests that the genders show more similarities than differences in identity development; however, the content of their identity choices might differ (Waterman, 1993; Collins & Steinberg, 2006).

Sexual Identity and Sexual Activity

With the onset of puberty, young adolescent girls typically begin to explore their sexuality and sexual identity (Collins & Steinberg, 2006). Sexual identity is often more fluid among adolescents than some might expect (Stewart, Spivey, Widman, Choukas-Bradley, & Prinstein, 2019). In fact, approximately a quarter of the adolescent girls in Stewart et al.'s (2019) study reported fluidity in their sexual identity over a course of three years. These adolescent females reported fluidity in their sexual and romantic attractions and this supports earlier findings from Savin-Williams and Ream (2007). They reported that around 50 percent of adolescents have some form of sexual experience with same-sex peers. The development of an adolescent's sexual orientation, whether for same or opposite sex partners, is typically a central feature of sexual development and romantic and sexual relationships generally are concentrated foci for adolescents.

Most identity development theories include some elements of exploration and commitment. The same applies to sexual identity development. For gay, lesbian, and bisexual adolescents, sexual questioning and disclosure have been identified by Savin-Williams and Diamond (2000) as two central identity development processes. These developmental processes resemble exploration and commitment stages of other identity development; however, individuals' paths through such phases might be extremely diverse, related to gender, minority status, religion, socioeconomic status, and parental acceptance or rejection. Moreover, individual case histories suggest that sexual identity and orientation can evolve and change across the lifespan (Lips, 1997). For example, some women transition to lesbian identity in adulthood; other lesbian women transition to heterosexual identity later in life (Bart, 1993). The time and nature of sexual identity development varies despite the fact that young adolescent girls begin to disclose their sexual orientation shortly after puberty or toward the end of adolescence (Broderick & Blewitt, 2014). Many adolescent girls struggle to come to terms with their own sexual orientation, especially when it is not one that they feel will be accepted by family or peers. Therefore, clinicians need to be knowledgeable about and sensitive to issues related to such complex identity development when working with their clients. They also must be prepared to help clients who are wrestling with exploration and experimentation with sexual partners of any gender.

Given our cultural focus on sexuality, it is not surprising that adolescents are sexually active, but there have been shifts in the prevalence of sexual activity among this age group. According to the Youth Risk Behavior Surveillance System (Kann et al., 2018), the percentage of ninth- through twelfth-grade students who reported having sexual intercourse has decreased (47 percent in 2007 compared to 40 percent in 2017). Ten percent of high school students reported having four or more sexual partners, and 30 percent reported having had sexual intercourse during the previous three months. Of these adolescents, 46 percent did not use a condom, 14 percent did not use any form of contraception, and 19 percent had used alcohol or drugs prior to their most recent incidence of sexual intercourse. Although there has been a decline in sexual intercourse, young adolescents are engaging in sexual experimentation in greater numbers and at earlier age than generations before them (Zimmer-Gembeck & Helfand, 2008). Even though sexual intercourse may be less frequent for teens, risks for sexually transmitted diseases are still a concern. Thus, clinicians may need to provide adolescent clients with information on preventing disease as well as preventing unwanted pregnancies. In addition to changing relationships with potential sexual partners, family relationships may also be an area of concern for adolescent girls.

Relationships with Parents

Parents continue to play a crucial role in their children's lives as they enter adolescence and emerging adulthood. Parents' involvement in their children's lives is crucial to healthy development during puberty and the use of an authoritative parenting style (e.g., high in responsiveness and high in demandingness) has been linked to higher academic achievement (Ahuja & Goyal, 2006) and higher levels of self-esteem, self-confidence, self-control, and social adjustment (Broderick & Blewitt, 2014).

Despite the fact that adolescents will strive for independence and autonomy and prefer their peers over their parents, it is clearly beneficial for parents or caretakers to stay involved in appropriate ways. The harder parents try to restrain their adolescent daughters, the harder many might struggle against their parents' efforts to control them. When young women feel that their autonomy-seeking behaviors are being threatened, they may try to assert their independence. Therefore, they may choose to engage in unmonitored activities with peers in which they may encounter more opportunities for risky behaviors (Tilton Weaver et al., 2010). Other researchers have suggested that a link exists between parental restrictive behaviors and adolescent girls' relational aggression (Centifanti, Fanti, Thomson, Demetriou, & Anastassiou-Hadjicharalambous, 2015). Longitudinal and cross-sectional studies of young and late adolescent girls reveal a negative correlation between parental promotions of autonomy and their daughters' depressive symptoms (Soenens, Park, Vansteenkiste, & Mouratidis, 2012). This link has been found repeatedly across cultures. Clinicians working with adolescent girls and their families should communicate to parents that the greater the perception of their promotion of their daughter's autonomy, the less likely she is to experience depressive symptoms (Manzi, Regalia, Pelucchi, & Fincham, 2012; Sheldon, Abad, & Omoile, 2009). Adolescence is a time when relationships with both parents may shift, and the changes in relationships with mothers are often quite different from those between daughters and their fathers.

Mother–Daughter Relationships

The relationship between a mother and a daughter can shift dramatically with the onset of puberty. What was once observed as a loving, kind, and friendly relationship might become more competitive and stressful during the adolescent years. Through the process of separation from her mother, a daughter seeks to establish her own identity and draws influence and engagement from a wider world (e.g., peers, school) than just her home and immediate family. Generational differences can produce wide disparities in values such as independence and sexuality, which can predictably lead to mother–daughter conflict. Not surprisingly, studies have found that a supportive approach to adolescent girls' autonomy seeking was associated with fewer conflicts (Missotten, Luyckx, Vanhalst, Nelemans, & Branje, 2017). In some cases, mothers may over-identify with their daughters or feel jealous of a daughter's youth and attractiveness; unsurprisingly, these feelings often result in a violation of boundaries (Williams, 1987). As daughters strive for increasing levels of autonomy and choose not to confide in their mothers but rather a friend or a relative, mothers may find this separation process rather painful. Once daughters mature, grow into adulthood, and accrue more life experience, the competition or rivalry may diminish and a new intimacy may set in from knowing and understanding each other (Degges-White & Borzumato-Gainey, 2011).

Father–Daughter Relationships

Due to gender differences and possibly time constraints, fathers typically relate to their daughters differently than mothers do. There is a spectrum of the level of fathers' involvement in their daughters' lives, and therefore their relationship will vary. Having a positive father-daughter relationship can significantly influence an adolescent's sense of self and her engagement in risky behaviors. Despite the fact that many fathers might not have a lot of time to spend with their daughters, a father's influence on an adolescent daughter is significant; in fact, it was found that a father has greater influence on his daughter's self-esteem than he does on his adolescent son's development (Keizer, Helmerhorst, & van Gelderen, 2019). Sentino, Thompson, Nugent, and Freeman (2018) found that an adolescent girl's perceptions about her father's levels of care and communication were related to the number of sexual partners with whom she engaged. The higher the quality of the perceived relationship, the fewer the number of partners she had. In light of the many ways in which family constellations may vary through blended families, reconstituted families, and other diverse arrangements, it is worth to note that stepfathers can forge strong and supportive relationships with their adolescent stepdaughters that are equal in positive qualities as those between biological fathers and daughters (Campbell & Winn, 2018). Fathers have significant influence on their adolescent daughters, and clinicians should encourage the families with whom they work to foster healthy relationships between both parents and their children. Even as relationships with parents may change, relationships between adolescent girls and their friends grow more intense.

Friendships

Adolescent girls tend to spend increasing amounts of time with their friends, and they shift their dependency onto them as they grow away from their parents (Degges-White & Borzumato-Gainey, 2011). Peers become the most significant source of support for many adolescents, and it is through these relationships that adolescents construct their identity. They rely on social comparison and attribution substitution, such as trying on or borrowing various behaviors of their friends to shape their own sense of identity (Degges-

White & Borzumato-Gainey, 2011). Girls tend to seek more connection, support, and understanding in relationships they develop and maintain (Gilligan, 1982; Jordan, Kaplan, Miller, Stiver, & Surrey, 1991), and these are selected from available peers (e.g., classmates, block friends). In groups or cliques, girls will operate according to the principles of group dynamics, such as norms, roles, selections, and expectations (Cohen & Prinstein, 2006); therefore, they are easily influenced by others, even if it is in a negative way. Adolescent girls can also be a source of stress rather than support to each other. They can perpetrate aggression by spreading rumors, gossiping about others, attempting to ruin relationships, and manipulating and excluding others (Centifanti & Modecki, 2013). Clinicians should help adolescents assess their support networks and friendships groups to determine whether or not the relationships are providing the support she would prefer.

Romantic Relationships

As mentioned earlier, the adolescent years are full of exploration and trial-and-error learning and this includes romantic relationships, as well. Today's "hook-up culture" opens up many adolescents to engagement in low/no-attachment sexual intimacy but at a potentially high cost. In fact, most sexual encounters occur within non-dating relationships (e.g., with friends or ex-partners) (Centers for Disease Control and Prevention, 2019). Young women who engage in "friends with benefits" relationships have noted that these types of alliances actually give them a sense of empowerment, control, and safety in that both partners are cognizant of the purpose and the limits of their relationships (Jovanovic & Williams, 2017). More serious romantic relationships, however, become increasingly preferable in late adolescence into the emerging adult years as the desire for a deeper connection and commitment from a partner grow in significance.

Relationship with Self and Media

Adolescent girls may experience many more stressors growing up compared to their male counterparts. For example, body image, double standards in sexuality, female gender roles being valued less than male roles, lower expectations of success for girls, earlier onset of puberty, and rumination tendencies are only some of the factors influencing girls' self-esteem and self-perceptions, which tend to decline in adolescent years. As young girls are trying to figure out who they are, they are constantly bombarded with messages about who they need to become. Their relationship to self is rather fragile and often unacknowledged due to frequent peer and media pressure of expected norms for looks and behaviors. There is little room for introspection on their own strengths, talents, and values.

Social media plays a significant role in the world of adolescent girls and it can have a significant impact on their sense of self. Nowadays, the majority of adolescents are connected to social media through technology (e.g., computers, smart phones). What they see and hear on social media platforms shapes their views, perspectives, and experiences significantly. Research indicates that 71 percent of adolescents use more than one social media platform, and the average time spent on social media is about nine hours a day (Department of Health and Human Services, 2016). The most common platforms are Facebook, Instagram, and Snapchat. Girls were found more likely than boys to use visually oriented platforms such as Instagram, Pinterest, and Tumblr. Social media use is consistently and positively associated with negative body image, and longitudinal studies suggest that this association may strengthen over time; young women who spend a significant amount of time viewing music videos are especially at risk for increased perceived importance of appearance and increased weight concerns (Fardouly & Vartanian, 2016). The majority of social media platforms expose adolescents to violent, sexual, and materialistic images, which often serve as a social comparison; this creates expectations for normative behaviors and values that might be incongruent with those of most families (Comstock & Scharrer, 2006). In the last few years, text messaging and chat rooms have become a norm for communicating not only with friends but also with the larger society, often anonymously. This presents another opportunity for risk taking and aggressive behaviors, such as cyberbullying. To navigate such a complex and challenging environment while establishing an identity, adolescent girls require support and guidance primarily from their immediate family circle but also from school personnel and the larger community. It is through constant negotiations between all factors mentioned above (e.g., risk factors and protective factors) that young girls will develop a clear sense of self and continue with healthy biopsychosocial development. It is a team effort to raise a child and support a growing adolescent. No school or family can do it alone. Parents, professionals, and nonprofessionals have a huge obligation to create environments that promote healthy growth opportunities for all adolescents.

BEST PRACTICES

Referrals for adolescent counseling are frequent and there are seldom enough practitioners who specialize in this area. According to the Department of Health and Human Services (2016), most adolescent girls struggle at some point with symptoms of depression, anxiety, attention deficit and hyperactivity disorder, or eating disorders. The National Survey on Drug Use and Health (Center for Behavioral Health Statistics and Quality, 2018) found that 13.3 percent of all youth have experienced a major depressive episode. Overall, almost 35 percent of youth at some point struggle with mood disorders, and two-thirds who do are girls. Findings from a meta-analysis of psychological treatment outcomes for depressed youth indicated that cognitive behavioral therapy (CBT) and interpersonal therapy (IPT) were the two most efficacious treatments (David-Ferdon & Kaslow, 2008). It is imperative to note that many adolescent girls might not present with typical symptoms of depression (e.g., hopelessness, isolation, weight gain, weight loss). On the contrary, children and adolescents may have symptoms of depression that manifest with a great deal of anger, arguing, physical fighting, and outrageous behaviors. As behaviors are purposeful, adolescent behaviors can often be expressions of unmet needs closely related to adolescents' developmental stage. See chapter 16 for additional information on counseling women with mood disorders.

To be as effective as possible in counseling adolescent girls, it is necessary to keep in mind their emotional, cognitive, and psychosocial development and the developmental tasks (e.g., competence, autonomy, intimacy, formation of identity) they are managing. These developmental tasks are linked to specific behaviors that are easily detectable. For example, arguing with and disobeying teachers and parents may stem from frustration related to an inability to succeed in school. Other young women may opt for "sensation seeking" activities in order to avoid boredom, avoid being put down, and overcome feelings of being ignored and unimportant. These behavioral functions are linked to the developmental task of achieving competency. Acting out behaviors, such as causing trouble in school, making threats, choosing outrageous clothing, or using profanity, are potentially related to an adolescent's need to make a personal statement and to be recognized as a capable and worthy individual. In such instances, counselors should focus on validating needs and the developmental tasks at hand while helping the client to develop more appropriate and healthier alternatives. For example, allowing girls to participate in rule and decision making, exploring ways they can contribute to society, teaching them to identify and express anger and other feelings more appropriately, and teaching them negotiations skills are ways to validate and redirect their efforts at identity development and competence achievement. Lastly, clinicians should bear in mind that the expression of needs and the actions taken to fulfill them are determined to a large extent by a client's cultural background.

CULTURAL CONSIDERATIONS

No matter a young woman's age, an individual's culture plays a significant role in shaping her values, perceptions, and experiences. Racial, ethnic, and religious background and socioeconomic status can greatly influence development and counselors should be careful to consider intersectionality and its effects on development. While many practitioners may have completed a course in cultural diversity, it is important for clinicians to think beyond broad brush strokes when considering the influence of cultural identity on clients. Every client is the product of a unique set of circumstances, influences, and background.

ETHICAL CONSIDERATIONS

Despite the exercised independence that adolescents show in many realms of life, it is important to remember that adolescents are still minors. Informed consent, confidentiality, reporting, and counselor competence are four issues of concern when counseling children and adolescents (Lawrence & Kurpius, 2011). Informed consent gives formal permission for treatment, and parents need to give consent for treatment. It is also recommended that counselors obtain adolescent verbal or written consent, but the parents enter into the contract by their consent. Juvenile court can order counseling for adolescents (e.g., give permission to treatment without parents' or minor's consent). At sixteen, adolescents are considered mature minors, and that gives them specific rights under special circumstances. Such circumstances or exceptions from parental consent include emancipation, birth control, pregnancy, sexually transmitted diseases, treatment for drug use, and alleged sexual assault of a minor over twelve. Confidentiality is limited, and parents or legal guardians have a right to be informed about treatment and any assessments that are being administered. Counselors working with young girls need to be aware of their responsibility, as highlighted in the ACA Code of Ethics (ACA, 2014) as they are ethically obligated to obtain adolescent permission to release information. Every clinician working with adolescents walks a fine line here to ensure that their clients do not lose trust in the counselor. Trust can be jeopardized when personal information is disclosed without informing the client beforehand. However, by informing the parent, the counselor is obeying the laws of the state in which they practice. Mandatory reporting is related to reporting child and adolescent abuse and neglect. Counselors are obligated to report any suspected negligence or abuse; otherwise, they fail to obey the law and follow ethical standards. Bean, Softas-Nall, and Mahoney (2011) reported that 27 percent of clients dropped out of therapy after their counselor broke confidentiality for mandatory reporting. Thus, it is important to ensure that adolescent clients are made aware of your intent to disclose and the ways this might influence the client's life.

ADVOCACY OPPORTUNITIES

Considering their age and developmental tasks, such as striving for more independence, competence, and exploring identities, adolescent girls should be first acknowledged and validated for their feelings and experiences, as it is challenging to navigate this period today. Social media and entertainment media can negatively influence their development. Messages of what is the "right look," the "right weight," and the "right outfit" surround them daily, creating constant pressure to conform to cultural standards. As they are creating their identities, it is important to highlight their uniqueness, celebrate their strengths and talents, and bring into their awareness the significant potential that every girl possesses. Further, counselors can advocate for egalitarian approaches to education, career, and personal success. Also, addressing double standard in sexuality is a crucial advocacy piece for everyone, including creating safe environments for members of the LGBT population. Counselors should also promote assertiveness and self-advocacy in their clients to help them navigate today's sociopolitical climate.

Case Vignette Wrap-Up: Sofia

Sofia started to trust her counselor as the counselor demonstrated empathy and validation of Sofia's feelings of being lost and out of place: "I don't want to go to school, I am forcing myself to go every day. I don't fit in. I wear the same clothes over and over again and other girls have new outfits every week. They go out together and I don't get invited. Some boys made fun of me when I didn't bring art supplies. I feel nervous before any presentation because I know kids are going to think that I am an outcast." Anna looked at Sofia, whose eyes were watery and said, "It looks like you are going through a lot, and it must be very hard facing so many difficulties, especially when it comes to not having your own home and feeling out of place." Sofia's tears were running down her cheeks at this point, but she continued: "I don't want to feel like this. . . . My mom tells me to get a job. . . . But I can't. I don't want to feel the same way while working. I know we need money, but I don't care." Anna maintained her eye contact, took some time to respond, and after some silence said, "It sounds like there is a conflict between you and your mom, and such conflict is not helping you at all. Am I right?" Sofia nodded and said, "I wish my mom could understand." "You don't feel supported by your mom," Anna reflected. Anna then asked if there was anything else bothering her at the present time. Sophie shook her head to signify that there was not.

Interventions: Strength-Based Approach

Anna began, "I have heard a lot about your difficulties and how hard it is for you to manage all these sad feelings. I would like to pause that discussion for a bit and focus on your hobbies, likes, and strengths. Would that be okay?" Sofia nodded and said that she liked painting and that she especially enjoyed drawing and designing clothing. She also made some jewelry from "found" materials. After further encouragement to talk more about her skills and strengths, Sofia said she was helping at home and with her little brother. She could cook, shop, and do laundry. She considered herself good in math but did not want to show it. Anna stepped in and said, "I also heard you say that you don't want to go to school, but you do go every day and that shows me that you are committed and responsible. And the things that you have been through, and that you are here talking to me, means that you are resilient and courageous. Could that be true?" Sofia wiped her eyes, looked at Anna and said, "I guess." Anna encouraged Sofia to think about some small things she would like to change about her feelings and situations. As Sofia shared her wants. Anna wrote them down so that they could cocreate some basic goals and objectives for Sofia to accomplish. The list looked like this:

1. *Have a place to call home*
2. *Have some friends to hang out with and enjoy their company*
3. *Have some happy feelings and feel good about myself*
4. *Have a better relationship with Mom*

Brief Conceptualization

Before any further work, here is a current developmental understanding of Sofia as a sixteen-year-old, Hispanic, homeless adolescent with only one parent, a history of past physical abuse, and currently residing in a facility for adolescent girls.

Sofia is in a unique position that many adolescent girls do not experience on a daily basis. Her reality is less than her ideal and is causing her significant distress. Everyone has a need to belong—especially teenagers. Sofia does not have a stable residence, only one parent present in her life, and no friends. Her identity is being shaped by rather tough circumstances over which she has little control. She does not want to be homeless and without friends. This is causing her to feel shame and embarrassment; therefore, she avoids any contact with classmates and does not want to present in front of the class. Such feelings undermine her self-esteem and feelings of competence. She partially satisfied the need for independence by leaving home and being placed in the independent living facility for teenage girls, but that was not as satisfying as she might have expected it to be. She wishes for a real home and an improved relationship with her mother. Further, her sense of self as a competent young woman was attacked by boys when they made fun of her for not having art supplies, something that is beyond her control due to her financial situation. As a result of multiple factors, she withdraws, refuses to participate, does not do her schoolwork, and has a very low sense of worth. Therefore, it will be crucial for her counselor to address developmental tasks such as identity, competence, and independence over the course of her counseling.

Final Wrap-Up

Anna and Sofia went into detailed discussion about each goal and described what success would look like. Since having a home is not really in her control, they discussed how to make her current room feel more like home for the present. For the long term, they would explore how to get her mom involved and explore referrals to agencies that can help and assist with housing. They talked about some strategies to make friends, but Anna wanted Sofia to understand that it is imperative that Sofia feels good about herself and improves her sense of worth before trying to make friends. In order to boost Sofia's self-esteem, Anna encouraged Sofia to explore some of her negative and irrational thoughts about herself and replace them with more neutral or positive ones. Finally, as Sofia became ready to focus on relationships, Anna and Sofia explored what aspects of relationships were missing and ways for Sofia to establish the kind of relationships she needed, including with family and friends.

QUESTIONS FOR REFLECTION

1. What are some risks and protective factors that are present in Sofia's life?
2. What are some additional issues that Sofia needs to address, such as physical abuse, failing grades, or other risks?
3. What are some ethical and multicultural considerations?
4. What approach would you take when working with Sofia as her counselor?
5. What might a prognosis for Sofia look like?

REFERENCES

Ahuja, M., and Goyal, S. (2006). Subject wise achievement of adolescents in relation to parental involvement and parental aspirations. *Indian Journal of Community Guidance and Research, 23*, 30–57.

American Counseling Association. (2014). *ACA code of ethics*. Alexandria, VA: Author.

Bachman, J. G., Safron, D. J., Sy, S. R., & Schulenberg, J. E. (2003). Wishing to work: New perspectives on how adolescents' part-time work intensity is linked to educational disengagement, substance use, and other problem behaviours. *International Journal of Behavioral Development, 27*(4), 301–15.

Bart, P. (1993). Protean woman: The liquidity of female sexuality and the tenacity of lesbian identity. In S. Wilkinson & C . Kitzinger (Eds.), *Heterosexuality: A feminism and psychology reader* (pp. 246–52). London: Sage.

Bean, H., Softas-Nall, L., & Mahoney, M. (2011). Reflections on mandated reporting and challenges in the therapeutic relationship: A case study with systemic implications. *Family Journal, 19*(3), 286–90. https://doi.org/10.1177/1066480711407444

Benner, A. D., Graham, S., & Mistry, R. S. (2008). Discerning direct and mediated effects of ecological structures and processes on adolescents' educational outcomes. *Developmental Psychology, 44*(3), 840–54. doi: 10.1037/0012-1649.44.3.840

Broderick, P. C., & Blewitt, P. (2014). *The life span: Human development for helping professionals* (4th ed.). Boston, MA: Pearson.

Bureau of Labor Statistics. (2017, May 22). 69.7 percent of 2016 high school graduates enrolled in college in October 2016. *The Economics Daily*. Retrieved from https://www.bls.gov/opub/ted/2017/69-point-7-percent-of-2016-high-school-graduates-enrolled-in-college-in-october-2016.htm

Campbell, C. G., & Winn, E. J. (2018). Father–daughter bonds: A comparison of adolescent daughters' relationships with resident biological fathers and stepfathers. *Fam. Relat., 67*, 675–86. doi:https://doi.org/10.1111/fare.12342

Center for Behavioral Health Statistics and Quality. (2018). 2017 National Survey on Drug Use and Health: Detailed tables. Substance Abuse and Mental Health Services Administration, Rockville, MD.

Centers for Disease Control and Prevention. (2018). *National vital statistic report, 67*(1). Retrieved from https://www.cdc.gov/nchs/data/nvsr/nvsr67/nvsr67_01.pdf

Centers for Disease Control and Prevention. (2019). Sexual risk behaviors can lead to HIV, STDs, and teen pregnancy. Retrieved from https://www.cdc.gov/healthyyouth/sexual behaviors/index.htm

Centifanti, L., Fanti, K., Thomson, N., Demetriou, V., & Anastassiou-Hadjicharalambous, X. (2015). Types of relational aggression in girls are differentiated by callous-unemotional traits, peers and parental overcontrol. *Behavioral Sciences, 5*(4), 518–36.

Centifanti, L. C. M., & Modecki, K. (2013). Throwing caution to the wind: Callous-unemotional traits and risk taking in adolescents. *Journal of Clinical Child & Adolescent Psychology, 42*(1), 106–19. doi: 10.1080/15374416.2012.719460

Cohen, G. L., & Prinstein, M. J. (2006). Peer contagion of aggression and health risk behavior among adolescent males: An experimental investigation of effects on public conduct and private attitudes. *Child Development, 77*(4), 967–83.

Collins, W. A., & Steinberg, L. (2006). Adolescent development in interpersonal context. In N. Eisenberg, W. Damon, & R. M. Lerner (Eds.), *Handbook of child psychology: Social, emotional, and personality development* (vol. 3), 6th ed. (pp. 1003–67). Hoboken, NJ: John Wiley & Sons.

Comstock, G., & Scharrer, E. (2006). Media and popular culture. In K. A. Renninger & I. E. Sigel (Eds.), *Handbook of child psychology: Child psychology in practice* (vol. 4), 6th ed. (pp. 817–63). Hoboken, NJ: John Wiley & Sons.

David-Ferdon, C., & Kaslow, N. J. (2008). Evidence-based psychological treatments for child and adolescent depression. *Evidence Based Psychological Treatments for Children and Adolescents: A Ten Year Update, 37*, 62–104. https://doi.org/10.1080/15374410701817865

Degges-White, S., & Borzumato-Gainey, C. (2011). *Friends forever: How girls and women forge lasting relationships*. Lanham, MD: Rowman & Littlefield.

Department of Health and Human Services. (2016, February). Teens' social media use: How they connect and what it means for health. Retrieved from https://www.hhs.gov/ash/oah/news/e-updates/february-2016-teens-social-media-use/index.html

Erikson, E. (1968). *Identity: Youth and crisis*. New York, NY: W. W. Norton.

Fardouly, J., & Vartanian, L. R. (2016). Social media and body image concerns: Current research and future directions. *Current Opinion in Psychology, 9*, 1–5.

Gilligan, C. (1982). *In a different voice.* Cambridge, MA: Harvard University Press.

Gutman L. M., Peck S. C., Malanchuk O., Sameroff A. J., & Eccles, J. S. (2017). Moving through adolescence: Developmental trajectories of African American and European American youth. Chapter 4 in *Monographs of the Society for Research in Child Development, 82*(4), 70–82.

Jovanovic, J., & Williams, J. C. (2017). Gender, sexual agency, and friends with benefits relationships. *Sexuality & Culture, 22*, 555–576.

Jordan, J. V., Kaplan, A. G., Miller, J. B., Stiver, I. P., & Surrey, J. L. (1991). *Women's growth in connections: Writings from the Stone Center*. New York, NY: Guilford Press.

Kann, L., McManus, T., Harris, W. A., Shanklin, S. L., Flint, K. H., Queen, B., . . . Ethier, K. A. (2018). Youth risk behavior surveillance—United States, 2017. *MMWR Surveillance Summaries, 67*(8), 1–114.

Keizer, R., Helmerhorst, K. O. W., & van Gelderen, L. (2019). Perceived quality of the mother-adolescent and father-adolescent attachment relationship and adolescents' self-esteem. *Journal of Youth and Adolescence, 48*, 1203–17. doi: 10.1007/s10964-019-01007-0

Lawrence, G., & Kurpius, S. E. R. (2011). Legal and ethical issues involved when counseling minors in non-school settings. *Journal of Counseling & Development, 78*, 130–136.

Lewis, G., Srinivasam, R., Roiser, J., Blakemore, S., Flouri, E., & Lewis, G. (2019). Risk taking to obtain reward: Gender differences and associations with emotional and depressive symptoms in a nationally representative cohort of UK adolescents. bioRxiv. doi: https://doi.org/10.1101/644450

Lips, H. (1997). *Sex & gender: An introduction* (3rd ed.). Mountain View, CA: Mayfield.

Manzi, C., Regalia, C., Pelucchi, S., & Fincham, F. D. (2012). Documenting different domains of promotion of autonomy in families. *Journal of Adolescence, 35*, 289–98. doi: 10.1016/Journal of Adolescence.2011.10.011

Marcia, J. E. (1980). Identity in adolescence. In J. Adelson (Ed.), *Handbook of adolescent psychology* (pp. 159–87). New York: Wiley.

Mazzer, K., Boersma, K., & Linton, S. J. (2019). A longitudinal view of rumination, poor sleep and psychological distress in adolescents. *Journal of Affective Disorders, 245*, 686–696. doi: 10.1016/J.JAD.2018.11.053

McGuire, T. C., McCormick, K. C., Koch, M. K., & Mendle, J. (2019). Pubertal maturation and trajectories of depression during early adolescence. *Frontiers in Psychology*, 12 June 2019. https://doi.org/10.3389/fpsyg.2019.01362

Medina, M. A., Rivas-Drake, D., Jagers, R. J., & Rowley, S. J. (2019). Friends matter: Ethnic-racial identity and school adjustment among African American and Latino early adolescents, *Applied Developmental Science*, doi: https://doi.org/10.1080/10888691.2018.1524712

Missotten, L., Luyckx, K., Vanhalst, J., Nelemans, S. A., & Branje, S. (2017). Adolescents' and mothers' conflict management constellations: Links with individual and relational functioning. *Personal Relationships, 24*, 837–57. doi: 10.1111/pere.12216

Piaget, J. (1965). *The moral judgment of the child*. New York, NY: Free Press.

Robins, R. W., & Trzesniewski, K. H. (2005). Self-esteem development across the lifespan. *Current Directions in Psychological Science, 14*(3), 158–62.

Romer, D., Reyna, V. F., & Satterthwaite, T. D. (2017). Beyond stereotypes of adolescent risk taking: Placing the adolescent brain in developmental context. *Developmental Cognitive Neuroscience, 27*, 19–34. doi: 10.1016/j.dcn.2017.07.007

Rubin, K., Bukowski, W., & Parker, J. (2006). Peer interactions, relationships, and groups. In W. Damon, R. Lerner, & N. Eisenberg (Eds.), *Handbook of child psychology: Social, emotional, and personality development*, 6th ed. (pp. 571–645). New York, NY: John Wiley & Sons.

SAMHSA. (2017). Slides for the 2017 NSDUH annual national report. Retrieved from https://www.samhsa.gov/data/report/slides-2017-nsduh-annual-national-report

Savin-Williams, R. C., & Diamond, L. M. (2000). Sexual identity trajectories among sexual-minority youths: Gender comparisons. *Archives of Sexual Behavior, 29*, 607–27.

Savin-Williams, R. C., & Ream, G. (2007). Prevalence and stability of sexual orientation components during adolescence and young adulthood. *Archives of Sexual Behavior, 36*, 385–94.

Sentino, P., Thompson, P. L., Nugent, W. R., & Freeman, D. (2018). Adolescent daughters' perceptions of their fathers' levels of communication and care: How these variables influence female adolescent sexual behaviors. *Journal of Human Behavior in the Social Environment, 28*, 632–646.

Sheldon, K. M., Abad, N., & Omoile, J. (2009). Testing self-determination theory via Nigerian and Indian adolescents. *International Journal of Behavioral Development, 33*, 451–59. doi: 10.1177/0165025409340095

Soenens, B., Park, S., Vansteenkiste, M., & Mouratidis, A. (2012). Perceived parental psychological control and adolescent depressive experiences: A cross-cultural study with Belgian and South-Korean adolescents. *Journal of Adolescence , 35*, 261–72. doi: 10.1016/j.adolescence.2011.05.001

Stewart, J. L., Spivey, L. A., Widman, L., Choukas-Bradley, S., & Prinstein, M. J. (2019). Developmental patterns of sexual identity, romantic attraction, and sexual behavior among adolescents over three years. *Journal of Adolescence, 77*, 90–97.

Tilton Weaver, L., Kerr, M., Pakalniskeine, V., Tokic, A., Salihovic, S., & Stattin, H. (2010). Open up or close down: How do parental reactions affect youth information management? *Journal of Adolescence, 33*, 333–46.

Twenge, J. M., Joiner, T. E., Rogers, M. L., & Martin, G. N. (2018). Increases in depressive symptoms, suicide-related outcomes, and suicide rates among U.S. adolescents after 2010 and links to increased new media screen time. *Clinical Psychological Science, 6*(1), 3–17. https://doi.org/10.1177/2167702617723376

Walker, E. F. (2002). Adolescent neurodevelopment and psychopathology. *Current Directions in Psychological Science, 11*(1), 24–28. https://doi.org/10.1111/1467-8721.00161

Waterman, A. S. (1993). Two conceptions of happiness: Contrasts of personal expressiveness (eudaimonia) and hedonic enjoyment. *Journal of Personality and Social Psychology, 64*(4), 678–91.

Williams, J. (1987). *The psychology of women* (3rd ed.). London: W. W. Norton.

Zimmer-Gembeck, M. J., & Helfand, M. (2008). Ten years of longitudinal research on U.S. adolescent sexual behavior: Developmental correlates of sexual intercourse, and the importance of age, gender and ethnic background. *Developmental Review, 28*, 153–224. doi: 10.1016/j.dr.2007.06.001

Chapter Five

Counseling Emerging and Young Women

Marcela Kepic

CASE VIGNETTE: AGNESHKA

Agneshka is a twenty-four-year-old white female born to Polish immigrant parents who have been divorced for the past fifteen years. She lives with her father, stepmother, and two younger half siblings. She is a fourth-year college student and the first in her family to go to college. Agneshka is studying nutrition; unfortunately, her parents are not supportive of her academic major and are pushing her to pursue medical school. She is an honor student, but she does not believe she can handle medicine. Currently, Agneshka and her stepmother have been experiencing significant conflict and frequent arguments. Agneshka isn't as helpful with her younger siblings or housekeeping as her stepmother would like her to be. Agneshka's father only steps in if an argument is growing intense, and then he tends to take the side of his wife. This leaves Agneshka feeling very much alone, and she is contemplating a move out of her father's home. She works part-time as a waitress to cover the expenses related to her car, and she is considering taking on more shifts in order to save money for a place of her own.

Agneshka is currently dating a thirty-three-year-old Polish divorced father with two young children who live with him. Agneshka loves to spend time with him but is disappointed that he has so little time available to spend with her. She finds herself helping him around the house but does not feel like she spends quality time with him. Similar to the dynamics between Agneshka and her stepmother, she and her boyfriend argue a lot over housework and other random issues. Overwhelmed and undecided about what she will do with her college major, what she will do with her home situation, and what she will do with her "not so happy" relationship, Agneshka reaches out for assistance from a counselor.

* * *

Arnett (2000) offered a developmental perspective on emerging adulthood (roughly spanning from eighteen to twenty-five years of age) and posited that the period is conceptually distinct from both adolescence and young adulthood. Role balance during this time frame is important. There has been an interdependent relationship found between residence, finances, and romance where when greater responsibility is assumed in one area it occurs in other areas as well (Bishop, Welsh, Lounsbury, & Norona, 2016). While many associate Erickson's theory as focusing on sexual development during this time frame, the focus on psychosocial intimacy is also about building deeper and more meaningful relationships with peers that are not necessarily of a sexual nature (Weisskirch, 2018). Traditionally, mate selection and relationship satisfaction are prioritized developmental tasks; however, changes in educational paths, jobs, or living situation occur as well, for many emerging adults (Arnett, 2006). Developing one's identity and attending to various areas of life can be a bit overwhelming, yet these challenges can help with overall identity development and growth. There are also areas within physical development that occur during this time frame.

Physical Development

Unlike the onset of puberty in early adolescence, emerging adulthood lacks physical signs of maturation and is more of a social construct determined by cultural criteria that must be met before one is called an adult (Broderick & Blewitt, 2014). Certain achievements and timing might be important for many cultures, such as completing an education, entering the workforce, or getting married. Despite the fact that adolescents and emerging adults are active sexually much earlier than prior generations, the path to independent adulthood often takes longer. Role transitions, such as marriage and chronological age, have less significance, but accepting responsibility for the consequences of one's actions and making independent decisions, including around finances, have grown in their importance as signifiers of entry into adulthood (Arnett, 2004, 2007). A sense of independence and autonomy seems be in primary focus as emerging adults transition to full adulthood. Emerging adults have completed their physical growth and are reaching peak physical performance. However, parenting style has been correlated to physical well-being (Reed et al., 2016). Maintaining a high level of physical fitness may or may not be seen as important to an individual. Weight gain is common during emerging adulthood and monitoring one's weight can be beneficial in addressing this issue (Gorin et al., 2019). The need to consider physical well-being and adapt healthy lifestyle choices is important during this time frame. However, it is also critical to consider that changes in the development of the brain continue well into young adulthood impacting emotional and cognitive development.

Emotional, Behavioral, and Cognitive Changes

Brain development continues through emerging adulthood, including the myelination of areas in the prefrontal cortex and the growth of synapses (Giedd et al., 1999), which improves skills of executive functioning, such as cognitive flexibility, inhibitory control (Miyake et al., 2000), and working memory. With exposure to different responsibilities, young adults transition from formal operations to postformal thought (Arlin, 1984; Sinnot, 1984, 1998), which is characterized by logical solutions to problems and the ability to understand the logic of each of the contradictory perspectives and integrate those perspectives into a large whole (Broderick & Blewitt, 2014). Emotional regulation in emerging adults has been linked to parenting style. Additionally, supportive parents tend to be a factor in the avoidance of risk-taking behaviors including sexual ones by emerging adults (Weisskirch, 2018). Research by Joseph, Zhu, Lynam, and Kelly (2016) confirmed previous research related to brain development in emerging adulthood but also indicated that personality might impact impulsive behaviors as well in emerging adults. Development is complex and there are various factors that need to be considered.

In understanding the complex nature of development, the use of theories can be highly beneficial. In a study by Linsenmeyer and Lucas (2017), Perry's theory of intellectual and ethical development was used to examine student behaviors. They found that college students moved through the various stages and that social justice issues allow students the opportunity to move towards high stages of development. This fits with the idea that during emerging adulthood a person's values, beliefs, and worldviews become clearer as reevaluation and self-examination occur (Haney & Rollock, 2018). These developments contribute to a young adult's ability to begin solidifying their sense of identity.

Identity Development

In Western cultures, the individual is encouraged to develop as an independent and competitive person who measures success through individuation and strength in isolation. Jean Baker Miller, Carol Gilligan, and Judith V. Jordan have questioned this widely accepted perception of human development and argued that this model does not fit for women (Miller, 1984). The differences between women's experience and portrayed human development in psychological literature appeared to only signify differences in women's development (Gilligan, 1982).

Women's identity development as described by Helms (cited in Ossana, Helms, & Leonard, 1992) focuses on how women move from an external, societal definition of womanhood to an internal, personally salient definition of womanhood. The Helms womanist model presents more general development, and its stages resemble Cross's black identity development model (Boisnier, 2003). Preencounter, stage one, is characterized by conformity to societal views about gender. Women think and behave in ways that devalue females and value males. In encounter, stage two, as new information and experience enters the woman's life, allowing her to be more salient, she starts to question accepted values and beliefs. Stage three, immersion–emersion, is characterized by the idealization of women and the rejection of male views of women. Women in this stage tend to search for a positive self-affirmation of womanhood and express an intense affiliation with other women. In the final stage, internalization, a woman fully incorporates into her own identity her own positive view of what it means to be a woman. She refuses to be bound by external definitions (Boisnier, 2003). Such transformation results in women adopting positive views of themselves and being able to value themselves as women in whatever role they may choose for themselves rather than any role dictated by any ideology. Despite advance in society and additional choices, there are still gender disparities that occur. For instance, women continue to be paid less them their male counterparts in the workforce and continue to be underrepresented in STEM fields (Kim, Sinatra, & Seyranian, 2018). Social identity theory has been used to explain the different trajectory of women's lives when it comes to career choice and development. While social membership can change, it is not always an easy process as it begins at an early age (Kim, Sinatra, & Sevranian, 2018). In addition to women's identity development, early in preadolescent years, sexual identity development starts to take place.

Sexual Identity

Gender identity and sexual identity are only two of many identity domains that are still being developed and crystallized during emerging adulthood. Sexual identity intersects with other domains as well, such as racial, ethnic, or religious identities. Sexual identity has been conceptualized as comprising emotional and cognitive understanding that individuals have about the meaning and significance of numerous aspects of their sexuality, such as their sexual attraction, desires, behaviors, values, and relationships (Horowitz & Newcomb, 2001). This understanding is being organized throughout adolescence into emerging adulthood, helping to create a meaningful sense of one's sexuality.

Over the past several decades, researchers have been proposing various models of sexual identity development, and most of them resemble a linear progression through stages, starting first with awareness of same-sex attraction, questioning and exploring such attractions, and eventually moving through acceptance, disclosure, and integration of identity (Cass, 1979; Fassinger & Miller, 1996; Meyer & Schwitzer, 1999; Minton & McDonald, 1984). Such models with linear progressions have been critiqued for failing to acknowledge the diversity of the coming-out process (Horowitz & Newcomb, 2001; Kitzinger & Wilkinson, 1995). Other models of sexual identity development attest to diversity of experiences, suggesting that there are multiple trajectories of sexual identity development for lesbian, gay, and bisexual individuals (Fassinger & Miller, 1996; Meyer & Schwitzer, 1999; Morris, 1997).

Simon, Vazquez, Bruun, and Far (2019) found that when it comes to sexual identity, women have greater latitude in deviating from the expected traditional norms and that societal structure is in place to prevent excessive deviation. They found no difference in the degree of exclusion experienced by sexual minority emerging adults based on gender. The challenge for these individuals is dealing with continued stereotypes and expectation in a society that tends to punish those who are different (Simon, Vazquez, Bruuns, & Farr, 2019). This is supported by research conducted by Luk et al. (2018) that found that sexual minority emerging adult females were less likely to enroll in college or complete college. This was due in part to the lack of social support, as indicated by potentially higher rates of bullying in high school (Luk et al., 2018). These negative experiences may impact the choices that a person makes and highlights the importance of relationships in life.

RELATIONSHIPS

During this period of life, women are growing increasingly sure of who they are, and while this involves a growing sense of independence, they are also learning to navigate relationships as adults. Significant changes can occur in both family and friendship relationships. In addition, romantic relationships may begin to receive greater attention and scrutiny as women may begin to plan for long-term commitments.

Relationships with Parents

Relationships with parents evolve and change throughout the lifespan. If the relationship with both parents is perceived as positive by the child before emerging adulthood, the relationship during emerging adulthood is perceived by the emerging adult as supportive. Thus, the bond between parents if supportive can lead to open communication and the transition to more of a peer type relationship (Kaniušonytė & Žukauskienė, 2018). It is often a struggle for parents to try to find a balance between protecting children and having them experience consequences of decisions to learn how to handle difficult situations. During emerging adulthood boundaries are tested and at times risk taking behaviors occur. For parents, this can provide the opportunity to engage in tough love, which can be difficult for emerging adults but can also serve as key transitional points as they move forward towards adulthood. These experiences help emerging adults to gain greater independence and understand the expectations for being an adult (Faw, Sonne, & Leustek, 2019).

Friendships

With the greater sense of self, young women are more aware of their values, likes, and preferences; therefore, they will choose their friends accordingly. Many earlier relationships from adolescent years may dissolve as women grow into their adult identities and responsibilities. Women also are more invested in choosing friends who fit their sense of self and who reflect the values and interests they have themselves (Degges-White & Borzumato-Gainey, 2011). Although romantic partners are taking up more space in young adult women's lives, they also still value the emotional support and connections they have with their platonic friends. Literature suggests that young women utilize self-disclosure as a major factor for growth in emotional closeness. Emotional support (e.g., being there for each other) and participation in some shared activities tend to help growing intimacy in friendships as well (Radmacher & Azmitia, 2006). For those young women who are not in a romantic relationship, friendships or having a best friend is predictive of happiness. When in a romantic relationship, friendship importance in happiness might be less pronounced if at all (Demir, 2009).

Romantic Relationships

During emerging adulthood, individuals build romantic relationship skills that will help them improve the quality of later long-lasting relationship. The lessons learned when a relationship dissolves can be valuable as a person moves forward in life (Norona, Roberson, & Welsh, 2017). For emerging adults, intimate romantic relationships are important despite the fact that a growing number of people are choosing to stay single. For some there is a very real fear of being alone, which can result in involvement in negative romantic relationship. Singles in society today tend to be viewed in a negative fashion (Timmermans, Coenen, & Van den Bulck, 2019).

However, due to multiple sociocultural factors, emerging adult women tend to postpone marriage and pregnancy even though they enjoy a fully active sex life. Many women choose to pursue higher education and enter the workforce at a later age than in the past as well. These choices may contribute to emerging adults' apparent delays in making formal commitments in their romantic relationships.

Although committed long-term relationships are common among emerging adults, the median age for first marriage is on the rise. In 2017, the median age was 27.4 for women and 29.5 for men; that's almost three years older than twenty years ago (U.S. Census Bureau, 2018). Striking racial differences exist regarding age at first marriage; black or African American women tend to marry at age 32, American Indian and Alaskan natives at age 28.7, Asians at 27.6, and white and Hispanic or Latina women at a median age of 27.5. While the marriage rate has fallen, the rate of cohabitation has risen 29 percent in twenty years.

Not only do women today tend to stay single longer, they also have much more flexibility in terms of whom to date or marry, and how to date and when to marry. They also tend to embrace new ideas about romance and family, not necessarily conforming to the ideas of institutionalized traditional marriage. More than thirty years ago, Williams (1987) suggested that traditional marriage might be considered a vehicle for the oppression of women and that women were hindered from growing into their full potential within this institution. While women's desire for full freedom and equality have not been fully met yet, there are many precursors that allow for much more liberation than previous generations achieved. Education allows women to enter the workforce in positions that were once reserved for men, birth-control technology helped with biological imperatives and allows women more control over their own bodies, and economic freedom liberates women from having to rely on another for basic needs. It was almost fifty years ago when O'Neil and O'Neil (1972) described the construct of the "open marriage." This was described as a relationship of intimacy based on equal freedom and identity of both partners. The open marriage model includes the expectations that both partners will grow and change, that the partners will be different persons due to ongoing development, that each partner will accept responsibility for self and grant it to the other, that one partner cannot fill all needs of the other partner, and that children are not needed as proof of love for each other; their liking and loving will grow out of the mutual respect that the open relationship allows (Williams, 1987). These expectations resemble the values of personal growth, individual freedom, and flexibility. Such models encouraged new kinds of behavior in a committed relationship, and although some partners may feel the line should be drawn at a marriage that is open to extramarital relationships, the concept of a relationship that encourages egalitarian and individualistic values appeals to many contemporary individuals. While women's entry into the workforce allows them to achieve significant occupational prestige, a stronger repertoire of socially valued competencies, and more economic independence, many still greatly value relationships and connectedness. They desire respect, trust, support, acceptance, emotional intimacy, loyalty, and security in their long-term romantic relationships and friendships as well.

Pursuing Commitment

Despite the fact that young women tend to commit to monogamous relationships or marriage much later nowadays, they still prioritize selection of a significant other during this phase of life. For many young women, this will be the most important choice they make. Mate selection is a complex process affected by a number of variables, including initial physical attraction, proximity, similarity, reciprocity, and complementarity (Lemme, 2006). Such factors may serve as various screens or filters through which young women select some individuals for continued consideration and eliminate others. Research continues to indicate that women place a higher priority on qualities other than physical attractiveness, such as socioeconomic status, ambition, character, and intelligence, while men primarily focus on physical attractiveness (Feingold, 1992; Lemme, 2006). Research shows that women tend to marry those similar to themselves in terms of age, physical attractiveness, personality traits, education, cognitive abilities, attitudes, and social class background. When a woman finds a potential partner who possesses desirable characteristics and shows evidence of reciprocal attraction, this potential mate may be perceived as presenting an opportunity for further self-expansion and self-enhancement through the psychological incorporation of the resources that he or she is bringing into a close relationship (Aron & Aron, 1986; Hartin 1990). In other words, we tend to fall in love with those who possess qualities we lack but who also complement us in some way and are relatively similar to us in values and background. Choosing a significant other may present itself as an exciting time; for others, it could be an anxiety-provoking process due to the challenges and risks inherent in relationship building. As with any transition, going from a single to a committed status requires compromises and adjustments that can be challenging for many women.

Transition to Committed Life and Family Life

Family relations can play a significant role in a woman's life from birth to death. According to the family life cycle model (Carter & McGoldrick, 2015), young adults typically leave their nuclear family, enter into a committed relationship, then build a family-of-creation. Learning to share your life and home with a significant other is not always easy. While dating, there are seldom arguments about whose turn it is to take the trash out, do the dishes or laundry, shop for groceries, or feed the cats; these can pop up quickly in some marriages. Another common challenge for couples is the maintenance of friendships outside of marriage. Single friends may not want to hang out with a couple, or perhaps one partner does not like the other's friends. Partners may be jealous of the time their spouse spends with friends or may simply dislike a partner's friend. Negotiating where time is spent during significant holidays can also cause conflict. For the couple, it can be challenging to learn how to function as a new family unit. Some couples may need to seek outside assistance, such as working with a counselor.

Another phase of the family life cycle—starting a family or childbearing—brings many new challenges. Just as the young couple becomes comfortable with committed or married life, a newborn baby throws that routine completely off. Suddenly, the centeredness around two partners shifts to centeredness around the newborn. Despite the fact that both partners are happily expecting the child and some changes associated with adding a new family member, the arrival of the baby changes the dynamics between the couple, where a new mom could completely be consumed by the needs of a newborn and deprived of sleep and a new dad or partner experiences feelings of being left out of the dyad. Such shifts contribute to feelings of being overwhelmed, exhausted, and not understood. Mothers after giving birth may experience either baby blues or postpartum depression, possibly stemming from fluctuating hormones and other environmental factors. According to the Centers for Disease Control and Prevention (CDC) (2019), approximately 70 to 80 percent of mothers will experience the "baby blues" after giving birth. Postpartum depression, something much more severe, is experienced by 10 to 15 percent of new mothers (CDC, 2019). The appearance of these can complicate adjustment to and the necessary shift in a couple's dynamics. If symptoms of either of these are present in your client, assess for depression and engage the client in appropriate treatment as quickly as possible.

Research suggests that marriage provides multiple benefits for couples. Women accrue more physical and mental health benefits from good marriages, whereas men benefit regardless of the quality of the marriage (Gottman & Gottman, 2015; Levenson, Carstensen, & Gottman, 1993). Some of the benefits include lower mortality, less risky behaviors, improved physical and psychological well-being, higher satisfaction with sex life, higher income, and more savings (Gottman & Gottman, 2015). However, not all women will choose married life or remain in a marriage for their lifetime.

Divorced and Single Mothers

Over the last decade or so, the U.S. divorce rate began falling and has continued this trend (U.S. Census Bureau, 2018). This change might reflect millennials' attitudes toward marriage, suggesting that young people are doing things differently. They tend to marry later in life, often after they have completed their education and are more financially stable; this contributes to marriage longevity. However, emerging and young women are more likely to divorce than older women (U.S. Census Bureau, 2018), leaving many of them single mothers, unless they marry again. About 75 percent of divorced women will remarry, usually around three years after a divorce (U.S. Census Bureau, 2018). Single mothers face multiple stressors associated with gender, work, socioeconomic status, and marital status. While two-thirds of single mothers are employed outside the home, only half of single mothers are employed full-time all year long. The median income for single mothers is $41,700 as compared to $90,380 for a married couple. Not only do single mothers earn less, only a third of them receive child support. Out of ten million low-income working families with children, 40 percent were headed by single working mothers. The proportion is much higher for African Americans (65 percent), compared to whites (36 percent). In terms of education, only 34 percent of single mothers have earned college degrees; a lack of funding for education can lead to a lifetime of earnings inequity. Despite all the challenges that single mothers might face, they are more likely than earlier generations were to choose divorce when they are stuck in an unhappy marriage.

In a society where access to and attainment in education have mushroomed for women, many will choose to postpone marriage and childbearing until much later than their mothers. They may also choose to raise a child on their own, a path that was dubbed "the single mother by choice" when it emerged in the 1980s. This choice may be driven by a variety of forces, such as the absence of a significant other and concerns about the "biological clock" ticking. To accomplish this, a woman must intentionally initiate and plan the conception of a child. Everything from technological advances or agreements and encounters with friends may produce the desired outcome. All in all, however, it is estimated that only 3 percent of women who are not cohabitating or are not married will choose to have a child on their own (Hayford & Guzzo, 2015). As social expectations have shifted, the expectations for relationship milestones have also changed as well. In addition, the timing of relationship developments may be affected by engagement in educational and occupational pursuits.

SCHOOL AND WORK TRANSITIONS

The world of work is changing rapidly as a result of economic and demographic trends along with technological innovations (Lemme, 2006). Lippert and Damaske (2019) found that for women who completed a college degree there were more job opportunities than for those who did not do so. They found that the health benefits for women who were able to successfully balance family and work tended to be more pronounced in women who were of a high SES group and had greater job flexibility and higher paying jobs. Women who did not have college degrees and had low paying jobs tended to have an increased level of stress and more difficulty balancing family and work. Career pathways for women are explored more fully in chapter 8 through a lifespan approach. However, it is important to note that emerging adulthood is when career starts, stops, and transitions may be frequent.

Challenges in the Workforce

As noted, women in the workforce are explored in more detail in chapter 8. However, it is worth noting in this chapter that regardless of their preparation and training, some women face unexpected challenges in the workplace due to such things as sexism and ageism, among other factors. Nelson, Sendroiu, Dinovitzer, and Dawe (2019) pointed out that traditionally marginalized groups will perceive discrimination more often than other groups. Additionally, women who have children tend to perceive discrimination in the workplace at a higher rate than other women and even men with children (Kay & Wallace, 2009). Stereotyping continues to be an issue that contributes to workplace discrimination and often goes unchecked and unaddressed (Nelson et al., 2018). Even if discrimination is occurring in the workplace it can be hard to prove due to narrow legal definitions. For women, this often results in the lack of opportunities to advance careers, lack of credit for ideas, and the sense they must perform at a much higher standard than their male colleagues and peers (Fink, 2018).

The workplace expectations can be confusing and frustrating for women. Women are expected to fit into workplaces that were designed for men. The structured system of workplaces requires that women find a way to fit into these environments and when they do, they often are not well received. Women are then stuck in a catch-22 when they face the possibility of being fired for demonstrating stereotypically male behaviors (Ballakrishnen, Fielding-Singh, & Magliozzi, 2019). Some women may then tend to maintain a low profile doing their jobs but not in a way that makes them noticed when it comes to promotions. For emerging adult women, figuring out and navigating the workplace can be challenging.

Emerging adults are in the midst of a busy time of life. Not only are they focused on solidifying their adult identities, they are also navigating the world of work and multiple relationships. There are multiple jokes about the trepidation that this age group has about "adulting," but it can be a daunting task to balance work along with family relationships, friendships, and romantic partnerships. These are just a few of the potential areas of concern that an emerging adult woman might present to her counselor.

BEST PRACTICES FOR WORKING WITH EMERGING ADULT WOMEN

Emerging and young adulthood can present women with challenging transitions that may shift their inner selves and external relationships. Women in this developmental stage are fully mature, independent, and at the peak of their physical development. However, they often seek counseling to help them better manage the transitions that occur during this potent period. Here are some suggestions for best meeting the needs of these clients:

1. Be familiar with the characteristics of a client's developmental stage; be cognizant of the typical progression of physical, cognitive, emotional, and psychosocial development.
2. Allow space for variation and uniqueness in every developmental theory. Theory is there to guide, not to prescribe. Some clients won't easily fit into the proposed stages or challenges but might present with unique "out-of-synch" struggles. It is necessary to be attentive to the client's presentation and their perceptions of the dilemma they are facing.
3. Be familiar with relational-cultural theory. Its tenets and practices are closely aligned with women's experiences and closely relate to women's ways of life, in which relationship and connection are key issues.
4. Listen carefully to your client's descriptions of her presenting problems and concerns. Encourage her to share her story in the way that she is experiencing it. Validate her feelings and her experiences.
5. Through active listening, paraphrasing, validating, and holding a nonjudgmental attitude, focus on building, promoting, and maintaining a safe space in which a client can feel comfortable expressing difficult experiences and feelings.
6. Explore further about her experiences, perceptions, thoughts, and feelings. Listen with a tentative ear, and paraphrase content and feelings to ensure you fully understand where she is coming from.
7. Pay attention to her personality and way of thinking. Not every woman prefers an emotionally focused approach to counseling. Strike a balance between a cognitive focus and a focus on feelings, as appropriate or necessary.
8. If you are a woman, do not assume that your client's experiences or needs are the same as yours; if you are a man, do not assume that you are not prepared to meet the counseling needs of women.
9. Avoid jumping into conclusion and or interpretations. Ask for possible explanations and possible solutions first before you share your own. Through this approach, your client might feel more empowered as she is finding her own ways to handle challenges she is facing.

10. Always consider the multiple layers of identity of each client, such as gender, culture, ethnicity, race, education, religion, socioeconomic status, and sexual orientation. Acknowledge the complexity and uniqueness of intersectionality with your client.
11. Help your client establish or maintain connections to social outlets, supports, and resources; social support is consistently related to mental and physical well-being.
12. Use role-play in sessions to help your client develop confidence in her ability to hold difficult conversations or to express parts of herself that she tends to suppress.
13. Use creative counseling interventions that allow your client to explore parts of herself that she may seldom have the time and space to uncover.
14. Provide her with tools and resources to fall back on in case of a need.

CULTURAL CONSIDERATIONS

Despite the fact that our counseling focus is on emerging and young women, not all will present the same spectrum of development and challenges. However, research has suggested that the common developmental tasks occur for most emerging adults regardless of race, culture, or SES background (Arnett, 2016). It is important to consider the uniqueness of each individual client and to realize that individual experiences due to her own diverse intersectionality of backgrounds will make her unique and special. This stage of life provides women with multiple pathways they may follow or circle back through, such as establishing themselves in their careers, graduating from schools, having their first child, or going through a divorce. One major challenge for individuals in this developmental period is career development. Individuals from lower SES backgrounds are less likely to go to college and this can have a profound impact on one's career and overall life (Arnett, 2016). Individuals will have different paths and counselors would do well to recognize the ways in which clients are diverse. It is the clinician's job, duty, and responsibility to explore and learn about their client in order to understand their perspectives instead of relying on learned stereotypes.

ETHICAL CONSIDERATIONS

All clinical professionals need to adhere to their own professional code of ethics. Clinicians need to pay attention to the type of presenting problem and issues associated with it and act accordingly. Since emerging women are already legal adults, confidentiality is handled differently than when counseling adolescent girls. However, clinicians still can encounter parental involvement when counseling a college student or an emerging adult mom who is still living with her parents or relying on her parents for help. Clinicians need to be sensitive to such matters and comply with the code of ethics (e.g., keep confidentiality) despite parents' involvement and potential requests for disclosure. At times, dual or multiple relationships might be at play, especially when it comes to romantic feelings for any party of the therapeutic dyad. In such cases, clinicians consult with their supervisors in order to take immediate appropriate action necessary to avoid mistreatment or negligence. There may be many other ethical concerns present when counseling emerging and young women. In any case of doubt, or just a simple question or wondering if a present issue might be an ethical concern, it is best to reach out and ask for help or consult with an immediate clinical supervisor.

ADVOCACY OPPORTUNITIES

There are many ways to advocate for emerging and young women based on the challenges that they might be facing. The spectrum is broad and complex and beyond this chapter's capacity to mention all possible issues and therefore advocacy components. Many specific challenges women might face are addressed in individual chapters of this book. However, advocacy at the client's level might simply consist of empowering her to speak up or share her perceptions and help other women with similar issues. At the community level, clinicians can organize presentations, training, or in-service educational opportunities at community agencies and organizations about challenges and issues emerging adult women face. These include topics such as sexual harassment, abuse, parenting skills, divorce, motherhood, work–life balance, and so on.

CASE STUDY WRAP-UP: AGNESHKA

Agneshka reached out to her counselor for support because she felt angry and depressed. After her counselor gathered a detailed history about her background and present situation, they started exploring some potential goals for counseling. Throughout the assessment process, the counselor made sure to empathize with Agneshka and validate her feelings of loneliness, anger, and relationship dissatisfaction. Considering Agneshka's background, her counselor paid close attention to her culture and asked relevant questions to ensure she fully understood Agneshka's cultural perspective. The counselor asked about gender and family roles in her life, the significance of family gatherings and celebrations, and family expectation of her as a child and, now, as an adult child. Agneshka clarified that their culture is family oriented and that the expectation is to stick together, help each other out, and be obedient to parents. She further stated that her Catholic religion plays a significant role in her family, and they celebrate all the holidays together with immediate and extended family. They share typical gender roles, such as the father working out of the house and the mother primarily responsible for kids, household, and some part-time work. Agneshka stated that she has no one to go to and has a hard time being at home. Her counselor asked, "How do you view such family roles, responsibilities, and family values?"

Agneshka took a deep breath and slowly started: "I like to go to church and spend time with family, but we fight most of the time. I understand that as a woman I will get married at some point and have kids, but I want to focus on my career first, get settled in my professional life, and then consider family. I know I need to help around the house and with the kids, but I want to be on my own. I don't like coming home and being asked where I was, where I go, what time I will be back . . . and then whatever I do to help, it's never good enough . . . so what's the point?" Agneshka's counselor nodded and reflected, "It must be frustrating to be treated as a child and then made to feel like you are not good enough." Agneshka nodded as tears welled up in her eyes.

Interventions: Strength-Based Approach

Agneshka's counselor suggested that they focus a bit on exploring her strengths and hobbies and things that might be going well in her life right now. Then she proposed they establish potential counseling goals and asked her if that would be okay with her. Agneshka nodded and shared that she likes traveling and camping and exploring new sites. She shared that she is good with kids and likes cooking and baking. Her grades are good, and she noted proudly that she had been on the dean's list. She is a supportive friend.

The counselor stepped in and added that she sees her as independent and responsible since she is holding a job while studying and paying for her own car and insurance. Agneshka reluctantly agreed. Her counselor encouraged Agneshka to think about some small things she would like to change about her feelings and her situations. Agneshka shared her wants, and together they cocreated some basic goals and objectives to accomplish. The list looked like this:

1. *To improve relationships through reducing conflicts: with my dad and stepmother and with my boyfriend*
2. *To improve mood: feel less anxious, less depressed, and therefore feel good about myself*
3. *To be more independent and eventually move out*

Brief Conceptualization

Before any further work, it is helpful to bear in mind Agneshka's current developmental status. As a young woman of Polish descent, her cultural background will play a role in her counseling work, even though she was raised in the United States. As an emerging adult, she has needs for independence and intimacy. She is also working on getting her education in order to establish her professional career. Cognitively, postformal thought allows her to consider multiple angles and contradictory perspectives. Further, her dualistic tendencies ("right vs. wrong" thought patterns) still persist until she moves into relativistic thinking that will allow her to honor different opinions. She might not have access to all possible information needed in order to make the best decision, and there are no preestablished answers. She has met with barriers related to her expected gender role and her own vision of her career path and identity. While she wants to become a wife and a parent, her independence and career come first. Such difference in views (gender, family, and culture) and tendencies for dualistic thinking contribute to frequent relational conflict, leading her to see only one possible solution to her problems, to move out of her parents' house. In relation to her stepmother, Agneshka's behaviors can be seen as a result of competition over her dad's attention. Further, feeling dismissed by her father and lacking a strong support network of female friends may contribute to her decision to date a man who is significantly older than she is and who is a father to two children; Agneshka may be seeking validation and support through this relationship.

Final Wrap-Up

While working with Agneshka, her counselor can best help her by doing the following: Show respect for Agneshka's thinking and keep in mind that promoting reflective thinking needs to be done in a supportive atmosphere. Encourage Agneshka to gather necessary information about a problem she is facing, evaluate the quality of the information she retrieves, and draw a conclusion based on evaluated facts. Assist Agneshka in concretely examining the assumptions she is using in making her decision about issues she is facing. Lastly, pay attention to Agneshka's culture and how this may be influencing her thinking and decision making. Agneshka and her counselor, besides working on already established goals, can also explore Agneshka's identity and facilitate a deeper self-understanding in order for Agneshka to navigate her relationships in a more meaningful and intentional manner.

QUESTIONS FOR REFLECTION

1. What additional information would you as a counselor like to gather about Agneshka, considering her developmental phase?
2. What are some additional issues Agneshka should address during counseling?
3. Are there any ethical considerations that are relevant to working with Agneshka?
4. What approach would you take when working with Agneshka as her counselor?

REFERENCES

Arlin, P. (1984). Beyond formal operations: Late adolescent and adult cognitive development. *Journal of Gerontology, 39*(6), 765–65.

Arnett, J. J. (2000). Emerging adulthood: A theory of development from the late teens through the twenties. *American Psychologist, 55*(5), 469–80.

Arnett, J. J. (2004, November 12). "Emerging Adulthood." *Chronicle of Higher Education*, p. B4.

Arnett, J. J. (2006). Emerging adulthood in Europe: A response to Bynner. *Journal of Youth Studies, 9*(1), 111–23.

Arnett, J. J. (2007). Emerging adulthood: What is it, and what is it good for? *Child Development Perspectives, 1*(2), 68–73.

Arnett, J. J. (2016). Does Emerging Adulthood Theory Apply Across Social Classes? National Data on a Persistent Question. Emerging Adulthood, 4(4), 227–35.

Aron, A., & Aron, E. N. (1986). *Love and the expansion of self: Understanding attraction and satisfaction.* New York, NY: Hemisphere/Harper and Row.

Ballakrishnen, S., Fielding-Singh, P., & Magliozzi, D. (2019). Intentional invisibility: Professional women and the navigation of workplace constraints. *Sociological Perspectives, 62*(1), 23–41.

Bandura, A. (1977). *Social learning theory*. Englewood Cliffs, NJ: Prentice Hall.

Betz, N. E., & Hackett, G. (1981). The relationship of career related self-efficacy expectations to perceived career options in college women and men. *Journal of Counseling Psychology, 28*, 399–410.

Bishop, J. L., Welsh, D. P., Lounsbury, J. W., & Norona, A. J. C. (2016). The individual and relational role balance scale (IRRBS): A preliminary scale development and validation study. *College Student Journal, 50*(4), 531–50.

Boisnier, A. D. (2003). Race and women's identity development: Distinguishing between feminism and womanism among black and white women. *Sex Roles, 49*, 211–18.

Broderick, P. C., & Blewitt, P. (2014). *The life span: Human development for helping professionals* (4th ed.). Boston, MA: Pearson.

Carter, B. A., & McGoldrick, M. (2015). *The expanded family life cycle*. Boston, MA: Pearson.

Cass, V. C. (1979). Homosexual identity formation: A theoretical model. *Journal of Homosexuality, 4*, 219–35.

Centers for Disease Control and Prevention (2019). Depression among women. Retrieved from https://www.cdc.gov/reproductivehealth/depression/index.htm#Postpartum

Chapman, B. E., & Brannock, J. C. (1987). Proposed model of lesbian identity development: An empirical examination. *Journal of Homosexuality, 14*, 69–20.

Collins, W. A. (2003). More than myth: The developmental significance of romantic relationships during adolescence. *Journal of Research on Adolescence, 13*, 1–24. doi:10.1111/1532-7795.1301001

Collins, W. A., & van Dulmen, M. H. M. (2006). "The course of true love(s) . . .": Origins and pathways in the development of romantic relationships. In A. C. Crouter & A. Booth (Eds.), *Romance and sex in adolescence and emerging adulthood: Risks and opportunities* (pp. 63–86). Mahwah, NJ: Erlbaum.

Degges-White, S., & Borzumato-Gainey, C. (2011). *Friends forever: How girls and women forge lasting relationships*. Lanham, MD: Rowman & Littlefield.

Demir, M. (2009). Close relationship and happiness among emerging adults. *Journal of Happiness Studies, 11*(3), 293–313.

Diamond, L. M. (2008). *Sexual fluidity: Understanding women's love and desire*. Cambridge, MA: Harvard University Press.

Fassinger, R. E., & Miller, B. A. (1996). Validation of an inclusive model of sexual minority identity formation on a sample of gay men. *Journal of Homosexuality, 32*, 53–78.

Faw, M. H., Sonne, J., & Leustek, J. (2019). Exploring tough love communication in parents' relationships with their young adult children. *Communication Studies, 70*(4), 470–91.

Feingold, A. (1992). Gender differences in mate selection preferences: A test of the parental investment model. *Psychological Bulletin, 112*, 125–39.

Fink, J. (2018). Gender sidelining and the problem of unactionable discrimination. *Stanford Law and Policy Review, 29*(1), 57–106.

Giedd, J. N., Blumenthal, J., Jeffries, N. O., Castellanos, F. X., Liu, H., Zijdenbos, A., . . . Rapoport, J. L. (1999). Brain development during childhood and adolescence: A longitudinal MRI study. *Nature Neuroscience, 2*(10), 861–63. https://doi.org/10.1038/13158

Gilligan, C. (1982). *In a different voice.* Cambridge, MA: Harvard University Press.

Gorin, A. A., Gokee LaRose, J., Espeland, M. A., Tate, D. F., Jelalian, E., Robichaud, E., . . . Wing, R. R. (2019). Eating pathology and psychological outcomes in young adults in self-regulation interventions using daily self-weighing. *Health Psychology, 38*(2), 143–50.

Gottman, J. S., & Gottman, J. M. (2015). *10 principles for doing effective couples therapy*. New York, NY: W. W. Norton & Co.

Gurrentz, B. (2018, November 15). For young adults, cohabitation is up, marriage is down. U.S. Census Bureau. Retrieved from https://www.census.gov/library/stories/2018/11/cohabitaiton-is-up-marriage-is-down-for-young-adults.html

Haney, A. M., & Rollock, D. (2018). A matter of faith: The role of religion, doubt, and personality in emerging adult mental health. *Psychology of Religion and Spirituality*.

Hartin, W. H. (1990). Re-marriage: Some issues for clients and therapists. *Australian and New Zealand Journal of Family Therapy, 11*, 36–42.

Hayford, S. R., & Guzzo, K. B. (2015). The single mother by choice myth. *Contexts, 14*, 70–72.

Horowitz, J. L., & Newcomb, M. D. (2001). A multidimensional approach to homosexual identity. *Journal of Homosexuality, 42*, 1–19.

Johnson, E. (2017). Erasing the scarlet letter: How positive media messages about sex can lead to better sexual health among college men and women. *American Journal of Sexuality Education, 12*(1), 55–71.

Joseph, J. E., Zhu, X., Lynam, D., & Kelly, T. H. (2016). Modulation of meso-limbic reward processing by motivational tendencies in young adolescents and adults. *Neuroimage, 129*, 40–54.

Kaniušonytė, G., & Žukauskienė, R. (2018). Relationships with parents, identity styles, and positive youth development during the transition from adolescence to emerging adulthood. *Emerging Adulthood, 6*(1), 42–52.

Kay, F. M., & Wallace, J. E. (2009). Mentors as social capital: Gender, mentors, and career rewards in law practice. *Sociological Inquiry, 79*, 418–452. doi: 10.1111/j.1475-682X.2009.00301.x

Kim, A. Y., Sinatra, G. M., & Seyranian, V. (2018). Developing a STEM identity among young women: A social identity perspective. *Review of Educational Research, 88*(4), 589–625.

Kitzinger, C., & Wilkinson, S. (1995). Transitions from heterosexuality to lesbianism: Discursive production of lesbian identities. *Developmental Psychology, 31*, 95–104.

Lemme, B. H. (2006). *Development in adulthood* (4th ed.). Boston, MA: Pearson.

Levenson, R. W., Carstensen, L. L., & Gottman, J. M. (1993). Long term marriage: Age, gender, and satisfaction. *Psychology and Aging, 8*, 301–13.

Linsenmeyer, W., & Lucas, T. (2017). Student development during the Occupy SLU Movement through the lens of Perry. *Jesuit Higher Education: A Journal, 6*(1), 44–53.

Lippert, A. M., & Damaske, S. (2019). Finding jobs, forming families, and stressing out? Work, family, and stress among young adult women in the United States. *Social Forces, 98*(2), 885–914.

Luk, J. W., Sita, K. R., Gilman, S. E., Goldstein, R. B., Haynie, D. L., & Simons-Morton, B. G. (2018). Adolescent sexual orientation and developmental transition in emerging adulthood: Disparities in school, work, residence, and transportation. *Journal of Adolescent Health, 63*(5), 649–51.

Meyer, S., & Schwitzer, A. M. (1999). Stages of identity development among college students with minority sexual orientations. *Journal of College Student Psychotherapy, 13*, 41–65.

Miller, L. H. (1984). Alternative approaches to measuring nursing: Gilligan's and Kohlberg's moral development scales. *Rehabilitation Nursing: The Official Journal of the Association of Rehabilitation Nurses, 9*(5), 22–26.

Minton, H. L., & McDonald, G. J. (1984). Homosexual identity formation as a developmental process. *Journal of Homosexuality, 9*, 91–104.

Miyake, A., Friedman, N. P., Emerson, M. J., Witzki, A. H., Howerter, A., & Wager, T. D. (2000). The unity and diversity of executive functions and their contributions to "frontal lobe" tasks: A latent variable analysis. *Cognitive Psychology, 41*, 49–100.

Morris, J. F. (1997). Lesbian coming out as a multidimensional process. *Journal of Homosexuality, 33*, 1–22.

Nelson, R. L., Sendroiu, I., Dinovitzer, R., & Dawe, M. (2019). Perceiving discrimination: Race, gender, and sexual orientation in the legal workplace. *Law and Social Inquiry, 44*(4), 1051–82.

Norona, J. C., Roberson, P. N. E., & Welsh, D. P. (2017). "I learned things that make me happy, things that bring me down": Lessons from romantic relationships in adolescence and emerging adulthood. *Journal of Adolescent Research, 32*(2), 155–82.

O'Neil, G., & O'Neil, N. (1972). *Open marriage.* New York, NY: Avon.

Ossana, S. M., Helms, J. E., & Leonard, M. M. (1992). Do "womanist" identity attitudes influence college women's self-esteem and perceptions of environmental bias? *Journal of Counseling and Development, 70*, 402–8.

Radmacher, K., & Azmitia, M. (2006). Are there gendered pathways to intimacy in early adolescents' and emerging adults' friendships? *Journal of Adolescent Research, 21*(4), 415–48.

Reed, K., Duncan, J., Lucier-Greer, M., Fixelle, C., & Ferraro, A. (2016). Helicopter parenting and emerging adult self-efficacy: Implications for mental and physical health. *Journal of Child and Family Studies, 25*(10), 3136–49.

Simon, K. A., Vázquez, C. P., Bruun, S. T., & Farr, R. H. (2019). Retrospective feelings of difference based on gender and sexuality among emerging adults. *Psychology of Sexual Orientation and Gender Diversity*.

Sinnott, J. D. (1984). Postformal reasoning: The relativistic stage. In M. Commons, F. Richards, & C. Armon (Eds.), *Beyond formal operations* (pp. 298–325). New York: Praeger.

Sinnott, J. D. (1998). *The development of logic in adulthood: Postformal thought and its applications*. New York: Plenum Press.

Timmermans, E., Coenen, L., & Van den Bulck, J. (2019). The Bridget Jones effect: The relationship between exposure to romantic media contents and fear of being single among emerging adults. *Psychology of Popular Media Culture, 8*(2), 159–69.

U.S. Census Bureau. (2018, November 17). The majority of children live with two parents, Census Bureau reports. Retrieved from https://www.census.gov/newsroom/press-releases/2016/cb16-192.html

Weisskirch, R. S. (2018). Psychosocial intimacy, relationships with parents, and well-being among emerging adults. *Journal of Child and Family Studies, 27*(11), 3497–3505.

Williams, J. H. (1987). *Psychology of women: Behavior in a biosocial context.* New York, NY: W. W. Norton.

Worthington, R. L., Savoy, H. B., Dillon, F. R., & Vernaglia, E. R. (2002). Heterosexual identity development: A multidimensional model of individual and social identity. *Counseling Psychologist, 30*, 496–531. doi:10.1177/00100002030004002

Chapter Six

Counseling Midlife Women

Suzanne Degges-White

CASE VIGNETTE: CARA

Cara is a forty-seven-year-old woman who identifies as a multiracial, Hispanic woman. Before coming out as a bisexual at twenty-eight, Cara had married in her late teens and given birth to two children by the time she was twenty-five. Cara's divorce was final shortly after her twenty-ninth birthday, and she was able to maintain primary custody of her children. Currently, Cara is in the middle of her second significant romantic breakup, as she and her partner of fifteen years, Sandy, have determined that their marriage is no longer viable. Sandy is a decade younger than Cara and had told Cara that she wanted to experience the world in ways that she had not been able to before, since she and Cara had moved in together when Sandy was only twenty-two. Cara recognizes that she is not the same woman she was in her early thirties and feels overwhelmed by Sandy's departure, her adult children's unexpected response of sadness at Sandy's departure, and their placement of blame on Cara for the relationship breakup. Cara is bemused at her own sense of helplessness, fatigue, and sadness.

Cara decided to reach out to a counselor to help her make sense of the unexpected turn of events in her life. She arrived on time for the appointment and is eager to have someone help her figure out how to handle what feels to Cara like a total disintegration of her life as she knew it. When she entered the office of Sarah, her counselor, Cara sat down on the edge of the couch. When Sarah invited her to share what has brought her into counseling at this point in time, Cara burst into tears. Sobbing, she said to Sarah, "I thought I knew where my life was going. I have a decent part-time job, two grown children, and until a few weeks ago, I had a spouse that I thought I would spend the rest of my life with. Now, I'm looking at a second divorce. I'm worried that my kids will hate me forever. I'm worried that I won't be able to pay my bills. I'm terrified that I'll end up in a tiny apartment with not enough money for food. I haven't slept through the night in months, my emotions are all over the place, and I feel like I'm either about to go off on people for no reason or just burst into tears like I did today. I don't know who I am or where I'm going anymore."

* * *

The stage of life known as "midlife" describes the years between somewhere around late thirties or early forties through the midsixties. Due to our lengthening lifespans, the midlife period grew into a discrete stage of life that precedes the "older adult years." Roughly a century ago, this period of life would have been, effectively, the late adult years as life expectancy hovered around the early fifties (Grove & Hetzel, 1968). When this period of life began to take on its own identity, forty was the age at which midlife began according to many theorists (Jung, 1971; Levinson & Levinson, 1996; Neugarten, Moore, & Lowe, 1965; Sheehy, 1993). Midlife women are a sizable population, as women aged forty to sixty-four accounted for approximately 33 percent of the total U.S. female population in 2010 (U.S. Census Bureau, 2010). Further, midlife women make up the bulk of the client population for an exceptionally large number of counselors (Shallcross, 2012). Therefore, this chapter will provide a comprehensive review of the changes and challenges that women in this age group experience.

Although midlife was traditionally, and negatively, associated with a major life crisis (Jacques, 1965; Levinson & Levinson, 1996), it has also been described as a period of psychological awakening and significant inner development (Brehoney, 1996; Jung, 1971) and a time in which individuals may begin to direct their energy into generative pursuits (Erikson, 1968). These enduring but conflicting views may contribute to the ways women respond to their arrival in this period of life. While it would be ideal if women embraced the arrival of menopause with "postmenopausal zest," a term Margaret Mead reportedly coined, not every woman is ready to experience these age-related changes regardless of the potentially positive outcome that awaits. Following is an overview of the ways the transition into and through the midlife period may influence women's lives physically, cognitively, and emotionally.

PHYSIOLOGICAL CHANGES THAT OCCUR DURING THE MIDLIFE PERIOD

It can be very useful for helping professionals to understand the vast array of changes that are taking place in women's bodies as they move through midlife. Stereotypes of midlife women abound, and many are related to their appearance, their moods, and the aging process. While not every woman will experience the same level of upset or distress with perimenopause and menopause, it is helpful for clinicians to understand the midlife-based challenges that may motivate women to seek counseling.

Perimenopause and Menopause

Perhaps the most iconic event associated with women at midlife is the experience of menopause. Menopause is considered to have taken place after the passage of twelve months since a woman's most recent menstrual period. Sadly, many women perceive their arrival into menopause as a marker of reaching "middle age" and a portent of a barren future. Menopause can be experienced as a natural transition or be a medically induced outcome due to removal of a woman's ovaries. The average age for experiencing this transition naturally is approximately fifty-one, no matter where a woman resides around the globe (Rahman, Akesson, & Wolk, 2015). While the prediction of a woman's age at menopause might inspire research, the most reliable predictor for most women is the age at which their own mothers reached menopause (Depmann et al., 2016). Some women are eager for menopause to arrive and celebrate it as a badge of honor of their arrival at a new stage of life; other women dread it as a sign of defeat.

It was only in the last two decades that any significant information was disseminated regarding the hormonal changes taking place prior to the arrival of menopause. *Perimenopause* describes the years that precede the final cessation of a woman's menstrual cycles. It is during this period that a majority of the symptoms that are typically ascribed to menopause actually begin to appear, including hot flashes, sleep difficulties, and other physiological changes (Delamater & Santoro, 2018).

Hot Flashes

Hot flashes and night sweats are two of the most frequently noted symptoms of perimenopause (Ying, Zhangbin, & Minfang, 2015). Whether or not a woman is able to joke about her "own personal summer" is generally tied to the level of disruption that these experiences generate. When night sweats are keeping a woman from getting adequate sleep, any other menopausal symptoms may be exacerbated by her sleep deficit. Irritability, moodiness, and fatigue are also symptoms of insufficient sleep, and when coupled with other menopausal symptoms, a woman may believe menopause to be an exceedingly challenging transition. Hot flashes, too, can create frustration and irritability in some women. When these experiences are normalized and their transitory nature understood, they may be less likely to create significant distress. Unfortunately, this is not always the case. When these symptoms are compounded with the sleep disturbances that occur during midlife, women may be challenged in feeling stable and emotionally sound.

Sleep Disturbances

The midlife years will bring on sleep difficulties for most individuals, whether male or female (Pearson, 2017). However, the period surrounding the perimenopause and menopause transition has been shown to be particularly deleterious to women's sleep hygiene (Jones, Zak, & Lee, 2018). While severe sleep disturbances may require referral to a physician, counselors can provide assistance to clients suffering from sleep problems. Cognitive-behavioral strategies related to relaxation can be as effective as medication (Pearson, 2017). Encourage clients to utilize free, downloadable apps (such as Calm, which includes relaxation, meditation, and sleep aids; Sleep; or a white-noise generator) that provide affordable relaxation scripts and "sleep stories." These can be helpful in moving clients toward a state of relaxation at bedtime, which is highly beneficial. Educate clients about the importance of regular sleep–wake cycles and encourage them to limit any type of electronic stimulation (such as email, Candy Crush, Twitter, and so on) that is keeping their brain from slowing down in the hour before they want to fall asleep. Some clients also benefit from basic reminders about avoiding caffeine or large amounts of liquids close to bedtime. Some clients have irrational fears about missing sleep or being unable to fall asleep; help clients let go of these thoughts and encourage them to practice exercises such as "drop that thought." When their brains get stuck in a loop of negative thoughts about missing sleep, which are on continuous playback at night, tell them to consciously and figuratively "drop that thought" and imagine themselves picking up their negative thought and "dropping it" off the edge of a cliff or the earth. The more clients are able to relax at bedtime, the more likely it is that they are able to drift off to sleep.

Not only does inadequate sleep decrease subjective well-being and mood, it is also linked to a greater risk for obesity (Jean-Louis et al., 2014). With the cultural messages regarding youth, size, and beauty, women's aging bodies may be a significant cause of emotional distress.

Aging Bodies

Throughout the midlife period, many physical changes occur. For instance, menopause signals the end of fertility for women, and it also is a harbinger of other physical changes that women are often unprepared to acknowledge and accept. As the body's production of estrogen winds down, health risks may increase and physical processes are altered. When fertility's end is appreciated as freedom from the risk of pregnancy, some women perceive this as a gift. Other women perceive the loss of fertility as a symbol of the loss of their feminine power and sexual attractiveness. Concerns about sexual well-being can be exacerbated by the vaginal dryness that can accompany menopause, as it can negatively affect women's desire for or pleasure in sexual intercourse (Waetjen et al., 2018). Unfortunately, the female body's transition into midlife can be accompanied by changes that can be of both psychological and medical concern. Following is an overview of some of the most concerning outcomes of hormonal changes, such as bone density changes, cardiovascular changes, and changes to the skin and hair. While the majority of these are related to physiological changes that counselors are not able to address, it can benefit clients to have their concerns validated by a counselor and to normalize the changes that they are undergoing. In addition, if they are comparing themselves negatively to media images of beauty and feel that they are lacking, encourage them to focus on what their experience in life has taught them about their strengths and skills, and remind them that external appraisals of worth or value do more to damage all women than they do to help a single one.

Bone Density

Bone density changes over time, peaking in the midthirties but decreasing much more rapidly once menopause has been reached (Condon, 2004). Lower bone density can lead to osteoporosis as well as result in more fragile and breakable bones. Other risk factors identified for decreased bone density include cigarette use, inadequate physical activity, and insufficient vitamin D intake or lack of sufficient exposure to natural sunlight (van Dijk, Kavousi, Troup, & Franco, 2015). In addition to the skeletal system, the cardiovascular system and integumentary system (skin and hair) also change during this time.

Cardiovascular System

The heart and circulatory system are also negatively affected by the cessation of estrogen production in women. Thus, older women are at an increased risk of heart disease than younger women. In addition, as the body transitions into menopause, many women experience heart palpitations that can be alarming when they arise. Headaches are related common complaints of women during this stage (Inayat, Danish, & Hassan, 2017). Choices that women make regarding diet, exercise, smoking, and alcohol consumption can positively or negatively affect their cardiovascular health. Educating clients on the intensified risk of heart disease during menopause is especially important when they are engaging in behaviors that present increased health risks in themselves. The skeletal system and the cardiovascular system are internal targets of the aging process, but for some women, the more outwardly visible signals of their advancing age, such as skin, hair, and weight changes, may be their primary concern.

Skin and Hair

Outward signs of advancing age include changes in skin, which includes both a thinning of the skin and a loss of elasticity, which contribute to the development of wrinkles. The desire of women to stave off the physical signs of aging can be measured in dollars; a recent research report projected annual spending for antiaging products and services would reach over $330 billion by 2021 (Orbis Research, 2017). This is a phenomenal amount of money, and it reflects the current cultural perceptions regarding the worth of women once they reach midlife. Encourage your clients to challenge media stereotypes about beauty as you encourage them to value the life experience and depth that maturity bring. Women's skin, at menopause, also tends to weaken in its ability to ward off infections and is more subject to irritation (Condon, 2004). Age spots and discoloration also begin to appear in midlife, and these can generate strong emotional reactions in some women who are afraid of the natural aging process. For women who are still premenopausal, it might benefit them to know that sun exposure and smoking are two identified risk factors for substantial wrinkling that can both be avoided for multiple health-related reasons.

In addition to changes in the skin's texture and appearance, hair also undergoes similar changes. A woman's head of hair, just like a man's, can begin to thin in midlife, and as pigmentation cells die, it loses its usual color and changes to gray or white (Baran & Maibach, 2017). While gray hair may be seen as "trendy" today by some women, it is often seen as a marker of advancing age that many women believe promotes ageism toward them or leaves them virtually "invisible" to others (Cecil et al., 2018). There's a joke about a midlife woman who complains, "I'm losing hair from where it should be, and it's showing up in places that it shouldn't!" As estrogen production slows down, facial hair growth often increases. Most women today are already familiar with and practiced at removal of unwanted hair from other parts of the body. The same methods, such as tweezing, bleaching, or electrolysis, are generally the most effective for unwanted facial hair as well. Sudden hair growth, however, could suggest something more significant that the typical hirsutism of midlife, and a visit to a physician might be recommended to a client (Blume-Peytavi, 2011). Hormonal changes can affect appetite as well.

Weight Gain

Weight gain is also typically associated with the midlife period, and the average woman will gain approximately five pounds during the menopause transition. Weight gain is often seen as an inevitable part of the aging process, but it is important to encourage clients to avoid using menopause as an excuse to overeat to the point of an unhealthy weight. Obesity has been linked to the development of adult-onset diabetes and multiple types of cancer, and the risks for these diseases increase during midlife (van Dijk et al., 2015). Women also tend to devalue their worth when they are unhappy with their weight, which can lead to emotional distress and lowered self-esteem. While healthy support networks are the key to a sense of satisfaction in life and happiness, healthy relationships can also promote positive behaviors and healthy choices. In fact, Chen and colleagues (2018) found that a supportive marital relationship was directly linked to healthy body weight and less weight gain for midlife women. Assessing for relationship quality and exploring any related concerns can be useful for clients in multiple ways. Being actively engaged in social support networks can encourage clients to stay healthy and stay engaged. However, if clients report that their support networks encourage unhealthy behaviors and choices, encourage them to seek out new social connections where healthy choices will be reinforced.

Please also note that contrary to some beliefs, midlife women may continue to suffer from long-term eating disorders or experience the initial onset of an eating disorder (Baker & Runfola, 2016; Mangweth-Matzek et al., 2014). Counselors should be alert to clients' expression of weight-related concerns or if they note any significant changes in client weight. For additional information on eating disorders or body image concerns, please refer to chapter 14. Perhaps one of the most beneficial interventions that counselors can offer is helping the client understand the changes that are occurring.

Suggestions for Client Education

Although there are certainly many books addressing menopause as well as online resources that women can access for more information, it can be helpful for counselors to be prepared to discuss the ways perimenopause and menopause may be influencing clients' health and well-being (Huffman & Myers, 1999). Helping clients understand the connection between their lifestyle choices and their health, especially in terms of addictive habits (smoking, drinking, and so on) or a sedentary lifestyle, may provide the motivation for clients to choose healthier behaviors.

While some symptoms of perimenopause and menopause, and associated hormonal and physical changes, can be controlled by medical means today, counselors should encourage clients to thoroughly review the benefits and risks of hormone replacement therapy (HRT), medical procedures, and other forms of treatment, including complementary and alternative treatments. In addition to the physiological changes, the passage into menopause and midlife are as much a psychological and emotional transformation for most women today.

PSYCHOLOGICAL AND EMOTIONAL CHANGES THAT MAY OCCUR DURING MIDLIFE

In addition to the significant physical changes that occur during this period of life, hormonal changes along with health and appearance-related changes can lead to significant emotional disruption and psychological distress.

Mood Swings and Irritability

Women of all ages understand the connection between their menstrual cycle and their moods. During perimenopause and menopause, women's moods are also labile and unpredictable. In addition to, and likely exacerbating, mood swings are the lethargy, fatigue, irritability, and difficulty concentrating that typically occur during this period of life (Inayat et al., 2017). Menopause is often accompanied by memory problems and forgetfulness as well (Devi, Hahn, Massimi, & Zhivotovskaya, 2005; Inayat et al., 2017), which can lead to additional frustration and irritation. Unfortunately, the middle adult years may bring about mood changes that are simply a normal aspect of hormonal shifts. Counselors should validate clients' feelings related to noted mood swings or irritability while normalizing their presence in client's lives. Some clients are happily surprised at their newfound ability to say what they think without worrying about consequences as they once might have. Counselors can encourage clients to share instances where their irritability might have been a positive force or surprising in a good way. In a culture obsessed with youth, or at least a youthful appearance, women reaching midlife may also express emotions and behaviors that are due, in part, to their changing bodies as well as the cultural messages and expectations they face. Combined, these symptoms may influence the development of depression.

Depression

While not every woman who experiences menopause is going to suffer from depression, it is true that depression is more common during the perimenopausal (Mulhall, Andel, & Ansley, 2017) and early postmenopausal period than at any other times in a woman's life (Georgakis et al., 2016). A report from the Harvard Women's Health Watch (2018) suggested that a woman's risk for depressive symptoms is quadrupled during this period of life. Of note, however, is the finding that the longer a woman's reproductive period lasted (the years from first period to menopause), the smaller the likelihood she will experience menopause-related depression (Georgakis et al., 2016).

Unfortunately, the emotional losses that midlife may present can also contribute to the incidence of depression during these years. Relationships and the family constellation can undergo significant transformations during midlife. Personal identities that have held great import may change as children exit the family home to create their own new family systems. Loss of parents or of others close to the client may be difficult to assimilate, as these deaths can often bring into focus a midlife woman's own sense of mortality. When a woman's primary role in life, whether it was mother, partner, or employee, changes dramatically, she may feel that the meaning her life once held has lost its value. For detailed information on counseling women experiencing depression, please refer to chapter 16.

Anxiety

For some women, the midlife years may bring on new levels of anxiety. Research indicates that symptoms of anxiety are increasingly prevalent during the postmenopausal period (Mulhall et al., 2017). The hormonal changes that trigger anxiety in some women can also be accompanied by the new challenges and concerns that appear in midlife and that would naturally heighten feelings of stress and anxiety. Just as losses can trigger depression, new expectations and responsibilities related to caregiving for others can trigger anxiety.

Perceptions about exactly what midlife should "look like" for a woman are often filtered through cultural messages and media representations of midlife, and the mismatch between these images and an individual woman's sense of self can generate anxieties about exactly what midlife *should* look like for her. As noted in other chapters, cultural representations of the "ideal" female, regardless of age, can be detrimental to the development or maintenance of a woman's healthy self-esteem and self-confidence. This can generate body dissatisfaction, which can generate appearance-related anxieties (McLaren & Kuh, 2004). For detailed information on counseling women experiencing body image concerns, please refer to chapter 14; for low self-esteem, please refer to chapter 15; and for anxiety, please refer to chapter 17.

RELATIONAL CHALLENGES THAT MAY APPEAR DURING MIDLIFE

Midlife women have traditionally spent their adult lives employed, and the majority of them have also been wives and mothers. The role expectations that midlife women have experienced on the home front, on the work front, and in the community can be overwhelming and, over time, take a toll. Midlife women, too, tend to make up the bulk of a counselor's client load (Shallcross, 2012), and it is important for counselors to be careful not to minimize the concerns of a midlife client. Many women are taught to bear their burdens and refrain from complaints, so these clients may be hesitant to share the full weight of the load that they carry. Understanding the physiological and emotional stressors that your clients may be facing will allow you to do a more thorough assessment.

Relationship to Self and Purpose in Life

While midlife women today have greater freedom in their life choices than generations before them, their lives are not without stress and their choices not without risk. While popular media likes to encourage ideas such as "fifty is the new thirty" or that "reinvention" of oneself at midlife is easily achievable, many women do not embrace this period in life as lustily as cultural messages suggest they might. In fact, there are harrowing statistics that suggest that midlife is an increasingly troubling time for women. The suicide rates for women aged forty-five to sixty-four has increased dramatically in the past two decades; in fact, the rate jumped 60 percent between 2000 and 2016 (Curtin, Warner, & Hedegaard, 2016). Although there is seldom a single reason that a person attempts suicide, it is known that approximately 60 percent of people who die by suicide suffered from depression. It is also true that menopause-related hormonal changes can trigger depression. Be alert to any warning signs or mixed messages that your clients might express regarding life purpose or life meaning or value to others. Every client's experiences differ, and it is important for counselors to assess for client well-being and support systems in place. Assess for self-harm, and if the client is at risk and feels unsafe, ensure that your client is transported to a hospital or other in-patient facility.

Intrapersonal Concerns

The arrivals of perimenopause and, subsequently, menopause affect each woman in an individual and unique manner. Some women actually welcome the transition and perceive it as freedom from concerns about reproductive health. They are relieved to leave behind concerns about unplanned pregnancy and the hassles related to monthly menstruation. They may be grateful for the newly experienced "invisibility" that is typical of this new life stage. Being removed from the "sexual gaze" in the professional arena, due to their graying hair and aging bodies, can be perceived as an opportunity to be taken more seriously on the job (Isopahkala-Bouret, 2017). When working with clients in midlife, it is important to remember that each client will have a unique experience and attitude regarding this period of development. Encourage clients to express their feelings or beliefs about aging and validate their viewpoints while also encouraging them to expand their perspectives, if necessary, to enlarge their views of what is possible.

There's an old saying that the older you get, the more like yourself you become. As Jung (1971) suggested, midlife is a time when individuals begin to own traits and characteristics that might not be as pleasing to others as the ones women tend to display throughout the first half of their lives. When coupled with the hormonal changes of midlife, midlife women may feel like they have been unfettered from societal expectations and feel more free to express themselves more authentically with their families, their friends, and their colleagues.

Most people find themselves formally or informally taking stock of their lives at some point during the midlife years, and they also begin to assess whether they are making headway or have become "stuck" (Erikson, 1968). The desire to stay vital and involved can encourage midlife women to become mentors for younger colleagues, volunteer in their communities, become patrons of good causes, and become advocates for others. There is much mention of "menopause zest" in online communities, and this references the motivation that many women feel to stay active and engaged in the world around them—especially if their primary roles in the home or workplace have lost their centrality or power. Transitions, whether unexpected or normative, can cause stress, but transitions also provide opportunities for new beginnings.

Jung's Perspective on Midlife Development

Traditional theories about adult development suggested this period is a time of transition, most surely, but a transition in which people come to know themselves more clearly and to integrate aspects of their personality that they may have previously ignored or somehow sublimated (Jung, 1971). Jung developed a construct of identity that included the *persona*, the face that people show to the world, and the *shadow*, the aspects of self that are kept hidden from others and often from the individual herself. During midlife, according to Jung, the individuation process takes place. This is the conscious realization and integration of all the various qualities and potentials present in an individual. Jung proposed that this is accomplished through the recognition of one's less attractive qualities (the shadow self), the ones kept hidden from the outer world as well as oneself, and through an effort toward acceptance and integration of these attributes into an amicable union with one's more pleasing qualities, as represented by the persona.

Erikson's Perspective on Midlife Development

Erikson (1968) proposed that people face specific developmental crises throughout eight predictable stages of life. The crisis that falls at midlife is described as a crisis of generativity versus stagnation. A person facing this developmental task must choose whether or not to give back to others through procreation, community service, professional service, or comparable approaches. Erikson theorized that midlife adults are driven to find meaning in their lives through being productive, but that they must be careful of giving in to self-absorption, which would lead to stagnation and diminished personal growth.

There are few species in which the female outlives her fertility, and there are many hypotheses regarding the value of this arrangement in humans. One idea that has received research support is the notion that women's roles as grandmothers greatly increases the likelihood of the survival of the species, giving support to a belief that women actually keep the world spinning and the species surviving. Unfortunately, the individual tasks that women must address during midlife seem much more mundane and have much less glamour, but require significant investment of time and energy. Thomas, Mitchell, and Woods (2018) found that the primary tasks of midlife include changing family relationships, the balance between work and personal life, self-exploration and discovery, resource acquisition (financial, housing, etc.), and coping with stressors. As counselors, you may work with clients presenting with one or many of these issues. In addition, some of the specific stressors clients experience may include relationship breakups, health problems, or bereavement.

RELATIONSHIPS WITH OTHERS

Individuals are dynamic creatures, and as an individual changes, her relationships with others often change as well. Flexibility is an important quality for women to cultivate as their own midlife changes may surprise others, as well as themselves.

Romantic Relationships

The number of women who are facing a transition such as "wife" to "divorcee" or "single woman" to "partner" has risen over recent years, which can be the cause of adjustment issues and challenges regardless of the overall positive value of the role change itself. A Pew Research Study indicated that the divorce rate for people fifty and over has climbed dramatically in the past decade (Stepler, 2017). For every one thousand married persons who are fifty or older, ten divorced in 2015; this is exactly twice the number who divorced in the same age group in 1990. While the reasons for divorce vary greatly across relationships (Crowley, 2017), simplified divorce procedures and lengthened lifespans may play a role in their frequency.

Sexual Relationships

Regardless of sexual orientation, women acknowledge that their sexual relationships change over time as interest and engagement in sexual behaviors diminish (Paine, Umberson, & Reczek, 2018). Not surprisingly, physical changes as well as changing responsibilities were perceived to contribute to these changes. More specifically, one of the most frequently voiced concerns about menopause is the perceived negative effect that it can have on sexual activity and intimacy. From the United States to Saudi Arabia (Al Mehdar et al., 2017), women express the desire for a more satisfying sex life postmenopause. Hormonal changes can bring about multiple causes of sexual dissatisfaction, including vaginal dryness, compromised arousal and difficulty reaching orgasm, decreased sexual satisfaction, and lower levels of sexual desire (Nappi & Lachowsky, 2009). Clearly, there are multiple challenges that menopausal women face in terms of decreased sexual pleasure.

Although women have been more vocal in expressing their experiences related to sexual activity in middle adulthood, there may be a parallel experience for men. A term coined by Jannini and Nappi (2018), *couplepause*, was used to describe the shared experience that aging can take on a midlife couple. While a lesbian couple, depending on age, might experience simultaneous menopausal symptoms, it was only recently that researchers acknowledged that a heterosexual couple may also battle waning sex drives and physiological, age-related sexual dysfunction. Menopausal women might experience symptoms such as vaginal dryness, vaginal irritation, and insufficient lubrication, which can all contribute to pain during intercourse. However, as men age, they also experience sexual dysfunctions, including erectile problems and, potentially, testosterone deficiency.

When working with a midlife client who is concerned about her level of sexual attractiveness to her partner or her own sexual performance, counselors can encourage her to discuss her concerns with her sexual partner. If her partner is at a similar developmental stage, it can be normal for both partners to lose interest in sexual activity. Counselors can help normalize this experience, and if a couple-centric focus is employed, it can be a positive support for a client who feels stigmatized for her age or menopausal status. Other relationships, beyond a primary romantic relationship, also may undergo significant changes during this period of life.

Caring for Others

Midlife is typically a period in life in which a woman's children are now leaving home and creating space in a woman's life to focus on new activities or in new directions. Many women, however, assume the role of caregiver of the older adults in their families. As lifespans have lengthened, so have the caregiving responsibilities of the women in each generation. Women may take on the role of caregiver voluntarily or as a result of geographical proximity or some other practical circumstance. Women in the caregiving role may face a significant number of challenges to their own well-being as they often feel that they must sacrifice their own needs for the needs of others (Halinski, Duxbury, & Higgins, 2018).

It was in 1981 that the term *sandwich generation* was coined to describe adults caring for their parents while also caring for their own children (Danson & Hardill, 2006). A new variation, the "club sandwich generation," describes those women who care for their parents but also are heavily involved in the lives of their adult children and their own grandchildren. It probably isn't a surprise, but researchers found that if a woman is caring for only one other generation, it is less stressful to provide childcare than it is to provide eldercare (Halinski et al., 2018). With children, parents have much more authority than they might with their own or their partners' parents.

Caregiving for others when a woman has reached a point in her life at which she believed she might finally have time for herself can be an emotionally charged challenge. For more information on working with clients who are caregivers, please refer to chapter 20. In addition to caregiving role changes, other family relationships may also shift.

Family Relationship Changes

Midlife is a time when relationship roles and boundaries take on more of an elastic nature as new people move into the circle and others move out. The traditional trajectory of a woman's life was to go from youth to bride to parent to grandparent. Although these transitions are considered part of the normal cycle of life, the transition from parent to grandparent or mom to "mom-in-law" can bring emotional challenges that may be unexpected. Some clients may welcome these new roles, while others may feel that their place in their children's lives is being usurped by their children's partners or in-laws. Grandparenthood—or longing for it but not having it occur—may challenge some individuals as well. Every individual responds differently to life events and "nonevents."

Some women have difficulty letting go of their children and wrestle with the "empty nest" that is often faced at midlife. This period can be a time of bereavement as the primacy of the role of mother may shrink in size. If married, some women may feel that their partners are strangers—this is common when childrearing has been the focus for the past couple of decades. Encourage clients to reacquaint themselves with their partners through "dates" or shared activities. Invite clients to explore hobbies or interests that were "put on the shelf" once their children arrived on the scene.

Other family roles that can cause upset include clients becoming the mother-in-law to disliked spouses of their children. Some women resent a child's changing allegiance from their parents to their partner. If your client is having difficulty accepting a child's partner, invite your client to discuss her concerns as well as her fears about the changing relationship with her child. Encourage her to reflect on how her relationship to her own mother changed when she became half of a couple herself. Enlarging a client's perspective on the transition as well as helping her expand her own vision of what "family" means as children grow up can help her shift her beliefs and decrease her distress.

The role of grandmother can be difficult for some women as they feel that this transition is a further marker of advancing age. Validate your client's fears and normalize her concerns by noting the wide range of feelings that entry into grandparenthood can bring. Help your client brainstorm the positive aspects to grandparenting and ways she might be different with the grandchild than she was with her own children.

Wanting to be a grandparent, but not getting that opportunity, can also be distressing for some clients. The "fear of missing out" may be especially strong if your client's social support system is peopled with friends who are already grandmothers. Again, normalize your client's feelings and then encourage her to share ways she might be able to fill the time she "thought" might be taken up by the grandmother role.

Although research suggests that women no longer feel the need to conform to specific timelines for transitions (Degges-White & Myers, 2006), any transition has the potential to create difficulties that motivate a woman to seek a counselor's support. Counselors working with midlife women should avoid preconceived notions about what midlife "used to" or "should" look like, as the experience is unique to each individual woman.

Friendships and Social Support Networks

For many women, midlife can offer the opportunity to explore new activities, let go of old responsibilities, and, potentially, enjoy the freedom to edit their social relationships as they desire (Degges-White & Borzumato-Gainey, 2011). As midlife brings a new awareness of the finiteness of time (Neugarten et al., 1965), women may be more selective in the relationships in which they invest time and energy. Women often become more discerning in their choices and are comfortable prioritizing the friendships that are the most authentic and rewarding. Although it is normal for the number of friendships a woman maintains to decrease over time, it can be especially difficult for midlife women to find new friends due to the often shrinking social circles in which people move over time.

If a woman's social connections and support life have revolved around their children and their children's friends' families, midlife can be a lonely time as children grow up and those parent-to-parent friendships fade. If a marriage or long-term partnership dissolves at this period in life, a woman may also experience a crumbling or rearrangement of her social support network, if other couples made up the majority of her friendscape. These two situations can be especially challenging for midlife women, as they will be coping not only with the "empty nest" their children leave behind, or the loss of a life partner, but also the loss of their primary support system.

Working with clients who are experiencing this type of complicated social loss requires counselors to encourage the client to seek out new friendships while taking care to ensure that you, as the counselor, are not put into the position of "standing in" as a friend for a client or being perceived as the client's primary support. Help your client brainstorm opportunities she could use to meet new people. Ask her to make a list of activities that she used to engage in that she could pick back up so that she can build new relationships with potential friends. If she is feeling the losses that accompany a newly "empty nest," encourage her to volunteer for a cause she cares about to provide a place to invest her "caretaking" energy if that's an aspect of motherhood that she misses. For some women, just starting small and joining an online support group or attending informational sessions at the local library or "Y" might be the most appropriate "first steps" in building up a friendscape. In addition to individual client factors, social dynamics must also be considered in light of cultural considerations.

CULTURAL CONSIDERATIONS

Cultural backgrounds greatly influence the ways an individual views and experiences development over the lifespan. Expectations about the weight and meaning of transitions varies across cultures. For instance, while regular physical activity is empirically proven to have strong physiological and psychological benefits for many of the concerns and symptoms for which midlife women seek treatment, a woman's ethnic identity influences her attitude toward exercise and activity engagement (Im et al., 2013). Both Caucasian and Asian women felt that engagement in fitness activities would positively affect their appearance and their ability to meet cultural standards of beauty, while both African American and Hispanic women noted that they did not feel the same pressure and voiced acceptance of their own individual appearances.

Wray (2007) noted that it is the individual and cultural experiences of women that truly determine the meaning of this period in life. She noted cultural expectations of a woman's role can influence the ways midlife is navigated, and when individual concerns, such as widowhood or caregiving, are present, it is not life stage but life tasks that command attention. Thus, counselors must consider the needs of the client and avoid imposing their values onto the client while considering cultural norms.

ETHICAL CONSIDERATIONS

The current cultural response to the natural physical changes women's bodies undergo over the passage of time is often to apply a medical model through which to view and "fix" things that are not disease-saturated changes. Midlife and its associated processes and outcomes should not be assumed to be problematic unless clients have determined them to be so. Helping professionals should assess whether or not their clients want to learn more about medically based care or treatment options. As in all cases, helping professionals must be careful to avoid letting their own values and perspectives influence the treatment their clients receive.

ADVOCACY OPPORTUNITIES

In a culture that exalts beauty and eternal youth, women coping with normal and natural changes to their bodies and their appearance may well benefit from advocacy efforts on their behalf. Advocacy efforts to assist women in the employment and earnings arena would be equally beneficial. Additionally, there is a need to encourage health organizations to catch up on the researching of women's health needs and care. While there are multiple studies that focus on men's health and men's pharmaceutical needs, less attention has been given to the unique needs of women. Working in your community to promote initiatives for women's well-being, services for older adults, and health forums are also ways to advocate for the well-being of midlife women.

CASE VIGNETTE WRAP-UP: CARA

Sitting across from Cara, Sarah recognized the significant distress Cara felt, and she responded to her with empathy: "It's clear that you're facing some unexpected challenges in life, and they seem pretty overwhelming for you right now. It's great, though, that you're here. I can tell that you're ready to begin to get back on top of things and figure out how to handle all of these unpredictable changes and emotions that are coming your way."

Cara affirmed, "I've got to do something. . . . I really don't know what I'll do if I can't get a grip on things soon. I'm running out of energy and ideas; those are two things I do know for sure."

Sarah answered, "Well, then, we know what our starting point is going to be. Share a little bit more about your current situation, and then we can figure out where you want to be. That will give us the goals you want to work toward—and once we know where you're headed, it's a lot easier for us to work together on a plan to help you get there."

Cara described her goal of becoming financially self-sufficient as well as figuring out "who she wanted to be" as she felt the relational breakup was showing her that it was time she "grew up." Cara also sought normalization of her emotions and her frustration with herself for feeling "old."

Intervention Strategy: Reframing Negative Self-Assessment

When Sarah heard Cara call herself "old" a couple of times in session, Sarah interjected, "Cara, when you call yourself 'old,' what are you getting out of the negative self-labeling?"

Cara was confused by the question and stammered, "Getting out of it? What do you mean? I don't think it's a benefit to get old!"

Sarah countered, "You're right. The way you're using the word, aging and maturing are negative events, not good things. But it sounds to me like you call yourself 'old' as an excuse for not succeeding or not going after what you want in life. What do you think?"

Cara agreed, "Yeah, okay, I see what you're saying. I'm so afraid I'll fail that I guess I'm already making up excuses in case I do."

Sarah responded, "Yep, I think you're right. I think we need to reframe things. How about instead of saying 'I'm old,' why not switch it up and say what that really means? Maybe something like, 'I've got years of experience,' or 'I have a mature outlook and can handle responsibility.' How do those sound?"

"A whole lot more positive. When I see myself through that perspective, I begin to believe that I have something that employers will want," Cara stated.

Sarah then provided information related to midlife development and the ways it affects women cognitively, emotionally, and physically. She encouraged Cara to learn more about perimenopause and its symptoms and encouraged Cara to contact her physician if she felt that the symptoms were keeping her from functioning effectively in her life roles.

Career Skills and Fantasy Focusing

Sarah and Cara discussed Cara's career goals. Sarah invited Cara to brainstorm all of the skills she believed she possessed. Sarah then asked Cara to talk about what activities she enjoyed most. Then Sarah asked Cara what she wanted to be known for as an employee. Many of the qualities and aspira-

tions revolved around caregiving. Sarah ended the session with a homework assignment for Cara. She asked her to spend some time looking at online career sites (such as Indeed.com) and to develop a résumé that she was to bring to the next session.

The next week, Cara shared her résumé and talked about some entry-level jobs in a nursing home that would cover the cost of training. Cara acknowledged that the most pleasurable part of her life had been when she was caregiving for her children when they were young and when she provided care to her partner's parents before they moved into an assisted-living community.

Sarah was pleased to see how Cara's attitude and self-assessment had begun to shift when Cara began to focus on where she was going, not where she had been or what she had lost. As Cara's knowledge and self-confidence increased, Cara became more confident in her relationships with her children as well. As Cara began her new career, she took pride in how courageous she had been, and Sarah reminded her that she was a strong role model for her kids in how to move forward and grow from adverse experiences.

QUESTIONS FOR REFLECTION

1. What are the stereotypes of menopause and midlife that you see in the media?
2. How might negative stereotypes influence women's feelings about themselves as they reach middle adulthood?
3. What are your own expectations about what midlife should be like? Do you have negative expectations that you need to change?
4. How might you advocate for women in this age group at the local level or at the national level?

REFERENCES

Al Mehdar, A. A., Hariri, M. O., Alotaibi, F. F., Abdullah, A. L., Alyani, T. A., Matary, . . . Sattam, M. H. (2017). Features of menopause and menopausal age among Saudi women. *Egyptian Journal of Hospital Medicine, 69*(7), 2809–13. doi:10.12816/0042570

Baker, J. H., & Runfola, C. D. (2016). Eating disorders in midlife women: A perimenopausal eating disorder? *Maturitas, 85*, 112–16.

Baran, R., & Maibach, H. I. (2017). *Textbook of cosmetic dermatology* (5th ed.). Boca Raton, FL: CRC Press.

Blume-Peytavi, U. (2011). An overview of unwanted female hair. *British Journal of Dermatology, 165*, 19–23. doi:10.1111/j.1365-2133.2011.10632.x

Brehoney, K. A. (1996). *Awakening at midlife*. New York, NY: Riverhead Books.

Cecil, V., Pendry, L. F., Salvatore, J., Kurz, T., Barak-Brandes, S., & Kama, A. (2018). Women's grey hair as an abomination of the body: Conceal and pass, or reveal and subvert.

In S. Barak-Brandes & A. Kama (Eds.), *Feminist interrogation of women's head hair: Crown of glory and shame.* London: Routledge.

Chen, Y., Kawachi, I., Berkman, L. F., Trudel-Fitzgerald, C., & Kubzansky, L. D. (2018). A prospective study of marital quality and body weight in midlife. *Health Psychology, 37*(3), 247–56. http://dx.doi.org/10.1037/hea0000589

Condon, M. C. (2004). *Women's health: An integrated approach to wellness and illness*. Upper Saddle River, NJ: Pearson.

Crowley, J. E. (2017). Gray divorce: Explaining midlife marital splits. *Journal of Women & Aging, 31*(1), 49–72. doi:10.1080/08952841.2017.1409918

Curtin, S. C., Warner, M., & Hedegaard, H. (2016, April). Suicide rates for females and males by race and ethnicity: United States, 1999 and 2014. NCHS Health E-Stat. National Center for Health Statistics.

Danson, M., & Hardill, I. (2006). Introduction: Demography, ageing and activity. *Population, Space and Place, 12*, 317–32.

Degges-White, S., & Borzumato-Gainey, C. (2011). *Friends forever: How girls and women forge lasting relationships*. Lanham, MD: Rowman & Littlefield.

Degges-White, S., & Myers, J. E. (2006). Transitions, wellness, and life satisfaction: Implications for counseling midlife women. *Journal of Mental Health Counseling, 28*(2), 133–50.

Delamater, L., & Santoro, N. (2018). Management of the perimenopause. *Clinical Obstetrics and Gynecology, 61*(3), 419–32.

Depmann, M., Broer, S. L., van der Schouw, Y. T., Tehrani, F. R., Eijkemans, M., Mol, B. W., & Broekmans, F. J. (2016). Can we predict age at natural menopause using ovarian reserve tests or mother's age at menopause? A systematic literature review. *Menopause, 23*(2), 224–32.

Devi, G., Hahn, K., Massimi, S., & Zhivotovskaya, E. (2005). Prevalence of memory loss complaints and other symptoms associated with the menopause transition: A community survey. *Gender Medicine, 2*(4), 255–64.

Erikson, E. (1968). *Identity, youth and crisis*. New York, NY: W. W. Norton.

Georgakis, M. K., Thomopoulos, T. P., Diamantaras, A., Kalogirou, E. I., Skalkidou, A., Daskalopoulou, S. S., & Petridou, E. T. (2016). Association of age at menopause and duration of reproductive period with depression after menopause: A systematic review and meta-analysis. *JAMA Psychiatry, 73*(2), 139–49. doi:10.1001/jamapsychiatry.2015.2653

Grove, R. D., & Hetzel, A. M. (1968). *Vital statistics rates in the United States, 1940–1960*. Washington, DC: U.S. Government Printing Office.

Halinski, M., Duxbury, L., & Higgins, C. (2018). Working while caring for mom, dad, and junior, too: Exploring the impact of employees' caregiving situations on demands, control, and perceived stress. *Journal of Family Issues, 39*(12), 3248–75. doi:10.1177/0192513X18777839

Harvard Women's Health Watch. (2018, May). When the arrival of menopause brings symptoms of depression. Retrieved from https://www.health.harvard.edu/womens-health/when-the-arrival-of-menopause-brings-symptoms-of-depression

Huffman, S., & Myers, J. E. (1999). Counseling women in midlife: An integrative approach to menopause. *Journal of Counseling and Development, 77*(3), 258–66.

Im, E.-O., Ko, Y., Hwang, H., Chee, W., Stuifbergen, A., Walker, L., & Brown, A. (2013). Racial/ethnic differences in midlife women's attitudes toward physical activity. *Journal of Midwifery & Women's Health, 58*(4), 440–50. http://doi.org/10.1111/j.1542-2011.2012.00259.x

Inayat, K., Danish, N., & Hassan, L. (2017). Symptoms of menopause in peri- and postmenopausal women and their attitude towards them. *Journal of Ayub Medical College Abbottabad, 29*(3), 477–80.

Isopahkala-Bouret, U. (2017). "It's a great benefit to have gray hair!": The intersection of gender, aging, and visibility in midlife professional women's narratives. *Journal of Women & Aging, 29*(3), 267–77. doi:10.1080/08952841.2016.1142773

Jacques, E. (1965). Death and the mid-life crisis. *International Journal of Psychoanalysis, 46*, 502–14.

Jannini, E. A., & Nappi, R. E. (2018). Couplepause: A new paradigm in treating sexual dysfunction during menopause and andropause. *Sexual Medicine Reviews, 6*, 384–95.
Jean-Louis, G., Williams, N. J., Sarpong, D., Pandey, A., Youngstedt, S., Zizi, F., & Ogedegbe, G. (2014). Associations between inadequate sleep and obesity in the US adult population: Analysis of the National Health Interview Survey (1977–2009). *BMC Public Health, 14*(1). doi:10.1186/1471-2458-14-290
Jones, H. J., Zak, R., & Lee, K. A. (2018). Sleep disturbances in midlife women at the cusp of the menopausal transition. *Journal of Clinical Sleep Medicine, 14*(7), 1127–33.
Jung, C. G. (1971). *Psychological types*. London: Routledge & Kegan Paul.
Levinson, D. J., & Levinson, J. (1996). *The seasons of a woman's life*. New York, NY: Ballantine Books.
Mangweth-Matzek, B., Hoek, H. W., Rupp, C. I., Lackner-Seifert, K., Frey, N., Whitworth, A. B., . . . Kinzl, J. (2014). Prevalence of eating disorders in middle-aged women. *International Journal of Eating Disorders, 47*, 320–24. doi:10.1002/eat.22232
McLaren, L., & Kuh, D. (2004). Body dissatisfaction in midlife women. *Journal of Women & Aging, 16*(1–2), 35–54. doi:10.1300/J074v16n01_04
Mulhall, S., Andel, R., & Ansley, K. J. (2017). Variation in symptoms of depression and anxiety in midlife women by menopausal status. *Maturitas, 108*, 7–12. doi:10.1016/j.maturitas.2017.11.005
Nappi, R. E., & Lachowsky, M. (2009). Menopause and sexuality: Prevalence of symptoms and impact on quality of life. *Maturitas, 63*(2), 138–41.
Neugarten, B. L., Moore, J. W., & Lowe, J. C. (1965). Age norms, age constraints, and adult socialization. *American Journal of Sociology, 70,* 229–36. doi:10.1086/223965.
Orbis Research. (2017). *Anti-aging market by demographics, by products, by services, by devices, and by region-global industry analysis, size, share, growth, trends, and forecasts (2016–2021)*. Dallas, TX: Market Data Forecast.
Paine, E. A., Umberson, D., & Reczek, C. (2018), Sex in midlife: Women's sexual experiences in lesbian and straight marriages. *Family Relationships, 81*(1), 7–23. doi:10.1111/jomf.12508
Pearson, Q. M. (2017). Sleep and aging: Challenges and recommendations for middle-aged and older adults. *Adultspan Journal, 16*, 31–46. doi:10.1002/adsp.12032
Rahman, I., Akesson, A., & Wolk, A. (2015). Relationship between age at natural menopause and risk of heart failure. *Menopause, 22*, 12–16.
Shallcross, L. (2012, August). Working with women from all walks of life. *Counseling Today*, 30–38.
Sheehy, G. (1993). *Passages: Predictable crises in adult life*. New York, NY: Dutton
Stepler, R. (2017, March 9). Led by baby boomers, divorce rates climb for American's 50+ population. *Factank: News in the Numbers*. Pew Research Center.
Thomas, A. J., Mitchell, E. S., & Woods, N. F. (2018). The challenges of midlife women: Themes from the Seattle Midlife Women's Health Study. *Women's Midlife Health, 4*, 8. doi:10.1186/s40695-018-0039-9
U.S. Census Bureau. (1996). *65+ in the United States*. P23-190 Current Population Reports: Special Studies. Washington, DC: U.S. Government Printing Office.
U.S. Census Bureau. (2010). *Census 2000 Summary File 1 and 2010 Census Summary File 1.* Washington, DC: U.S. Government Printing Office.
U.S. National Center for Health Statistics. (2018). Vital statistics of the United States, annual, and National Vital Statistics Reports (NVSR). Retrieved from https://www.cdc.gov/nchs/products/nvsr.htm
van Dijk, G. M., Kavousi, M., Troup, J., & Franco, O. H. (2015). Health issues for menopausal women: The top 11 conditions have common solutions. *Maturitas, 80*, 24–30.
Waetjen, L. E., Crawford, S. L., Chang, P. Y., Reed, B. D., Hess, R., Avis, N. E., . . . Gold, E. B. (2018). Factors associated with developing vaginal dryness symptoms in women transitioning through menopause: A longitudinal study. *Menopause, 25*(10), 1094–1104. doi:10.1097/GME.0000000000001130
Wray, S. (2007). Women making sense of midlife: Ethnic and cultural diversity. *Journal of Aging Studies, 21*, 31–42.

Ying, Z. Z., Zhangbin, L., & Minfang, T. (2015). Characteristics of menopausal symptoms in menopausal women and analysis of influencing factors. *Chinese Journal of Endocrinology, 10*(4), 320–24.

Chapter Seven

Counseling Older Adult Women

Marcela Kepic

CASE VIGNETTE: JORDAN

Jordan is a seventy-one-year-old, divorced African American female who retired six years ago from an aviation company. She is proud of her career accomplishments as well as having been clean and sober for approximately forty years. She has a forty-six-year-old daughter who is emotionally and financially unstable. Jordan has another daughter whom she gave up for adoption right after her birth. During her intake session with Chandra, her counselor, Jordan explained that when she realized she was pregnant with her second child, she needed to stop drinking. She started her recovery immediately and acknowledged that it had been a struggle. Jordan was overwhelmed with taking care of a newborn and her six-year-old daughter as a single parent, keeping her job, and participating in full recovery. Feeling lonely and exhausted, she made a decision and sought out an adoption company and gave up her second child. It took her a few years to get stable and function independently. Eventually, she found a job in the aviation industry and slowly climbed the career ladder. Later, she married a Hispanic man, but the marriage lasted only two years. After her divorce, she stayed single but was involved in a few casual romantic relationships. She is still helping her daughter financially. She is a great support to her daughter, but she recognizes that there is only so much she can do.

Jordan attended individual and group counseling when recovering but has been out of therapy for twenty years. She still attends AA meetings. Last week, she felt overwhelmed and thought her depression might be returning. She had a hard time getting out of bed, she did not go to see her friend, and she did not respond to her sister's phone call. Her sister came over and convinced Jordan to make an appointment with her primary-care physician and a psychiatrist. Jordan has been losing weight lately without trying. She also revealed that she has been experiencing mobility issues for the past few months. Jordan reported no energy throughout the day, no desire to go out, and no need or desire to interact with people.

* * *

Older adulthood typically refers to the period in life that begins around age sixty-five (Fields & Casper, 2001). This segment of the population is growing at a rapid pace, but there are many unfortunate misconceptions and stereotypes about older adults and aging (Fullen, Granello, Richardson, & Granello, 2018). Aging can be explained from biological, psychological, and sociocultural perspectives. This chapter focuses on psychological models of aging but explains some major physiological changes as well.

Older women experience many gains and losses in this period, but aging can look different for every individual. Primary aging is considered normal and intrinsic because it is genetically programmed and takes place with the passage of time despite good health and the absence of disease (Busse, 1969; Lemme, 2006). Secondary aging refers to age-related declines that are pathological and result from extrinsic factors, including disease, environmental influences, and behavior. For example, poor nutrition, smoking, and high levels of stress may contribute to disease and accelerated aging. These nutritional and psychosocial factors (e.g., stress, personality, and surrounding environment) can act as risk factors that accelerate aging or as resilience factors that decelerate aging (Aldwin & Gilmer, 2013; Lemme, 2006). Regardless of the unique ways each individual may age, there are positive and negative stereotypes about this period. These vary from older adults being loving and patient to being dependent and in ill health (Chen, Joyce, Harwood, & Xiang, 2017). The variety of perceptions reflects the many forces at work in the aging process.

Besides biological and psychosocial changes, many older adults may have also gained valuable knowledge and skills and have extensive job experience. At the same time, older adults may be dealing with physical, cognitive, and social changes that can, at times, adversely affect their daily functioning.

PHYSICAL DEVELOPMENT

Biological changes begin earlier than many anticipate. After the body reaches maturity around age thirty, subtle changes begin that become more noticeable over time. These visible changes, such as the graying and thinning of hair, change in body proportions, and changes in skin tone, are only a few exterior changes. For many women, external signs carry significant emotional weight. Women especially seem to be threatened by overt signs of aging, such as wrinkles or sagging body parts, because of the emphasis traditionally placed on women's appearance. Older women tend to have a lower body satisfaction than younger women due to the high emphasis society tends to place on youthfulness as a requisite for attractiveness (Sabik & Cole, 2017). In addition to visible changes in the skin, there are also other changes taking place throughout the body. Predictable changes may occur within the skeletal system, the muscular system, the cardiovascular and respiratory systems, the gastrointestinal and urinary tract systems, and the nervous system. Declines in all of the senses are also common.

With advancements in medicine and related fields, older adults live longer than prior generations, thus leaving implications for both prevention and interventions. Clinicians may not be able to address physical disease, but they can counsel their clients to incorporate a healthy diet, low stress, and exercise as crucial components of their lifestyle. These promote optimal aging and can help prevent the premature development of illnesses and disabilities and decelerate aging processes, thus maintaining good physical, mental, and cognitive health (Buchman et al., 2012; Devore, Kang, Breteler, & Grodstein, 2012; Hahn & Andel, 2011).

PSYCHOSOCIAL DEVELOPMENT

Late adulthood typically provides an opportunity for older adults to enjoy more leisure time and to maintain existing skills and hobbies and to develop new ones. Individuals have meaningful experiences throughout life. Older adults continue to find purpose in their lives; this is important to support as having a sense of purpose is critical to having a meaningful life (Isik & Üzbe, 2015). During this developmental stage, reflection regarding one's life path and choices often occurs. Erik Erikson (1968) described the last stage of life as reflective and evaluative. The eighth stage of Erikson's psychosocial development model is marked by the crisis of *integrity versus despair* as older adults typically are motivated to reflect on and evaluate their lives to that point. People who feel satisfied with the choices they've made along the way, or feel a sense of peace with their choices, experience a sense of integrity. If a person is unable to find that sense of self-acceptance, they may experience an overwhelming sense of disappointment or dissatisfaction that generates despair. In many cases, a matured perspective allows older adults to resolve lingering conflicts or mend estranged relationships, especially as they are more acutely aware of the finiteness of life. Janus and Smrokowska-Reichmann (2019) found that faith and family relationships were extremely important to women who were sixty or older. Women who seek counseling support might wish to focus on issues related to family, spirituality, or religion or to seek a sense of closure and peace related to relationships and past choices.

When clients seek assistance in working through these significant issues, counselors must support these efforts with an eye toward the role they play in overall client well-being. Women who feel a sense of ego integrity tend to have higher marital satisfaction, better relationships with their adult children, and are more willing to give and receive help from others (James & Zarrett, 2005). Further, experiencing this sense of generativity predicted higher likelihood of achieving ego integrity in later years. A constant theme in the lifespan development literature is the emphasis women place on relationships and connection to others (e.g., Gilligan, 1982; Jordan, 1997). This may suggest that women find generativity, integrity, and self-actualization through their relational bonds with others. Historically, caring for children, family, household, and others provided a means of primary fulfillment. The contemporary sociopolitical climate, as well as advancements in our society, have shifted this fulfillment to some extent; this affects women's self-perceptions and self-expectations. With greater appreciation, self-understanding, self-acceptance, and a continuing focus on fulfilling relationships, older women may continue to be engaged in many different roles (e.g., grandparent, caregiver, partner, relative, friend) that bring fulfillment in ways that are equivalent to, but broader than, prior generations.

OPTIMAL VERSUS SUCCESSFUL AGING

Successful aging has been a frequently used term to describe what was conceived of as the ultimate goal in older adulthood. While there is no standard definition of successful aging, it is typically assumed to include physical and mental well-being and the presence of social support (Bosnes et al., 2019). Reality and life circumstances are different for everyone, thus "successful aging" may actually present as an unobtainable goal for many. Thus, *optimal aging* has become the preferred term as it recognizes good physical functioning, cognitive abilities, and mental health, but also includes recognition of the development of illnesses and limitations. It captures the myriad of ways of aging well. Moreover, the word *optimal* avoids connotations of competition that the word *success* suggests (Aldwin & Gilmer, 2013).

There's a saying that "old age is state of mind." This is reflected in the level of attention that theories of aging pay to perspectives and behaviors. These include disengagement theory, activity theory, continuity theory, and selective optimization and compensation theory (SOC). For many older adults, engagement in leisure activities continues as they age. However, advancing age may also require additional medical care and decreasing levels of self-sufficiency. This typically occurs between the ages of seventy-five and eighty, as adults enter what has been termed the "fourth age." The transition can occur slowly or quickly (Kafková, 2016) and events related to this transition are reflected in the experiences that are described by the disengagement theory of aging.

Disengagement Theory

In understanding aging, some have used the disengagement theory of aging, which was developed in 1961 by Cumming and Henry. This theory is based on the idea that as one ages, one becomes increasingly disengaged from others and contact with friends, relatives and social organizations diminishes over time. Thus, older adults may grow increasingly lonely and physically inactive (Asiamah, 2017). Having less physical energy contributes to moving at a slower pace and, psychologically, there is also a diminished interest in the world. Social interactions and social investments often become less frequent with age. Such slowing down or disengagement is reinforced by society. However, as medical care and overall health have improved over time, there are many older adults who remain vitally invested and active in life. Thus, disengagement theory may not be as appropriate moving forward as it seemed to be in the past. A counter perspective is provided in activity theory.

Activity Theory

Activity theory asserts that older adults are able to maintain active lifestyles that keep them engaged in the world and in relationships (Lemon, Bengston, & Peterson, 1972). This theory highlights the importance of social engagement that can continue throughout the lifespan. While this theory appears to be in direct opposition to disengagement theory, the way in which a person ages is dependent upon a number of individual factors. Those who remain social engaged with others in older adulthood tend to function within environments where involvement is supported by social and economic conditions (Asiamah, 2017). This theory emphasizes that despite some slowdowns and disengagement from wider society, older adults continue to remain active and engaged in many areas of life.

Continuity Theory

Continuity theory proposes that people tend to continue with the same lifestyle, habits, and preferences that they have practiced throughout adulthood. The assumption is that people will continue to enjoy the same activities they have in the past. While changes do occur, they tend to be more gradual over time and later life is not significantly different from earlier years. Older adults continue to use the coping skills they've used throughout their lives, which can be unfortunate if they have always relied on negative coping skills

(Guyette, 2018). Through the development of stable patterns, people remain engaged in these patterns of behavior throughout their lifespan.

Continuity may also serve as an adaptive coping strategy when facing negative life events in older age. Familiar leisure activities as well as continued engagement in significant relationships have great importance in restoring meaning and direction after negative life events. Most researchers who have investigated continuity, change, and adaptation in later life have supported the importance of continuity as a main characteristic of healthy aging (Janke, Nimrod, & Kleiber, 2008). However, there are times when some activities shrink in importance or are forfeited for various reasons.

Selective Optimization and Compensation Theory

Baltes and Baltes (1990) proposed the selective optimization and compensation (SOC) theory of aging. The SOC theory stems from a goal-oriented approach to development and can be viewed as an extension of continuity theory because it not only describes the need for continuity and adaptation but also explains how this adaptation in continuity may be achieved (i.e., selection, compensation). Baltes and Baltes (1990) stressed the balance between gains and losses in the aging process. Aging is perceived as a process, not a series of stages, in SOC theory (Baltes, 1987). With limited or reduced resources, Baltes (1987) contended, older adults will select preferred goals or activities and optimize their performance by applying their limited resources to those particular goals, while compensating for deficiencies that could interfere with goal achievement (e.g., life satisfaction after spousal loss).

According to Baltes and Baltes (1990), adaptation to life changes can be accomplished through several means: (1) being selective when choosing activities based on personal abilities and meaning, (2) optimizing one's abilities by working harder and focusing resources on desired goals, and (3) compensating for loss of meaningful activities by adapting how desired goals are achieved in times of struggles and limitations.

Psychological theories of aging explain only one aspect of aging, and it is necessary to consider other aspects (i.e., biological) when it comes to helping individuals with their struggles. To best understand growth and aging, a complex, multidimensional approach is more effective at explaining and understanding the intricacy of our human development, especially in the area of counseling for enhanced well-being.

COUNSELING APPROACHES WITH OLDER WOMEN

Not every adult development theory fits all individuals, and not every counseling theory or approach is effective with all clients. Clinicians must adapt their interventions and perspectives based on a client's identity and developmental stage. Knight and Satre (1999) advised that clinicians bear in mind the contextual identities and cohort-based aspects in counseling due to the ways culture and related events shape identity. When working with older adults, the literature supports guided autobiography, reminiscence, and life review as appropriate interventions (Aldwin & Gilmer, 2013). These strategies align with the later developmental stages, when older adults typically look back and evaluate their life choices.

Reminiscence

Reminiscence focuses on the recall of memories and past events and experiences. Retelling or recalling is focused on remembering past events and experiences instead of sharing recent memories (Ingersoll-Dayton, Kropf, Campbell, & Parker, 2019). Reminiscence can also increase peer interactions through focused conversations and identifying commonalities (Burnside & Haight, 1992) but can be challenging and may require clinical support when negative memories surface with regards to how to handle them (Ingersoll-Dayton et al., 2019). Lin, Dai, and Hwang (2003) described a five-stage framework for reminiscence: antecedents, assessment, purpose setting, treatment modality, and outcome. The antecedent stage refers to a period when there is a situation that triggers an interest in reminiscence. For example, someone relocated and or is going through stress, and such sharing will probe further remembrance of similar experiences in the past. In the assessment stage, psychometric self-reports or other observational instruments are used. In the purpose setting stage, the process for the reminiscence intervention is determined. In the treatment modality stage, the clinician and client will choose which traditional reminiscence activity to use (e.g., guided autobiography, life review). Lastly, the outcome stage includes assessment of short-term and long-term goals (Lin et al., 2003). Coleman (2005) identified many different functions of reminiscence: life review, identity maintenance, disengagement, reengagement, obsession, avoidance, and rumination. While younger clients tend to reminisce to reduce boredom, to develop identity, or to problem solve, older clients tend to reminisce to maintain intimacy, to teach or inform, and to prepare for death (Webster & Gould, 2007). Reminiscence work can be done in an individual or group setting.

Life Review

Life review is one of the major reminiscence types, and it is focused on the "search for meaning through reflection on one's life's experience" (Coleman, 2005, p. 305). Further, life review encompasses not only a "recall" of what happened but evaluation of what happened. Clinicians should listen and help clients with keeping track, to review, to address their feelings, and to evaluate their sharing (Burnside & Haight, 1992). Life review has been associated with creativity, spirituality, and generativity, as well as with personal growth, problem solving, and identity exploration (Coleman, 2005). Structured life review typically takes up to eight sessions to complete, as it reflects Erikson's eight stages of psychosocial development. The goal is to reconcile or reframe memories of a given stage (Haight & Haight, 2007). Such an approach in reminiscence is distinguished from other approaches due to its length and the presence of evaluation.

Guided Autobiography

Guided autobiography is a structured approach that helps older women explore meaning found in their lives. This activity can promote the client's belief in the significance of her life and the ways she has mattered and continues to matter to others (Birren & Deutchman, 1999). There is not a focus on problem solving; instead, the focus is on remembering life experiences. Specific areas of focus can include coping and adaptation, acceptance of death, generativity, depression relief, integration, personal connection, reconciliation, meaning, role clarification, self-esteem and self-actualization, and spiritual and general well-being (Birren & Deutchman, 1999).

This intervention involves the writing down of the client's story and the counselor asking the client to write and to share her writing with others. Guided autobiography often takes place in group settings, where clients compose an essay based on an assigned topic and then share with others and discuss their writing. Common themes include career, major transitions, family, finances, health, love, death, sexuality, death, and aspiration. Questions that might be used to focus the writing include the following: What was your first job like? How old were you? How was it to get used to your work environment? What did you learn about yourself from working at the job? How was it for your family while you were working? How did that job help you with other jobs (career) in your life? Or related to family, how was it for you to start your family? How did the dynamics change between you and your partner? How was it for you to see your child grow, and how did that affect you?

Client benefits from this activity include improved self-worth and a greater sense of personal influence, realizing adaptive strategies that can still be helpful, achieving rapprochement with one's own history, letting go of negative feelings, reengaging in former activities, increased social networking and friendship, and finally gaining a greater sense of meaning in one's life and its impact on the world (Birren & Deutchman, 1999). In addition, this intervention has been shown to decrease symptoms of depression, improve coping mechanisms, enhance ego integration, increase the sense of continuity, orient clients to the future, foster greater connection with future generations, and increase death acceptance (Birren & Deutchman, 1999). However, clinicians are cautioned not to use guided autobiography as a therapy; do not probe into emotions beyond what has been spontaneously shown. Space should be allowed for emotions to emerge rather than seeking them out. Older clients are in charge of their stories, and coherence helps them with developing a greater sense of integrity in the story of their lives.

Reminiscence approaches utilize memories of life events and experiences to help clients understand life, make meaning, and find their place in the world. These activities can be incorporated into multiple therapeutic approaches. In addition to exploration of individual identity, understanding the ways older adult women engage in relationships is also important.

WOMEN IN RELATIONSHIPS

Through their relationships, women develop connections, resources, and coping mechanisms that eventually may lead to a broader social life and possibly richer connections when compared to men (Janke et al., 2008). Despite the many losses women can experience in older age, they still maintain relationships, develop a new identity, and master new skills, new roles, and new lives (Holtslander, Bally, & Steeves, 2011; Wilson & Supiano, 2011). In fact, although relationships change, relationships are extremely important for older women (Janus & Smrokowska-Reichmann, 2019). Older women typically maintain their relationships with family members, especially with their partners, children, grandchildren, friends, and neighbors, and, most importantly, their relationship with themselves.

Relationship with Self

The transition into older adulthood is not always as simple as younger adults assume. In our society, women may become an "invisible" or "forgotten" population as they exit the workforce, reduce productivity, and lose their youthful appearance. Stereotypes about older women are often surprisingly harsh. Some women tie their value to their appearance, and aging can be especially challenging for them. However, robust self-esteem is not typically based on chronological age but on subjective age and feeling good about who you have become at whatever age you are now. In fact, research suggests there is significant stability in self-esteem and self-concept with increasing age (Baker & Gringart, 2009; Baltes & Baltes, 1990; Lemme, 2006). While late midlife and older adulthood typically present adjustments, transitions, and losses, women seem able to manage these events in such a way that they feel good about themselves and their ability to handle these challenges. Older adult women tend to be more emotionally stable and balanced than earlier in life and more openly embrace who they are, what they have accomplished, and their roles in relationships to self and others. The multitude of transitions that women experience throughout their lives, in personal, social, and career contexts, and associated relationships, resources, and coping strategies likely serve to build resilience that allows them to adjust to their ever-changing bodies and environments. Possessing a sense of belongingness, social connectedness, and healthy relationships are key attributes in feeling comfortable within one's own skin and within a greater network of support.

Relationships with Friends

Friendships are opportunities to enjoy leisure time with others, but they are also vital to physical and mental well-being and longevity. Loneliness is a major risk factor for functional challenges for older adults (Singh & Misra, 2009). Older women (and men) who are involved in positive relationship tend to have a higher sense of control in life and greater independence. They are also less negatively affected by everyday challenges. Unfortunately, being involved in poor relationships or lacking relationships altogether leads to isolation and feelings of depression, which are risk factors for negative self-perceptions and lack of motivation to change (Birmingham & Holt-Lunstad, 2018; Hanson & Carpenter, 1994. Thus, a vicious cycle of loneliness is set in place. Friendships in older age are related to better overall functioning, and strained relationship in older adulthood contribute to more chronic illness (Chopik, 2017). Counselors should encourage their older adult clients to reach out to others and be open to others reaching out to them in order to support protective factors for well-being.

The number of close friends a woman has rises and falls depending on life stage, but it tends to decrease in older adulthood (Degges-White & Borzumato-Gainey, 2011). In young adulthood, women are surrounded by others, including family, friends, neighbors, colleagues, mentors, rivals, and peers. However, due to changes in health, living situation, mobility, and other factors, a woman's social landscape changes greatly over time. Even as the size of social support networks shrink, women tend to have more friends than men (Lemme, 2006), and this is most likely because women have richer, more extensive, and more complex social networks then men, which may guard women against isolation. Women tend to offer more emotional support, nurturance, and intimacy in their friendships, whereas men tend to have activity-based friendships. In older adulthood, many women take pleasure in "just talking" with friends, providing a means of staying emotionally connected and maintaining a sense of belonging. Men typically engage in instrumental rather than emotional support with their friends. Women tend to maintain their friendships much longer than men do, so it is not surprising that many older women keep in contact with best friends from childhood or adolescence. Women report that as they get older, good friendships tend to grow in importance due to the shortening of their available time (Lemme, 2006). Women appreciate meaningful relationships in which harmony and a sense of similarity are present; this can include shared values and morals and similar life experiences and perspectives. Friendships may outlast many other relationships, and because of the gender discrepancy in longevity, women value their friendships as support networks especially in widowhood.

Relationships with Partners

Couples who have been together for decades, aging together, often seem to have their routines clearly well established. They know each other intimately and are capable of responding to each other's needs accordingly. Many times, older adult couples are at a place of nearing or achieved retirement and are able to focus on leisure activities as well as the business of aging and planning for the end of life. Discussions about health needs, relocation and housing, finances, and social engagement are crucial components of such transition to older age and retirement.

In many instances, however, older adulthood does not offer protection against challenging and unsatisfying marriages or long-term relationships. Some women choose to remain with their partners even in the face of abuse, addictions, extramarital affairs, financial difficulties, and other challenges. In some cases, partners live separate lives under a shared roof. There are also couples who will wait until their adult children grow up and become independent before they choose to take formal steps of separation and divorce. Women who are experiencing this transition may seek counseling and support. For some women, a later life relationship termination can produce feelings of significant liberation as they leave their dysfunctional relationships and begin to live more peaceful, independent, or fulfilled lives.

Sexuality

Although there are multiple physiological changes in the reproductive system over the lifespan, the majority of women still experience sexual desire and engage in sexual activities of some type. In fact, sexual activity is common in older adults and research has indicated it can potentially help reduce cognitive decline (Allen, 2018). Negative stereotypes regarding older adults and their sexual activity are still too common, but this is gradually changing. Unfortunately, these attitudes may lead some to not engage in sexual activity or feel ashamed about dating or sexual involvements (Berdychevskya and Nimrod, 2017). It is not unusual for older adults to desire education and support regarding sexual health and dating relationships (O'Connor & Kelson, 2017). Clinicians should normalize sexual desire, intimacy, and sexual activities throughout the lifespan.

While age-related physical changes in the reproductive organs may create some minor challenges to sexual intimacy and sexual fulfillment, it's been found that it is the availability, or lack of availability, of a partner that has the greatest influence on an older woman's opportunity for regular sexual expression (Aldwin & Gilmer, 2013). Widows outnumber widowers four to one, and only one-third of women over sixty-five in this country are married compared to two-thirds of the men (Berdychevskya & Nimrod, 2017). For older women, body appreciation tends not to change with age, and high levels of body appreciation have been linked to high levels of sexual satisfaction (Robbins & Reissing, 2018). In addition to the relationships that women create independently over time, with friends and romantic partners or spouses, familial relationships continue to play a role in the lives of older adult women.

Relationships with Parents

With medical advancements, older adults are living longer, especially those ninety and over (Aldwin & Gilmer, 2013). Thus, it is not uncommon for older adults, sixty-five and above, to still have living parents. Typically, relationships between adult children and their older parents are influenced by culture, family values and history, gender, and cohort. In some cultures, it is common to see two or three generations still living together, whereas in more Western cultures such a phenomenon is less common. Many times, as a parent advances in age, older adult children must assume caregiving responsibilities. This can be especially challenging when the adult children are facing their own age-related health issues. These situations present an array of potentially conflicting priorities and challenges that require multiple factors and needs to be considered. It is typical for women to outnumber men in family caregiver roles, and this is most likely due to the traditional gender role of a woman as a caregiver and *kinkeeper*. Women usually maintain closer relationship with parents than men do and often are more willing to stay geographically proximal to their parents, or to relocate when their parents' health begins to fail (National Alliance for Caregiving, 2015). For more information on working with caregiving clients, please see chapter 20.

Relationship with Adult Children and Grandchildren

Empirical research on families shows that aging parents and their adult children typically remain involved with one another over the life course; however, older women tend to be in closer relationships with their adult daughters and receive more caregiving from them than they do their sons (Grigoryeva, 2017). As women age, relationships with adult children and grandchildren increase in importance. There is a need for help, advice, encouragement, and frequently, emotional and moral support continue to be sought by adult children. Fingerman (2003) described "the paradox of a distant intimacy" (p. 26). This concept reflects very frequently observed situations in which adult children move apart and establish more distinct boundaries, but their relationships with aging parents grow closer. Despite the fact that tensions have existed and will exist in ongoing relationships between aging parents and adult children, they are considered normative and many times are the result of discrepancies in developmental needs that vary by age, generation, and gender (Birditt, Miller, Fingerman, & Lefkowitz, 2009).

Mother–Adult Daughter Relationships

In our culture, there is a tendency to oversimplify and idealize the mother–adult daughter relationship. The reality, though, is that these relationships are very complicated, especially considering culturally diverse families and relationships. The mother–daughter relationship will change over time in significant ways (Degges-White & Borzumato-Gainey, 2011). They can vary from harmonious and affectionate to conflictual and bitter. Regardless of the ages or stages of mothers and daughters, there is a definite need for healthy boundaries. Understanding that an adult daughter now will do things her way and that she does not need to ask for permissions is necessary. Older women who are able to maintain strong relationships with their daughters reap the greatest benefits as they age, in terms of friendship, connection, respect, and care.

Grandparents

As adults age, one of the expected later life roles is grandparent. About 94 percent of older adults are grandparents (Jayson, 2017). Many older women will step in and help, in some ways, with their grandchildren; some research suggests the presence of a grandmother has significant positive benefits for children and adults. Some grandparents take on full-time parenting responsibilities for their grandchildren. About three million grandparents assume custodial (i.e., guardian) responsibility (U.S. Census Bureau, 2010). Grandparents raising grandchildren tend to be female and from lower SES backgrounds and this can create additional financial stress and negatively affect overall health (Peterson, 2018).

From a theoretical perspective, grandparenting offers benefits to older adults. This role allows older adults to remain engaged with younger generations and more socially involved as well. There is a sense of purpose that feeds the need to experience generativity and integrity (Erikson, 1968). However, when grandparents are unprepared to take on the custodial raising of their grandchildren, this role may be marked by stress, limited time for themselves, and lack of resources to support grandchildren (Dunn & Wamsley,

2018), especially if the role must be assumed early and unexpectedly. A newly retired older adult may feel that the new role of grandmother limits or delays her retirement plans for leisure and hobby activities. While joy may be experienced at the arrival of the new life, it may be tempered by fears of loss of freedom. Some women may feel unsure in determining how to navigate their new roles in their child's new family. For example, a grandmother may be eager to be involved in caring for a child, but may feel that her help is not wanted by the new parents. This type of internal conflict may be resolved through open and honest communication of expectations from members of both generations.

Sibling Relationships

Because of the multiple ways families may be created, blended, and reconstituted over the lifespan today, it is imperative to avoid generalizations about family constellations. Especially in the counseling context, clinicians need to account for individual and group differences in their own experiences and knowledge associated with family and sibling dynamics. Clients may possess full siblings, half siblings, stepsiblings, adoptive siblings, and fictive siblings. As individuals age, sibling relationships grow in importance (Cicirelli, 1991; Connidis & Campbell, 2011). While the relationships may wane and wax over the lifespan, sisters often offer significant support, instrumental and emotional, in older adulthood (Connidis & Campbell, 2011). Counselors should consider the vast variety of sibling relationships and help older adult clients explore ways to leverage these support systems.

BEST PRACTICES

Older women present a unique population with a changing identity as our cultural expectations of women and older adults has shifted. Due to the increasing number of aging adults and the growing diversity of the country, being prepared to work with a diverse population of older adults is advised for all clinicians. In order to be effective in helping older women, the following are recommended guidelines for sound practice.

1. Be familiar with psychosocial developmental stages and physical and cognitive changes in older adulthood, their characteristics, and associated gains and losses.
2. Bear in mind the differences between primary and secondary aging and what contributes to or accelerates secondary aging.
3. Be familiar with preventative measures and health promotion in later ages across all areas of mental and physical well-being.

4. Have an understanding of the functional capacity of older women, and psychoeducate those that are unsure of what they "should" and "should not" be able to do.
5. Do not be limited solely by theory; consider diversity and variability in the aging process, especially unique influences of sociocultural factors on physical and psychological health in older age.
6. Be aware of your own attitudes and beliefs about aging and the older population and seek consultation and further education on emerging issues or areas in which you feel limited by your own biases or experiences.
7. Be familiar with counseling approaches that have proven to be appropriate with older adults, such as reminiscence interventions and relational-cultural theory.
8. Have knowledge about appropriate assessments for older adults and maintain the skills necessary for administering, scoring, interpreting, and sharing results of such assessments, recognizing the cognitive abilities of your clients.
9. Be familiar with the latest trends and research pertaining to aging and gender-related issues in aging.
10. Incorporate interventions and practice skills that are culturally sensitive and modifiable to fit the needs of older women.
11. Have knowledge of ethical and legal issues pertaining to practice with older women as well as public policy issues and advocacy opportunities.
12. Have age and issue appropriate resources and referrals ready. Be an advocate and ready to be a member of an interdisciplinary team.
13. Acknowledge age differences, if appropriate. Through active listening, paraphrasing, validating, and maintaining a nonjudgmental attitude, focus on building, promoting, and maintaining a safe space and a strong therapeutic alliance.
14. Do not practice outside of your scope of competence. Gain training and necessary supervision to competently work with older women.

CULTURAL CONSIDERATIONS

The aging population is growing increasingly diverse as the population in the United States grows increasingly diverse. Clinicians need to be aware of many disadvantages and challenges that diverse women face in order to provide support and necessary resources. Regardless of cultural identity, each client's experiences and support system may be different from what the counselor would "expect." Ask questions to better understand your client's experiences, support network, roles, and expectations.

One population that warrants special concern are women who reside in rural settings. While the majority of older adults prefer to remain in their homes as long as possible, the geographical placement of rural women presents greater challenges. Many times they are isolated and lack access to health care, transportation, and nutritional services. In rural areas, there are minimal or no options for appropriate housing, civic engagement, or social services. In such circumstances, technology-assisted counseling is possible. Clinicians need to be aware of such options and actively be involved in advocacy for specific needs of rural populations.

ETHICAL CONSIDERATIONS

Informed consent and confidentiality may present an important concern when counseling older women, especially those well advanced in age. Clinicians must ensure a client's capacity to understand consent forms and make informed decisions about their treatment. Race, ethnicity, and cohort-specific beliefs about counseling and mental health might influence their views about services. Other older clients might have a guardian who has power of attorney and will be involved in making decisions on behalf of the client. Clinicians may want to include their client and their guardians in consent form acknowledgment and signing and have them collaborate in treatment as well. Issues pertaining to confidentiality, such as self-harm, neglect, and elder abuse, are high on the list in counseling older women. Clinicians need to pay attention to any signs or suspicious observations and thoroughly assess for suicide risk, negligence, and abuse.

End-of-life issues may show up when working with older women who suffer from terminal or chronic illness. Older women and their family members might have great difficulties approaching these difficult conversations and clients may turn to counselors for support as they consider their choices. Clinician have the option of maintaining confidentiality if older adults are considering hastening their own deaths, depending on applicable state laws. Clinicians are always advised to consult with their supervisors and relevant legal parties.

Technology-assisted counseling and distance counseling might be excellent options for those who are in rural areas and have limited access to mental health services. Clinicians must pay attention to state regulations when engaging in technology-assisted counseling and ensure that the privacy and confidentially of their older clients are ensured.

ADVOCACY OPPORTUNITIES

Clinicians can empower older adults and advocate on their behalf in areas such as career issues, grandparenting issues, retirement, ageism, and health access. Counselors and other professionals can take action by reaching out to their legislators to support bills and laws that would benefit older adults.

CASE VIGNETTE WRAP-UP: JORDAN

Jordan sought out a counselor with a background in relational-cultural theory and training for work with older adults. During the intake with Chandra, her new counselor, Jordan answered questions about her history and was pleased that Chandra validated her feelings. Chandra is aware of physical, social, and cognitive changes in older adults; therefore, she explored Jordan's physical and cognitive issues. Jordan reported that her vision has been deteriorating but that she has not had it checked for almost a year. She described her difficulties with mobility, stiffness, and joint pain. Chandra encouraged Jordan to schedule a routine checkup with her doctor. Jordan reported some random forgetfulness, and Chandra decided to assess her cognitive functioning by giving Jordan a mini–mental status exam. Next, they moved on to gathering additional history and family history. Jordan took a deep breath before stating, "I messed up my daughter's life." Chandra responded, "Sounds like you feel responsible for your daughter's situation." After a brief pause, the counselor continued: "Would you be willing to tell me a bit more about your responsibility for your daughter's 'messed up' life?" Jordan did not look up from the floor as she quietly revealed that she was drinking and using drugs for the first six years of her daughter's life. She stated she was not emotionally or physically present as much as she should have been and that she did not care for her daughter as a mother should. Her daughter stayed at Jordan's mother's house much of those first six years. Later, when Jordan got her life together, she tried to improve her relationship with her daughter, but it was rocky. Her daughter didn't listen and also caused trouble at school. Jordan helped make sure her daughter graduated high school, but her daughter didn't pursue further education. She was already drinking and using drugs "just like me," Jordan admitted. Her daughter, now forty-six, has no job, struggles with health issues, and continues to use drugs. Jordan feels like she did everything for her daughter and can't help her anymore. Jordan shared that she still feels guilty for her daughter's early years. Chandra asked, "How is it for you to talk about such responsibility and guilt?" Jordan kept her eyes on the floor as she quietly replied, "It is very difficult. I don't share this with anyone."

Interventions: Strengths-Based Approach

After some difficult exploration and sharing, Chandra stayed with Jordan for just a bit longer to process her feelings. She used validation and silence as well. Chandra then proceeded with exploring Jordan's strengths, hobbies, and talents. She asked her about her successes in life and asked Jordan to share a detailed story from her first career success. Here, focused on her strengths, the counselor introduced reminiscence as a part of her counseling approach. After hearing the details of Jordan's story, Chandra proposed the following for the remainder of the session: "We can briefly focus on exploring what you would like to accomplish in sessions with me so we can have a plan ahead. We also will finish the risk assessment, and then we can focus on planning your doctor's visit. How does that sound?" Although Jordan expressed some hesitation, she and Chandra cocreated the following goals:

1. *To improve overall satisfaction with life*
    a. *Stabilize her mood by decreasing her depressive symptoms*
    b. *Stabilize her physical complaints by following up with medical doctors*
2. *To improve self-concept*
    a. *Increase her self-esteem*
    b. *Alleviate feelings of guilt*
3. *To improve her sense of generativity and integrity*
    a. *Enlarge social life*
    b. *Expand on daily activities*

Brief Conceptualization

Jordan is a seventy-one-year-old African American woman and presents with symptoms of depression. Based on the brief history that was gathered, Jordan seems to be an accomplished retired woman who feels responsible for her adult daughter's poor choices. As a result, Jordan feels significant guilt. She attributes her daughter's addictive and unstable personality to her own earlier addiction and absence as a parent. Further, as an older and retired woman, she might feel that she is stagnating as she is no longer contributing to society. She does not have a large social support network and is not very physically active due to physical and possibly medical challenges. Jordan seems to perceive herself as incompetent and feels her life is a failure, which corresponds with her despair. More importantly, she had a successful career and retired at age sixty-five. She is still helping her daughter and had some success in relationships. Such strengths and positive attributes are necessary in her stabilization.

Final Wrap-Up

Due to feelings of guilt, regret, and possibly shame, Jordan might be at risk for self-harm. It is necessary to complete a risk assessment and suicide assessment prior to ending her session. The counselor may assist her with setting up her doctors' appointments and provide her with resources and referrals if needed. Lastly, after completing a mini–mental status exam, the counselor will share the results and take appropriate action. It is imperative to stay strengths-based and incorporate a reminiscence approach with Jordan as this will help her see the many accomplishments in her life, assist her with redefining purpose and meaning, and help her make sense out her life experiences.

QUESTIONS FOR REFLECTION

1. What thoughts come to mind first when you think about working with a woman in her sixties? Seventies? Eighties?
2. How might you explore meaning in life and purpose with a woman who is in the midst of a divorce from her partner of fifty years?
3. What are some ways you might advocate for older adults in your community?
4. What are your feelings about end-of-life issues, including clients who might choose to refuse medical care?

REFERENCES

Aldwin, C. M., & Gilmer, D. F. (2013). *Health, illness, and optimal aging: Biological and psychological perspectives.* New York: NY, Springer.

Allen, M. S. (2018). Sexual Activity and Cognitive Decline in Older Adults. *Archives of Sexual Behavior, 47*(6), 1711–19.

Asiamah, N. (2017). Social engagement and physical activity: Commentary on why the activity and disengagement theories of ageing may both be valid. *Cogent Medicine, 4*(1).

Baker, L., & Gringart, E. (2009). Body image and self-esteem in older adulthood. *Ageing and Society, 29*(6), 977–95. doi: 10.1017/S0144686X09008721

Baltes, P. B. (1987). On the incomplete architecture of human ontogeny: Selection, optimization and compensation as foundation of developmental theory, *American Psychologist, 52*(4), 366–80.

Baltes, P. B., & Baltes, M. M. (Eds.) (1990). *Successful aging: Perspectives from the behavioral sciences.* New York: Cambridge University Press.

Barlow, M. A., Wrosch, C., Gouin, J.-P., & Kunzmann, U. (2019). Is anger, but not sadness, associated with chronic inflammation and illness in older adulthood? *Psychology and Aging, 34*(3), 330–40.

Berdychevsky, L., & Nimrod, G. (2017). Sex as leisure in later life: A netnographic approach. *Leisure Sciences, 39*(3), 224–43.

Birditt, K. S., Miller, L. M., Fingerman, K. L., & Lefkowitz, E. S. (2009). Tension in the parent and adult child relationship: Links to solidarity and ambivalence. *Psychology and Aging, 24*(2), 287–95.

Birmingham, W., & Holt-Lunstad, J. (2018). Social aggravation: Understanding the complex role of social relationships on stress and health-relevant physiology. *International Journal of Psychophysiology, 131*, 13–23.

Birren, J. E., & Deutchman, D. E. (1999). *Guiding autobiography groups for older adults: Exploring the fabric of life*. Baltimore, MD: Johns Hopkins University Press.

Bosnes, I., Nordahl, H. M., Stordal, E., Bosnes, O., Myklebust, T. Å., & Almkvist, O. (2019). Lifestyle predictors of successful aging: A 20-year prospective HUNT study. *PLoS ONE, 14*(7), 1–12.

Buchman, A. S., Boyle, P. A., Yu, L., Shah, R. C., Wilson, R. S., & Bennet, D. A. (2012). Total daily physical activity and the risk of AED and cognitive decline in older adults. *Neurology, 78*(17), 1323–29.

Burnside, I., & Haight, B. K. (1992). Reminiscence and life review: Analyzing each concept. *Journal of Advanced Nursing, 17*, 855–62.

Busse, E. W. (1969). Theories of aging. In E. W. Busse & E. Pfeiffer (Eds.), *Behavior and adaptation in later life* (pp. 11–31). Boston, MA: Little, Brown.

Carstensen, L. L. (1992). Social and emotional patterns in adulthood: Support for socioemotional selectivity theory. *Psychology and Aging, 7*(3), 331–38.

Chen, C.-C., Seo, D.-C., & Lin, H.-C. (2018). Longitudinal state-level effects on change in body mass index among middle-aged and older adults in the USA. *Health Education Journal, 77*(1), 59–72.

Chen, C.-Y., Joyce, N., Harwood, J., & Xiang, J. (2017). Stereotype reduction through humor and accommodation during imagined communication with older adults. *Communication Monographs, 84*(1), 94–109.

Chopik, W. J. (2017). Associations among relational values, support, health, and well-being across the adult lifespan. *Personal Relationships, 24*(2), 408–22. https://doi.org/10.1111/pere.12187

Cicirelli, V. G. (1991). Sibling relationships in adulthood. *Marriage and Family Review, 16*(3–4), 291–310.

Coleman, P. (1995). "Reminiscence within the study of ageing: The social significance of story." In J. Bornat (Ed.), *Reminiscence Reviewed: Perspectives, Evaluations, Achievements*. Buckingham: Open University Press.

Coleman, P. G. (2005). Uses of reminiscence: Functions and benefits. *Aging & Mental Health*, 9: 291–94.

Connidis, I. A., & Campbell, L. D. (2011). Closeness, confiding, and contact among siblings in middle and late adulthood. In A. Walker, M. Manoogian-O'Dell, L. McGraw, & D. L. White (Eds.), *Families in later life* (pp. 149–55). Thousand Oaks, CA: Pine Forge Press.

Degges-White, S., & Borzumato-Gainey, C. (2011). *Friends forever: How girls and women forge lasting relationships*. Lanham, MD: Rowman & Littlefield.

Degges-White, S., & Gainey, C. (2014). *Mothers and daughters: Living, loving, and learning over a lifetime*. New York: Rowman & Littlefield.

Devore, E. E., Kang, J. H., Breteler, M. M., & Grodstein, F. (2012). Dietary intakes of berries and flavonoids in relation to cognitive decline. *Annals of Neurology, 72*(1), 135–43.

Dunn, B., & Wamsley, B. (2018). Grandfamilies: Characteristics and needs of grandparents raising grandchildren. *Journal of Extension, 56*(5).

Erikson, E. (1968). *Identity, youth and crisis*. New York, NY: W. W. Norton.

Fields, J., & Casper, L. M. (2001, June). America's families and living arrangements. U.S. Census Bureau. Retrieved from https://www.census.gov/content/dam/Census/library/publications/2001/demo/p20-537/p20-537.pdf

Fingerman, K. L. (2003). *Mothers and their adult daughters: Mixed emotions, enduring bonds*. Amherst, NY: Prometheus Books.

Fullen, M. C., Granello, D. H., Richardson, V. E., & Granello, P. F. (2018). Using wellness and resilience to predict age perception in older adulthood. *Journal of Counseling and Development, 96*(4), 424–35.

Gates, G. J. (2011, April). How many people are lesbians, gay, bisexual, and transgender? Williams Institute. Retrieved from https://williamsinstitute.law.ucla.edu/wp-content/uploads/Gates-How-Many-People-LGBT-Apr-2011.pdf

Gilligan, C. (1982). *In a different voice: Psychological theory and women's development.* Cambridge, MA: Harvard University Press.

Grigoryeva, A. (2017). Own gender, sibling's gender, parent's gender: The division of elderly parent care among adult children. *American Sociological Review, 82*(1), 116–46. https://doi.org/10.1177/0003122416686521

Guyette, F. (2018). Successful aging: Social theory, scripture, church teaching. Journal of Religion, *Spirituality and Aging, 30*(3), 199–211.

Hahn, E. A., & Andel, R. (2011). Nonpharmacological therapies for behavioral and cognitive symptoms of mild cognitive impairment. *Journal of Aging and Health, 23*(8), 1223–45. doi: 10.1177/0898264311422745

Haight, B. K., & Haight, B. S. (2007). *The handbook of structured life review*. Health Professions Press.

Hanson, R. O., & Carpenter, B. N. (1994). *Relationships in old age: Coping with challenge transition.* New York: Guilford.

Holtslander, L., Bally, J. M. G., & Steeves, M. L. (2011). Walking a fine line: An exploration of the experience of finding balance for older persons bereaved after caregiving for a spouse with advanced cancer. *European Journal of Oncology Nursing, 15*(3), 254–59.

Ingersoll-Dayton, B., Kropf, N., Campbell, R., & Parker, M. (2019). A systematic review of dyadic approaches to reminiscence and life review among older adults. *Aging and Mental Health, 23*(9), 1074–85.

Isik, S., & Üzbe, N. (2015). Personality traits and positive/negative affects: An analysis of meaning in life among adults. *Educational Sciences: Theory and Practice, 15(*3), 587–95.

James, J. B., & Zarrett, N. (2005). Ego integrity in the lives of older women: A follow-up of mothers from the Sears, Maccoby, and Levin (1951) *Patterns of child rearing. Journal of Adult Development, 12*(4), 155–67.

Janke, M., Nimrod, G., & Kleiber, D. A. (2008). Leisure patterns and health among recently widowed adults. *Activities, Adaptation and Aging, 32*(1), 19–39.

Janus, E., & Smrokowska-Reichmann, A. (2019). Level of happiness and happiness-determining factors perceived by women aged over 60 years. *Journal of Women and Aging, 31*(5), 403–18.

Jayson, S. More grandparents than ever. *New York Times*, March 20, 2017.

Jordan, J. (1997). *Women's growth in diversity*. New York, NY: Guilford Press.

Kafková, M. P. (2016). The "real" old age and the transition between the third and fourth age. *Sociologia, 48*(6), 622–40.

Knight, B. G., & Satre, D. D. (1999). Cognitive behavioral psychotherapy with older adults. *Clinical Psychology: Science and Practice, 6*(2), 188–203.

Lemme, B. H. (2006). *Development in adulthood* (4th ed.). Boston, MA: Pearson.

Lemon, B. W., Bengston, V. L., & Peterson, J. A. (1972). An exploration of the activity theory of aging: Activity types and life satisfaction among in-movers to a retirement community. *Journal of Gerontology, 27*, 511–523.

Lin, Y.-C., Dai, Y.-T., & Hwang, S.-L. (2003). The effect of reminiscence on the elderly population: A systematic review. *Public Health Nursing, 20*(4), 297–306.

National Alliance for Caregiving. (2015). *Caregiving in the U.S. 2015 report.* Retrieved from https://www.caregiving.org/wp-content/uploads/2015/05/2015_CaregivingintheUS_Final-Report-June-4_WEB.pdf

O'Connor, D., & Kelson, E. (2017). Boomer matters: Responding to emotional health needs in an aging society. *Journal of Gerontological Social Work, 61*, 61–77.

Peterson, T. L. (2018). Future care planning by older grandparents raising adolescent grandchildren. *Families in Society, 99*(1), 67–77.

Pinquart, M., & Sorensen, S. (2001). Gender difference in self-concept and psychological well being in old age: Meta-analysis. *Journal of Gerontology, 56*(4), 195–213. https://doi.org/10.1093/geronb/56.4.P195

Robbins, A.-R., & Reissing, E. D. (2018). Appearance dissatisfaction, body appreciation, and sexual health in women across adulthood. *Archives of Sexual Behavior, 47*(3), 703–14.

Rodrigue, K. M., & Kennedy, K. M. (2011). The cognitive consequences of structural changes to the aging brain. In K. W. Schaie & S. L. Willis (Eds.), *Handbook of the psychology of aging* (7th ed., pp. 73–91). London: Academic Press.

Sabik, N., & Cole, E. (2017). Growing older and staying positive: Associations between diverse aging women's perceptions of age and body satisfaction. *Journal of Adult Development, 24*(3), 177–88.

Sha, S. H., Talaska, A. D., & Schacht, J. (2009). Age related changes in the auditory system. In J. B. Halter, J. G. Ouslander, M. Tinetti, S. Studenski, K. P. High, & S. Asthana (Eds.), *Hazzard's geriatric medicine and gerontology* (6th ed., pp. 525–34). New York, NY: McGraw-Hill.

Singh, A., & Misra, N. (2009). Loneliness, depression and sociability in old age. *Industrial Psychiatry Journal, 18*(1), 51–55. doi: 10.4103/0972-6748.57861

Umberson, D. (1992). Relationships between adult children and their parents: Psychological consequences for both generations. *Journal of Marriage and Family, 54*(3), 664–73.

U.S. Census Bureau. (2010). People and households. Retrieved from http://www.census.gov/population/www/socdemo/grandparents.html

Webster, J. D., & Gould, O. (2007). Reminiscence and vivid personal memories across adulthood. *International Journal of Aging and Human Development, 64*(2), 149–70.

Wilson, S. C., & Supiano, K. P. (2011). Experiences of veterans' widows following conjugal bereavement: A qualitative analysis. *Journal of Women & Aging, 23*(1), 77–93.

Part III

Career Counseling

Chapter Eight

Career Counseling over the Career Span

Wendy Killam

CASE VIGNETTE: MARIA

Maria is a first-generation college student from a Hispanic family who received little guidance from her family regarding the world of work. She applied herself in college while also working a part-time waitressing job. Maria's family had been disappointed when she chose school over marriage after high school. Her family's expectations did not match Maria's aspirations. During her time at Global University, Maria was involved in the accounting club and completed an internship at a Fortune 500 company. Despite financial challenges and limited family support, Maria graduated with a degree in business in five years. Upon graduation, she began an accounting position at a major corporation. After a year on the job, she realized that to further her career she would need to take and pass the CPA exam. John, her supervisor, encouraged her to prepare and complete the exam. She was nervous and lacked confidence, but John's support and guidance were instrumental in her decision to strive to achieve her professional goals. Maria passed the exam on her first attempt, and her supervisor rewarded her success with a promotion, which entailed a commitment to overtime hours. Her circumstances allowed her to accept, and she would routinely work sixty or more hours each week. Maria received a pay increase for her efforts and felt a great deal of satisfaction in her career. As her supervisor continued to mentor her, he began to encourage her to consider furthering her education by earning a graduate degree. She is seeking counseling to help her consider the pros and cons of entering graduate school. Her employer offers educational benefits that would help defray the costs of her education. While Maria feels that it is the right time to start a part-time MBA program, she is concerned about taking out additional student loans and worries that if she were to marry and start a family, it would interfere with her earning her MBA.

* * *

The expense of college is a major factor for many, and it is a significant reason for selecting a trade instead. Many students rely on student loans, which can be crippling to graduates who must begin their careers in poorly compensated entry-level careers. This has resulted in an increasing interest in jobs that do not require four-year degrees. Community colleges are becoming a popular choice due to their low cost and diverse training programs. A growing number of students take dual-credit courses in high school (Grundmann, 2013), thus reducing the cost of attending college and allowing an earlier entry into the workforce. However, even after accruing college credit in high school, obtaining a college degree often takes time. In fact, less than 40 percent of people who start college right out of high school graduate in four years.

Professional development opportunities and internships can be instrumental in preparing college students for full-time jobs (Blau & Snell, 2013). In some fields, internships are required; in others, students must actively seek out this experience. For students who lack connections, this can be challenging. Networking and making connections early on, even while still in college, can pay benefits over the entire course of one's career. In some states, high schools have programs that provide students opportunities to explore various career options, collaborate with business leaders, and gain hands-on experience. These connections can yield college scholarships and opportunities for part-time employment (Hackmann, Malin, & Gilley, 2018). Whether a student chooses to pursue a college degree, full- or part-time, or enter the workforce immediately after high school graduation, she may need support from individuals beyond her family to help her get a strong start on her career. Career counseling can be beneficial in helping a person embrace her strengths and understand areas for continued growth. For counselors, it is important to be sensitive to the needs of clients and to understand the factors that influence each unique woman's career choices.

EARLY CAREER DEVELOPMENT

Research continues to indicate that some women may choose careers that require less effort than men because they are planning ahead for future families (Gronlund, 2017). Many women seek jobs that allow for flexibility and balance. This is due, in part, to the primary responsibility that women continue to carry for childcare and housework in families today, although the gender divide is shrinking (Bianchi, Sayer, Milkie, & Robinson, 2012). Unfortunately, women continue to face unequal pay and discrimination in the workplace on a regular basis (Hegewisch & Hartmann, 2019). Minority women, unfortunately, face double marginalization and additional challenges with stereotypes that are often roadblocks to career opportunities and advancement (Dickens & Chavez, 2018).

For many individuals, career is a significant aspect of overall identity. In early adulthood, women are often still trying to solidify their identities as they work to define their primary priorities in life. This period of emerging adulthood can be exciting and full of promises but also overwhelming and difficult as one begins to navigate uncharted territory (Murphy et al., 2010). Women especially benefit from social and professional connections with others as these provide emotional and instrumental support as they deal with life and career-related transitions (Yang, Chawla, & Uzzi, 2019). Being able to connect with others at work in a positive fashion is important for job success, but for women it can sometimes be challenging due to traditional views and values within organizations (Dickens & Chavez, 2018). One way individuals can learn unwritten organizational rules and make connections is through mentorship.

Importance of Mentorship in Early Career Development

Mentoring has been shown to increase job success and provide avenues for connections and development for employees. Research shows that mentorship is especially valued and productive when a mentor takes time to understand all facets of a mentee's identity, including career aspirations and cultural identity (Cross et al., 2019). While some organizations provide a very formal process for mentorship, that is not the case everywhere. In fact, many organizations may not have formal mentorship programs. Taking advantage of formal programs is important, but reaching out to other relevant formal or informal mentors can help women gain support and assistance as they move forward in their careers (Turner-Moffatt, 2019). Ideally, mentors do not serve as evaluators or supervisors of their mentees as this complicates the mentor–mentee relationship. Within many organizations, informal mentoring occurs, and counselors may need to encourage clients to seek out appropriate mentors, even if it is an intimidating process (Evans-Galea & Galea, 2014). In order to garner as many benefits as possible, women should be encouraged to remain open to various types of mentorship, including peer and group situations (Turner-Moffatt, 2019). Research indicates that informal mentoring tends to be more positive and growth-oriented, while formal mentoring can result in negative interactions. This may be attributed to the voluntary nature of informal mentoring, without the presence of employer demands and expectations, which can negatively influence a mentor's engagement in the process (Liang & Gong, 2013). Effective mentors provide feedback that is not always easy to hear as well as support and encouragement (Evans-Galea & Galea, 2014). Ruff (2013) found that female mentors tend to be more connected and have a higher level of intimacy with their mentees. This fits with developmental models that indicate relational connections are highly valued by women and a critical component of productive mentorship. To maximize the benefits of mentoring, mentees must possess, or develop, the ability to critically analyze themselves and their performance (Liang & Gong, 2013). The overall goal of mentorship is to help a person grow and learn both professionally and personally. Thus, mentors can provide support and guidance beyond just policies and procedures in the workplace to include life-balance issues as well.

Revisiting the Case of Maria: Family Life

Maria has continued to work for the same company for the following three years. John, her former supervisor, has continued to provide Maria with guidance even after leaving the company. At a business conference, Maria met Suzi, who has been working at another company a few years longer than Maria has been employed. Suzi has become a mentor and friend. During this time, Maria also meets Jack, a retail sales manager with whom she falls in love and whom she eventually marries. Maria's parents and extended family are delighted that she has married a good man, but they begin to badger her and ask when she is going to quit work and start a family. They assume that Maria will stay home and raise children. Her parents often ask her why she continues to work and, between themselves, wonder if Jack does not earn enough money to support both of them. Maria enjoys her job, continues to work long hours, and advances to an assistant director position. She then decides to pursue her MBA online.

When Maria is halfway through her MBA coursework, she becomes pregnant. Her pregnancy is not an easy one, and she is put on bed rest in her eighth month. This causes her anxiety regarding her job. She feels that she will be less valued by her team due to her absence from the job. She struggles to determine how she will balance caring for her newborn and maintaining her career. In fact, her new boss, Ross, has made negative comments in the past regarding children and how they tie parents down and affect potential career opportunities. Recalling these comments, Maria grows more upset, and she calls her friend Suzi for guidance. Suzi shares that some companies offer free daycare and seldom require employees to work beyond their scheduled shifts. She suggests that Maria might consider finding a new employer that provides more visible support for working mothers. She also suggests that Maria be realistic in her expectations of herself as she contemplates balancing childcare, employment, and graduate education aspirations. Suzi reminds Maria that she spent ten years off her career path to stay at home while her children were younger; Suzi also notes that she felt like her return to work was actually starting over at the bottom. She describes how males with less education and experience were promoted over her when she came back due to the gap in her paid employment history. Suzi explains that on one hand she was glad she had her time to raise her twins, but she regrets taking off so much time that it negatively affected her career. Suzi affirms that it is a personal decision for everyone, and she would certainly support her friend no matter what Maria chose to do. Maria shares that her husband, Jake, supports a quick return to work because of financial and investment opportunities they enjoy due to their dual-income status. Jake grew up in a dual-income home and feels it is the way a marriage should be so that he and Maria can afford the things they enjoyed doing without going into debt.

PRIORITIES IN LIFE

Current research indicates that women fit into one of three groups in terms of prioritizing paid employment: work centered, family centered, or adaptive, which means they adjust throughout their careers (Gronlund, 2017). Counselors should help women determine their own priorities in view of any external influences that affect these, including religious beliefs, cultural norms, and perception of gender roles, which can all affect the way a woman views her priorities. Reassuring women that their priorities may shift over time can help women determine what is best for where they are in life without feeling like they are shutting down future opportunities.

For women who prioritize family, guide them to seek employment with companies that have family-supportive work environments. In such settings, administrators are visibly supportive of family obligations and responsibilities of workers and seldom place demands on employees that would negatively affect family life. This is noticeably different from companies that have expectations of excessive overtime hours, working on holidays, and frequent contact and availability during off hours, such as 24/7 emails and texts that are expected to be answered quickly. Additionally, family-supportive employers do not penalize their employees due to their involvement with their families (Wayne & Casper, 2016). Each woman must determine her own priorities and use these as a guide to job hunting; the counselor can remind a client that her own needs should come before those of anyone else. Career paths do not always follow straightforward, linear trajectories, and clients should be reassured that their own path may vary greatly as they move through subsequent life stages.

Work–Life Balance

Work–life balance is often a challenge for women, regardless of their parenting status. It can be difficult for women who feel torn trying to meet financial responsibilities, maintain a career, and meet personal responsibilities (Schilling, 2015). Women may feel like they have to choose between caretaking for others and career advancement for themselves. Trying to find a balance can be frustrating and result in significant levels of fatigue, symptoms of depression, and stress (Maqsood, Sohail, Qureshi, & Kausar, 2017). In some environments, taking time off to care for parents or children can have a negative impact on how employees are perceived by others in the workforce. In addition, trying to balance everything may lead some women to feel as if they have two full-time jobs since most women who work full-time indicate that they are also primarily responsible for the home and children (Roy, 2016). This sense of being overwhelmed can contribute to compromised health and decreased job satisfaction.

When work–family conflicts are low, there is often a higher level of job satisfaction. Thus, what happens at home affects how well one is able to perform at work. Women often feel overwhelmed and have reported higher stress levels than males in terms managing family responsibilities that conflict with work schedules (Higgins, Duxbury, & Lyons, 2010). Balancing work against the needs of children can be especially difficult for women. Recent studies have indicated that nearly 60 percent of first-time mothers return to work before or at twelve weeks of maternity leave. Yet women may need a year to two to recover both emotionally and physically from having a child (Shepherd-Banigan, Bell, Basu, Booth-LaForce, & Harris, 2016). The United States continues to lag behind other countries in terms of paid leave (Adema, Clarke, & Frey, 2016). For some women, just the thought of going back to work can be extremely stressful, and they will sacrifice financial benefits to remain home with their children. In some cases, cultural and religious beliefs play a role (Rogers & Franzen, 2014). Regardless of the reasons for their choice, women are definitely less likely than men to be employed once they become a parent (Adema et al., 2016). Unfortunately, if a woman decides to return to the workforce when her children are older, she may be unpleasantly surprised by the reception she receives.

Women who return to work after a long break due to family obligations may be viewed as less valuable employees due to the extended gap in their work experience (Schilling, 2015). Some women may be paid less when they take time off from work to care for family, choose jobs that are more flexible, and pass up promotions due to time constraints (Kahn, García-Manglano, & Bianchi, 2014). In some cases, women feel like they are starting over at the beginning as their household management experience is not viewed as significant in the workforce. Unfortunately, the larger the gap between paid employment positions, the more of an impact it might have on future employment earnings and retirement funding. This creates the need for women to carefully consider the impact of decisions to take extended time off from work to stay home with children or care for older relatives.

Challenges and Opportunities

Career satisfaction isn't found only in the paycheck. According to Wayne and Casper (2016), younger employees place a high priority on jobs that provide flexibility and allow for work–life balance over opportunities for advancement and higher salaries. Additionally, companies that offer paid leave for parents of any gender along with subsidized childcare increase the likelihood that parents will remain in the workforce and contribute to the industries in which they work (Adema et al., 2016). Unfortunately, many U.S. companies are behind the curve and offer only minimal parental benefits and little flexibility. This contributes to the need for women to set boundaries in an online world that is always awake to avoid burnout. Whiston, Feldwisch, Evans, Blackman, and Gilman (2015) emphasize the need to set boundaries between "working hours" and "off-the-clock hours." Learning to refrain from taking work home can be a challenge for many as they try to manage work–life boundaries, and when a person works from home, that boundary becomes even fuzzier. However, Adema and colleagues (2016) found that women with young children who work from home have a lower level of stress, gain a higher level of job satisfaction, and feel less depressed than those who did not do so. Unfortunately, not every employer or every job lends itself to working from home; this might be a consideration for women who are seeking a better work–life balance as they return to work from parental leave. Sadly, in some organizations, getting ahead is not based solely on ability but also on availability and inferred commitment, which may be viewed as less substantial for women due to underlying biases in the workplace (Turner-Moffatt, 2019). As noted, women continue to earn less than men (Clark & Bower, 2016), and counselors can engage in and support advocacy efforts related to social policies that promote the value of all employees and help to minimize work–family conflicts. Employees and employers benefit when a workplace promotes job satisfaction, as happier employees are more productive and more likely to stay on the job for a longer time.

Revisiting the Case of Maria: A Return to Work

Maria hates the thought of returning to work yet feels overwhelmed caring for a newborn. She is not sure what to do. She knows that working long hours will not be good for overall wellness. After discussing her situation with Suzi,

Maria also reaches out to an EAP counselor through her husband's employer to explore her career concerns further. Maria's work with her counselor leads her to return to work. However, her counselor has helped her develop a clear idea about the kind of environment she feels would be best for her and her family. Maria is able to find a company that has a daycare on-site at a reduced cost for employees. This allows Maria to see her young son when she takes breaks and when she is on her lunch break. Maria is happy with her new job and also enjoys working at a company that supports work–life balance. Although she is earning a somewhat smaller salary than her previous position paid, she has fewer responsibilities, and the family-centered benefits are worth the lost compensation. Unfortunately, she does have concerns about long-range advancement at her new job, and she occasionally wonders how her current position might affect her long-term career opportunities.

CHANGES IN THE WORKPLACE

Today, there are increasing numbers of women in the workplace as well as the largest number of employed mothers, with over 70 percent of mothers in the workforce (Bureau of Labor Statistics, 2018). There are more women enrolled in colleges than there are men, and more women are attending graduate school, which results in more women in a variety of positions in the workforce (Donnelly et al., 2016). Today's recent graduates were raised in a time when women were trying to find balance and wanted to have both personal and professional lives in a manner that was fulfilling. Thus, they want work flexibility as well as meaningful activities outside work (Tajlili & Baker, 2018). Millennials tend to focus on individual achievement rather than organizational goals and tend to be quicker to change jobs. This results in companies having to retrain employees more frequently than they once would have done (Calk & Patrick, 2017), which can be expensive for business. As the employment environment has also shifted to a "gig economy" setting, individuals are often more entrepreneurial and motivated to create unique career paths that flex as they move through adulthood. When clients are feeling trapped in positions and settings that they find too constricting, counselors can encourage them to think outside the once-traditional "nine to five" work setting. Additionally, if counselors are working with clients who employ others and are having a difficult time finding suitable employees, counselors can advocate for change in the workplace. As businesses are forced to rethink policies and practices that no longer serve the contemporary workforce, developing a structure that helps women find a solid and acceptable work–life balance will be important.

MIDCAREER

Over the course of a career, workers gain experience that can create opportunities for both personal and professional success. For women in early midlife or at midcareer, this can be a period of self-examination and priority realignment. Some women would prefer not to seek advancement into administrative positions due to the potential work–family conflicts that could be created. Other women might not want to be responsible for other employees or deal with the politics involved (Ward & Wolf-Wendel, 2016). In some fields, gender may place women at a disadvantage throughout their careers; for instance, in STEM academic positions, women have reported feeling more pressure to engage in higher levels of service than male colleagues (Hart, 2016). Within the engineering field, men have reported feeling threatened by females in the field, and women report gender discrimination (Morris, 2016). Additionally, women may feel devalued and unacknowledged for their achievements in midcareer as well as lose the mentors that helped them at the start of their careers (Grove, 2015). This is a time of adjustment for many women as they strive to prioritize their lives and make decisions about their careers that will shape their career trajectory through the remaining years.

While women have no doubt made many strides toward equality in the workplace, it is evident that more work needs to be done. Part of the issue perhaps goes back to what was previously discussed regarding the need for companies and organizations to consider workplace policies that not only allow but also encourage employees to find a balance between work, family, and leisure time. Midcareer for women is often a balancing act with the demands of family. Handling those demands will vary for each individual. Trying to have it all, though, may come with a heavy price. Midcareer women who are in administrative or leadership positions are much more likely to suffer from chronic stress and depression than their male counterparts (Salgado, 2015). There is also a connection between physical health and mental health that might lead to women feeling overwhelmed. Doing it all well might not be possible, and sometimes choices might need to be made. This can be difficult for the woman who loves her career yet wants to spend significant time with her family. As children grow older, women might be more inclined to take on leadership and administrative positions, yet due to waiting might be at a disadvantage when they elect to do so.

Revisiting the Case of Maria: Her Family Grows

Maria and her husband have a second child, Jasmine, and they decide that Maria should stay home for a few years to raise their children. When her daughter enters second grade, and after having been out of the workforce for seven years, Maria decides to return to the work. Despite having earned her

MBA, she feels like the jobs she is being offered do not allow her the to reach her potential or use the skills she has developed over her career. Maria is frustrated with having to basically restart her career and feels devalued. She reaches out to the counselor with whom she had worked previously. Together, they work to help Maria sort out her priorities for a new position. The counselor asks Maria to make three lists to guide her job search: "Nonnegotiables," "Wish List," and "If I Must." The last list included items that Maria would only accept "if she must" do so to meet her other needs. Once Maria has sorted what she is looking for into these three categories, she feels better about the control she has in her search.

Maria finally finds a position that meets her "nonnegotiable" requirements and a couple of her "wish list" items. Her new supervisor is someone with less experience than Maria and is also younger. After Maria has worked at this job for two years, a position opens that would be a promotion. Maria applies, but she is not selected. Someone without an MBA is selected who has been at the company for four years. Her years off have had a negative impact on her career, and even when looking for other jobs, the seven-year gap in her résumé is viewed as a detriment. Maria stays at her current position for another year and then finds a job with a different company that has additional flexibility and allows her to work from home several days a week, an item from her original "Wish List." This allows her to pick her children up from school and attend their extracurricular activities. While it is still challenging to find a balance, Maria is happy to have flexibility in her work schedule. Yet, at the same time, her status as a partial remote employee offers little opportunity for advancement as well as many missed opportunities for networking. Both of these factors can affect a person's long-term career. Maria, though, is happy for now with her decision and is enjoying finding a balance to her multiple life roles.

CAREER ADVANCEMENT

There continues to be a gender disparity in leadership and administrative positions within companies despite the growing number of women in the workforce (Turner-Moffatt, 2019). Whiston and colleagues (2015) found that women in traditionally male-dominated professions indicated higher levels of discriminatory practices regarding recognition, promotions, and job duties than women in female-dominated professions. When it comes to career advancement, networking is critical. However, women tend to have less visibility and less powerful networks than men do (Fernando & Cohen, 2014). For marginalized women, there may be additional barriers to career success, decision making, and advancement. These include affordable daycare, mental health issues, and the negative career impact of pregnancy (Clark &

Bower, 2016). Career counseling tends to be focused on the middle class. For those in lower socioeconomic groups, getting ahead is difficult, as they may face greater challenges in soft skills such as networking and finding effective mentors, two activities that greatly influence career success.

Career advancement is greatly facilitated by networking and business connections. It can be essential for women to recognize their worth in their fields and to seek out networking opportunities with those who can help them advance. Unfortunately, compared to men, women often lack confidence in their abilities and may tend to devalue their own skills. Additionally, they tend not to self-advocate to the same degree as men (Turner-Moffatt, 2019). Perception is another factor that can negatively influence career advancement. Women tend to perceive more barriers when it comes to career advancement than males, and this may cause them to continue to devalue the worth of their skills and abilities. This can result in missed chances for advancement (Novakovic & Gnilka, 2015). Their lack of success may stem from their self-perceptions of being inadequately qualified for promotions or advancement opportunities.

Thus, women are put at a disadvantage when it comes to making the most of opportunities for career advancement. Mentors can play a vital role in helping women understand that it is acceptable to advocate for oneself and to better understand the benefits they bring to an organization (Turner-Moffatt, 2019). If a woman reaches out to a counselor at this juncture in her life, the counselor can encourage the client to seek out an effective mentor who can facilitate her career confidence and development. Counselors, too, can effectively work with clients who need to build their career confidence through such means as interview or networking role plays, facilitating job exploration and career changes, and encouraging clients to acknowledge and strengthen their skills and unique abilities. Due to socialization, many women are hesitant to emphasize their strengths in business settings. However, being confident and being able to discuss their qualifications and accomplishments can be key to career advancement.

Revisiting the Case of Maria: Ten Years Later

Maria's youngest child, Jasmine, is preparing to leave for college. Maria's focus has begun to shift back to her career as her children have grown into young adults. This is a normal development as priorities tend to shift throughout life depending on life stage and development. Maria finds that she is excited about the possibilities of her future and freedom from having to be as available for her children as she had been when they were in school. She has enjoyed the flexibility of working from home but has now applied for a key managerial position that would require her presence in the office on a regular basis. When she is rejected for the job, she reaches out to her former counselor again.

Maria and her counselor review her résumé and qualifications to see if Maria can develop a stronger "on-paper identity" before she applies for another position. Her counselor notes that her years working from home and the seven-year gap may still create barriers in some settings, so they create a résumé that highlights Maria's skills and accomplishments and then presents her experience history. Maria sends out her freshly updated resume to multiple employers and receives a handful of follow-up interviews. She is disappointed that she is passed over for job offers for positions she knows she is qualified to assume. After much reflection, however, Maria accepts a new job that is just a lateral move rather than a promotion. Maria is hopeful that working on-site at this new company will provide an opportunity for her to excel and begin to climb the job ladder again. A promotion does not materialize as soon as she had hoped, and she is now thinking about starting her own business. She is unsure if she is willing to take this type of risk, so she and her husband begin to assess the potential risks and benefits of her doing so. Right now, Maria feels stuck, devalued, and frustrated. She is beginning to experience some regret for having chosen to prioritize her family's needs now that she is finding out what a strong and lasting influence they have had on her career.

WORKING LONGER

People are working longer and retiring later, if they are able to retire at all. However, career counseling theories have often ignored the issues faced by older workers as they begin to sunset their careers, especially the issues faced by women (Whiston et al., 2015). This creates challenges and opportunities for counselors working with older adults as they transition through the later stages of a career. While women may hold similar jobs and career spans equal to those of men, they often have a different trajectory when it comes to their careers than men, such as career gaps and more flexible jobs at different points in their careers. Younger adults tend to hold many negative stereotypes about older workers, and ageism, in addition to sexism, can negatively affect older women on the job. While retirement and exiting the workforce may be a desired path, increased longevity may result in women "outliving" their retirement savings (Frank-Miller, Lambert, & Henly, 2015). In addition, more years on the job delays access to social security benefits (Gillen & Heath, 2017), stretching retirement out even further.

Dealing with Younger Bosses

While older workers may bring expertise to the workplace, they often are undervalued by younger bosses, and older women may face an additional layer of discrimination and minimization in some industries (Killam & Weber, 2014). It is important for older women to be able to clearly articulate their skills and expertise when interviewing for new positions or expressing their interest in opportunities for career advancement. It is also important to seek out opportunities to enhance current skills and add new ones, including keeping up with changes in technology (Whiston et al., 2015). Even as the culture has seemed to shift regarding what aging looks like today, stereotyping continues to be a major problem for older workers. Many women have indicated that marketing and advertising about menopause has increased negative stereotypes about women (Kemp, 2018). As a group, older workers may be perceived as less productive, physically frail, and resistant to change. They also may be viewed as unmotivated and with little potential to move forward in the organization (Frank-Miller et al., 2015).

In terms of physical health, there may be some legitimate concerns related to some workers' ability to continue the jobs they took when younger. Due to safety rules and laws in some fields, hearing acuity, reduction in cognitive abilities, and reaction time are factors that are viewed when it comes to safety in the workplace (Kirk & Belovis, 2005). While older workers are less likely to take sick leave than younger workers, the number of days they take off due to an illness is higher than that of younger workers (Henkens, Cozijnsen, & van Solinge, 2009). While health benefits are a reason that many continue to work, stereotypes regarding ability and health have a major impact on relationships in the workplace. And despite formal and informal efforts to eliminate discrimination against older workers, it still occurs. The ramifications of workplace discrimination against older workers goes beyond the workplace. Discrimination at the workplace can have a profound negative impact on an individual's physical and psychological health (Chou, 2012). Counselors working with older adult women may need to assess for issues related to their employment settings as well as functioning in other aspects of their lives.

Revisiting the Case of Maria: Unexpected Changes Arise

Maria has continued to work at the same company over the past few years and was finally promoted to a midlevel management position. She likes her job, the people with whom she works, and the benefits her company provides. She has just learned, however, that her daughter, Jasmine, has dropped out of college due to issues related to substance abuse and is pregnant. Jasmine also asked to move back home. The baby is due soon, and Maria is not sure Jasmine will be able to care for a baby. Jasmine's substance abuse resulted in legal troubles, and this has taken a toll on the family. Maria and Jake have experienced significant conflicts with one another as they differ in how they should handle these new developments in their family. Jasmine gives birth to a healthy child but is unable to parent her son, and the child's father has never been spoken of or seen by Maria and Jake. Maria recognizes that she is the only one in a position to care for the infant. Once the child is three months old, Maria returns to her job and the child is placed in daycare. Maria and Jack find themselves in the position of raising a grandchild when Jasmine leaves the home and drops out of their lives.

Maria and Jake had been planning for retirement in a few years, but they accept that their new responsibilities will require they work longer than anticipated to support a grandchild. Maria reaches out to her counselor for support when she realizes how strong her feelings of frustration are. Maria's counselor helps her make sense of the choices she has made and helps her develop healthy ways to cope with the career frustration that she is experiencing. Maria is encouraged to find a creative outlet outside of her professional role that will allow her to enjoy herself and develop a new skill. Maria acknowledges that this could provide a needed outlet, and she revisits some of the hobbies she once enjoyed as an adolescent, recognizing that she cannot let her frustration get in the way of her relationship with Jake or their grandchild. She and the counselor work through the unexpected return of the work–life balance challenge. Her counselor notes that when Maria was in counseling ten years ago she was wresting with trying to prioritize her family time and how she wanted to ensure her professional and individual identity was not lost in caring for her family. Maria affirms that she does not want to lose her sense of self; she also knows her grandson needs her. She acknowledges that she wishes her grandson wasn't spending so many hours in daycare, but also notes that her position brings her pride and that she has worked hard to reach this point in her career after her earlier break. The counselor normalizes her conflicted feelings and reminds Maria that no career path is the "right one" for everyone and that doing what feels right for herself will be the path that brings her the most satisfaction.

Delaying Retirement

There are a number of factors that influence the age at which a woman retires. If a woman has a spouse that is working, she is more likely to work than a woman who has a retired spouse. Some women, however, work even longer when their spouses retire due to their desire to avoid spending every day in the company of their spouses. Women who have degrees are more likely to work longer than those who do not have degrees (Gillen & Heath, 2017). The once sought-after "gold watch and comfortable pension" are more myth than truth today as well. This can be a major reason people are working longer, due to the need to ensure financial resources are available. Changes in social security laws keep more adults in the workforce than in the past; for many, full social security benefits are not available until age sixty-seven (Wenger & Reynolds, 2009). People are also more willing than before to leave one job to take another or to relocate for a job (Smith, 2009).

Retirement is a very personal decision, and some older adults are simply not ready, or financially able, to take the pay cut that typically occurs at retirement. Many older workers are highly skilled and highly paid due to having unique skill sets along with experience that comes with longevity in the workforce. However, their higher salaries might place them higher on the list of employees targeted for downsizing when cost savings are needed (Sweet, 2007). Although there are laws that are designed to prevent discrimination against older workers, employers can be stealthy in decision making concerning older workers. Not everyone is offered the metaphorical "golden parachute," and retirement may be accompanied by financial exigencies for some workers who are forced to retire before they are ready. For some potential retirees, the impending loss of affordable health care may keep them employed longer than they like. The major financial challenge with retirement is that no one knows exactly how much money will be needed or what sort of expenses will be required beyond basic necessities. In some cases, retirees may be asked to assume the responsibilities of raising their grandchildren.

Grandparents as Parents

A growing number of grandparents are now raising their grandchildren. Unfortunately, children being raised by grandparents tend to experience a greater number of behavioral problems, and grandparents experience higher levels of stress than grandparents who are not raising grandchildren (Pilkauskas & Dunifon, 2016). It is important to consider that grandparents often step into the caregiver role unexpectedly and may not realize everything that this role will entail (Shovali, Emerson, & Augusta, 2019). They also may not realize how it can impact retirement plans and financial resources. The need to financially help or support grandchildren is another reason some women delay retirement (Miller, Tamborini, & Reznik, 2018). Older women may have thought that family-life conflicts would be avoided at this stage in their career but now find themselves trying to balance childcare with work again. While this can lead to feelings of frustration and stress, by developing the trait of adaptability, the conflict can be better managed.

Reframing

Career adaptability is an important skill as women mature, and it provides flexibility as they must respond to changing situations and circumstances that occur with age (Whiston et al., 2015). Mental health issues affect career adaptability, and counselors working with older adults in transition should bear this in mind (Killam & Weber, 2014). Ideally, older adults will be employed in settings that allow them to continue to work as long as they feel able. Unfortunately, the "ideal job" seldom exists, and women may need to reframe their current job or the job for which they would be hired as more suitable or closer to "ideal" than they might have felt at a different life stage. Being flexible and able to adapt to a changing professional landscape can allow a woman to remain in the workforce longer. However, while retirement may occur earlier or later, depending on personal circumstances, it is important to plan for retirement earlier than later.

RETIREMENT

Retirement typically presents challenges and opportunities. In the past, research on retirement focused on men's experiences, but as baby boomers have reached retirement age, the focus of research has widened as a record number of women are now retiring (Sherry, Tomlinson, Meika, Johnston, & Feeney, 2017). During their retirement, baby boomer women focus on navigating their shifting identities as well as their shifting relationships (Loe & Johnston, 2016). For couples who retire together, spending more time together can be a major change, and roles tend to change in terms of household responsibilities. Counselors should encourage clients struggling with this new level of togetherness to create a sense of daily structure and make time for open and honest communication (Cooley & Adorno, 2016). Some women may experience a sense of loss related to the role they had at work, in addition to the frequent tension with a spouse that results when retirement occurs (Sherry et al., 2017). Making major life transitions can be challenging and can negatively affect overall well-being and contribute to compromised mental health.

While retirement was once considered a career "grand finale" after decades spent with a single employer, today it is often seen as a doorway into a new role. Not everyone is as happy to reach retirement as some might believe. Research indicates that a person's reaction to retirement varies from increased life satisfaction to increased feelings of depression and loneliness (Olds et al., 2018). This variance demonstrates that retirement alone is not the only consideration that must be taken into account when working with a client. There are several factors that affect overall mental health, wellness, and well-being, including perception and interpretation of life events. This highlights the need for counselors to take a holistic approach when working with clients on career and retirement issues. It is important also to note that women experience less divide between areas of life, perhaps due to their selection of jobs and having different work trajectories than their male counterparts (Sherry et al., 2017). This might mean that the needs of women are different from the needs of men when it comes to career retirement counseling.

Revisiting the Case of Maria: Retirement

Maria and her husband continue to work until their grandson is ten years old. They have full custody of their grandchild, and it is for him that they felt the need to work longer than anticipated. They have set up a college savings fund for him and increased their retirement investment contributions. They are now able to be present at his extracurricular activities and to provide for him. Maria has time to do things she always wanted to do, such as get more involved in gardening and join a gardening club. She also has begun to paint and has taken several painting classes at the local art museum and is finding new ways to express her creativity and desire to remain active in life.

IMPLICATIONS FOR COUNSELORS

Career self-management is a dynamic process and places responsibility for career success fully on the individual rather than on an employer, to whom employees once dedicated their entire career span. This can be extremely challenging for women when they may be excluded from critical opportunities to network and will typically also bear the brunt of domestic and family responsibilities (Fernando & Cohen, 2014). In working with women, it is important for counselors to consider the needs of women in all of their various relational identities. Interpersonal relationships are important to consider when working with women's career issues, especially in the context of cultural differences (Whiston et al., 2015). As one considers the various roles a woman takes on throughout her career, here are some key points to consider to best meet the needs of women at each stage of their careers:

Early Career

- Encourage women to seek both informal and formal mentors to help build connections and networks and establish strong relationships.
- Consider priorities both long term and short term and determine what will be needed to reach career goals.

- Be proactive in considering potential life-changing events such as marriage and children when planning for the future.
- Determine and implement ways to engage in activities that promote overall wellness.

Midcareer

- Help female clients to consider current priorities and life choices.
- Have clients consider jobs that offer flexibility if work–life conflict is an ongoing issue.
- Encourage women to continue building solid support systems and networking with colleagues in the field.

Career Advancement

- Work with the client to determine what she wants in terms of her career. Does she want to take on an administrative or leadership position, or is she content with a job that may offer her flexibility?
- Encourage the client to continue networking with others in her profession and to be open to new job possibilities that will further her career.

REFERENCES

Adema, W., Clarke, C., & Frey, V. (2016). Paid parental leave and other supports for parents with young children: The United States in international comparison. *International Social Security Review, 69*(2), 29–51.

Bianchi, S. M., Sayer, L. C., Milkie, M. A., & Robinson, J. P. (2012). Housework: Who did, does or will do it, and how much does it matter? *Social Forces, 91*(1), 55–63.

Blau, G., & Snell, C. M. (2013). Understanding undergraduate professional development engagement and its impact. *College Student Journal, 47*(4), 689–702.

Bureau of Labor Statistics. (2018). *Current population study*. Washington, DC: Author.

Calk, R., & Patrick, A. (2017). Millennials through the looking glass: Workplace motivating factors. *Journal of Business Inquiry, 16*(2), 131–39.

Chou, R. J. (2012). Discrimination against older workers: Current knowledge, future research directions and implications for social work. *Indian Journal of Gerontology, 2*, 25–49.

Clark, M. E., & Bower, J. D. (2016). Career experiences of women with major financial barriers. *Career Development Quarterly, 64*(4), 373–86.

Cooley, E. L., & Adorno, G. (2016). Advice from working women with retired partners. *Journal of Women and Aging, 28*, 141–49.

Cross E. S., Riddoch K. A., Pratts J., Titone S., Chaudhury B., & Hortensius R. (2019). A neurocognitive investigation of the impact of socializing with a robot on empathy for pain. *Philosophical Transactions of the Royal Society B: Biological Sciences, 374*(1771). https://doi.org/10.1098/rstb.2018.0034

Dickens, D. D., & Chavez, E. L. (2018). Navigating the workplace: The costs and benefits of shifting identities at work among early career U.S. black women. *Sex Roles, 78*(11–12), 760–74. https://doi.org/10.1007/s11199-017-0844-x

Donnelly, K., Twenge, J. M., Clark, M. A., Shaikh, S. K., Beller-May, A., & Carter, N. T. (2016). Attitudes toward women's work and family roles in the United States, 1976–2013. *Psychology of Women Quarterly, 40*(1), 41–54.
Evans-Galea, M. V., & Galea, C. A. (2014, October). The value of mentoring. *Chemistry in Australia,* 26–29.
Fernando, W. D. A., & Cohen, L. (2014). Respectable femininity and career agency: Exploring paradoxical imperatives. *Gender, Work & Organization, 21*(2), 149–64.
Frank-Miller, E. G., Lambert, S. J., & Henly, J. R. (2015). Age, wage, and job placement: Older women's experiences entering the retail sector. *Journal of Women & Aging, 27*(2), 157–73.
Gillen, M., & Heath, C. J. (2017). Effects of receipt of social security retirement benefits on older women's employment. *Journal of Women & Aging, 29*(5), 448–59.
Gronlund, A. (2017). On different tracks? Gender, professional strategies, and early career wage gaps. *Nordic Journal of Working Life Studies, 7*(2), 9–25.
Grove, J. (2015, September 10). "Neglected" mid-career women need recognition, study suggests. *Times Higher Education,* 11.
Grundmann, O. (2013). Career readiness: An old idea revived? *Journal of College Science Teaching, 43*(1), 8–9. https://doi.org/10.2505/4/jcst13_043_01_8
Hackmann, D. G., Malin, J. R., & Gilley, D. (2018). Career academies: Effective structures to promote college and career readiness. *Clearing House, 91*(4/5), 180–85. https://doi.org/10.1080/00098655.2018.1480196
Hart, J. (2016). Dissecting a gendered organization: Implications for career trajectories for mid-career faculty women in STEM. *Journal of Higher Education, 87*(5), 605–34. https://doi.org/10.1353/jhe.2016.0024
Hegewisch, A., & Hartmann, H. (2019, March 7). The gender wage gap: 2018 earnings differences by race and ethnicity. Institute for Women's Policy Research. Retrieved from https://iwpr.org/publications/gender-wage-gap-2018/
Henkens, K., van Solinge, H., & Cozijnsen, R. (2009). Let go or retain? A comparative study of the attitudes of business students and managers about the retirement of older workers. *Journal of Applied Social Psychology, 39,* 1562–1588.
Higgins, C. A., Duxbury, L. E., & Lyons, S. T. (2010). Coping with overload and stress: Men and women in dual-earner families. *Journal of Marriage and Family, 72*(4), 847–59.
Kahn, J. R., García-Manglano, J., & Bianchi, S. M. (2014). The motherhood penalty at midlife: Long-term effects of children on women's careers. *Journal of Marriage & Family, 76*(1), 56–72. https://doi.org/10.1111/jomf.12086
Kemp, N. (2018, September). Marketing's menopause. *Campaign,* 54–56.
Killam, W., & Weber, B. (2014). Career adaptation wheel to address issues faced by older workers. *Adultspan Journal, 13*(2), 68–78.
Kirk, J. J., & Belovics, R. (2005). Recommendations and resources for counseling older workers. *Journal of Employment Counseling, 42,* 50–59.
Liang, J., & Gong, Y. (2013). Capitalizing on proactivity for informal mentoring received during early career: The moderating role of core self-evaluations. *Journal of Organizational Behavior, 34*(8), 1182–1201.
Loe, M., & Johnston, D. K. (2016). Professional women "rebalancing" in retirement: Time, relationships, and body. *Journal of Women & Aging, 28*(5), 418–30. https://doi.org/10.1080/08952841.2015.1018047
Maqsood, H., Sohail, T., Qureshi, U., & Kausar, T. (2017). Work–family conflict, job stress and job satisfaction among teachers. *Journal of Arts & Social Sciences, 4*(1), 40–60.
Miller, M., Tamborini, C. R., & Reznik, G. L. (2018). Parental retirement timing: The role of unanticipated events in the lives of adult children. *Journal of Population Economics, 31,* 747–81.
Morris, C. (2016). Study underscores bias obstacles for women, minorities in engineering. *Diverse: Issues in Higher Education, 33*(22), 7.
Murphy, K. A., Blustein, D. L., Bohlig, A. J., & Platt, M. G. (2010). The college-to-career transition: An exploration of emerging adulthood. *Journal of Counseling & Development, 88*(2), 174–181. https://doi.org/10.1002/j.1556-6678.2010.tb00006.x

Novakovic, A., & Gnilka, P. B. (2015). Dispositional affect and career barriers: The moderating roles of gender and coping. *Career Development Quarterly, 63*(4), 363–75.

Olds, T., Burton, N. W., Sprod, J., Maher, C., Ferrar, K., Brown, W. J., . . . Dumuid, D. (2018). One day you'll wake up and won't have to go to work: The impact of changes in time use on mental health following retirement *PlusOne, 13*(6), 1–14.

Pilkauskas, N. V., & Dunifon, R. E. (2016). Understanding grandfamilies: Characteristics of grandparents, nonresident parents, and children. *Journal of Marriage & Family, 78*(3), 623–33.

Rogers, J. G., & Franzen, A. B. (2014). Work–family conflict: The effects of religious context on married women's participation in the labor force. *Religions, 5*(3), 580–93.

Roy, G. (2016). Impact of mobile communication technology on the work life balance of working women: A review of discourses. *Journal of Contemporary Management Research, 10*(1), 79–101.

Ruff, J. (2013). Sisters of the heart along the way: The power of the female mentoring relationship. *Women & Therapy, 36*(1–2), 86–99.

Salgado, S. (2015). A woman's view from the top might be a sad one. *Utne Reader, 186*, 14–18.

Schilling, E. (2015). "Success is satisfaction with what you have"? Biographical work–life balance of older female employees in public administration. *Gender, Work & Organization, 22*(5), 474–94.

Shepherd-Banigan, M., Bell, J., Basu, A., Booth-LaForce, C., & Harris, J. (2016). Workplace stress and working from home influence depressive symptoms among employed women with young children. *International Journal of Behavioral Medicine, 23*(1), 102–11. https://doi.org/10.1007/s12529-015-9482-2

Sherry, A., Tomlinson, J. M., Meika, L., Johnston, K., & Feeney, B. C. (2017). Apprehensive about retirement: Women, life transitions, and relationships. *Journal of Women & Aging, 29*(2), 173–84.

Shovali, T. E., Emerson, K. G., & Augusta, M. (2019). School-aged children living in grandfamilies: Grandparent caregiver confidence in community resources matters. *Child Welfare, 97*(2), 79–94.

Smith, D. I. (2009). Changes in transitions: The role of mobility, class and gender. *Journal of Education and Work, 22*, 369–390.

Sweet, S. (2007). The older worker, job insecurity, and the new economy. *Generations, 31*, 45–49.

Tajlili, M. H., & Baker, S. B. (2018). The future work–life balance attitudes scale: Assessing attitudes on work–life balance in millennial college women. *Journal of Asia Pacific Counseling, 8*(2), 57–74. https://doi.org/10.18401.2018.8.2.2

Turner-Moffatt, C. (2019). The power of mentorship: Strengthening women in leadership roles. *Professional Safety , 64*(8), 17–19.

Ward, K., & Wolf-Wendel, L. (2016). Academic motherhood: Mid-career perspectives and the ideal worker norm. *New Directions for Higher Education, 2016*(176), 11–23. https://doi.org/10.1002/he.20206

Wayne, J., & Casper, W. (2016). Why having a family-supportive culture, not just policies, matters to male and female job seekers: An examination of work–family conflict, values, and self-interest. *Sex Roles, 75*(9–10), 459–75. https://doi.org/10.1007/s11199-016-0645-7

Wenger, J. B., & Reynolds, J. (2009). Older married workers and nonstandard jobs: The effects of health and health insurance. *Industrial Relations, 48*, 411–431.

Whiston, S. C., Feldwisch, R. P., Evans, K. M., Blackman, C. S., & Gilman, L. (2015). Older professional women's views on work: A qualitative analysis. *Career Development Quarterly, 63*(2), 98–112.

Yang, Y., Chawla, N. V., & Uzzi, B. (2019). A network's gender composition and communication pattern predict women's leadership success. *PNAS, 116*(6), 2033–38. doi:10.1073/pnas.1721438116

Part IV

Counseling Concerns of Relational Focus

Chapter Nine

Counseling Women Dealing with Family-of-Origin Issues

Lucy Parker and Dana T. Isawi

CASE VIGNETTE: RANIA

Rania, a twenty-five-year-old woman, appears for her first counseling appointment dressed in a hijab and a loose dress, wearing very little eye make-up. From first impressions in your early interactions, Rania does not appear to have any obvious or egregious presenting issues. She shares with you that she is from Dammam, Saudi Arabia, and that she moved to the United States after earning her MBA, only six months ago. Rania continues to share her personal history and elaborates that she was once married in her home country but is now separated from her husband. Rania shares that she is "not seeking treatment for my separation necessarily" but from issues due to her decision for separation. She elaborates that she is seeking treatment for "issues I'm having because I don't know how to cope with my decision to separate and with my family stress."

When asked various open-ended questions about her disclosure, Rania shares that in her family of origin, her father is currently undergoing chemotherapy and her brother is currently suffering from alcoholism. Rania went on to share that although she has a very supportive family that actually encouraged her to move to America and to separate from her husband, she often feels pressured by her family. She extends this conversation by confessing that "I am not there to hold the family together, and every day I remember this."

After sharing this intimate information, Rania expresses her concerns that an American counselor may not understand her feelings of "pressure" because "in America, people are much more career focused than family focused." She begins to cry and share that she, too, wants independence from her family but feels "guilt" and "pressure," due in part to her decision to separate from her husband and in part to her decision to move to America and start a new life.

* * *

When working with any client, it is salient to learn about the context of her presenting issues; in family-of-origin-related issues, it is essential. Narrative therapy (NT) has been shown to be one of the most effective therapeutic practices for helping women and other clients cope with family and other issues. NT helps clients to cope without over internalizing or pathologizing the issues they experience (Epston & White, 1992; Griffin, 2003; White, 1995). Various techniques to help women with family-of-origin issues will be presented and are intended to provide contemporary psychoeducational and insightful methods for working with clients. Cultural inclusion and phenomenological understanding are particularly emphasized with the use of narrative theory and narrative techniques for women dealing with family-of-origin issues. Rania will be featured, and ways to help her theoretically and practically will be discussed below.

FAMILY-OF-ORIGIN ISSUES

Although many of us would like to believe that growing up means we grow out of unhealthy beliefs or conflictual experiences that were embedded within our families of origin, it is not uncommon for vestiges of unhealthy patterns to remain. We are all shaped by our early relationships and experiences; sometimes, however, we do not realize the influence these have over us until we are well into adulthood. Family patterns that can be detrimental to healthy development include the use of demeaning or disrespectful communication between adults in the family or by adults with the children. Some women may harbor feelings of low self-worth, low self-esteem, and insecurity that were planted by the significant adults in their lives when they were children. Abuse at the hands of family members, regardless of its type (e.g., physical, emotional, sexual, and so on), can create patterns for relationships in which a woman may unconsciously seek out relationships in which her partners treat her as she was as a child. Witnessing abuse between adults can be equally detrimental to healthy development and healthy adult relationships. Living in a home in which a parent or caregiver is addicted to alcohol or other substances can also leave lasting consequences on children. As children grow into adolescents and young adults, even supportive and loving parents may create challenges for their daughters if they are hesitant to let them grow up and grow into adult women, show favoritism to a particular child or children in the family, expect an unusually high emotional or instrumental investment in the family of origin even as a woman enters into a significant relationship and begins a family of her own, or exhibit unnatural levels of desire to control an adult daughter's life.

In working with clients who are trying to navigate patterns of behavior that they attribute to early experiences or trying to manage current conflicts between themselves and their family of origin, counselors should invite clients to discuss how they felt treated by their parents as they grew up, expectations they feel their parents continue to place on them, current relationships between themselves and their parents and any siblings, and any current conflicts or tensions between them and their family of origin. If counselors notice patterns about which the client appears unaware, it is helpful to state what you have heard in a tentative way to check in with the client (Kopal & Keitel, 2012). A counselor might inquire, "I wonder if you notice any patterns between the way your parents treated you when you wanted to take risks and the way you treat yourself now, as an adult, when you want to take risks or try new things?" If a woman experiences guilt because she is wrestling with a choice that she feels will displease her parents, you might state something like, "It seems that your parents are still able to generate feelings of guilt in you even though you know that the choice you want to make is the best one for your current situation." Often, clients may not realize the ways their early experiences affect their adult relationships and choices. One way to help a client begin to tease out the influence of their family of origin on their adult behaviors and relationships is through narrative family counseling.

FOUNDATIONAL THEORY OF NARRATIVE FAMILY COUNSELING

In working with adult clients who are dealing with issues related to their family of origin, it is often useful to utilize interventions from narrative theory (Epston & White, 1992; White, 1988/9). This theory was founded with a focus on the relationship between the client and others in her life and positions the client as the expert. In NT, people are recognized within the context of their own phenomenological worldview as well as within time-relevant social contexts (White, 2007). According to Simon (2003), narrative therapy is identified by five main dimensions that are used to construct one's worldview. These dimensions include the following: (1) being an individualist-based theory, (2) exhibiting a view of *freedom from* (i.e., eudaimonistic), (3) accepting people as vessels that are primarily "good" and not defined by their mistakes, (4) viewing individuals as intellectual and eager to use the facilitation provided in counseling, and (5) treating clients as people who are also becoming as they continue to create and re-create new life narratives.

Narrative therapy purports that positive interactions (i.e., positive family integration or positive individual integration in society) can come from learning through past negative experiences and responses (White, 1995). This therapeutic orientation states that there are multiple truths that exist for family members, and regardless of how these truths diverge across individuals, each family member's perception is valid. Regarding family therapy, narrative family therapy recognizes that the excessive use of "shame and blame" immobilizes families in their goal of reunification. One of the most significant aims of narrative family therapy is for a balance to be created by individual family members between self, family, and problems. Narrative therapy also normalizes any problems a client may reflect as old stories to be transitioned out of rather than medical abnormalities to be diagnosed. In other words, a problem is something a person has, not something a person is. Also, many times, families' and individual client's issues are influenced by social, political, and cultural preexisting story lines. Despite social influences and current family and individual circumstances, narrative therapy aims to help clients accept and find hope in the present life stories.

Furthermore, issues and patterns unique to different families still bring truth, and no family is "abnormal." As Epston and White (1992) referenced, there is no absolute truth or one monolithic way of being according to a narrative-oriented worldview. The narrative counselor does not create normality or pressure a client to assimilate to some socially constructed norm; however, the role of the counselor is simply to facilitate the values and truths that are within the core of the client.

NARRATIVE THERAPY BEST PRACTICES

Narrative therapy assumes that the counselor's role includes being a facilitator and an investigator. Techniques and theory information about narrative therapy include separating a person from his or her problem. A foundational narrative technique that helps counselors separate the person from the problem includes an intervention called externalization (Erford, 2015). This technique focuses on the counselor's use of language to identify the client's problems as separate entities outside of the client. In other words, narrative theorists often say "the problem is the problem, the person is not the problem" (Epston & White, 1992; Jill, & Combs, 1996; Suddeath, Kerwin, & Dugger, 2017; White, 2011). Externalization includes allowing the client to separate themselves from their problem. Some examples of externalization mediums that counselors may use include client-facilitated and -created journaling, rapping, and artwork (Suddeath et al., 2017).

Metaphors

In addition to demonstrating the technique of externalization, counselors may also use metaphors, including specifically client-generated stories that serves as metaphors of their lives (Erford, 2015; Hannen & Woods, 2012; Pomerantz, 2007). Though story creation and re-creation may look different when used with different clients with different cultural or presenting issues, this intervention is a themed intervention, universal to NT. Other populations that have been seen to benefit from story creation and re-creation specifically include clients dealing with feelings of hopelessness, such as those who may experience suicidal or depressive symptoms (note however that NT does not conceptualize clients with symptoms but rather with problems; thus, depressive problems) (Hannen & Woods, 2012; Marsten & Howard, 2006; Pomerantz, 2007). This therapy technique would also serve as helpful with clients with family-related issues, as story creation allows family members and individual clients to rely on their own skills to express and then metaphorically re-create their desired future stories. Specifically, Hannen and Woods (2012) described how externalization, story creation, metaphor usage, and other practical NT interventions have worked well with clients dealing with intrapersonal issues and crises including self-harm.

Other narrative-related techniques that can be effective in helping clients address issues related to their family of origin include the "miracle question," which is a component of solution-focused therapy; psychoeducation about systems and the concept of "unfinished business," which is borrowed from Gestalt therapy; the "empty chair technique," also from Gestalt therapy; and "genogram" creation (Erford, 2015).

The Miracle Question

The miracle question is a technique in the form of a direct question that helps a client focus on "what they want" versus the current foci of their problems, in other words "what they don't want" (Erford, 2015, p. 18). One direct example and form of the miracle question is this: "Suppose that, one night, you went to sleep and when you woke, the problem was solved. What would be different?" (de Shazer, 1988, p. 5; cited in Erford, 2015, p. 18).

Psychoeducation and Unfinished Business

In addition to the miracle question, a counselor may use psychoeducation, which includes educating the client about family patterns and family roles and the ways these can influence individuals long after they have moved from childhood into adulthood. Particularly important is psychoeducation that facilitates a client's understanding of her own personal unfinished business and her family's unfinished business (Macaulay & Angus, 2019; Paivio

& Greenberg, 1995). *Unfinished business* is a term that was created by counseling theorist Fritz Perlz, who was the key developer of Gestalt therapy (Macaulay & Angus, 2019; Paivio & Greenberg, 1995). Unfinished business describes a client's unexpressed feelings or thoughts regarding current or past events or personal exchanges. Unfinished business could also include unexpressed tension, conflict, communication, or secrets between family members. Regarding the case vignette that opened this chapter, it could be beneficial for Rania's counselor to encourage Rania to express, in session, the unfinished business that she has with her family.

The Empty Chair Technique

One concrete way to help Rania or similar clients understand how to process unresolved family patterns and unfinished business includes facilitating a technique called "the empty chair" (Macaulay & Angus, 2019; Paivio & Greenberg, 1995). The empty chair technique includes having a client role-play a conversation with an imagined other person. When applying the empty chair technique with Rania, a counselor may tentatively structure a session so Rania can express aloud feelings that she has been unable to express to a family member from whom she feels the most pressure or tension. The counselor invites the client to state their feelings, directing them toward a literally empty chair, while imagining the person with whom the client has unfinished business is sitting there. Processing the content of this conversation and exploring what the client says and does during this intervention would follow the imagined conversation. The purpose of the empty chair technique is to provide clients with a chance to come to some sense of closure regarding family business that has been left unfinished between the client and the family. One of the key benefits of using this technique is self-insight. In addition to an increased self-understanding and greater awareness of her feelings regarding an issue, the client is also given the opportunity to speak aloud her thoughts and feelings that she has been unable to previously share. Although the empty chair intervention does not include the physical presence of the other person, it does provide an opportunity for clients to release their feelings and experience some sense of catharsis regarding their issues.

Genograms

A genogram is a graphic representation of how family members are biologically, legally, and emotionally related. Typically, at least three generations are depicted in a genogram since family patterns can be transmitted across generations. Genograms summarize complex multigenerational patterns over time and allow counselors to understand the family's history and view current issues within the context of family patterns. Genograms also can help the counselor understand family interactional patterns, reframe family issues, and make hypotheses regarding clients' issues in the context of their family. Squares and circles represent family members, and various lines are used to depict their relationships. Other information that may be depicted in the genogram includes critical life changes (e.g., transitions, life-cycle changes), roles, illnesses, mental health issues, loss or trauma, genetic patterns, and other cultural factors (e.g., religion, immigration status). Genograms have been used both as a practical assessment tool as well as an intervention. The genogram facilitates client insight through viewing issues in their current and historical context. Both the counselor and the client often notice themes, rules, and multigenerational patterns that may be influencing current concerns (McGoldrick, Gerson, & Petry, 2008).

Genograms are widely used in clinical practice and have been established as a culturally appropriate intervention (Thomas, 1998). They have been used to elicit family narratives where the therapist bears witness to the client's narrative (Sherman, 1990). Genograms can be applied to multiple issues, such as family members' temperaments, career choices, religion/spirituality, dominant/submissive relationships, and financial patterns. Cultural genograms focus specifically on the cultural aspect of a client's history and are used to understand the culture and worldview of family members (Congress, 1994; Thomas, 1998). Using genograms is especially appropriate with Rania since she comes from a collective culture that places tremendous emphasis on family relations, and her presenting concerns stem from family-of-origin issues.

In the case of Rania, the counselor could use a genogram and ask her to include cultural factors such as ethnicity, race, immigration status, socioeconomic status, gender, and spirituality since these can influence family functioning. The counselor could ask the following questions: What family rules are determined by ethnicity? What roles, rules, or responsibilities are determined by race? What difficulties did you face during immigration? Has there been a change in current social class? How are gender roles divided in your family (Thomas, 1998, pp. 26–30)? In addition, the counselor could ask, "What meaning does religion or spirituality have for you in your everyday life? In your family's life? In times of danger or crisis?" (McGoldrick et al., 2008, p. 55).

In Rania's case, the counselor can facilitate creating separate genograms to focus on different aspects of the client's life. A gender genogram, a socioeconomic status genogram, a spirituality genogram, and a gender genogram. Another way to use genograms is to transform current relationships and empower clients in the current time. The counselor could work with Rania to develop a sense of meaning and continuity through connecting the present with her past. After depicting Rania's family genogram, the counselor could ask her to write letters to her family members (McGoldrick et al., 2008).

Conclusion

Externalization, story creation, metaphor usage, the miracle question, psychoeducation about unfinished business, usage of the empty chair technique, and family genograms are various best practices often associated with various postmodern theories, especially narrative therapy. These best practices are helpful to clients, especially clients such as Rania, as through NT clients may be empowered to form their own story and identity.

CULTURAL CONSIDERATIONS

Consideration of clients' needs, which are elicited from the commonly created humanistic and egalitarian relationship that NT provides, is important. In fact, consideration of client needs, including the need for *all* counselors, regardless of primary theory, to be culturally competent, is crucial for counseling to be efficacious and promote change. Another advantage of narrative theory, as was introduced earlier, is that this theory has been extensively researched with a variety of diverse clients (Epston & White, 1992; Griffin, 2003; Patterson, Sprenkle, Williams, Grauf-Grounds, & Chamow, 2009; Simon, 2003; White, 1995). It is important to note that NT is efficacious with many client types because of its focus on strengths and externalizations (but not invalidations) of problems.

Contemporary NT researchers and clinicians have held that, because NT is categorized as postmodern or, also referenced, is fourth force of counseling, this theory already innately incorporates multicultural elements (Cashin, 2008; Zimmerman & Beaudoin, 2015). However, other holistic evaluations of NT support that though such theory is intentional in incorporating culture, such an orientation may still be too focused on a Westernized, individualized worldview (Stebleton, 2010). In fact, NT recognizes humans as "nonnormative" (Jill & Combs, 1996). With the concept of being nonnormative in mind, narrative theorists as well as other postmodern theorists emphasize that change occurs with collaboration and an egalitarian, goal-focused relationship (Jill & Combs, 1996; White, 2011).

ETHICAL CONSIDERATIONS

Narrative theory and related interventions create a space where clients are considered the experts on themselves and their lives. Particularly, when considering ethics, one of the largest concerns when working with Rania as well as all clients is to maintain client beneficence through promoting client autonomy (or, as narrative theorists encourage, for clients like Rania to be the expert on herself) (American Counseling Association [ACA], 2014). Furthermore, the ACA Code of Ethics requires that counselors be continually ethically and culturally competent. These competencies are specifically aligned in the ACA Code of Ethics Standards A.2.c., B.1.a, C.2.f., E.5.b., E.8., F.2.b., F.11.c., and H.5.d (ACA, 2014). Outside of the ACA standards and professional jargon, client beneficence means to "do good" for the client. In order for all counselors to "do good" for our clients, we must maintain continued education on techniques, such as those listed above, and remember to not impose our own values. One way to help ourselves not impose our own values on clients is to maintain a genuine sense of curiosity without interrogating our clients. Additionally, with clients such as Rania, we must remember not to impose various ethnocentric, American values and instead see what values Rania, as her own person with a unique phenomenological identity, holds within her worldview. NT is also ethically congruent for a client such as Rania, as NT interventions recognize that social changes and contexts may empower or, unfortunately often, inhibit individuals. Rania, depending on her own unique individual worldview, may feel inhibited by a Westernized society where current societal pressures and issues such as Islamophobia exist (Haque, Tubbs, Kahumoku, Brown, & Kahumoku-Fessler, 2019).

ADVOCACY OPPORTUNITIES

Advocacy for clients like Rania is not a single act but rather an ongoing conversation or a learned set of skills or behaviors (Dollarhide, Gibson, & Moss, 2013; Hollenbaugh, 2015). In and outside of sessions with clients, we as counselors must reinforce ethical and social justice to counteract potential oppression our clients may be facing. One way that we may advocate is to remember and consider the ACA Code of Ethics Standard E.5.c., which is to "recognize historical and social prejudices." As referenced briefly above, for example, Rania may or may not identify as having experienced current Islamophobia in society (Haque et al., 2019). One small step to help Rania advocate for herself includes providing an affirming clinical environment for this and all of our clients despite intersectional differences (Hurt-Avila & Castillo, 2017).

Case Vignette Wrap-Up: Rania

Narrative therapists focus on acceptance for the client through teleology and story creation. Furthermore, narrative family therapy (NFT) focuses on helping families reorient their energy to win their familial relationships versus emotional energy generated toward winning arguments within the family (Epston & White, 1992; Griffin, 2003; Patterson et al., 2009; Simon, 2003; Suddeath et al., 2017; White, 1995). NFT specifically provides a structure for clients like Rania not to overpathologize and instead externalize their problems. It is best practice for counselors also to reinforce to female clients that all families have concerns and to offer empowerment to cope with these family concerns. Holistically speaking, techniques that a narrative therapist could use with Rania to cope with various family-of-origin issues include (1) to help Rania become self-aware of her family issues and her reactions to these issues through story creation, miracle questing, and other NT interventions; (2) to help Rania externalize some of her emotions to expressed issues in her family, if needed; and (3) to empower Rania in her desired worldview, in her family, and in society (Erford, 2015).

Some guiding questions that could prove efficacious in Rania's narrative therapy session include these: If life were perfect, what would your family look like (i.e., the miracle question)? What are the times when you felt you were not present for your family? What are the times when you felt you were present for your family? What does a good daughter look like? What is the most difficult emotion to cope with regarding your family? What are three adjectives to describe your family? What does family mean to you? If you had to pick a symbol, what symbol represents your relationship with your family?

QUESTIONS FOR REFLECTION

1. Reflect on your own family-of-origin issues. Are there specific issues you would find difficult to work with as a counselor? What steps will you take to ensure that you are effective in working with the client?
2. NT has been shown to be one of the most effective therapeutic practices for helping women and other clients cope with family and other issues. What are other therapeutic approaches you find appropriate for helping women cope with family-of-origin issues?
3. What are some of the challenges counselors could encounter working with women who are seeking counseling due to family-of-origin issues?
4. What are advocacy opportunities that you have engaged in when working with women who are seeking counseling due to family-of-origin issues?

REFERENCES

American Counseling Association. (2014). *ACA code of ethics*. Alexandria, VA: Author.

Cashin, A. (2008). Narrative therapy: A psychotherapeutic approach in the treatment of adolescents with Asperger's disorder. *Journal of Child and Adolescent Psychiatric Nursing, 21*(1), 48–56.
Congress, E. P. (1994). The use of culturagrams to assess and empower culturally diverse families. *Families in Society, 75*(9), 531–40. doi:10.1177/104438949407500901
de Shazer, S. (1988). *Clues: Investigating solutions in brief therapy.* New York, NY: W. W. Norton.
Dollarhide, C., Gibson, D., & Moss, J. (2013). Professional identity development of counselor education doctoral students. *Counselor Education and Supervision, 52*, 137–50. doi:10.1002/j.1556-6978.2013.00034.x
Epston, D., & White, M. (1992). *Experience, contradiction, narrative, and imagination: Selected papers of David Epston and Michael White, 1989–1991.* Adelaide: Dulwich Centre Publications.
Erford, B. T. (2015). *40 Techniques Every Counselor Should Know.* New York, NY: Pearson Higher Education.
Griffin, M. (2003). Narrative behavior therapy: Integration in practice. *Australian and New Zealand Journal of Family Therapy, 24*(1), 33–38.
Hannen, E., & Woods, K. (2012). Narrative therapy with an adolescent who self-cuts: A case example. *Educational Psychology in Practice, 28*(2), 187–214. doi: 10.1080/02667363.2012.669362
Haque, A., Tubbs, C., Kahumoku, F. E., Brown, M., & Kahumoku-Fessler, E. (2019). Microaggressions and Islamophobia: Experiences of Muslims across the United States and clinical implications. *Journal of Marital and Family Therapy, 45*(1), 76–91.
Hollenbaugh, K. M. (2015). Increasing leadership behaviors in counselor education doctoral students via study abroad experiences: A single case study approach. *Journal of Counselor Leadership and Advocacy, 2*(2), 170–83. http://dx.doi.org/10.1080/2326716X.2015.1066277
Hurt-Avila, K., & Castillo, J. (2017). Accreditation, professional identity development, and professional competence: A discriminant analysis. *Journal of Counselor Leadership and Advocacy, 4*(1), 39–51.
Jill, M. S. W., & Combs, G. (1996). *Narrative therapy: The social construction of preferred realities.* New York, NY: W. W. Norton.
Kopal, M., & Keitel, M. A. (2012). *The handbook of counseling women.* Thousand Oaks, CA: Sage.
Macaulay, C. B., & Angus, L. (2019). The narrative-emotion process model: An integrative approach to working with complex posttraumatic stress. *Journal of Psychotherapy Integration, 29*(1), 42–53.
Marsten, D., & Howard, G. (2006). Shared influence: A narrative approach to teaching narrative therapy. *Journal of Systemic Therapies, 25*, 97–110.
McGoldrick, M., Gerson, R., & Petry, S. S. (2008). *Genograms: Assessment and intervention.* New York, NY: W. W. Norton.
Neukrug, E. (2010). *Counseling theory and practice.* Belmont, CA: Cengage Learning.
Paivio, S. C., & Greenberg, L. S. (1995). Resolving "unfinished business": Efficacy of experiential therapy using empty-chair dialogue. *Journal of Consulting and Clinical Psychology, 63*(3), 419–25. http://dx.doi.org/10.1037/0022-006X.63.3.419
Patterson, J., Sprenkle, D., Williams, L., Grauf-Grounds, C., & Chamow, L. (2009). *Essential skills in family therapy: From the first interview to termination.* New York, NY: Guilford.
Pomerantz, K. A. (2007). Helping children explore their emotional and social worlds through therapeutic stories. *Educational and Child Psychology, 24*(1), 45–55.
Sherman, M. H. (1990). Family narratives: Internal representations of family relationships and affective themes. *Infant Mental Health Journal, 11*(3), 253–58.
Simon, G. M. (2003). *Beyond technique in family therapy.* Boston, MA: Pearson Education.
Stebleton, M. (2010). Narrative-based career counseling perspectives in times of change: An analysis of strengths and limitations. *Journal of Employment Counseling, 47*, 64–78.

Suddeath, E., Kerwin, A., & Dugger, S. (2017). Narrative family therapy: Practical techniques for more effective work with couples and families. *Journal of Mental Health Counseling, 39*(2), 116–31.

Thomas, A. J. (1998). Understanding culture and worldview in family systems: Use of the multicultural genogram. *Family Journal, 6*(1), 24–32. doi: 10.1177/1066480798061005

White, M. (1995). *Re-authoring lives: Interviews and essays*. Adelaide: Dulwich Centre Publications.

White, M. (1988/89). The externalizing of the problem and the re-authoring of lives and relationships. *Dulwich Centre Newsletter*, Summer.

White, M. (2007). *Maps of narrative practice*. New York, NY: W. W. Norton.

White, M. (2011). *Narrative practice: Continuing the conversations*. New York, NY: W. W. Norton.

White, M., & Epston, D. (1990). *Narrative means to therapeutic ends*. London: W. W. Norton.

Young, K. (2008). Narrative practice at a walk-in therapy clinic: Developing children's worry wisdom. *Journal of Systemic Therapies, 27*(4), 54–74.

Zimmerman, J., & Beaudoin, N. M. (2015). Neurobiology for your narrative: How brain science can influence narrative work. *Journal of Systemic Therapies, 34*(2), 59–74.

Chapter Ten

Counseling Contemporary Couples

Focus on Infertility

Rebecca Meeks, Jessica Shull, Ana Ulloa Estrada, and Bonnie Cardillo

CASE VIGNETTE: ARETTA

Aretta is a navy veteran currently working with children. Her husband, Lucas, is on active duty as a senior enlisted serviceman in the navy, and both are in their late thirties. She was diagnosed with unexplained first-line infertility after the couple had two failed IVF cycles. Aretta is a Christian and a first-generation Nigerian American who was raised in the Midwest. Although Aretta is a first-generation American, the strong Nigerian culture of her family continues to be a dominant force on her emotions and in her relationship. Lucas is a proud Texan of Mexican descent who exudes masculinity. They both longed to soothe the other and make the pain of their infertility go away; they just didn't know how. They presented as eager during their sessions, hoping to gain skills that could assist them moving forward. They both shared their emotional pain and continuous disappointment in failed medical procedures and pregnancies, labeling it as "unfair." They openly discussed how they chose to isolate from close family and friends and how this situation had become increasingly distressing.

Aretta shared that in her Nigerian culture, if she could not reproduce, the husband's side of the family would likely encourage him to take a different wife that could produce children. This childbearing expectation from her culture fueled her underlying fears of losing her husband and feelings of shame that she could not please and deserve him. Lucas's traditional Mexican Catholic family also voiced their expectations for grandchildren and constantly pushed the couple about having children. The couple decided to avoid their families and their probing questions and insensitive remarks rather than reveal Aretta's diagnosis. They dreaded the criticism and backlash they would receive from their family members.

* * *

The inability to conceive or carry a child to term affects over 12 percent of American women aged fifteen to forty-four, or 7.5 million, which reflects one in six couples (Centers for Disease Control and Prevention, 2019). The struggle to conceive frequently takes a heavier emotional and psychological toll on women than on their male counterparts. Infertility-related distress often turns into depression and left untreated can result in major depressive disorder (Koszycki, Bisserbe, Blier, Bradwejn, & Markowitz, 2012).

Female infertility patients report a significantly lower quality of life and higher levels of both anxiety and depression than their male partners (Zurlo, Della Volta, & Vallone, 2018). Among IVF patients, 30 to 44 percent of females and 10 percent of males received a psychiatric diagnosis (Noorbala, Ramezanzadeh, Abedinia, & Naghizadeh, 2008; Volgsten, Svanberg, Ekselius, Lundkvist, & Poromaa, 2008), and another alarming finding is that 39 percent of women undergoing unsuccessful fertility treatment over the course of eighteen months met the criteria for major depressive disorder (Hoff, Crawford, & Mersereau, 2018).

Women of color are overrepresented among people with infertility but are underrepresented among those who receive medical services. Tragically, marginalized women are more likely to receive medical care that impedes fertility, such as sterilization, and are less likely to receive care that facilitates fertility (King & Meyer, 1997). Szkupinski-Quiroga (2002) found that infertile women of color experienced infertility not only as a challenge to personal identity but also as an affront to their ethnic and cultural identity that celebrates the family. The media often represents the infertility patient as a middle-class white woman, implicitly depicting poor and nonwhite women as hyperfertile and not afflicted with infertility (Bell 2009, 2010; Sandelowski & de Lacey, 2002). These practices are consistent with the "implicit fertility policy" (King & Meyer, 1997) of the United States, which discourages births among poor women and women of color as it promotes births among white and middle-class women (Bell 2009, 2010; Sandelowski & de Lacey 2002). These disturbing patterns not only withhold medical services from women of color and poor white women suffering from infertility but also reflect social values about who deserves to be a mother.

Infertility is defined as the inability to conceive after twelve consecutive months of unprotected intercourse (Psaros et al., 2015). The term *infertility* is broad and, for the purposes of this chapter, is generally categorized as primary or first-line infertility and secondary infertility. Primary or first-line infertility applies to cases where no prior conception or full-term pregnancy had resulted in a live birth. First-line infertility includes all conditions leading couples to abandon the quest for a biological child, including but not limited to endometriosis, pelvic inflammatory disease, chlamydia, hormonal disorders, genetic anomalies, cancer, ovulation problems, pregnancy loss, advanced maternal age, unexplained infertility, the ability to conceive but the inability to carry a child to term, and male infertility. Secondary infertility is defined by at least one successful pregnancy followed by a failure to conceive, carry, or deliver a live birth (Gibson & Myers, 2000). Women are much more likely than their male partners to seek out mental health services while seeking or undergoing medical interventions for infertility, though their efforts are not often successful (Greil, Slauson-Blevins, & McQuillan, 2010; Psaros et al., 2015; Wischmann, 2008). Further, it is uncommon for women with infertility to receive referrals for individual, group, or couples counseling from their physicians (Greil et al., 2010).

Infertility may result from a wide range of causes. In 2015, the breakdown in etiology of infertility cases in the United States was reported to be 40 percent attributed to female factors, 40 percent to male factors, and 20 percent to a combination or unexplained etiology (Centers for Disease Control and Prevention, 2019). The cause of infertility will largely dictate the treatment protocol, which can include but is not limited to medication (oral or intramuscular injections), surgery to attempt to restore fertility, and assisted reproductive therapy (ART), which commonly involves forms of intrauterine insemination (IUI) and in vitro fertilization (IVF) (Chazan & Kushnir, 2019).

At least 17 percent of reproductive-aged women in the United States have sought medical attention for infertility (Chandra, Copen, & Stephen, 2014). Medical treatment protocols are invasive and often painful, lasting from months to years, and can involve early morning monitoring, appointments at the doctor, daily injections, blood sampling, and laparoscopic surgery. Infertile couples subject themselves to a stressful regime of programmed sexual relations and monitoring that places a burden on their everyday life and adversely affects their sexual, emotional, social, physical, and even intellectual life. Interpersonal communication and connection are strained. The costs are high, and failure can occur at any phase (Galst, 2018).

The experience of primary infertility is lifelong and is felt at each stage of life, such as pregnancy, giving birth, and having grandchildren. Fertility, also known as the fecundity rate, is strongest between the ages of twenty and thirty, with the natural fertility rate each month at about 25 percent. Interestingly, birth rates are dropping for eighteen- to twenty-four-year-old females as many are postponing starting their own families for schooling or careers until they are in their thirties and forties. The fertility rate dips below 10 percent after age thirty-five, and at age forty the chances of conceiving are 5 percent. By age forty, a woman is more than five times likely to have a stillbirth than a woman under thirty-five, and the risk of miscarriage is greater than the chance of a live birth. Despite the risks, the prevalence of giving birth later in life has increased for women. From 2000 to 2014, the proportion of first births to women aged thirty-five and over increased 23 percent (Mathews & Hamilton, 2016).

Infertility is a deeply distressing experience and often is perceived as a daunting departure from the expected developmental trajectory of adulthood. The infertility process from suspicion to diagnosis to treatment takes place over an extended period of time and is disruptive for couples. This time period introduces repeated fluctuations between hope and delusion, loss of control, low self-esteem, inability to plan for the future, difficult social interactions, and pivotal changes in identity and worldview. Infertile couples are pressured to use their resources, knowledge, and skills to address infertility challenges and at the same time preserve their individual and relational quality of life (Zurlo et al., 2018).

Based on the literature, infertility reflects an unprecedented opportunity for counselors to address the needs of *all* women and couples struggling with infertility. Counselors are uniquely poised to address the social isolation, regret, grief, and loss related to miscarriages, stillbirths, and the realization that an aspiring mother will never be able to conceive or carry her own biological child (Solinger, 2005).

FOSTERING HOPE PROGRAM

The Fostering Hope Program is a six-week, ninety-minute evidence-based psychoeducational support group. It was developed as a weekly group intervention for women and their partners struggling with infertility and considering adoption or foster care through the county. Participants in this group were heterosexual couples; however, the applicability of the group to diverse couples is addressed in a later section in this chapter. Women attended the first three weeks in order to build an alliance, receive psychoeducation about infertility, and create a safe space for processing their emotions with other women also diagnosed with first-line infertility. Men joined the group for the last three sessions. The interventions included psychoeducation, health education, communication training, mindfulness, and spousal support with the goals of decreasing isolation and infertility-induced emotional and psychological stress and increasing hope, positivity, mindfulness, and self-care. The group worked on reimagining their families by reflecting on the meaning of parenthood, revisiting family decision making, boosting communication, and strengthening coping and problem-solving skills. At the end of the program, couples were able to discuss alternative options to building their own families, including fostering and adopting children or remaining childless. The program was approved by the local university institutional review board and the county. Following is a detailed outline of the Fostering Hope group protocol.

Isolation and Connection

During the first session, infertility was introduced to the female participants as a "major life crisis" that is often accompanied by social and relational isolation. The aim of this group session was to decrease isolation and nurture an open and healing environment and community. Facilitators encouraged group members to share experiences and acknowledge their infertility, as well as to develop skills to combat the ongoing pattern of isolation from friends and family outside of the group.

Infertility often disrupts one's self-image, body image, self-esteem, and concept of normative sexuality. It can reintroduce unresolved issues from the past, prevent healing for the future, and result in personal and social isolation. Facilitators presented (1) definitions for primary and secondary infertility, (2) infertility base rates, and (3) the incidence and description of "silent grief" that often accompanies infertility.

The group discussed different forms of isolation that occur with infertility, including romantic, relational, familial, community, or cultural isolation, which can lead to depression, anxiety, or simply avoidance. Also, the decision to stop attempting to conceive is quite disruptive, pressing women to scrutinize their gender identity in regard to motherhood, womanhood, what family looks like, and a range of related issues (Lockerbie, 2014). In closing, the group facilitators invited each participant to share something that resonated from the evening's discussion.

Anger and Regret

The session began with members reflecting on the previous session's discussion and how they were affected throughout the week. Anger and regret were then introduced as discussion topics with the goal of increasing awareness of emotions and identifying anger as a primary or secondary emotion. Often the loss of someone or something can feel unfair, and individuals can experience anger, resentment, or regret. Examples include receiving uncontrollable results of pregnancy failures and medical outcomes, feeling "robbed" of jointly conceiving or parenting a child, or missing the emotional or physical gratification of pregnancy.

Sometimes, people attribute blame for the injustice to a source such as God, a doctor, a partner, or even themselves. Facilitators discussed with the group that placing blame is a way to transfer feelings onto another source in order to alleviate sorrow or loss. For many, working through grief is an exercise in forgiveness or identifying their emotions. Unresolved anger can lead to a pattern of negative behavior that may damage relationships, careers, and mental and physical health. It is important to learn how to manage feelings and develop tools for effectively resolving and working through anger.

Gottman's "anger iceberg" was introduced as a visual way for the group to understand the complexity of anger and to explore primary and secondary emotions (Gottman & Gottman, 2019). Using the metaphor of an iceberg, members discussed how it is easy to see a person's anger but more difficult to see the many other emotions hidden beneath the surface, such as disappointment, embarrassment, loneliness, depression, or fear. In closing the group, members were asked what they learned during the session, including how they express their anger and whether they see anger as related to other (secondary) emotions. Group members were encouraged to notice their feelings throughout the week and to practice identifying emotions.

Grief and Loss

This session opened up with members sharing thoughts and emotions from previous sessions. The topic for the session was then introduced: the silent grief and trauma of miscarriages, and what these losses represent to group members. This session emphasized the importance of grieving when confronted with trauma, crisis, loss, or infertility. The discussion began with a review of Kübler-Ross's (1997) five stages of the grieving process, which are denial, anger, bargaining, depression, and acceptance. It was emphasized that each person processes grief uniquely, and one person's progression may differ from that of their partner. For example, some people accept loss as a normal and natural part of their life. Others seek substitutions for the loss, choose to isolate themselves, or try to find control in other situations.

Silent grief was a pivotal discussion point and was defined as a reaction to the loss of something that was never present to begin with. This is a powerful topic, as silent grief relates strongly to the isolation that accompanies infertility. In dominant Western cultures, most losses are tangible. For example, if someone loses their house to a fire or loses a three-year-old child, there is a social standard where family and friends lend support. Since the loss of fertility is not tangible, this may result in family and friends not lending much-needed support. Loved ones may even avoid the issue because they are unsure how to be supportive. The couple is then left to grieve alone and in silence.

Six losses related to infertility were discussed with members: (1) genetic continuity, (2) potential children with life partner, (3) self-esteem, (4) security, (5) control over one's body, and (6) emotional gratification of pregnancy and other childbearing experiences such as parenting and breastfeeding. With these forms of loss in mind, participants were invited to write a letter to someone or something that had deeply impacted their infertility journey. Examples included an unborn or lost child, their body for failing them, a doctor that let them down, or a partner. Following the letter-writing exercise, members were invited to share their experience of writing the letter with the group and were given the option to read their letter aloud. The goal of this exercise was to empower members to give voice to their grief, how it is related to their loss of dreams and hopes for having biological children, and to recognize that they are not alone in their infertility grief or survival. Bringing closure to the group, a loving-kindness meditation and visualization were offered.

Expectations and Hope for Family Planning

At the fourth session, facilitators welcomed group members, shared introductions, and oriented the women's partners into the group. A fishbowl technique was utilized to facilitate the discussion and to distinguish the speaking roles from (nonspeaking) observer roles during the discussion. First, women in the group and one facilitator form an inner circle. An outer circle surrounding them was formed with their partners and one facilitator. The members of the outside circle were asked to remain silent and simply relax, listen, and observe what their partners had to say. The inner circle members were invited to summarize the themes of each of the prior three sessions, including what they had learned, what was most powerful for them, and issues they really wanted their partners to hear about. After they had reviewed the previous sessions, the inner facilitator praised them for openly sharing these difficult thoughts and feelings. Then the women were asked to give the same courtesy to their partners and simply relax, listen, and observe.

The outer facilitator guided a discussion on what the men had observed and their reactions to the women sharing such raw emotions and experiences. Once the men's discussion was complete, the women moved their chairs back to create a single large circle with their partners and facilitators. All members had the opportunity to clarify and process what they noticed and heard from their partners and were invited to share their overall experience of the fishbowl activity. The hope of this exercise was for partners to experience increased vulnerability as a couple. Then, with greater emotional closeness, they formed a single cohesive group.

The group discussed desires related to family planning, adoption, or fostering children. Parenting issues that can emerge in the adoption or fostering process were explored. Couples were queried about their expectations for fostering or adopting children with the following questions: What expectations have been placed on you? What expectations have you placed on each other? What expectations need altering?

Societal myths regarding adoption were discussed, including (1) stereotypes regarding birth parents, (2) assumptions that adopted children are less emotionally healthy, (3) adoption as the second best alternative, (4) parents' struggles to love adopted children that are not genetically linked to them, and (5) families that choose adoption not being "real" families. Couples then discussed how they might empower themselves to become adoptive parents. What would it take for them to feel confident in setting healthy boundaries for their adopted or foster children?

The session concluded with a discussion surrounding the couples' hopes for their family's future, recognizing that infertility and adoption are lifelong journeys and commitments and one does not simply substitute one for the other. With this in mind, couples explored ways to increase their confidence as future parents. Couples were challenged to consider the possibility of holding their infertility story and adoptive story at the same time. What might they hope for? What would they like their family story to look like moving forward?

Partner Support and Communication

This group session focused on developing open and healthy communication and building mutual support between partners dealing with infertility. Understanding the gender differences in how infertility is experienced and processed and its impact on the partnership or marriage were highlighted. The disruption infertility had on couples' communication and relationship satisfaction was discussed, and couples were encouraged to communicate their needs to their partners in clear and adaptive ways. Psychoeducation on communication was presented, members reflected on current communication patterns with their partners, and then they identified areas in need of additional work. Couples were encouraged to continue monitoring their communication, offer support to each other, and set aside time to refine communication skills that were targeted during the session.

Reimagining partnership and marriage are crucial when dreams and desires for the relationship have been shattered. Facilitators reminded couples that commitment to their partners came before choosing to start a family together, beginning infertility treatment, or starting the adoption process. Fondness, admiration, love, and respect between partners was the foundation that prompted them to envision starting this family. Couples were encouraged to take a moment and reflect on what initially brought them together and reaffirm to one another their relationship.

Facilitators brought attention to how infertility subjects couples to stressful and continual doctor visits, pharmacological treatments, programmed sexual relations, psychological screenings, and surgical interventions that place a burden on their everyday life. All of these stressors can affect their emotional, social, physical, and intellectual life and introduce difficulties in their relationship.

Facilitators highlighted how men and women experience infertility differently and introduced research findings that 49 percent of the female participants cited infertility as the most upsetting experience of their lives, whereas only 15 percent of the male participants cited infertility as upsetting (McQueeney, Stanton, & Sigmon, 1997). In other words, men and women experience different emotions, which can be a source of confusion, isolation, anger, and resentment between couples dealing with infertility, who also face the possibility of not sharing biological children. Developing a shared vision of their infertility is paramount for couples. This requires them to accept their own experiences of infertility and that of their partners, without judgment or resentment.

Creating opportunities to listen and accept their partner's needs, worries, and pain without trying to "fix it" is the first step to fostering effective communication. Facilitators also acknowledged the complexity involved when fertile partners sacrifice their own fertility and freely choose to support their infertile partner in adopting, fostering, or remaining childless. Facilitators encouraged couples to acknowledge these significant sacrifices and decisions in their relationships.

Couples were then asked the following questions: Keeping partner support in mind, how has this infertility journey affected your relationship? What do you think you need from one another? How do you receive and give love? How do you communicate as a couple about your infertility? How do you acknowledge the sacrifices that each of you have made in relation to infertility?

Mindfulness, Self-Compassion, and Self-Care

Mindfulness teaches a person to become aware of their feelings in a nonjudgmental way and to deal more effectively with stress, pain, illness, psychological distress, and the demands of daily life. It provides ways to respond to stressful situations in an emotionally regulated, calm, and "mindful" manner. An evidence-based method of mindfulness called mindfulness-based stress reduction (MBSR) has been successfully applied to individuals with a number of medical issues to decrease stress levels, anxiety, and depression (Kabat-Zinn, 1990), which are common feelings associated with infertility. Women with infertility often experience invasive medical procedures, deep grief, severe distress, dissatisfaction with physical functioning, and feelings that their body has failed them. The session began with a guided meditation to introduce mindfulness.

Self-compassion and self-care exercises were then introduced and practiced. Self-compassion calls one to practice kindness and understanding when confronted with personal failings. Facilitators led a discussion regarding three components of self-compassion: (1) the flexibility to treat oneself with kindness and compassion in the face of struggles rather than with self-criticism, (2) recognizing that individuals are not alone in their suffering as suffering is a common part of humanity, (3) the process of mindfully reflecting on thoughts and feelings in order to avoid overidentification with negative emotions (Neff, 2019).

Coping with infertility is a physically and emotionally taxing experience. Self-care is essential to finding balance and peace in the midst of distressing life situations. Facilitators generated and discussed positive self-care techniques to reasonably adopt in daily life. Facilitators initiated a closing discussion on how infertility spans the lifetime, then prompted members to consider and share how mindfulness may assist them in their infertility journey.

CULTURAL CONSIDERATIONS

Creating a safe space for women and couples with infertility to share themselves fully is key to addressing infertility. Especially salient are family and cultural prescriptions and wishes, spoken and unspoken, about bringing children into the family. This requires some background knowledge about the culture, customs, and social norms that have been passed down in the family from one generation to another. Below are a few examples related to Aretta and Lucas.

While Nigerian and Mexican cultures are clearly distinct, both are generally ordered by gender and age, highly value family, and hold many family expectations. Both cultures are traditionally patriarchal, with extended family members having varying levels of acculturation, such as language, immigration history, and adherence to traditional culture, yet holding more influence than usual in comparison to most American families. Children are very important to Nigerian and Mexican families because parents believe that their children will support them in their old age. Family relationships are mostly guided by a strict system of privileged, male seniority where men have the most say in family matters. Historically, male members of the family mattered more because of their rights to both family inheritance and extend their family lineage and name. In Nigerian culture, women typically bear the blame for childlessness in marriage. In a recent study, women in Nigeria who did not fulfill expectations of motherhood through having children of their own were more likely to be ostracized from their community than men. Infertile women were often regarded as immoral, suspected of having undergone clandestine abortions and blamed for their childlessness. Nigerian women who fail to bear any children could be divorced, even if there was no evidence that it was the woman who was the infertile partner in the marriage (Ibisomi & Mudege, 2014). Infertility and acceptance of nonbiologically related offspring generate anxiety and confusion in all levels of the family system.

Finally, acculturation, or the balancing of two cultures while adapting to the U.S. culture, was identified as a source of strength and creativity for couples planning their families beyond infertility. Aretta and Lucas were successful at navigating and setting clear boundaries between them and their families of origin to give Aretta the respect and space she and Lucas needed to plan their family beyond infertility. These are some of the most salient issues addressed by Aretta and Lucas in navigating patriarchal values, family legacy, generativity, and the continuity of their family system.

ETHICAL CONSIDERATIONS

The presentation of an infertility diagnosis can vary widely for each woman. Addressing the clinical needs of women and couples with infertility always requires adherence to the Codes of Ethics of the American Counseling Association (ACA, 2014) and the American Mental Health Counselors Association (AMHCA, 2015). Below are some ethical issues and complexities that may arise in working with infertility.

Medical knowledge of infertility diagnoses, treatments, and psychosocial repercussions is vital to effectively addressing the needs of this population. Establishing a strong therapeutic alliance with clients is key. Advanced preparation for meeting with clients is required and should include collaborating with physicians and reviewing the clients' medical chart. This will also reduce the potential to retraumatize clients by overquestioning them about their infertility history and treatment.

Screening clients with a thoughtful and clear criterion for group membership is key to building a safe, cohesive, and effective group for members to explore infertility in an open and vulnerable manner. Including women with various forms of infertility such as first-line and second-line infertility can be iatrogenic and is not recommended.

Counselors must increase their awareness and knowledge about cultural traditions, attitudes, and biases related to infertility. Differing cultural and familial expectations and levels of support should be explored with clients. In working with clients, it is important for counselors to simultaneously hold onto both their clients' infertility status and their deep desire to create a family, as one does not preclude the other. Remaining open to a range of experiences, emotions, and possibilities for building families beyond infertility is essential.

Counselors must respect and understand how one's religious or spiritual beliefs inform and make meaning of infertility. Most religions view children as a central part of forming one's family, and faced with infertility, individuals might begin bargaining with God or question their faith and destiny in the midst of pregnancy failures. It is important to be prepared to address the pronatalist values and social norms of many religions, which can lead to feelings of shame and isolation for infertile individuals (Chan, 2018; Collins, Kim, & Feske, 2012).

Infertility affects one's entire lifespan. Counselors need to recognize and acknowledge the pain and isolation of a woman with infertility who attends many friends' and family members' rituals around pregnancy, including parties, holidays, school events, sports, and becoming grandparents, while she remains infertile. Having a keen awareness of these issues and providing support and coping skills to an individual or couple are critical during stressful and discouraging times.

As clients work through their emotions regarding infertility, it is important to acknowledge that adoption will not cure infertility. It is unfair and unwise to place biological expectations on a nonbiological child, especially a child who has been exposed to trauma in utero or after birth. Family planning beyond infertility can look quite different for each person and each family. Providing permission for individuals to mourn their infertility while allowing a space for joy with the placement of a child is complex but so important for parents and their child(ren).

ADVOCACY OPPORTUNITIES AND REFLECTIONS

Women and their partners are suffering alone and silently with infertility, with 17 percent of women seeking fertility meeting the clinical criteria for major depressive disorder. Marginalized, poor women, and communities of color are at particular risk, suffering from infertility without receiving medical or psychological care. And yet many of these women and their partners are interested and motivated to pursue these services. Given the counseling profession's values of social justice and cultural diversity, counselors are in a unique position to bring awareness, advocacy, and counseling to clinically underserved women and couples with infertility.

Women and their partners need an integrated, multidisciplinary team approach where physicians and clinical counselors coordinate care in the best interest of individuals with infertility. Counseling referrals at the outset of a medical diagnosis of infertility should be a standard part of the medical treatment protocol. Referrals to counselors who are knowledgeable about the medical etiologies, available treatments, and risks associated with infertility are recommended. Developing a strong collaboration between the medical treatment team and counselor is critical to help patients traverse their family-building journey during and beyond infertility (Galst, 2018).

The Fostering Hope Program raised many issues about the lack of information and opportunities for women, young and old, to learn about and openly discuss female reproductive and sexual health. A woman's age is the most critical factor in infertility, and as more women are delaying childbirth as they attend school and launch careers, the tensions between fertility windows and career opportunities are rising. Yet many women are not prepared to make these decisions or pursue other options to start a family. Many reproductive options exist that were not available a generation ago, including freezing eggs during the most fertile years, surrogacy, egg donors, embryo donation, sperm donors, open and closed adoptions, international adoption, and foster care. Again, there is a pressing need for counselors to offer groups and individual consultation on sexual health, female reproduction, and infertility.

Fostering Hope represents a call to counselors to provide strength-based and evidence-based group treatment where affordable and accessible groups are offered widely to individuals and couples in diverse communities. It is our hope that more groups will be developed where all individuals, including LGBTQIA+ (lesbian, gay, bisexual, transgender, queer, questioning, intersex, asexual, and others such as nonbinary and pansexual identities) and their partners can communicate, develop coping skills, and explore options for their families beyond infertility. We have presented many emerging themes and strategies for counselors to foster hope for *all* women and couples facing infertility.

CASE VIGNETTE WRAP-UP: ARETTA

The group's ability to validate and normalize Aretta and Lucas's shared experiences were an integral part of their healing and meeting their previously stated goals. Their religious backgrounds and beliefs came into play while another woman in the group was sharing her deep anger toward her own husband because he did not share equally in her pain and loss. She brought up the story of Hannah from the Bible, who was devastated about her own infertility. Hannah's husband replied to her, "Am I not enough?" While this woman was speaking, the facilitators noticed Aretta's visceral reaction and inquired if she would like to share her experience. Aretta simply faced Lucas and asked him, "Have I ever made you feel this way, like you are not enough?" He replied, "At times, yes." They both became tearful, and Aretta assured Lucas that he was more than enough for her and promised that she would work on continuing to remind him about how much he meant to her. The couple committed to working on their communication skills and reporting at each session how they were progressing.

Following the fishbowl technique (described above), Aretta and Lucas arranged their chairs so they could turn toward each other to maintain eye contact and physical contact, resulting in an intensified vulnerability when expressing their emotions. Later, a conversation regarding anger as a secondary emotion led to important insights about one another. Aretta identified that much of her hurt and disappointment was expressed as anger. She stated, "I never thought of anger as a secondary emotion and that my anger is really a deep-rooted hurt!" Lucas replied humorously, "So I guess you're not just the Hulk."

While the women processed and shared their own struggles with silent grief and isolation, the topic of infertility was introduced. Manifesting the strength to own their infertility was a powerful moment, giving permission to one another to use whatever term (for infertility) was most consistent with their values. Aretta felt empowered by the group to own her infertility and to share her condition with her close friends in a direct, calm, and vulnerable manner.

After working on communication and support, the couple decided to share their diagnosis with their families and, in a unified way, state their decision to pursue adoption. Acknowledging the cultural expectations and judgments surrounding infertility, Lucas expressed his commitment and support for his wife in sharing their news and that he would stand by and protect her if needed throughout this process. They both looked forward to adopting children, recognizing that it would not cure their infertility.

Lucas and Aretta grew together as a couple and realized their mutual pain and disappointment regarding the infertility. Throughout the course of the group, the couple developed an understanding that they process pain differently. At the same time, they learned that if they can communicate their individual experiences to one another in a healthy and productive manner, they will be better equipped to support one another moving forward.

REFERENCES

American Counseling Association. (2014). Code of ethics. Retrieved from https://www.counseling.org/knowledge-center/ethics#2014code

American Mental Health Counselors Association. (2015). Code of ethics. Retrieved from https://www.amhca.org/publications/ethics

Bell, Ann V. (2009). It's way out of my league: Low income women's experiences of medicalized infertility. *Gender and Society, 23*, 688–709.

Bell, Ann V. (2010). Beyond (financial) accessibility: Inequalities within the medicalisation of infertility. *Sociology of Health & Illness, 32*, 631–46.

Centers for Disease Control and Prevention. (2019). Reproductive health. Retrieved from https://www.cdc.gov/reproductivehealth/data_stats/index.htm

Chandra, A., Copen, C. E., & Stephen, E. H. (2014). Infertility service use in the United States: Data from the National Survey of Family Growth, 1982–2010. *National Health Statistics Report, 73*, 1–21.

Chazan, L., & Kushnir, T. (2019). Losses and gains of psychosocial resources: Effects on stress among women undergoing infertility treatments and participating in social network systems. *Psychiatric Quarterly, 2019*, 1–16. https://doi-org.sandiego.idm.oclc.org/10.1007/s11126-019-09661-0

Collins, S. C., Kim, S., & Chan, E. (2018). Racial and ethnic differences in the utilization of prayer and clergy counseling by infertile US women desiring pregnancy. *Journal of Religion and Health, 57*(6), 2230–40. doi: 10.1007/s11126-019-09661-0

Engel, G. L. (1977). The need for a new medical model: A challenge for biomedicine. *Science, 196*(4286), 129–36. doi: 10.1126/science.847460

Feske, M. C. (2012). Rachel's lament: The impact of infertility and pregnancy loss upon the religious faith of ordinary Christians. *Journal of Pastoral Theology, 22*(1). doi:10.1179/jpt.2012.22.1.003

Galst, J. P. (2018). The elusive connection between stress and infertility: A research review with clinical implications. *Journal of Psychotherapy Integration, 28*(1), 1–13. doi: 10.1037/int0000081

Gibson, D. M., & Myers, J. E. (2000). Gender and infertility: A relational approach to counseling women. *Journal of Counseling & Development, 78*(4), 400–410.

Gottman, J., & Gottman, J. (2019). *Clinician's toolkit*. Seattle, WA: Gottman Institute.

Greil, A. L., Slauson-Blevins, K., & McQuillan, J. (2010). The experience of infertility: A review of recent literature. *Sociology of Health & Illness, 32*(1), 140–62. http://doi.org/10.1111/j.1467-9566.2009.01213

Hoff, H. S., Crawford, N. M., & Mersereau, J. E. (2018). Screening for psychological conditions in infertile women: Provider perspectives. *Journal of Women's Health, 27*(4), 503–9. doi:10.1089/jwh.2017.6332

Ibisomi, L., & Mudege, N. N. (2014). Childlessness in Nigeria: Perceptions and acceptability. *Culture, Health & Sexuality, 16*(1), 61–75.

Kabat-Zinn, J. (1990). *Full catastrophe living: The program of the stress reduction clinic at the University of Massachusetts Medical Center*. New York, NY: Delta.

King, L., & Meyer, M. H. (1997). The politics of reproductive benefits: U.S. insurance coverage of contraceptive and infertility treatments. *Gender & Society, 11*, 8–30.

Koszycki, D., Bisserbe, J., Blier, P., Bradwejn, J., & Markowitz, J. (2012). Interpersonal psychotherapy versus brief supportive therapy for depressed infertile women: First pilot randomized controlled trial. *Archives of Women's Mental Health, 15*(3), 193–201. doi: 10.1007/s00737-012-0277-z

Kübler-Ross, E. (1997). *On death and dying*. New York, NY: Scribner Classics.

Lockerbie, S. (2014). Infertility, adoption and metaphorical pregnancies. *Anthropologica, 56*(2), 463–71.

Mathews, T. J., & Hamilton, B. E. (2016). Mean age of mothers is on the rise: United States, 2000–2014. Centers for Disease Control and Prevention.

McQueeney, D. A., Stanton, A. L., & Sigmon, S. (1997). Efficacy of emotion-focused and problem-focused group therapies for women with fertility problems. *Journal of Behavioral Medicine, 20*(4), 313–31. doi: 10.1023/A:1025560912766

Neff, K. (2019). Self-compassion. Center for Mindful Self-Compassion. Retrieved from https://self-compassion.org/the-three-elements-of-self-compassion-2/

Noorbala, A. A., Ramezanzadeh, F., Abedinia, N., & Naghizadeh, M. M. (2008). Psychiatric disorders among infertile and fertile women. *Social Psychiatry and Psychiatric Epidemiology, 44*(7), 587–91. doi: 10.1007/s00127-008-0467-1

Psaros, C., Kagan, L., Shifren, J. L., Willett, J., Jacquart, J., Alert, M. D., . . . Park, E. R. (2015). Mind–body group treatment for women coping with infertility: A pilot study. *Journal of Psychosomatic Obstetrics & Gynecology, 36*(2), 75–83. doi: 10.3109/0167482X.2014.989983

Sandelowski, M., & de Lacey, S. (2002). The uses of a "disease." *Infertility around the Globe: New Thinking on Childlessness, Gender, and Reproductive Technologies*, 33–51.

Solinger, R. (2005). Choice and coercion: Birth control, sterilization, and abortion in public health and welfare [Review]. *Journal of Interdisciplinary History, 38*(2), 309–10. doi: 10.1162/jinh.2007.38.2.309

Sormunen, T., Aanesen, A., Fossum, B., Karlgren, K., & Westerbotn, M. (2018). Infertility-related communication and coping strategies among women affected by primary or secondary infertility. *Journal of Clinical Nursing, 27*(1–2), e335–e344. doi:10.1111/jocn.13953

Szkupinski-Quiroga, S. (2002). *Disrupted bodies: The effect of infertility on racialized identities.* San Francisco, CA: University of California, San Francisco.

Volgsten, H., Svanberg, A. S., Ekselius, L., Lundkvist, O., & Poromaa, I. S. (2008). Prevalence of psychiatric disorders in infertile women and men undergoing in vitro fertilization treatment. *Human Reproduction, 23*(9), 2056–63. doi: 10.1093/humrep/den154

Wischmann, T. (2008). Implications of psychosocial support in infertility: A critical appraisal. *Journal of Psychosomatic Obstetrics & Gynecology, 29*(2), 83–90.

Zurlo, M. C., Della Volta, M. F. C., & Vallone, F. (2018). Predictors of quality of life and psychological health in infertile couples: The moderating role of duration of infertility. *Quality of Life Research: An International Journal of Quality of Life Aspects of Treatment, Care & Rehabilitation, 27*(4), 945–54.

Chapter Eleven

Counseling Women Facing Contemporary Family Challenges

Elizabeth R. O'Brien

CASE VIGNETTE: ELEANOR

Eleanor is a forty-three-year-old female who identifies as a Caucasian bisexual woman. She has been married to a man since her late twenties and has a ten-year-old daughter, Julie. In her late twenties, Eleanor was diagnosed with schizoaffective disorder; for many years, she managed the symptoms of her illness well and was able to engage in work and home life with only occasional interruptions caused by hallucinations that required hospitalization. In her late thirties, her illness became increasingly unmanageable, requiring frequent hospitalizations and changes in medications, and it resulted in Eleanor having to cease working and go on long-term disability. As the frequency of Eleanor's symptoms increase, she struggles with a sense of self—the guilt and shame that she is experiencing regarding how her illness is affecting her family and increasing her depression and passive suicidal ideation.

Eleanor was referred after her last hospitalization to a counselor, Carmen, to begin working on self-stabilization and to help her negotiate the family-relational issues that have emerged from her illness and affect the family system. She attends the first appointment and is somewhat reticent to speak. She reports that she is feeling stable on her medications and that her hallucinations have quieted, but she is still sometimes unsure if she is fully grounded in reality or if she is experiencing hallucinations. When she questions her reality in the therapy room, she checks in with Carmen to confirm her experiences are real. When Eleanor is asked about her social supports and her family during the initial assessment questionnaire, she becomes emotional. She states that she is struggling to connect with her family as she once again begins stabilizing on her new medications. She reports the family's income is lower since she is on disability now, and her husband is working overtime at his job to make up the shortfalls. He has become increasingly distant and has mentioned that perhaps it would be better if he and Eleanor consider some time apart or file a formal separation.

She also reports that her daughter, Julie, is experiencing high levels of anxiety toward her mother's hospitalizations. Julie's anxiety, and some students' knowledge of her mother's "problems," has resulted in bullying at school. In addition, Eleanor reports that she and her husband were checking Julie's iPad and realized their daughter has downloaded pornography, and the content suggested to them that she is bi-curious. Although Eleanor reports that she has no issue with this as she self-identifies as bisexual, she is concerned about how to speak with her daughter since Julie's anxiety is so high and she cries when confronted with any of these subjects. Eleanor finishes her story and looks to Carmen for help in untangling this web.

* * *

According to the Census Bureau (2010), men and women are delaying marriage or cohabitation and women are delaying having children. The average age of mothers at the birth of their first child was twenty-six, and approximately 25 percent of mothers were thirty years or older at the birth of their first child. Overall, census data reveals the following trends: Americans are having children later in life, having fewer children than in previous decades, and are planning the conception of their children at an increasing rate. These changes can have an impact on the family unit and functioning, as well as the types of interventions that are useful for women seeking counseling.

The abovementioned trends also mean that the range of children's ages and their temporal place in family life cycle can be far more variable than it has been in the past. Mothers who delay childbirth or adoption until later in life may have very young children in their forties, whereas mothers who had children earlier in life may have older teenagers or have launched their children at a trajectory that leaves them with empty nests in their midforties to early fifties. The aforementioned is a descriptive range that does not include variety of familial combinations that exist in between these two ends of the spectrum. Each family presents with its own set of circumstances that must be contextualized so that helpers can tailor interventions to the needs of individuals and families seeking counseling.

THE FAMILY LIFE CYCLE

Understanding individual development is an integral part to working effectively with individuals and families. Developmental processes are important in understanding how clients function in their world and allows the helper to conceptualize ways individuals may not be functioning optimally. Individual stage models were created so that professionals in a variety of settings could utilize a common lexicon to understand how individuals develop (physically, cognitively, socially, etc.), identify behaviors that may be indicative of slower or faster development, and use common benchmarks to determine particular stages that most people move through across the lifespan. Erikson's psychosocial development model is one example and articulates eight stages throughout the lifespan to describe individuals' personality development in relation to the self and society (Erikson, 1968).

Although individual development models are useful when working with all clients, it is imperative that helpers have a working knowledge of the family life cycle and their specialized iterations (such as the single-parent family life cycle), as these conceptualizations can be very informative in understanding how a family is functioning in relation to the members' developmental levels. In its original conception, the family life cycle was a six-stage cycle that illustrated the major transitions a family experienced and attempted to explain the overlay of individuals' personal development that occurred along with the overall development of the family unit (McGoldrick, Carter, & Garcia-Preto, 2011). The original family life cycle model is systemic in nature and based on a Caucasian, heterosexual, two-parent, nuclear family.

The overarching limitation of the original model is its lack of applicability to families that look different from the traditional nuclear unit. Now there are many more family life cycle models that are able to guide helpers and families seeking to understand the nature of their development in relationship to their unique circumstances (Hill, 1986). Helpers should seek research and family life cycle models that more closely mirror the experiences of their clients so that issues presented in counseling are understood in the appropriate context and interventions are tailored to the unique needs of the presenting individual or family (McGoldrick, 1992). For example, Donaldson (2000) completed a qualitative study on midlife lesbian mothers who were negotiating their roles as parents with the intersectionality of their minority status (or statuses). The article highlights specialized considerations that counselors will likely want to consider when working with same-sex parents as they negotiate mainstream culture while raising children.

Parental Separation and Divorce

Parental separation and divorce mark the end of one iteration of family and a new dynamic for all the members involved. According to data from the Centers for Disease Control (CDC), both marriage and divorce rates in the United States have declined in the last twenty years (CDC, 2002b). The CDC issued another report in 2002 that focused on a survey of women regarding marriage, cohabitation, divorce, and remarriage, and found that approximately 54 percent of women remarried approximately five years after a divorce, and 75 percent of women remarried after ten years (CDC, 2002a). Although more recent national data regarding remarriage rates is lacking, one could extrapolate from these reports that remarriage rates for women are still relatively high, particularly among white and Hispanic women.

Parental separation and subsequent divorce can have consequences for all members of the family. For adults within the family, it means the loss of supports and stability that a two-parent household can provide, such as time, monetary resources, and shared responsibilities. For children, this can result in a fracturing of familial relationships and bonds with one or both biological parents, as well as sibling relationships. This is not to say that there cannot be benefits to separation and divorce in families; families of a "good divorce," where parents engage in cooperative coparenting, tend to have children with fewer behavioral issues and maintain strong relationships with their biological fathers (Amato, Kane, & Spencer, 2011).

Blended Families

Given the aforementioned statistics regarding remarriage, it makes sense that blended families comprise approximately 15 percent of families with children seventeen and younger living in the United States (Pew Research Center, 2018). Blended families can have many configurations; however, they are typically formed by two partners, with one or both bringing children into the newly formed family. In the past, this may have been due to the death of a spouse, although in more recent history it is usually due to marital separation and divorce. Additionally, the constellation can further grow if the newly formed couple add their own biological or adoptive children to the family.

Blended families may face challenges in promoting cohesion within the new unit. Adults in blended families may have biological children or may be bringing stepchildren into their family unit. Biological parents of children can feel caught, or triangulated, between the demands of the spouse and their children. The parent–child relationship that predated the newly formed adult relationship can create a sense of safety for the child, but it can also create a barrier for the new couple.

In addition, the biological coparents' relationship has an impact on the blended family. Biological parents who have positive relationships and a strong commitment to cooperative coparenting tend to have more success in their newly formed relationships, as well as in their relationships with their children. Unfortunately, this is more the minority, with more biological parents reporting negative coparenting relationships with their ex-spouses, particularly as it relates to finances, reliability, cooperating, and attitude toward the new partner (Cartwright & Gibson, 2013). Ex-spouses can be viewed as undermining the new family when they are perceived as coercing biological children toward their "side" or create an emotional cutoff from the remarried biological parent.

Stepparents face particular challenges as nonbiological family members who are brought into the family and can face challenges while joining the family unit. Coleman, Ganong, Russell, and Frye-Cox (2015) found that stepchildren classified their stepparents into three distinct categories: claimed, disclaimed, or unclaimed. Claimed stepparents were looked upon as family members, while disclaimed and unclaimed were not. Disclaimed stepparents were those who left the familial relationship through subsequent divorce, and unclaimed stepparents were never looked upon as family members by children. It stands to reason that the type of attachment that children form for stepparents can evolve over time and that stepparents can move from one category to another; it can be particularly important for family cohesion and expressed family happiness if stepchildren are able to "claim" stepparents over time. But the movement from unaccepted to accepted member of the family (if it occurs) can take a large emotional toll on the nonbiological parent and create emotional stress for other members of the family.

The role of stepparent is a difficult one, and adult partners can work together to delineate specific roles for stepparents and set realistic boundaries and expectations for family members. Even with the best intentions, the transition to blend a family is challenging, particularly for the adult women, both mothers and stepmothers.

Stepmothers are not portrayed positively in popular culture, beginning with fairy tales such as Cinderella and Snow White. Although no family is required to buy into this paradigm, the reality is that it is an easily accessible archetype that children and adults in the family system can latch onto when angry or lashing out at the new family member. Negotiating the roles and alliances between biological mothers and stepmothers is particularly difficult for children and former partners. The nuances of the mother–child relationship are quite complicated, and even the most cooperative coparents can experience conflict when a new female figure is introduced into the system.

Making the situation even more complicated, women engaging as stepmothers can often experience the double bind of not being a "real" parent while also experiencing higher levels of expectations from their partners, and from other members of the blended family, to nurture children. Craig, Harvey-Knowles, and Johnson (2012) found that stepmothers felt underprioritized in the blended family, felt ignored when decisions were made that directly affected them, and experienced mixed emotions regarding their partner and stepchildren, particularly feeling anger and guilt over wanting the partner and not necessarily the children that came with the package.

In order to increase successful bonding and blending of the family, the adults in the family unit must have realistic expectations for themselves and those around them. Particularly, adults must commit to behaving as responsibly and as civilly as possible. Moreover, when working with a blended family, a counselor must look outside of the traditional family life cycle and consider an alternative cycle that accommodates the process of a blended family.

Kumar (2017) proposes a revised stage model that can help counselors conceptualize blended families. This stage model highlights many of the changes that are common for blended families and can help counselors and families work through some of the developmental paths that families encounter along the way. These stages are the following:

> (a) separation, divorce, or death; (b) establishment of parenting agreements; (c) re-partnering; (d) pre-blended family counseling to solidify the couple relationship; (e) defining expectations and roles for the new stepparent; (f) having the stepparent meet the ex-spouse, if appropriate; (g) having children and stepparent meet; (h) making any necessary changes to parenting agreements to accommodate the new blended family system; (i) meeting with the children to define boundaries and roles; (j) cohabitation or marriage; and (k) preparation for the possible entrance of new child. (Kumar, 2017)

A preblended or blended family can move through some or all of these stages, skipping some that may not be relevant or pertinent to the particular unit. Although it is ideal to have an entire family come to counseling during familial dissolution and family blending, the reality is that many families are not able to make this commitment for a variety of reasons. Often one member of the family, likely the mother or stepmother, attends counseling sessions and "brings" the rest of the family through stories and problems. Although counselors can encourage family sessions, having techniques that women can use to help themselves and possibly influence the system through their own behaviors can be extremely powerful.

Ultimately, the focus of this counseling should be the individual in session, and assessing the woman's experience of her family is imperative to understanding her thoughts, feelings, and behaviors around the people who are in her life. This can be accomplished by using the structural family therapy technique called family mapping (Minuchin, 1974). Family mapping is similar to Bowen's genogram; however, instead of a large visualization of intergenerational familial relationships, mapping gives counselors and clients a way to map the relationships and power structures that influence family functioning (McGoldrick, Gerson, & Perry, 2008). Of particular importance in blended families is determining the types of boundaries that exist (rigid, clear, diffuse), how power is distributed in the family (how decisions are made, whether emotions or thoughts prevail in power struggles), and the nature of relationships within the family and among its members.

The map is cocreated by counselor and client and can act as a guide for therapeutic talk and interventions when the client is attempting to change how she functions within the family system. For example, a client I worked with realized that when her older daughter she shares custody of comes to visit, her younger daughter begins to escalate and act out. This behavior intensified when the older daughter moved in permanently. After completing a family map that compared the mother's perceptions of her boundaries and relationships with both daughters before they were living in the home together and after, the mother realized that her boundaries with her younger daughter were more rigid and disengaged than they had been when the older daughter was not a permanent fixture in the home. This insight allowed the mother to examine her behavior in her relationship with both of her daughters and how her nonverbal messages were contributing to her younger daughter's escalating behavior, which was a bid for her attention.

Every blended family story is unique and comes with its own set of challenges and opportunities for the new family. The reality is that if counselors can engage in flexible thinking beyond the traditional family life cycle, they have a better chance of meeting family members where they are and asking pertinent questions that can help assess the process and progress of the blended family's formation. Even more important, women can be powerful change agents within their families. In individual counseling, they can understand who and how they are within the dynamics of the family, gain insight into how they contribute to problematic patterns within the family, learn to engage or disengage in communication cycles as needed, learn self-care techniques and process feelings of acceptance and rejection for members of the family, and quite possibly influence the family's willingness to participate in the therapeutic process so that even more change can occur.

SOCIAL INFLUENCES AND THE FAMILY

Regardless of a family's status—intact, single-parent led, blended—social influences are a powerful force that every family must reckon with. The proliferation of information, via the Internet through social media and in the news, inundates people daily with both real information and misinformation. As of 2018, the Pew Research Center states that approximately 69 percent of American adults use some form of social media platform. However, this medium is not the sole means of influencing families; peers, organized religion, community, and extended family also influence the mores and norms in a family and can govern how they function.

A norm is an informal, unwritten rule or guideline for behavior that is expected to be followed; mores are also unwritten, but they are more serious in nature and when violated can result in punishments or sanctions. For example, in the American South, it can be a norm to hold the door open for the person behind you when coming out of a building; although there is no punishment for not doing this, it is generally accepted to be good manners. Conversely, mores violations can create a strong sense of shame and result in serious social sanctions, such as shunning. Examples of mores violations can include adultery, abuse of drugs and subsequent addiction, or stealing.

It is important to consider social influences, such as information or peer pressure, in tandem with the rules that govern the social contracts within a family and outside of the family. These ideas are most succinctly encapsulated in Bronfenbrenner's ecological systems theory, which gives a holistic view of how society and culture can influence an individual's experience of her world. It is through this lens that I will explore some of the social influences that can affect women and their families.

Bullying and Hazing

Bullying and hazing are systemic issues facing children, families, school systems, and communities. Acts of aggression, which are intentional behaviors intended to cause physical or psychological harm, are common, difficult to address, and impact all players involved, including the victim, aggressor(s), bystanders, and interveners. Bullying is characterized by an imbalance of power, intentional acts, and repetition over time (Olweus, 1994). Bullying is intended to ostracize individuals in order to force them outside of the group, whereas hazing is sanctioned acts of aggression intended to create a sense of belonging inside a group.

Both bullying and hazing can take place through multiple mediums, including face-to-face aggression, online intimidation (via email or social media platforms), and inclusion or exclusion from groups (such as teams, cliques, clubs). Bullying and hazing are a part of social life, and in some ways overcoming these types of conflicts is necessary for children to build resiliency and learn negotiation tactics that will help them as they mature. However, when these dynamics are ongoing and individuals are caught within a cycle (particularly with bullying), it is difficult to change the social situation or systemic dynamics in order to extinguish the aggressive behavior.

Recognizing the signs of bullying and hazing is imperative for all caregivers. There is some overlap in the signs and symptoms of both situations; for instance, both bullying and hazing can be characterized by the following: increased or decreased sleep and appetite patterns, decreased energy level, withdrawing or decreased communication with friends and family, unexplained injuries, loss or destruction of personal items, and loss of interest or avoidance of school or other activities (in the case of hazing, for a specific club or team the child is attempting to join) (Stopbullying.gov, 2019).

Counselors should communicate the appropriate ways parents can support their children whom they suspect of being bullied. One of the most powerful tools parents have is that they are the experts in their children's lives. They know their children and can observe subtle changes in behavior; however, the biggest challenge is then to address these changes. One of the byproducts of bullying and hazing is creating a sense of shame in victims, leaving them feeling vulnerable and defensive. Breaking down those walls can be difficult, even in very stable parent–child relationships. In my experience, mothers who are facing these issues with their children can oscillate between overprotection and anger toward the aggressor, which is both justifiable and sometimes counterproductive. Another coping strategy in this situation is to avoid it altogether, telling children that this is a normal part of growing up and that they will need to "toughen up" for the real world. As noted earlier, some conflict is necessary to children's growth, but when adversity becomes insurmountable, children can fall into a danger zone of depression, anxiety, or worse.

Mothers can harness their nurturing tendencies to help their children by engaging with them and the organizations in which the bullying and hazing are taking place. Women are highly relational and can leverage those skills when working with teachers, administrators, and organizational coaches to open discussions that center on understanding the situation from the worldview of their child and their family, then moving outward to the worldview of the individuals who represent the microsystems and mesosystems of the child's world.

An example of this from my professional practice was a mother whose child was bullied due to her physical size. Through therapeutic dialogue, the mother and I discussed how she could best focus her anger at the children and school toward a solution to the problem. The conversation resulted in awareness regarding the mother's anger as a parallel process to the daughter's feelings of anger, shame, and impotence to change the problem. Through conversations, mother and daughter were able to understand that their feelings in this situation were parallel, and they were able to find solace and heal wounds within the shelter of the parent–child relationship. Once they both felt stronger, they were better able to communicate their concerns to school administrators and teachers in an effort to change the situation, not only for the one child but to communicate concerns regarding the systemic oppression that young adolescent girls were experiencing in the school that were not being appropriately addressed by school administrators. It should be noted that changes were slow to come and took place over time; this was not a situation that was resolved in the span of a few weeks but rather took months and a great deal of healing and rebuilding trust between the family and the educational organization.

Peer Pressure

Social, cognitive, and emotional development are heavily influenced by peers beginning in childhood. Particularly in later childhood into middle adolescence, peer reference groups become more influential than family groups and can have both positive and negative consequences for young people. On the positive side, peer groups can help individuals develop social skills and moral reasoning skills; conversely, negative consequences can include joining noncompliant peer groups or social rejection. The consequences of joining noncompliant peer groups can result in behavioral disturbances and maladjustment. Examples of maladjustment include drug and alcohol use, smoking, and increased sexual activity.

Parenting children who are experiencing peer pressure is difficult because developmentally children and adolescence are primed to reject parental influence in favor of peers in order to develop an identity outside of the family system. This is a point at which children are experimenting with their identities and "trying out" different roles and reference groups to discover their authentic selves. The opportunities to engage in novel experiences at this age and stage are plentiful because so many things are new at this point in an adolescent life. Acquiring new experiences at this stage can contribute to impulsive behavior, particularly if young people are attempting to engage in new experiences and sensations that are gratifying (Romer, 2010).

Similar to bullying and hazing, parents and caregivers must be vigilant regarding peer pressure and influence groups. Positive peer pressure can aid in positive development, such as associating with an academically high achieving peer group, but taken to an extreme even these influences can be unhealthy, for example, when striving for achievement results in unrealistic expectations, risk aversion, and fear of failure.

Drugs and Alcohol

The gender gap that existed between men and women using substances, including alcohol, nicotine, marijuana, illicit drugs, and nonmedical prescription drugs, is closing (McHugh, Wigderson, & Greenfield, 2014). Compared to men, women are more susceptible to negative medical, psychiatric, and social consequence of drug use, and their illness progression toward substance use disorder (SUD) can occur much more rapidly. Additionally, women of childbearing age using substances can affect their reproductive health, as well as the health of their child if they are engaging in substance use while pregnant. Women also experience more barriers when attempting to enter treatment for addiction. Among women, there are higher incidences of co-occurring substance use disorders and psychiatric disorders, particularly depression and anxiety (Khan et al., 2013). Often individuals report utilizing substances as a way to cope with symptoms of depression or anxiety.

Drugs and alcohol can affect individuals and families at any age and stage in their development. For example, substance use by pregnant mothers can impact their children's cognitive, physical, and emotional development, which can impact the family over time. Moreover, substance use by parents can create a chaotic home life that can include abuse and neglect, affecting children's development and sense of security. Finally, children who grow up in a home with individuals who are addicted to drugs and alcohol are more susceptible to developing a substance use disorder themselves.

Therapeutic treatment for families who have members with SUDs are dependent on who in the family is using, as well as the attitude of family members regarding addiction (Lander, Howsare, & Byrne, 2013). For example, a teenager who is addicted to illicit drugs may have a parent who believes that drug use is a character flaw and that the teenager could control her use with willpower. Counselors must assess individuals and families to determine the level of knowledge they possess regarding specific substance use and SUDs; the medical, psychiatric, and psychological side effects of substance use; and the effects of substance use on the family system. In light of the information gathered, counselors must then educate family members where there are gaps in knowledge and validate that not all family members will see SUDs in the same manner, which may impact both the individual's and the family system's ability to engage in recovery.

From a family systems theory perspective, it is important to remember that a family must remain in balance or homeostasis in order to maintain its functioning. Homeostasis is defined as "the tendency toward a relatively stable equilibrium between interdependent elements, especially as maintained by physiological processes" (Merriam-Webster, n.d.). When one considers family members as interdependent elements that function together to maintain a physiological process (the family unit), it becomes clear that members can work in ways that may or may not be healthy in order to maintain the peaceful function of the whole—for example, the younger brother who covers for his older brother when he comes home drunk so that their parents won't confront the negative behavior and fight themselves regarding his behavior. For families in midlife, this example may be very familiar. Because substance use behavior in teenagers is sometimes considered a "rite of passage," it may be taken less seriously than it should be and warning signs may be ignored or go unaddressed, to the detriment of the individual. Counselors working with individuals and families must be aware of the risks of SUDs, assess for substance use, and be aware that addressing substance use and SUDs will disrupt the homeostasis of the family; many individuals and families are resistant to change and will continue the unhealthy functioning in order to avoid the discomfort of change.

Sexuality and Sexual Identity Formation

Sexuality and sexual identity evolve throughout the course of the lifespan. For women in midlife, biological changes including perimenopause and menopause contribute to feelings around their own sexuality and esteem regarding their attractiveness to others. Along with these feelings come the inherent physical changes, including increased risks for diseases, changes in metabolism, and changes in physical ability in terms of exercise and endurance. Psychologically, women may experience increased levels of self-knowledge and awareness that contribute to their confidence in certain areas of their life, while in other areas they may experience feelings of loss or reformulating of their sexual identity.

Just as women are managing these changes, their children are recognizing and beginning to formulate their own sexual identity as adolescents and emerging adults. Identity formation is an important step in adolescence, as shown in Erikson's stage development model (Erikson, 1968). Marcia (1980) took this idea a step further and introduced two processes that are inherent to identity formation, *exploration* and *commitment*. Exploration connotes trying a variety of identities to see what fits, whereas commitment delineates a choice of a specific identity. It is important to note that exploration in relationship to sexuality encompasses not only erotic and romantic relationships but also reproductive health and contraceptive practices, body image, sexual orientation, and gender identity, as well as life satisfaction (World Health Organization, 2010).

Sexuality exploration can be helped and hindered by culture, diversity, and socioeconomic status, along with many other factors. For example, in the United States in 2019, there are ongoing debates and legislative decisions regarding women's rights and accessibility for certain forms of contraception. At intersections of sexuality and gender, exploration can create discomfort in families, whether members are exploring heterosexual dating relationships or nonbinary gender identity. It should be stated that some adolescence and families can readily identify and know that family members have a certain gender identity or sexual orientation, while for some individuals their sexual identity evolves over time. There is no one way to determine certain aspects of sexuality or sexual identity, and counselors can help families a great deal to normalize this reality.

Often individuals are ignorant of certain developmental and biological facts regarding sexuality and sexual identity, which can cause many emotions, including fear and anger. For example, as a counselor, I have educated and normalized for parents that young children do engage in sex play and masturbation and that this is normal development and exploration. Open communication and boundaries on what is healthy and not healthy regarding sexuality can help foster a sense of personal control in a nonshaming environment. As children become adolescents, parents may see sexual exploration that is outside of the family's chosen value set, and this can cause conflict. There is no easy way to handle this, and often it is individuals who seek counseling for sexual issues rather than families. Unfortunately this may not alleviate the systemic issues that are occurring in the family, which in some cases can feel unbearable. It is difficult to be congruent to your sexual identity when the people who are supposed to love you are not supportive of this identity, regardless of knowing it or not. Counselors can help families in midlife by educating individuals and systems regarding what is developmentally appropriate, how to communicate in a nonshaming way regarding sexuality, encouraging clear communication between members, understanding how values play into the family's life, and ensuring that members have appropriate resources for support and safety as needed.

BEST PRACTICES WHEN WORKING WITH FAMILIES

Assessment is an invaluable tool when working with a family. When working with one member of a family (about the workings of the entire family) or working with a family whose members are all attending counseling, assessment can help a counselor sift through the stories, relationships, and problems that brought the system to counseling. Additionally, assessment tools can be used throughout the therapeutic process to show changes and stuck patterns of engagement and to formulate goals for moving the family through treatment.

Depending on where a family is at in the process, one invaluable tool for adults who are remarrying or recoupling is participating in premarital counseling and assessment, such as Prepare and Enrich, SYMBIS, or Relate. Each of these assessments gives couples information regarding their communication style; conflict style; relationship strengths; attitudes regarding roles, sex, religion, and the like; areas of improvement for the relationship; and more based on their individual answers to specific questions. The composite answers for the couple are generated as part of an overall report that can be used in couples counseling so that topics can be discussed and worked through with the guidance of a counselor. Many of these assessments can also be taken by a couple who is already together and want to work on their relationship, which can be helpful for the therapeutic process. It should be noted that many of these assessments are normed on predominantly white, heterosexual individuals, and many are intended for use with specific religious traditions in mind; therefore, counselors should keep this in mind when researching the appropriate assessment tool.

Other tools that are helpful in working with families include genograms, family mapping, and family sculpting. I will attempt to describe these tools and their use in family counseling below. Genograms and family mapping can be used with individuals who are attending counseling and need to work on family issues, as well as entire families; family sculpting is intended to engage many members of a family and therefore requires as many family members to attend as possible.

Genograms

Genograms were developed by Murray Bowen as part of his intergenerational family systems theory approach to therapy. At its heart, a genogram is a map that provides an organizational structure to delineate the individuals, relationships, and nature of those relationships that make up a family. Note that a genogram is flexible in that individuals can map social relationships as well as those that are familial, honoring the notion that family is not necessarily a blood tie. Moreover, the process includes a fairly comprehensive analysis of relationships that denotes how people relate to each other emotionally and gives a way to view generations over time, so that patterns of behavior can be documented or discovered. McGoldrick, Gerson, and Shellenberger (1999) provide a comprehensive guide to genograms that walks practitioners through constructing a genogram, conducting a genogram interview, and interpreting the genogram. Of particular importance to a counselor are the organizational structure and genogram legend used to document relationships accurately.

The magic of a genogram is that it is only limited by two things: imagination and paper space. A genogram can hold a plethora of information, from familial relationships to the nature of the relationships (conflictual, harmonious, disengaged), as well as intergenerational patterns of behavior (drug and alcohol addiction, patterns of domestic abuse, career choice, marriage and divorce patterns, etc.). A genogram can be a highly interactive part of the therapeutic process, making it engaging and dynamic, with all participants playing an active role. Creating a genogram can be done fairly easily with an easel pad of paper that has adhesive so the paper can be placed on a wall. This, in conjunction with markers, can create an opportunity to map out the client's family, paying particular attention to how the presenting problem plays into how the family functions. For example, one client came to counseling with the concern that she is dependent on her husband financially and emotionally, in a way that she believed was stifling her and would ultimately destroy the marriage. Through genogram work and counseling, we discovered a pattern of women in her family of origin who sought relationships that provided a refuge or "safety" that ultimately ended up in either unhappy marriages or divorce. This insight allowed the client to realize that she was "just doing what my mother always did" and to consider how this pattern of behavior did not have to be her future functioning.

Although genograms are a powerful visual tool, the counselor must have the skills and abilities to make connections from the patterns that emerge within the map. Because creating the genogram allows the client to be the expert in their family history, the counselor is able to take a curious approach with the client and ask questions beginning with, "I wonder," and explore hunches or the temporal place impressions of family function emerged. For example, "I wonder if the reason that you can't see yourself growing into a matriarch is because many of the women in your family defer to their husbands to make family decisions."

Family Mapping

Similar to genograms, family mapping emerged from Salvador Minuchin's structural family therapy (Minuchin, 1974). Within this theoretical framework, Minuchin and his colleagues utilized an ecological model to describe the family, with layers of subsystems overlapping to perform family functions and create stability (or instability, as the case may be). Family mapping is somewhat difficult to use on multiple generations of a family; however, it is invaluable for documenting relational and power dynamics occurring in the present with a family in counseling. Lynch and Lynch (2000) offer an excellent text that gives practitioners a more in-depth explanation of symbols to use in outlining the structure and functioning of the family, how to create a working relationship with the family, and ways to intervene with the family in a structural framework. For the purposes of this chapter, focus is on family mapping specifically.

Many practitioners have heard terms that are aligned with structural family therapy and mapping particularly when referring to boundaries. Minuchin employed the terms *disengagement/rigid boundaries*, *flexibility/clear boundaries*, and *enmeshment/diffuse boundaries* when he described how families structured boundaries between and among members. Additionally, and similar to genogram work, Minuchin created a set of symbols to describe emotional responses and consistent patterns of interaction that family members have with each other. The symbols delineate coalitions, conflict, overinvolvement, and the like. Mapping is particularly useful in family counseling when the struggles that the family faces include power, privileges (such as attention), and a sense of fairness.

To some degree, members of families wish to get their individual needs met, which may not align with harmonious family (group) functioning. Examples of individual needs versus family needs may include parents sending one child to soccer camp while another child is not sent to a camp, one member of a couple having opportunities to travel with their job while the other member is home with their own job and the bulk of the family responsibilities, or a male child being given different privileges than his female siblings. To clarify, there can be very logical reasons for the aforementioned examples to occur, but problems can arise when family members begin to sense that individual needs are met more often than collective needs or when the distribution of met needs is not perceived to be equal or consistent among all members.

Take the example of one child who is sent to camp and one who is not; imagine that one child is an elite athlete with potential for professional success, and the second child is fairly average in his development. The parents make a choice to funnel resources to help the athletic child so that she is given many opportunities to be successful and live up to her potential. Moreover, the athletic child receives a great deal of attention due to her prowess. Eventually, the second child could experience some anger or resentment toward his parents or sibling, and ultimately he may experience issues around self-esteem or self-worth. In this case, the second child coming to counseling may have some trouble articulating how he is feeling. But by having the guidance and power to utilize symbols and cocreate the relational power dynamics within his family, he may create a map that shows his parents and sister in enmeshed (overinvolved) relationships, while he experiences his relationship with his parents and sister as disengaged (underinvolved). In summation, the second child describes relationship patterns in which he feels left out much of the time.

As a counselor in this situation, it is imperative to get one or both parents into session so that the family can explore this child's experience of his family's dynamics. It would also be helpful to ascertain if the parents see the power differentials that the child articulates or if they experience something different, and if so to map this experience so that comparisons can be made and family members can cultivate a sense of understanding and empathy for each other. More importantly, mapping is an opportunity to show how members relate to each other within the whole—that there cannot be a "whole" family without each member represented and contributing to the group. In counseling, when perceived inequities are unearthed and explored, there is an opportunity to renegotiate power and privilege distributions so that the whole can function more cohesively.

Family Sculpting

Virginia Satir's work discusses family sculpting, which is considered a valid intervention for individuals, couples, and families (Loeschen, 1998). Within her work, Satir utilized sculpting as a way to describe the emotional expression and communication that occur in a room, as well as a tool to coach clients in new patterns of behavior. By eliciting help from family members, she creates a picture of family functioning that makes a powerful image that clients see, experience, and manipulate to create a different way of being. Satir creates stances within her work that are exaggerated poses to help clients express specific behaviors such as blaming or placating. These stances can be helpful when attempting to get clients into their roles in the family, but it is not required to use them within a sculpture.

Sculpting is extremely useful when working with families, particularly when talk therapy has become bogged down in too many voices or when individuals aren't speaking. It is an opportunity for members to express themselves in a different, kinetic way that can provide greater insight into how other family members experience them. One example is a blended family with mother, stepfather, and two half sisters. One half sister lived full-time with her mom and stepdad, while the older half sister lived primarily with her father and stepmother. The custody arrangement changed quite suddenly, however, and the older half sister has come to live with her mom and family full-time. The family has continued with their normal, busy lives. While there were fights between the sisters, none of these were addressed until the younger half sister acted out at home and the parents brought the family to counseling. The first session was stilted, with parents talking and attempting to encourage the daughters to speak, but both refusing to do so.

To break the tension in the room, sculpting was introduced as a way to help family members express how they were feeling in that moment. As the counselor, I asked the younger daughter, who is the identified patient due to her acting out, to sculpt her family and create a picture of how she feels her relationships are with her family at this time. Her sculpture placed her and her mother very far away from each other, with her older sister between them and closer to the mom, blocking the younger sister's view. The stepfather was more aligned with the younger daughter, standing to her side and creating a triangle between the mom and the younger daughter, although not directly aligned with the older daughter.

The initial picture gave a great deal of insight into how the younger daughter was experiencing her relationships with her family, particularly with her mother. Beyond the sculpting, the counselor's next task is to ask process questions within the session of the individual completing the sculpture, as well as of the members who are sculpted. In this example, when asked about her feelings toward her mother, the younger daughter replied that she was angry and couldn't reach her mother if she tried. The younger daughter maintained a closed-off stance throughout the sculpting session, essentially closing herself off from other family members, which was indicative of how her behavior at home had been—closed off with occasional anger outbursts or major boundary violations.

As sessions progressed, the initial sculpture helped the family understand how the younger daughter was experiencing the family. This was important because the younger daughter's behaviors were the focus of the family and a reliable barometer for overall family functioning; in essence, the youngest daughter was manifesting the emotional output of the entire family. However, this is not a healthy situation for any family member, and so the counselor's work was to resculpt the family through questions, traditional talk therapy, and sculpting enactments to change the picture to one that was healthier. In this case, health meant that family members realigned to all see each other, adults aligned together as the parents and leaders of the household and the sisters moving closer to each other in order to begin negotiating their sibling relationship. Questions that aided in this resculpting process included the following. To the younger sister: What would happen if your sister moved and you were able to face your mother? To the older sister: If you and your sister were to figure out how to be sisters, how would this sculpture change? And to the couple: How are you able to coparent the girls if you are so far away from each other?

CULTURAL CONSIDERATIONS

All families have some aspects of diversity—it may pertain to family makeup, racial/cultural identity, abilities or disabilities, diagnoses, or the intersections of these and other markers of diversity. It is imperative that counselors are able to work outside the mainstream notion of nuclear, Caucasian, heterosexual, able-bodied family and integrate the unique aspects of each family in order to create interventions that will work for all members of the system. At this time, there are multiple models and theories available to counselors who are working with diverse families, and utilizing these can be helpful in creating successful working alliances and outcomes for those seeking services. Counselors should work with families to understand the unique gifts and challenges that their diversity experience brings to their system and follow research models and techniques that utilize the systemic paradigm and adapt these ideas to work successfully with families in the modern age.

Families often come to counseling because one member, perhaps the mother or stepmother, seeks help for disharmony in the system. Counselors can work within a family systems perspective with one member or many members of the family; creating change with one member can create change in the system. However, it is important that counselors are adaptable in order to include family members. This may mean utilizing online platforms such as Zoom (which is HIPAA compliant) to hold real-time and virtual meetings with family members who can come to the counseling room and those who may not be able to due to work or other obligations. At one time, it was a common thought that not attending counseling sessions meant a lack of commitment—this is shortsighted. The reality is that for many families there are barriers to attending counseling, including work schedules, transportation, monetary resources, or social support resources. Family members who are negotiating these issues are committed to their families, and counseling may not be the top priority because more pressing concerns are. Therefore, it is important to be as flexible as appropriate in a given setting in order to help families in ways that let them participate and grow.

ETHICAL CONSIDERATIONS

Ethical and legal issues that arise when working with families typically center on confidentiality, family safety, legal rights of guardians, informed consent, primary responsibility, and values conflicts. In the case of families, the whole system is considered the "patient," and yet the counselor must engage individuals in order to create changes. This can be particularly complicated with families in midlife who may have blended members for whom custody is shared or as children become older and the age of assent and consent may change, particularly in states whose statutes stipulate that minors can consent to treatment for certain services without the knowledge of their parents.

In order to best serve a family, counselors could create a brief checklist that can help the therapeutic process. Items on this checklist can include (1) requiring copies of legal paperwork for the clinical file that articulates custody agreements and custodial consents for treatment; (2) obtaining consent and assent (as appropriate) for all family members before commencing with counseling; (3) reminding families that consent and assent are ongoing and checking in regularly to reaffirm members' participation in counseling; (4) creating rules about confidentiality, respecting boundaries, and sharing limits for the family to follow outside of the counseling room; (5) reminding families of legal statutes that govern disclosures of information by minor clients if therapeutic work is occurring with only the children of the family; and (6) open dialogue that counseling may not produce positive results for the family. Note that guidance on many of these items can be found in the International Association of Marriage and Family Counselors (IAMFC) ethical codes, which are available for review online (IAMFC, 2017).

Surprises in family counseling may still arise even when counselors follow the above list. When counselors encounter families engaging in behaviors that conflict with their own beliefs, it can challenge professionals' ability to maintain a semblance of neutrality in order to give the family the autonomy to make choices that work best for the system. Family counselors can struggle with fairness in couples and family counseling. As stated in the section on family mapping, in order to meet the needs of the system, family members must sometimes cede their individual needs or wishes. Although this sacrifice occurs at some point with all family members, women are more likely to give up their personal needs in order to serve the system as a whole or to give resources to another member of the household—for example, the mother who forgos purchasing much-needed new clothes so that her child can have the latest shoes, or the wife who gives up her evening with friends so that her husband has a quiet night of rest without watching the children. In these examples, I review the IAMFC ethical code to remind myself of the following: "J.3. Couples and family counselors respect the rights of individual and members to define their relationships and family units beyond the boundaries imposed by dominant culture or tradition" (IAMFC, 2017). Family counselors are charged with the task of aiding families to achieve better functioning, as only they can define. This means that a family must live in the way that they believe is best for them, even when a counselor's perception is that individual members may not flourish within that environment.

ADVOCACY OPPORTUNITIES

Traditional psychology and counseling practice are largely based on individual interventions that treat people in isolation from the systems that affect them. However, people do not exist in isolation but instead are influenced by the people, communities, and cultures they are part of. Unfortunately, insurance and third-party reimbursement companies demand that an "identified patient" be delineated to "carry" the pathology of the family in order to pay for services. The individual who carries the primary diagnosis can feel stigmatized and believe that they are the problem and reason that the family is unwell. The *Diagnostic and Statistical Manual of Mental Disorders*, fifth edition (DSM-5), has Z codes, which are a group of diagnoses or factors that influence individuals' functioning. Included in the Z codes are family system issues that can be the focus of clinical treatment and can be used as either the principal diagnosis or secondary diagnosis. Using the Z code in individual and family treatment can be a more accurate way to describe the issues the family is experiencing and moves away from one person as the identified patient—rather, the "patient" is the family system as a whole. Advocating to accurately identify issues in a family, treat them accordingly, and decentralize the source of pathology from an individual to the system is important in destigmatizing family counseling.

CASE STUDY WRAP-UP: ELEANOR

Carmen begins her work with Eleanor by cocreating a genogram of Eleanor's family that goes back three generations. As they work together to map out family functioning, Carmen includes assessment questions about family members' psychiatric diagnoses, the role that these played in the household, and parenting styles, as well as the impact on marriages in Eleanor's family of origin. The patterns show that in each generation at least one or more family members were diagnosed with severe psychiatric disorders, and because treatment options were more limited those family members tended to utilize substances to cope with their symptoms. Carmen encourages Eleanor that she has found ways to cope with her symptoms that include counseling, medication, and recreational therapies rather than substances.

Eleanor also acknowledges that like other members of her family, when she feels overwhelmed or ashamed of her illness she tends to withdraw from both her husband and her daughter, in a similar manner to her father when he was coping with his mental illness. She recalls that this eventually destroyed their family, and her parent's divorce marked the end of her relationship with her father. She becomes tearful as she describes this because she fears that this is what will happen to her—her husband will leave her, she will be unable to care for her daughter, and she will lose her relationships with both of the people she holds most dear.

As Eleanor and Carmen work to uncover these family patterns that Eleanor is unconsciously re-creating in her current family, Carmen moves Eleanor to work on family mapping—in particular, the power differentials that Eleanor experiences with her husband and daughter in relationship to her mental illness. What is revealed in these maps is that Eleanor's mental illness has the greatest amount of power in the family. Although some of this power is by necessity (caring for Eleanor when she is unable to care for herself), the family has entered into a state of homeostasis by attempting to keep the home calm and serene in order to not trigger Eleanor's symptoms. Eleanor begins to cry as she considers how she contributes to this homeostasis by engaging in helpless behaviors at times when she is fully capable. Carmen and Eleanor work on Eleanor's conflicting feelings of fear of her illness and anger that she avoids living her life when she is feeling stable and healthy.

As their work progresses, Eleanor begins to have more good days than bad, and when she has good days she makes plans to engage with her family and enjoy life. Her change in behavior begins to change her family system—in some positive ways and some negative. Her daughter's anxiety has lessened, but she reports that her husband is still uncertain of how to interact with her on good days as opposed to bad days. Eleanor reports that she has suggested to her husband that they enter into couples counseling so that they can work on their relationship, and he is open to this.

QUESTIONS FOR REFLECTION

1. How can assessment questions be modified for use when cocreating a genogram?
2. How can social media influences affect the psychosocial functioning of the family?
3. What state legal statutes affect your work with children and families? Are you apprised of the latest regulations?
4. How can you adapt your counseling practices to include family members who may not be able to attend sessions physically but are valuable to the systemic health and functioning of the unit?

REFERENCES

Amato, P. R., Kane, J. B., & Spencer, J. (2011). Reconsidering the "good divorce." *Family Relationships, 60*(5), 511–24.

Cartwright, C., & Gibson, K. (2013). The effects of co-parenting relationships with ex-spouses on couples in step-families. *Family Matters, 92*, 18.

Centers for Disease Control. (2002a). *Cohabitation, marriage, divorce, and remarriage in the United States.* Retrieved from https://www.cdc.gov/nchs/data/series/sr_23/sr23_022.pdf

Centers for Disease Control. (2002b, June). New report sheds light on trends and patterns in marriage, divorce, and cohabitation. Retrieved from https://www.cdc.gov/nchs/pressroom/02news/div_mar_cohab.htm

Coleman, M., Ganong, L., Russell, L., & Frye-Cox, N. (2015). Stepchildren's view about former step-relationships following stepfamily dissolution. *Journal of Marriage and Family, 77*, 775–90.

Craig, E. A., Harvey-Knowles, J. A., & Johnson, A. J. (2012). Childless stepmothers: Communicating with other stepmothers about spouses and stepchildren. *Qualitative Research Reports in Communication, 13*(1), 71–79. https://doi.org/10.1080/17459435.2012.722164

Donaldson, C. (2000). Midlife lesbian parenting. *Journal of Gay & Lesbian Social Services, 11* (2–3), 119–38.

Erikson, E. H. (1968). *Identity: Youth and crisis*. New York, NY: W. W. Norton.

Hill, R. (1986). Life cycle stages for types of single parent families: Of family development theory. *Family Relations, 35*(1), 19–29.

International Association of Marriage and Family Counselors. (2017). *IAMFC code of ethics*. Alexandria, VA: Author.

Khan, S., Okuda, M., Hasin, D. S., Secades-Villa, R., Keyes, K., Lin, K.-H., . . . Blanco, G. (2013). Gender difference in lifetime alcohol dependence: Results from the national epidemiological survey on alcohol and related conditions. *Alcoholism: Clinical and Experimental Research, 37*(10), 1696–1705. https://doi.org/10.1111/acer.12158

Kumar, K. (2017). The blended family life cycle. *Journal of Divorce & Remarriage, 58*(2), 110–25.

Lander, L., Howsare, J., & Byrne, M. (2013). The impact of substance use disorders on families and children: From theory to practice. *Social Work Public Health, 28*(3–4), 194–205. doi:10.1080/19371918.2013.759005

Loeschen, S. (1998). *Systematic training in the skills of Virginia Satir.* New York, NY: Brooks/Cole.

Lynch, B., & Lynch, J. E. (2000). *Principles and practice of structural family therapy*. Gouldsboro, ME: Gestalt Journal Press.

Marcia, J. E. (1980). Identity in adolescence. In J. Adelson (Ed.), *Handbook of adolescent psychology* (pp. 159–87). New York, NY: Wiley.

McGoldrick, M. (1992). Ethnicity and the family life cycle. *Family Business Review, 5*(4), 437–59.

McGoldrick, M., Carter, B., & Garcia-Preto, N. (Eds.). (2011). *The expanded family life cycle: Individual, family, and social perspectives* (4th ed.). Boston, MA: Allyn & Bacon.

McGoldrick, M., Gerson, R., & Perry, S. (2008). *Genograms: Assessment and interventions* (3rd ed.). New York, NY: W. W. Norton.

McGoldrick, M., Gerson, R., & Shellenberger, S. (1999). *Genograms: Assessment and Intervention.* New York, NY: W. W. Norton.

McHugh, R. K., Wigderson, S., & Greenfield, S. F. (2014). Epidemiology of substance use in reproductive-age women. *Obstetrics and Gynecology Clinics of North America, 41*(2), 177–89.

Merriam-Webster. (n.d.). Homeostasis. Retrieved from https://www.merriam-webster.com/dictionary/homeostasis

Minuchin, S. (1974). *Families and family therapy*. Cambridge, MA: Harvard University Press.

Olweus, D. (1994). Annotation: Bullying at school: Basic facts and effects of a school based intervention program. *Journal of Child Psychology and Psychiatry, 35*, 1171–90.

Pew Research Center. (2018). Social media fact sheet. Retrieved from https://www.pewinternet.org/fact-sheet/social-media/

Romer, D. (2010). Adolescent risk taking, impulsivity, and brain development: Implications for prevention. *Developmental Psychobiology, 52*(3), 263–76.

Stopbullying.gov. (2019). Warning signs for bullying. Retrieved from https://www.stopbullying.gov/at-risk/warning-signs/index.html

World Health Organization. (2010). *Developing sexual health programmes: A framework for action.* Retrieved from https://www.who.int/reproductivehealth/publications/sexual_health/rhr_hrp_10_22/en/

Chapter Twelve

Counseling Survivors of Emotional and Physical Abuse

Anne Shragal

CASE VIGNETTE: MEREDITH

Meredith is a heterosexual Caucasian female in her late twenties, currently attending undergraduate school for elementary education. She resides in a rural area in Tennessee, where she has lived her entire life. She currently lives with her boyfriend of two years and their eight-month-old daughter. She works full-time at a daycare as a teacher assistant in the two-year-old classroom. Meredith has worked at this location for the past eight years but is ready to improve her professional career by working as a full-time elementary school teacher. She is halfway done with her program and is expecting to graduate next spring semester.

Meredith has had a history of both emotional and physical abuse. As a child, she was physically abused by her uncle. She had lost both parents in a car accident when she was a toddler, and her paternal uncle took her into his care. She lived with him and his two other children (both older than her by a few years) until she graduated high school. Physical abuse was not only directed at her, and she witnessed this abuse done to the other two children. The Department of Child and Family Services was contacted multiple times, but no response ever came of these reports. Most of the physical signs of abuse on her body were hidden, and she was required to wear clothing that would cover the bruising and burns.

Once she turned eighteen, she went on to community college, where she received her associate degree in early childhood education. She moved out of her uncle's home and into an apartment not far from school with one of her female friends. She received high honors and graduated one semester early.

In order to pay for schooling and living expenses, she worked as often as she could. Once graduated, she got a job immediately in the daycare where she works today. She very much enjoys her job and the people that she works with.

However, her home life is a different picture. Her live-in boyfriend is emotionally and physically abusive. He calls her names and requires her to cook, clean, and pay for all living expenses. He currently does not work and rarely leaves the home. He says that the reason he can't work is a back injury that occurred one year ago. He is also physically abusive, especially when he is either using drugs or drinking alcohol. She has shown up to work a few times with bruising on her arms and legs. When questioned, Meredith tells her coworkers that she fell or was clumsy. Thankfully, her eight-month-old daughter is able to go to work with her every day. Meredith never leaves her alone with her boyfriend, as she is fearful for her daughter's safety.

Meredith arrived at therapy wanting to discuss her concerns and looking for help in deciding if she should leave her boyfriend or try to fix things. She is currently in her undergraduate program and is fearful that she will not be able to complete the program if she leaves her boyfriend. She also mentions a few happy memories with him and feels that he might be able to change. She is concerned that her daughter will grow up in an environment similar to the one she did as a child and is adamant that she does not want to see that happen. Meredith is looking for the counselor's assistance on how to navigate this situation.

* * *

Abuse can happen to anyone at any time. Over time, the statistics of abuse for both children and adults have increased dramatically. Abuse does not occur just in physical form. There are many other types of abuse that can affect both physical and mental health. With abuse comes the repeated and recurring pattern. Those who have endured abuse as children are more likely to abuse or conduct criminal acts as adults. Those who are victims of abuse tend to revolve in a cycle of violence, allowing abuse to continue.

Abuse, regardless of age, could potentially be unknown and silent to the general public. According to the American Society for the Positive Care of Children (American SPCC, 2018), as of 2017 more than 4.1 million child maltreatment referrals were received; 74.9 percent of these reports are due to childhood neglect, 18.3 percent physical abuse, 8.6 percent sexual abuse, and 7.1 percent psychological maltreatment. There are many types of child abuse, including child neglect, physical abuse, emotional abuse, sexual abuse, negative childhood experiences, shaken baby syndrome, domestic violence, and trafficking and exploitation (American SPCC, 2018). According to the National Domestic Violence Hotline (2019), approximately twenty-four people per minute are victims of rape, physical abuse, or stalking by an intimate partner in the United States, that is, nearly three in ten women and one in ten men. Females aged eighteen to twenty-four and twenty-five to thirty-four experienced the highest rates of partner violence.

Abuse can happen to anyone and can manifest in many different forms. According to Silambuselvi, Abirami, Nandhini, Oneyekachi, and Jeevitha (2019), abuse can have implications for both physical and mental health, influencing health long after the abuse occurred.

> According to the World Health Organization, child abuse or maltreatment constitutes all forms of physical and/or emotional ill-treatment, sexual abuse, neglect or negligent treatment or commercial or other exploitation, resulting in actual or potential harm to the child's health, survival, development or dignity in the context of a relationship of responsibility, trust or power. (Silambuselvi et al., 2019, p. 23)

There is an association between domestic violence and post-traumatic stress disorder (PTSD). There is also an indication of elevated levels of emotional symptoms, especially anger and depression, which in turn increase the likelihood of suicide attempts. Others experience high rates of denial, fear, shame, embarrassment, and stigmatization (Lipford, Lawrence, & Lacking, 2016).

CYCLE OF ABUSE

The "cycle of abuse" theory was developed by Dr. Lenore Walker in 1979, consisting of four stages of abuse: tension building, incident, reconciliation, and calm (Kelly, 2018). These four stages form a continuous cycle that circles around on itself, and its starting point is typically the stage of tension building.

In the tension-building stage, conflict begins. Unfortunately, conflicts go unresolved, with the abuser never admitting to wrongdoing or attending to passive-aggressive behavior. The second phase, the incident, occurs when the abuser acts on their emotions, projecting it onto the victim in the form of emotional or physical abuse. The reconciliation phase happens once the abuse occurs due to the abuser being afraid of the consequences of his or her actions. This tends to come in the form of convincing through apologies and excuses. The final stage, according to Dr. Walker, is the calm phase, also known as the honeymoon phase. The abuser will go to extensive lengths to create a positive light for themselves and act in ways that they know will make the victim feel happy. However, the cycle of violence continues, returning to tension building over time (Anastasia, 2018).

The cyclical pattern of abuse has been researched extensively to understand why the cycle does not break. Maxwell, Callahan, Ruggero, and Janis (2016) found that several studies show a link between abuse as a child and later adulthood perpetrators. In fact, childhood physical abuse recipients were twice as likely to be physically violent with their intimate partners during adulthood than those who did not experience childhood abuse (Maxwell et al., 2016). Fagan (2005) found that maltreated children are at an increased risk for criminal activity later in life. Interestingly, the research also suggested these victims can become frequent, repeated criminal offenders. Many of these crimes include violent crimes, spousal assault, and drug and alcohol abuse (Fagan, 2005).

BEST PRACTICES

Given the neurobiological impact of early trauma, treatment should target multiple levels of processing. These levels include sensorimotor, cognitive, and emotional interventions. Studies have shown that abusers who were victims as children respond well to counseling treatment. If individuals who were victims of childhood abuse remain untreated, they are more likely to become more violent as adults. Therefore, research supports therapeutic interventions targeting childhood abuse experiences (Maxwell et al., 2016).

Trauma-Focused Cognitive Behavioral Therapy

Empirical literature suggests phase-oriented treatment as a best practice for abuse victims. The first phase of treatment is to create safety and work on regulation of core emotions and behaviors. It is recommended that this phase be established before moving on to the second phase, trauma processing. The goal of this phase is to integrate trauma memories into a cohesive sense of self. The final goal of this treatment, consolidation, focuses on resiliency. It promotes engagement in the community and with family. Note that phase-oriented treatment should incorporate caregivers and other support systems, be tailored to the client's specific developmental and cognitive profile, focused on symptom reduction, and create a positive, resilient trajectory (Dauber, Lotsos, & Pulido, 2015).

Trauma-focused cognitive behavioral therapy (TF-CBT) has shown increasing effective results specific to the treatment of abuse. This includes those who have experienced child sexual abuse, domestic abuse, traumatic grief, natural disasters, and complex trauma (Dauber et al., 2015). The TF-CBT model is a cognitive-behavioral and resiliency-building framework. There are nine phase-based components, spelling out the word PRACTICE. Phase-one, stabilization, include the components of the psychoeducation of trauma impact (including **p**arenting skills), **r**elaxation skills, **a**ffective skills (to address emotional dysregulation), and **c**ognitive processing skills. Phase-two, trauma processing, specifically reviews **t**rauma processing and narration. Phase-three, consolidation, provides clients with **i**n-vivo experiences (addressing overgeneralization of fears and memory avoidance), **c**onjoint parent–child sessions (enhancing communication), and **e**nhancing of future safety. Specific to child and adolescent TF-CBT, it is recommended that the therapist meet half of the time with the child and half of the time with the parent. The goal is to optimize recovery of the trauma primarily while increasing feelings of safety and rebuilding of trust with the parent (Cohen, Deblinger, & Mannarino, 2019).

Attachment-Based Therapy

Studies have also found that relational and attachment-based therapies have helped, specifically for children and adolescents with complex trauma and those in foster care. According to Scott, Diamond, and Levy (2016), attachment-based family therapy (ABFT) aims to recover and increase a more secure relationship with parents so that children and adolescents feel protected and safe with their parents. Attachment has been found as a protection factor for a range of maladaptive behaviors. When a child or adolescent feels confident of their caretaker's ability to provide protection and support, there is more communication, emotional regulation, and development of problem-solving skills (Kobak & Duemmler, 1994).

Scott and colleagues (2016) provide a case study involving the use of ABFT. Five ABFT tasks were identified, used by the therapist: relational reframe, adolescent alliance, parent alliance, attachment task, and promoting autonomy. The first task, relational reframing, involves identifying family ruptures and agreed upon family treatment goals. Next, in adolescent alliance, the therapist aims to understand the adolescent's current narrative first, then helps the adolescent identify how failures in attachment relationships have contributed to beliefs and expectations of self and others as well as behaviors in the future. The third task, parent alliance, asks the parents to become emotionally attuned to each other and their child and explores differences in parenting styles and the impact of trustworthiness in the parent–child relationship. The fourth stage, attachment task, is more of a corrective phase where the child witnesses and the parents demonstrate emotional attunement. Finally, ABFT looks to promote autonomy, which involves solidifying communication and relational trust. This will allow the adolescent to feel more comfortable exploring personal autonomy (Scott et al., 2016).

Somatosensory Interventions

Dauber and colleagues (2015) suggest somatosensory interventions (pertaining to the perception of sensory) to "promote modulation of regulatory processes and to access traumatic material that is thought to be stored in nonverbal parts of the brain" (p. 530). Somatosensory techniques include the incorporation of music, art, and play into the therapeutic session, especially for children with complex trauma (Dauber et al., 2015). Curreri (2013) suggests music therapy, promoting the growth of new synaptic connections, decreasing rigidity, and increasing openness to change. Results of his study indicated that participants in a music therapy group found music helped them gain insight into new experiences and an understanding that change is healthy for healing, happiness, and growth (Curreri, 2013). Additionally, Ikonomopoulos and colleagues (2017) found art therapy to be an effective technique for abused victims by helping to explore emotions and experiences without the risk of retraumatization. This study had participants attend a nine-session creative arts therapy program, which effectively reduced mental health symptoms and improved resiliency (Ikonomopoulos et al., 2017). Play therapy gives children the opportunity to express feelings, problems, insecurities, and confusion. As Singhal and Vahali (2014) write, "Play therapy, then, is to children what psychotherapy is to adults" (p. 134). Acting out a frightening or traumatizing experience symbolically provides the potential to change or reverse the outcome, moving toward inner peace and resolution.

Another type of sensorimotor treatment found in the literature is animal-assisted therapy (AAT, aka pet therapy):

> AAT is a goal oriented, planned, and structured therapeutic intervention directed and/or delivered by health, education and human service professionals. Intervention progress is measured and included in professional documentation. AAT is delivered and/or directed by a formally trained (with active licensure, degree or equivalent) professional with expertise within the scope of the professional's practice. AAT focuses on enhancing physical, cognitive, behavioral and/or socio-emotional functioning of the particular human client. (International Association of Human-Animal Interaction Organizations, 2014)

Studies have found that those struggling with PTSD, a mental health condition developed after trauma, find AAT improves symptoms. Altschuler (2018) found that AAT can dramatically improve PTSD conditions. He also noted that AAT does not require canine therapy and that there is a benefit in using a variety of animals. In addition, AAT can play a role in preventing suicide attempts. Bobby Peeker, a U.S. military veteran who had witnessed trauma, explained that his canine-assisted therapy "helped me get out of the house. . . . He pulled me out of a dark place" (Altschuler, 2018, p. 12). However, AAT does not just benefit those struggling with PTSD. Kelly and Cozzolino (2015) found that animals help all populations, including children, adolescents, adults, and the elderly. AAT is a helpful addition to talk therapy as clients transfer skills used in animal handling to their own behaviors. The aim is to help develop positive life skills and social interactions (Kelly & Cozzolino, 2015).

CULTURAL CONSIDERATIONS

Cultural diversity should be considered when working with those that have been physically or emotionally abused. Paone, Malott, and Maldonado (2008) suggest that counselors adjust interventions to match the diverse needs of clients. An essential component of working with cultural competence is an understanding of the client's culture as well as the therapist's self-awareness. The counselor should acquire more than just relevant cultural knowledge to avoid the creation of stereotypes. This expanded knowledge includes the client's environmental and multicultural influences. Counselors should be aware of any biases of particular populations and obtain continuing education in an effort to decrease these biases and increase multicultural competencies (Paone et al., 2008).

There are various recommendations of counseling diverse populations of abuse. For domestic violence, counselors could look at how cultural influences might affect the decision to leave an abusive relationship. By understanding these diverse variables, a counselor may be able to assist and provide resources throughout the framework of the victim's culture (Kasturirangan & Williams, 2003). For a child who has been maltreated or abused, counselors should find ways to support the child and foster the healthiest position for the child. Also, counselors should be open to the child's reality, not as it is imagined. For example, children may say they live with "mama," which to a counselor may seem like a mother, but a child could mean a grandmother (Fontes, 2005). Finally, when working with children, counselors should be mindful of providing culturally appropriate toys, a multitude of colors for art, and culturally diverse dolls and kitchen items (Paone et al., 2008).

ETHICAL CONSIDERATIONS

Various ethical and legal considerations apply when working with victims of physical and emotional abuse. The American Counseling Association (2014) Code of Ethics states that the primary duty of a counselor is to protect the welfare of the client. However, there are some instances, especially when working with the abused population, where this might not hold. As stated in code B.2.a. Serious and Foreseeable Harm and Legal Requirements:

> The general requirement that counselors keep information confidential does not apply when disclosure is required to protect clients or identified others from serious and foreseeable harm or when legal requirements demand that confidential information must be revealed. Counselors consult with other professionals when in doubt as to the validity of an exception. (p. 7)

Therefore, if a counselor is notified that the client may be in danger, they are required, by law, to notify the authorities as a means to protect the client from harm. Should the counselor be ordered by court to release privileged information, it is an ethical responsibility to obtain written consent from the client to share such confidential information. Should the counselor not be able to obtain this information, the ACA recommends the counselor take steps to either prohibit or limit disclosure of information (ACA, 2014).

In addition to the ACA Code of Ethics applying to victims of abuse, counselors should also prepare and provide, when necessary, safety plans. According to Kress, Protivnak, and Sadlak (2008), safety plans are tools counselors use to minimize risk and assist with client safety. The safety plan is designed to prepare in advance how to respond and get to safety. It should be designed to fit the unique needs of the client. Specific to domestic violence, a client in a physically abusive relationship should not leave the counseling session without a safety plan created. This session may be the only one to help protect the client as the client may not be able to or may choose not to return to counseling. Some examples to include in the safety plans are police protection, legal action, support networks, and resources (Kress, Protivnak, & Sadlak, 2008).

ADVOCACY OPPORTUNITIES

Part of the role of a counselor is to advocate for the counseling field and mental health. There are a variety of ways counselors can advocate for the physically and emotionally abused. According to Rivas and colleagues (2016), advocacy may reduce abuse by empowering victims to improve their situation. This can be done by providing counseling (both formal and informal), support for safety, and access to additional services. Advocacy may be solely through the health-care provider, assisting and referring to various resources. But it may also come in the form of a multicomponent intervention through staff and other individuals (Rivas et al., 2016).

There are a variety of resources available to both counselors and the public for victims of physical and emotional abuse. The National Domestic Violence Hotline is a free 24/7 call line providing tools and support for victims of abuse. Services include crisis intervention, referral services, and general information about domestic violence (National Domestic Violence Hotline, 2019). The Childhelp National Child Abuse Hotline is dedicated to preventing child abuse. Like the National Domestic Violence Hotline, Childhelp is staffed 24/7 with crisis counselors. Services include crisis intervention, educational information, and emergency, social service, and support referral resources (Childhelp, 2019). Counselors and the public can also research county, state, and federal governmental programs specifically designed to assist victims of abuse.

CASE VIGNETTE WRAP-UP: MEREDITH

Meredith: *I'm really not sure what I should do. He calls me names that don't make me feel respected and there have been times where I wondered if what he did was considered physical abuse. Now my uncle did abuse me as a child, so I know what that looks like. But this, I'm not sure. And if it is, and just generally overall, I'm not sure I want to be with him. But we have our daughter together. So that's part of the equation too.*

Therapist: *It sounds like you are unsure about what to do. Are you familiar with the cycle of violence? Basically, it starts with building of tension, then an incident happens, then there is reconciliation where the person tries to make the situation better, and then there is a state of calm. However, tension will build again, and this whole cycle starts over again. Do you think this is happening in your life, in your relationship?*

Meredith: *Yeah, I mean, I guess so. I always feel like I'm walking on eggshells. I don't know who I'm going to get sometimes, when he is going to switch into this man that I don't know. There certainly have been incidences and then he tries to make up, telling me that he is going to change and do better. Why do I always believe him? I guess I am in the cycle.*

Therapist: *I'm glad that you decided to come to counseling. It is very courageous of you to want to work on yourself. I think the first step is to create a sense of safety for yourself and your daughter.*

Meredith: *What do you mean? Like leave. I'm not sure I want to do that just yet.*

Therapist: *Well, I have to make sure I am doing my job and need to ask you a hard question. Do you feel like you are in harm's way or in danger currently?*

Meredith: *No.*

Therapist: *Okay, well then I recommend the next step is to make sure we have a safety plan in place just so that you know what to do if you are ever in that situation or feel that you or your daughter might be in a dangerous situation. Would that be okay with you to start with that?*

Meredith: *Sure.*

Therapist: *Okay, here are some resources for you and places to call if you need to speak with someone when I am not in the office. [Counselor hands over pamphlets.] I want to also write down for you the support systems you have available should you need them. Can you tell me who they are? [Client provides family and friends names and phone numbers.] I also want to include a few steps you can take if you are in danger. One, leave the home and find a secure place to go. [Client lists locations.] Two, contact your support systems. Three, call the hotline numbers to speak to someone if I am out of the office or with another client. Four, go to the nearest hospital emergency room or call 911 if you are in immediate danger. [Therapist hands a copy of the safety plan to the client to take with her.]*

Meredith: *Thanks. Sometimes I just don't know what to do, so this should help. I appreciate it. But I still don't know if I should leave or stay. I just don't know what to do.*

Therapist: *I'd like to spend a few sessions with you to try to sort this out. I feel as though there is a lot going on, and it might be good to spend some time sorting through everything. What do you think? Will that work?*

Meredith: *Yes, I think that is a good idea. Thank you.*

The therapist includes the safety plan in the client's file and writes in the client's chart to begin TF-CBT work with the client, adding somatosensory interventions when appropriate.

QUESTIONS FOR REFLECTION

1. Based on the statistical information on child and adult abuse presented in this chapter, what do you think your role as an advocate could be?
2. What therapeutic interventions would you implement when working with victims of abuse?
3. How is working with abused children different from working with abused adults? What might you implement that is similar for both populations? Different?
4. What additional information might you add to a safety plan for both children and adults?
5. What cultural, ethical, and legal obligations do you foresee when working with victims of abuse?

REFERENCES

Altschuler, E. L. (2018). Animal-assisted therapy for post-traumatic stress disorder: Lessons from "case reports" in media stories. *Military Medicine, 183*(1/2), 11–13. doi: 10.1093/milmed/usx073

American Counseling Association. (2014). *ACA code of ethics*. Alexandria, VA: Author.

Amerian SPCC. (2018). Child mistreatment statistics in the U.S. Retrieved from https://americanspcc.org/child-abuse-statistics/

Anastasia. (2018, December 10). The cycle of abuse: Definition, explained, examples. Cleverism. Retrieved from https://www.cleverism.com/cycle-of-abuse/

Childhelp. (2019). National child abuse hotline. Retireved from http://www.childhelp.org/hotline/

Cohen, J. A., Deblinger, E., & Mannarino, A. P. (2018). Trauma-focused cognitive behavioral therapy for children and families. *Psychotherapy Research, 28*(1), 47–57. doi: 10.1080/10503307.2016.1208375

Curreri, E. (2013). Aesthetic perturbation: Using a chance/aleatoric music therapy intervention to reduce rigidity in adult patients with psychiatric disorders. *Music Therapy Perspectives, 31*(2), 105–11.

Dauber, S., Lotsos, K., & Pulido, M. (2015). Treatment of complex trauma on the front lines: A preliminary look at child outcomes in an agency sample. *Child & Adolescent Social Work Journal, 32*(6), 529–43. doi: 10.1007/s10560-015-0393-5

Fagan, A. A. (2005). The relationship between adolescent physical abuse and criminal offending: Support for an enduring and generalized cycle of violence. *Journal of Family Violence, 20*(5), 279–90.

Fontes, L. A. (2005). *Child abuse and culture: Working with diverse families*. New York, NY: Guilford Press.

Ikonomopoulos, J., Cavazos-Vela, J., Vela, P., Sanchez, M., Schmidt, C., & Catchings, C. V. (2017). Evaluating the effects of creative journal arts therapy for survivors of domestic violence. *Journal of Creativity in Mental Health, 12*(4), 496–512. doi: 10.1080/15401383.2017.1328290

International Association of Human-Animal Interaction Organizations. (2014). The IAHAIO definitions for animal assisted intervention and animal assisted activity and guidelines for wellness of animals involved [White Paper]. Retrieved from http://www.iahaio.org/new/fileuploads/4163IAHAIO%20WHITE%20PAPER-%20FINAL%20-%20NOV%2024-2014.pdf

Kasturirangan, A., & Williams, E. N. (2003). Counseling Latina battered women: A qualitative study of the Latina perspective. *Journal of Multicultural Counseling and Development, 31*(3), 162–78.

Kelly, L. (2018). The ejusdem generis of A-B-: Ongoing asylum advocacy for domestic violence survivors. *National Lawyers Guild Review, 75*(2), 65–81.

Kelly, M. A., & Cozzolino, C. A. (2015). Helping at-risk youth overcome trauma and substance abuse through animal-assisted therapy. *Contemporary Justice Review, 18*(4), 421–34. doi: 10.1080/10282580.2015.1093686

Kobak, R., & Duemmler, S. (1994). Attachment processes in adulthood. In K. Bartholomew & D. Perlman (Eds.), *Advances in personal relationships* (pp. 121–49). London: Jessica Kingsley.

Kress, V. E., Protivnak, J. J., & Sadlak, L. (2008). Counseling clients involved with violent intimate partners: The mental health counselor's role in promoting client safety. *Journal of Mental Health Counseling, 30*(3), 200–210. doi: 10.17744/mehc.30.3.e0r8773472116016

Lipford, K. J., Lawrence, S., & Lacking, R. (2016). Community partnership curricular support through a domestic violence forum. *Researcher: An Interdisciplinary Journal, 29*(1), 105–26.

Maxwell, K., Callahan, J., Ruggero, C., & Janis, B. (2016). Breaking the cycle: Association of attending therapy following childhood abuse and subsequent perpetration of violence. *Journal of Family Violence, 31*(2), 251–58. doi: 10.1007/s10896-015-9765-z

National Domestic Violence Hotline. (2019). About us: The hotline. Retrieved from https://www.thehotline.org/about-the-hotline/

Paone, T. R., Malott, K. M., & Maldonado, J. M. (2008). Exploring group activity therapy with ethnically diverse adolescents. *Journal of Creativity in Mental Health, 3*(3), 285–302.

Rivas, C., Ramsay, J., Sadowski, L., Davidson, L. L., Dunnes, D., Eldridge, S., . . . Feder, G. (2016). Advocacy interventions to reduce or eliminate violence and promote the physical and psychosocial well-being of women who experience intimate partner abuse: A systematic review. *Campbell Systematic Reviews, 12*(1), 1–202.

Scott, S., Diamond, G. S., & Levy, S. A. (2016). Attachment-based family therapy for suicidal adolescents: A case study. *Australian & New Zealand Journal of Family Therapy, 37*(2), 154–76. doi: 10.1002/anzf.1149

Silambuselvi, K., Abirami, P., Nandhini, R., Oneyekachi, E., & Jeevitha, J. (2019). A comparative study to assess the knowledge on child abuse among mothers residing in urban and rural community. *International Journal of Nursing Education, 11*(2), 23–26. doi: 10.5958/0974-9357.2019.00033.3

Singhal, M., & Vahali, H. O. (2014). Building broken sandcastles: Explorations in play therapy with a sexually abused child. *Journal of Indian Association for Child & Adolescent Mental Health, 10*(2), 132–44.

Chapter Thirteen

Counseling Strategies for Building Healthy Support Networks

Suzanne Degges-White

CASE STUDY: TRINIDAD

Trinidad, a thirty-seven-year-old African American, moved to this area over a year ago and is seeking counseling to help her deal with a pervasive sense of loneliness that she describes as "overwhelming aloneness." She moved here from her hometown almost one thousand miles away with her husband, Marcus, who was transferred to the area for his job. Unfortunately, Marcus's job involves a great deal of overnight travel, as he is a regional sales executive and his territory covers multiple states. Due to the extended absences from home of her husband, Trinidad says that she feels "uprooted and isolated" from her family and friends. She reports that she has not felt ready to try to create a new social support network in her new town and has begun to feel that she might not ever be ready. Trinidad tells Shatoya, her counselor, that she feels like her life ended when she and Marcus moved to town. She reports that she doesn't have the energy or zest that she did before the move and wonders if she should just pack up and go back home where she knew everyone and everyone knew her. Trinidad states, "I'm so tired of being a stranger. You know, everyone back home called me 'T' or 'Trini.' Now, it hurts my heart that days can go by when Marcus isn't home, and there's no one around to call me Trini anywhere in this city. Please call me Trini in here." Shatoya responds with empathy and encouragement: "Trini, it's really been challenging for you to move to a new city and still feel like a stranger months later. It's hard for you to spend so much time alone at home. You said that you hadn't been ready before to work at establishing yourself or making friends in a new community. Because you're here today, though, I have a feeling that you're ready to begin building some new friendships and finding your place. Does that sound accurate?" Trini nods her head and affirms, "I either have to find a way to feel at home here or I'll have to leave Marcus and go back home." Shatoya responds, "So it sounds like we are ready to focus on some strategies you can use to expand your social network."

* * *

William Glasser (1999) once stated that there are really only two reasons that clients seek counseling: they have unsatisfying relationships, or they have no relationships. To thrive, humans need to experience belongingness with individuals with whom they share mutual respect, positive regard, and the absence of conflict. Seldom is there any relationship that is conflict free, but in healthy friend and family relationships, conflict can be addressed and managed in ways that unhealthy relationships do not support.

POSITIVE EFFECTS OF A HEALTHY SUPPORT NETWORK

Some research has suggested that many people underestimate just how important having an intact and healthy social support system can be (Haslam et al., 2018). Unfortunately, when social support systems are marked by discord or generate role strain, they are actually detrimental to psychological well-being (Kawachi & Berkman, 2001). However, there is no doubt that having an adequate social support network and a sense of belonging positively influence an individual's overall sense of well-being and mental health (Appau, Churchill, & Farrell, 2019; Kessler & McLeod, 1985). These are also important to physical health. In fact, loneliness and social isolation present risks to physical health, including cardiovascular disease, compromised sleep, cognitive decline, weakened immunity, and earlier mortality (Hawkley & Capitanio, 2015; Segrin, 2019). Some view loneliness and the lack of social connection as severe health hazards that might be as lethal as smoking or obesity.

LONELINESS

Loneliness is a function of affective need for companionship and belonging, and left unaddressed it can detrimentally affect a person's self-wroth (Hawkley, Browne, & Cacioppo, 2005). The presence of loneliness reflects the absence of connection, not the absence of people. That's why a person can feel lonely even in a crowd. In fact, being in the middle of a crowd can make some people feel even lonelier if none of the members of their known support network are present and they feel unable to connect with others around them. Individuals also experience loneliness when they feel that their support network isn't providing the support that they need at a given moment.

Types of Loneliness

- A little bit of existential loneliness is good for the soul and is definitely an inevitable part of the human experience. However, loneliness tends to stir up negative feelings, and while those can be helpful for self-exploration, they are also something to which we are averse and want to avoid as much as we can.
- Emotional loneliness is the feeling that you lack relationships or attachments. You might experience emotional loneliness when everyone has a romantic partner in your group but you don't.
- Social loneliness occurs when you don't feel a sense of belonging to a group beyond yourself. You might even feel social loneliness when you're in a romantic relationship with a partner you treasure. If you don't feel that your presence is valued in a wider circle, you might experience social loneliness.

There is also a chronicity factor of loneliness. It can be a transient feeling, a situational feeling, or a chronic feeling. Most everyone has experienced a fleeting feeling of loneliness on occasion. Situational loneliness can be a more acute feeling of absence, especially when it's accompanied by some other significant transition, such as being alone during lunch at a new job or moving to a new place as a trailing spouse and feeling abandoned when your spouse heads off to work and you're left in the new place with no connections. Chronic loneliness, however, can result from unabated situational loneliness that lasts more than two years.

Combating Loneliness

Acknowledging that loneliness can lead to depression and compromised physical health, researchers have explored multiple ways of minimizing feelings of loneliness. Some of the methods explored are these four modes (Masi, Chen, Hawkley, & Cacioppo, 2010):

- Social skill enhancement—teaching people how to interact and be more effective in social settings
- Social support enhancement—scheduling interactions and arranging social connections
- Social contact increase—facilitating additional opportunities for social interaction
- Changing thoughts/beliefs about social interactions/support

These researchers found that the most effective method for combating loneliness is not enhancing social skills or increasing social connection opportunities; the most effective way to combat loneliness is for individuals to change their thoughts about social situations and social interaction. Clients may already have the requisite skills for creating a stronger sense of connection with others but may need support in changing their perspective on their social support and interaction.

While a sense of loneliness can be felt by people even when surrounded by others, social isolation reflects a static and objective set of circumstances. Social isolation is believed to be more devastating to physical health than loneliness might be (Tanskanen & Anttila, 2016) and can even predict rehospitalization for some patients (Saito et al., 2019).

SOCIAL ISOLATION

Social isolation, similarly to loneliness, means different things to different people. For some, it is the absence of a sense of emotional connection to others. For others, social isolation describes a sense of social disconnection (Knight, Chisholm, Nigel, & Godfrey, 1988). In essence, social isolation occurs when someone has little to no interaction with others.

Most often we think of older adults as the most likely to experience isolation; as their families move away and their mobility lessens, older women may find themselves becoming housebound, whether it is their choice or not. However, researchers have found that young adults actually experience higher levels of social isolation than those in late middle age (Child & Lawton, 2017). The perception of satisfaction with one's support group was a predictor of feelings of isolation and loneliness. An interesting conundrum exists related to the use of social media and feelings of social isolation. Younger adults with higher social media usage reported higher levels of isolation; however, midlife and older adults reported their engagement in social media actually leaves them feeling less isolated and more connected to their social networks (Hajek & König, 2019). When working with clients, it is apparent that the effect of social media engagement may vary significantly based on age as well as other demographic and personality traits.

STRATEGIES TO INCREASE SOCIAL ENGAGEMENT AND SUPPORT NETWORKS

In past generations, mothers would tell their daughters that in order to have good friends, they must be a good friend to others first. When working with clients who are trying to build new relationships or improve existing relationships, it is important for the client to objectively assess her own role in social relationships. Being likable and self-confident are two important attributes when it comes to forging friendships and social connections. People gravitate toward people who seem familiar to them, which is why people are attracted to others they feel are similar to themselves in some way and to those with whom they have exchanged positive words or similar perspectives (Benoit, 2003). When people are meeting potential friends for the first time, the sharing of information about oneself provides opportunities to find commonalities, which also serve as the glue that holds friendships together. There are other traits beyond similarity that affect the future of potential friendship development. These traits typically are revealed as an acquaintanceship moves toward friendship, and the presence or absence of these traits tend to predict the eventual quality and depth of a friendship.

Friendship Traits Client Self-Assessment Intervention

Three categories of personal traits were found key to building healthy friendships (Degges-White & Borzumato-Gainey, 2011). These are the traits of integrity, caring, and congeniality. When clients reported frustrated attempts to establish new friendships or propel an acquaintanceship into a friendship, clinicians can encourage clients to take stock of what qualities they bring to the relationship and determine if there are areas in which personal development is needed.

Traits of Integrity

These five qualities are related to the core values held by most cultures: trustworthiness, honesty, dependability, loyalty, and, as an interrelated quality, the ability to trust others. Trustworthiness is often the "make or break" element in any interpersonal relationship. Any breach, regardless of perceived magnitude, can devastate a relationship. It is comprised of several components, including honesty, dependability, and loyalty. Although each is important to successful relationships, dependability and honesty have been identified as the most vital in the realm of friendships (Degges-White & Borzumato-Gainey, 2011). To assess for the presence of these traits, ask your client to respond to the following questions:

Trustworthiness: Am I someone that I would trust?
Honesty: Do I speak openly with objectivity with others?
Dependability: Can others count on me to do what I said I would do?
Loyalty: Do I stand by my friends and stand up for my friends?
Trusting of Others: Can I be vulnerable with friends and count on them to be there for me?

Traits of Caring

This cluster of traits includes empathy, the ability to withhold judgment, effective listening skills, and the ability to offer support in good times and bad. These require personal insight, self-discipline, and unconditional positive regard for our friends. To assess for the presence of these traits, ask your client to respond to the following questions:

Empathy: Do I show others that I understand what they are going through or feeling?

Lack of Judgment: Can I accept a friend's choices even if they are radically different from what I would do?

Listening Skills: Am I patient with others when they need me to listen and be present?

Supportive of Others in Their Bad Times: Do I show up for friends when they are in trouble or facing a challenge?

Supportive of Others in Their Good Times: Am I able to celebrate another's good fortune, or do I feel resentment, jealousy, or envy?

Traits of Congeniality

Self-confidence, the ability to see the humor in life, and being fun to be around make up this set of traits. This trio of traits has also been associated with overall well-being and happiness in life. To assess for the presence of these traits, ask your client to respond to the following questions:

Self-Confidence: Do I feel good about who I am, and do I help others feel good about who they are?

Fun to Be Around: Do I make life more pleasant for those around me, or do I spend more time bringing down my friends?

Ability to See the Humor in Life: Do I have trouble laughing about things, and do I take life too seriously?

Helping a client work through these questions can provide them with an opportunity to see themselves more objectively as well as to begin to understand which qualities they should look for in their current and future friends. When clients share anecdotes of prior failed relationships, counselors should listen for patterns across the incidents described. People tend to repeat relationship mistakes throughout their lives until they are able to recognize the patterns they follow.

Using these traits as a guide, help the client explore whether there are patterns or similarities in their failed or stalled relationships that reflect one or more of these necessary qualities. For example, if a client typically withdraws from relationships when their friends are moving forward and experiencing successes, whether in their careers, families, or other relationships, perhaps the client should explore their roadblocks to being able to celebrate others' success. On the other hand, if a client shares experiences in which they felt that they had been wronged by friends through misplaced trust or loyalty, they may be encouraged to explore their own expectations of others as well as their own boundaries. These traits provide rich areas for discussion when clients want to take all of the blame for failed relationships or try to place all of the blame on others.

Support Needs Self-Assessment Intervention

Not only do clients need to be able to honestly assess themselves and their strength and areas in need of development, they also need to develop a clear idea of the networking needs that they are trying to meet. Kahn and Antonucci (1980) developed the construct of the "social convoy," which is made up of the individuals who are people in our networks. The convoy is composed of concentric circles illustrating the closeness of the relationship. Not only do friendships differ in regard to intimacy between a person and her friend, they also differ in terms of the type of support a friend provides. We typically rely on people outside our family networks to provide one of two kinds of support, instrumental support and emotional support. Instrumental needs focus on the "nuts and bolts" of survival in our environment, such as lending things, carpooling our kids, and helping out when a task is too big to manage on our own. Our emotional needs relate to companionship, understanding, and a shoulder to lean on if we need it. Both are vital to our optimal functioning, but they serve different purposes. While friends who do "double duty" are especially appreciated, clients need to be assured that not any one friend can meet every need a person will have.

By helping a client deconstruct her social support networks and social support needs, the client will be in a more objective position to seek out and establish the type of relationships that are needed. Invite the client to create two lists on a sheet of paper; one list is titled "Instrumental Support," and the other "Emotional Support." With younger clients, you might term the subsets of a social support network as "Functional Friends" and "Fun Friends." Ask the client to list the needs she has under each category that are not being met. For instance, if a client needs someone to carpool her child to lacrosse practice, you can ask her to brainstorm ways to connect with other lacrosse parents. If she needs someone to talk to about her frustration with her job, her latest disagreement with her mother, and so on, you can challenge the client to invite a pleasant coworker to coffee or a lunchtime walk to see if there might be potential for friendship.

When clients feel alone or isolated due to illness, disability, relational status, and so on, counselors can challenge their clients to gather information on face-to-face or virtual support groups. While face-to-face groups provide an in-the-moment connection and vulnerability that online groups do not, when clients feel significant disconnect from others, even an online community can be of assistance to the client.

Strategies for Helping Clients Connect to Others

Not only is it common sense, research provides evidence that the more time we are able to spend with friends, the closer the friendship will grow (Hall, 2019). Not only does time together matter, so does the content of the communication between two people. Small talk may propel two people "from strangers to acquaintances," but it requires increasingly meaningful and rich conversations to take a pair of people into a mutual friendship.

Shyness and self-consciousness are two significant hindrances that limit a client's availability for new friendships. Encourage clients to start small by practicing their skills in opening conversations with "safe" strangers, such as clerks in stores, neighbors they pass while picking up their mail or walking their dogs, and coworkers. Encourage them to practice "opening lines," such as commenting on lighter topics such as the weather or local sports teams.

Practicing "soft openings" and casual pleasantries will prepare clients for engaging in conversations that will require increased self-disclosure and engagement. Some tips to share with clients include encouraging them to observe themselves in a mirror to ensure that their facial expression is open and approachable. Encourage clients to use the name of the person to whom they are chatting, as this builds the sense of connection and has a positive effect on another's openness to conversation. Remind clients that it takes time to build authentic friendships, and according to Hall's (2019) findings, it takes about forty-three contact hours before acquaintances will begin to feel like friends.

Suggestions for Finding Potential Friends

There are multiple online venues for connecting with new people, but remind clients that some means are safer than others. Several apps have been created to facilitate friendships, including Nextdoor, Hey! Vina, BumbleBFF, Peanut (for moms of young children), Meetup (which provides multiple interest-based groups from knitters to Mini Cooper owners to salsa dancers), and Friender. Other less "high tech" means include taking classes and engaging classmates in conversations before and after class to deepen potential friendships, volunteering for a cause that matters to the client, attending faith-based services or events, getting involved in community service opportunities, and taking dogs to the dog park or kids to a neighborhood park.

A Note about Social Media

While social media platforms were created to allow people to connect with others around the globe, the use of social media as a primary form of connection is not recommended. In fact, individuals who report the highest utilization of social media also report higher levels of social isolation (Primack et al., 2017). When newly transplanted individuals, such as those who relocate to a new town or young adults moving onto a college campus, spend a disproportionate amount of time connecting to or communicating with friends from their hometown, they may be slower to acclimate to their new home and slower to build new, local social support networks. Advising clients to stay in touch with their friends and family is good, but encouraging them to devote at least an equal amount of time engaging with people in their new hometown is important as well.

Social media can be a tool to access information about meet-up groups, local events, and so on, but reliance on social media does not protect against feelings of isolation. If social media is used to deepen relationships with new acquaintances, researchers have found that photo images, not just text messages, are more likely to heighten the sense of connection between people (Pittman & Reich, 2016). However, not all connections are positive.

Helping Clients Terminate Unhealthy Relationships

Sometimes clients share details about their relationships with acquaintances and friends that are clearly unhealthy and detrimental to their physical and mental health. When you have concern about the effects clients' relationships may be having on their well-being, broaching the topic of healthy relationships may be helpful. Encouraging a client to explore the benefits and costs of a friendship is an appropriate place to begin the discussion. Social relationships marred by conflict can be more damaging to well-being than the absence of relationships.

Reviewing key communication skills, such as using "I" statements, avoiding the placement of blame on the acquaintance, and being authentic and straightforward in as kind a manner as possible, can help the client prepare for a difficult conversation. Invite the client to rehearse their "friendship breakup speech" with you in the counseling office to allow them to gain a sense of familiarity with the content. Through behavior rehearsal, the client will be able to mentally refer to what they have planned to say, which will decrease the likelihood of going totally off script and using damaging or hurtful words.

DIVERSITY CONSIDERATIONS

Friendship and social connection are essential to health and well-being around the globe. Unfortunately, potential relationships can be prevented from forming due to perceived differences between individuals. When working with any client regarding any issue, counselors must allow themselves to see the world from the client's perspective. If a client feels uncomfortable with suggested interventions due to concerns about others' perceptions or biases, it is helpful to explore these perceptions or fears with the client.

ETHICAL CONSIDERATIONS

When suggesting interventions to encourage a client to meet new people or get more involved in social settings, it is important to encourage client safety in any unfamiliar setting. If the clinician suggests strategies that involve approaching new people, the client should be encouraged to follow guidelines related to personal safety. No strategies for establishing new relationships should put the client in any type of emotional or physical danger. Encouraging clients to utilize current friends and family members as pathways to new friendships may be advisable if clients do not feel immediately comfortable establishing relationships with less familiar acquaintances.

ADVOCACY OPPORTUNITIES

Perhaps the most impactful advocacy effort is offering your time to volunteer in your community. One can volunteer to provide companionship or assistance at women's shelters. Or one can offer babysitting services to the children of the residents at the shelter. Individuals who have been displaced from their homes and may feel very much alone or isolated from their prior social networks would welcome a friendly listener. One can volunteer to deliver meals to homebound individuals and take time to get to know the people, for whom one becomes a link in their lifelines. As women get older, their social networks often shrink; by making time to build relationships with older women, whose families may be far-flung, you are providing a much-needed gift of connection. If you work in settings where you see children being rejected by other children, reach out to that child. If you see someone standing alone at a party, walk up to her and open a conversation. Advocating for others, in terms of social connection, is as easy as introducing yourself and inviting someone to do the same.

CASE VIGNETTE WRAP-UP: TRINIDAD

Shatoya feels concern about the presence of depressive symptoms reported by Trinidad and the lack of interest in the activities that she once enjoyed, so Shatoya explores the level of subjective distress Trinidad is feeling. She asks Trinidad to put a number on her level of sadness, with 1 being as low as she's ever felt, and 10 being the best she's ever felt. Trinidad responds, "I guess I'm about a 4 or 5; I don't feel depressed really as much as overwhelmed by the job ahead of me. I want to get back to my old self, and I'm willing to do something now so that I don't turn tail and run back home. I love Marcus, I love our new house, but I just don't love this town yet."

Shatoya empathizes with Trinidad on a professional and personal level, as she has experienced several cross-country relocations in her own life. Shatoya chooses to self-disclose judiciously to provide support to Trinidad as they begin their work together. Shatoya shares, "Trini, I've experienced a few geographic shakeups myself, and I appreciate the challenges you are facing in trying to find your place in a new community."

Taking into account the sense of isolation that Trinidad describes, Shatoya focuses on ensuring that Trinidad is able to build and maintain new social support networks. Shatoya first invites Trinidad to assess her current support needs in terms of emotional support and instrumental support.

Trini reports that she doesn't have a long list of instrumental support needs as Marcus leaves her their car while he travels and they only have cats not kids. Trinidad wonders aloud whether connecting with her new neighbors might be a good way to find the best veterinarian for her cats and a dentist for her and Marcus.

Shatoya responds, "So it sounds like the type of instrumental support you could use most right now is information. That's usually something that others like to share with new neighbors. How might you go about reaching out?"

Trini smiles. "Oh, that's easy. My next-door neighbor has dogs; I've seen them walking them every evening when they get home. It's as easy as being out on my porch when they walk by and striking up a conversation. I don't like dogs, but I could ask them about local vets."

"Absolutely! Okay, by taking the first step for your instrumental needs, how might that connect to your emotional needs?"

"Well, like I said, I don't talk to too many people during the week. What with self-checkouts, ATM machines, and electronic everything, I isolate myself pretty much. If I take a chance and reach out, I'll at least be having a conversation with a face-to-face local. That would get me started on the path to building new friendships here. And, yeah, I know, I could begin going to the church down the street. I could maybe look into volunteering at the food pantry." Trinidad is smiling now. "The move was just so much, and with Marcus gone all day, I just felt stuck, ya' know?"

Shatoya affirms, "Moving to a new city and spending more time alone than you ever had before is a huge transition. It's normal for some people to feel paralyzed by that kind of change. Being aware of the need to do something different takes courage, and it's clear that you're ready to break the ice and begin reaching out and exploring the possibilities of new friendships."

QUESTIONS FOR REFLECTION

1. What are some situations that you have faced in which you had to build new social connections?
2. What are some barriers that clients might describe that would keep them from reaching out to new acquaintances?
3. What are some strategies you might suggest to older adult clients to help them build new friendships?
4. What are some volunteer activities you would suggest for young women, midlife women, new mothers, or older adults?

REFERENCES

Appau, S., Churchill, S. A., & Farrell, L. (2019). Social integration and subjective wellbeing. *Applied Economics, 51*, 1748–61.

Benoit, M. (2003). The warm glow heuristic: When liking leads to familiarity. *Journal of Personality & Social Psychology, 85*, 1035–48.

Child, S. T., & Lawton, L. (2017). Loneliness and social isolation among young and late middle-age adults: Associations with personal networks and social participation. *Aging & Mental Health, 23*(2), 196–204.

Degges-White, S., & Borzumato-Gainey, C. (2011). *Friends forever: How girls and women forge lasting relationships.* Lanham, MD: Rowman & Littlefield.

Glasser, W. (1999). *Choice theory: A new psychology of personal freedom.* New York, NY: HarperCollins.

Hajek, A., & König, H. H. (2019). The association between use of online social network sites and perceived social isolation among individuals in the second half of life: Results based on a nationally representative sample in Germany. *BMC Public Health, 19*(1), 40.

Hall, J. A. (2019). How many hours does it take to make a friend? *Journal of Social and Personal Relationships, 36*(4), 1278–96.

Haslam, S. A., McMahon, C., Cruwys, T., Haslam, C., Jetten, J., & Steffens, N. K. (2018). Social cure, what social cure? The propensity to underestimate the importance of social factors for health. *Social Science and Medicine, 198*, 14–21.

Hawkley, L. C., Browne, M. W., & Cacioppo, J. T. (2005). How can I connect with thee? Let me count the ways. *Psychological Science, 16*, 798–804.

Hawkley, L. C., & Capitanio, J. P. (2015). Perceived social isolation, evolutionary fitness and health outcomes: A lifespan approach. *Philosophical Transactions of the Royal Society B, 370*(1669), 1–12.

Kahn, R. L., & Antonucci, T. C. (1980). Convoys over the life course: Attachment, roles, and social support. In P. B. Baltes & O. G. Brim Jr. (Eds.), *Lifespan development and behavior,* vol. 3 (pp. 253–86). New York, NY: Academic Press.

Kawachi, I., & Berkman, L. F. (2001). Social ties and mental health. *Journal of Urban Health, 78*(3), 458–67.

Kessler, R. C., & McLeod, J. D. (1985). Social support and mental health in community samples. In S. Cohen & S. L. Syme (Eds.), *Social support and health* (pp. 219–40). San Diego, CA: Academic Press.

Knight, R. G., Chisholm, B. J., Nigel, V. M., & Godfrey, H. P. D. (1988). Some normative, reliability, and factor analytic data for the revised UCLA loneliness scale. *Journal of Clinical Psychology, 44*, 203–6.

Masi, C. M., Chen, H.-Y., Hawkley, L. C., & Cacioppo, J. T. (2010). A meta-analysis of interventions to reduce loneliness. *Personality and Social Psychology Review, 15*(3), 219–66.

Pittman, M., & Reich, B. (2016). Social media and loneliness: Why an Instagram picture may be worth more than a thousand Twitter words. *Computers in Human Behavior, 62*, 155–67.

Primack, B. A., Shensa, A., Sidani, J. E., Whaite, E. O., Lin, L., Rosen, D., . . . Miller, E. (2017). Social media use and perceived social isolation among young adults in the U.S. *American Journal of Preventive Medicine, 53*, 1–8.

Saito, H., Kagiyama, N., Nagano, N., Matsumoto, K., Yoshioka, K., Endo, Y., . . . Matsue, Y. (2019). Social isolation is associated with 90-day rehospitalization due to heart failure. *European Journal of Cardiovascular Nursing, 18*(1), 16–20.

Segrin, C. (2019). Indirect effects of social skills on health through stress and loneliness. *Health Communication, 34*, 118–24.

Tanskanen, J., & Anttila, T. (2016). A prospective study of social isolation, loneliness, and mortality in Finland. *American Journal of Public Health, 106*(11), 2042–48.

Part V

Individual Concerns

Chapter Fourteen

Counseling Women with Body Image Concerns

Rachel Brandoff and Marcela Kepic

CASE VIGNETTE: SADIE

Sadie is a thirty-four-year-old woman who presents as healthy, fit, and attractive. In her first session with Jamie, her counselor, she described herself as an overweight teen who grew into a taut and fitness-obsessed adult after battling self-injurious behaviors during her teen and early adult years. She spent the better part of seven years binging and purging and cutting herself. Sadie explained that she would cut in private in her room, usually on her lower stomach or upper thighs, where it would not show around her clothing. In later sessions, Sadie was able to identify that she started hating herself and her body when she was very young. She shared with Jamie that she thought these feelings corresponded to a sexual assault she endured when she was three-years-old at the hands of an older foster child placed with her family. Sadie seemed to try any means possible to develop control of her body. In addition to bulimia nervosa and cutting, Sadie engaged in strenuous and obsessive exercise and sexual promiscuity, and eventually she married an abusive and controlling man who would body shame her. However, on the outside to others, Sadie appeared to be the picture of health—eating well, exercising regularly, dressing stylishly, and taking care of her appearance.

* * *

Body image concerns take all forms and are frequently addressed in psychotherapy, both as the impetus for seeking treatment and as an emergent issue during treatment. Clients can develop body image issues due to a variety of issues. These include child abuse and neglect, teasing/bullying, relationship violence, sexual assault, rape, physical deformities and illness (both physical and psychological), surgery, accidents, marriage, divorce, social judgment, and rigid cultural norms. Body image concerns might accompany or cause depression, anxiety, social withdrawal, sleep disturbances, low self-esteem, eating disorders, chemical or behavioral addictions, and suicidal ideation. In this chapter, we provide foundational information regarding body image and treatment interventions for working with clients. While body image issues can occur in any individual at any point in life, this chapter focuses on adult women and treatment.

PREVALENCE AND RISK FACTORS

Body image concerns are not a new development, as cultural norms for appearance date back to earliest times. These concerns arise for a variety of individuals, and they exist for multiple reasons. The Body Image Therapy Center (n.d.) reported that 50 percent of women use unhealthy behaviors to control their weight and that 70 percent of eighteen- to thirty-year-olds do not like their body. It is believed that 89 percent of girls have dieted by the age of seventeen and that 81 percent of ten-year-olds are afraid of being fat (Body Image Therapy Center, n.d.). There is evidence that poor body image starts early and does not end for many women (Levens, 1995). Statistics have indicated that one thousand women die each year from eating disorders due to malnutrition, heart attacks, and suicide, and the rate of death for women with eating disorders is twelve times higher than women without an eating disorder in the same age range (Body Image Therapy Center, n.d.). There is a clear need for women to see themselves and their bodies in a positive light.

Positive body image supports good health, both physical and mental. In addition to the role that positive body image plays in boosting confidence and self-esteem, it promotes self-care and health practices that create a positive feedback loop. Similarly, thinking negatively about one's body tends to lead to more negative thinking. Negative body image can have a profound impact on thoughts, feelings, and behaviors; it is difficult to feel good about oneself when there is a part of the self that is intensely disliked. In fact, body dissatisfaction, or a negative body image, can lead to anxiety, depression (Hawkins, 2014), low self-esteem, self-consciousness (Maine, 2000), poor relationship and lifestyle choices (Hirschmann & Munter, 1995), and in extreme cases suicide. This can also negatively affect behaviors, activities, and relationships.

Body image is influenced by a variety of factors, including personality, family history and family environment, social media, and culture (Maine, 2000). Additional influences include abilities and normative development, such as growth, puberty, menopause, and physical decline. Paradoxically, body image concerns are experienced internally, but they are commonly prompted by external factors. In other words, the personal thoughts and feelings people have about their body image are frequently fostered by comments, criticisms, and overt and covert societal messages (Maine & Kelly, 2005). Many people report that they internalize the words they have heard others use, whether the message comes from people they know, magazines or print media, or online. Unfortunately, negative messages carry far more weight than positive messages (Hanna & Bond, 2006). While the exact origin of a negative body image is highly individual, many possible causes have been cited. Maine (2000) suggested factors such as social influences that promote poor body image in children, from dieting pressure to biased sport activities like dance, to the impact of Barbie dolls and similarly exaggerated doll icons. It is clear that by the time women grow up, they have been inundated with messages regarding the danger of imperfections in their appearance as well as messages that their bodies are problems to be corrected. Maine's (2000) groundbreaking research exemplified that in this culture women are devalued, disempowered, and even taught to hate their bodies. Maine's study also served as a sort of call to arms, encouraging a pushing back on the aspects and agents of a culture that endorses what the researcher called "body wars" (Maine, 2000).

It has become common for people to experience body dissatisfaction as well as shame, anxiety, and self-consciousness about their appearance. This is perhaps why someone like Sadie was able to engage in undetected cutting and disordered eating behaviors for so long. Clinicians who work with clients who have poor body image and eating disorders know that body dissatisfaction may have little to do with an individual's weight, shape, or appearance. Individuals with poor body image often compulsively compare themselves to others, further feeding their own feelings of inadequacy (Hawkins, 2014). In many cases, people are caught in a vicious cycle of wanting to lose weight or improve what they think is one small facet of their physical selves, only to find they are chasing an unattainable perfection forever. Their realistic perception of themself has already been distorted. Regardless of size or scale number, women who lack an acceptance of body and self are likely to continue to reapply their own critique, even if a perceived wrong has been righted.

There are risks that promote the likelihood of body image concerns in individuals; knowing these risk factors, counselors can preemptively address clients who may have greater likelihood of developing negative body image. Risks include childhood trauma, sexual assault and rape, deformities, medical illness, surgeries, childbirth, domestic violence, mental illness, drug use, and unsuccessful dieting (Hirschmann & Munter, 1995). Some of these risks are immensely broad and experienced by a large number of women. To help minimize the risk of hazardous body-image-related behaviors, some organizations and institutions are taking a proactive approach. School-based curriculums, treatment centers, and counseling providers are proactively offering classes, workshops, and tutorials on how to establish and maintain a positive body image, and how to identify the warning signs of disorder (Kater, Rohwer, & Levine, 2000; Piran, 1994; Polivy & Herman, 1991).

Body Image Concerns by Diagnosis and Behavior

Certain diagnoses listed in the fifth edition of the *Diagnostic and Statistical Manual of Mental Disorders* (DSM-5) are most readily associated with body image concerns. They are body dysmorphic disorder, muscle dysmorphic disorder, gender dysphoria, trichotillomania (hair-pulling) disorder, excoriation (skin-picking) disorder, substance abuse disorders, post-traumatic stress disorder, and feeding and eating disorders, including pica, avoidant/restrictive food intake disorder, anorexia nervosa, bulimia nervosa, binge-eating disorder, and unspecified eating disorders. However, body image concerns can be associated with any diagnosis, including mood disorders, psychotic disorders, and personality disorders. Here is a more in-depth look at the top three.

Eating disorders are perhaps the most well-known form of body-image-related concern. In these conditions, individuals generally try to control eating, weight, and caloric intake and output. Disorders have diagnostic criteria and defining features, but motivation and triggers can vary significantly. Anorexia nervosa (extreme food restriction) and bulimia nervosa (binge eating combined with purging) are the most documented eating disorders. Others include binge-eating disorder (eating an excessive amount, even when not hungry), compulsive eating (constant eating or grazing), orthorexia (compulsive consumption of health foods), other specified feeding and eating disorders, and unspecified feeding and eating disorders, which allows for additional variations in symptomology or insufficient support for a more specific diagnosis of eating disorder. Eating disorders can include a plethora of behaviors, including food restriction, fasting, fear of weight gain, excessive exercise, use of laxatives or diet aids, or vomiting after eating (Maine & Kelly, 2005). All counselors can provide education and early interventions aimed at prevention of the development of negative body image perceptions and eating disorders as these can affect anyone regardless of socioeconomic status, race, gender, or age (Shallcross, 2013).

Many women with body image concerns live normal lives and do not recognize that they may be engaging in disordered eating or receive a mental health diagnosis. That does not mean that they are not suffering from a disorder. Maine and Kelly (2005) wrote about what the real behavior of subclinical eating disorders looks like. With significant statistics to back up their implications for practice, they looked at women who use drugs and diet pills, smoke cigarettes, shop excessively, elect for plastic surgery, and resort to a variety of other behaviors in conjunction with dieting as a way of keeping control over their bodies and the concerns that plague them. Maine and Kelly (2005) presented a familiar list of behaviors that indicate subclinical disorders; perhaps these are common enough to be "excused" as normal. Their list included the following:

> Counting calories, fat grams, or carbohydrates every time she eats, chronic restrictive dieting, exercising obsessively in order to burn up calories consumed, skipping meals as often as possible, trying to go days without eating, repeated weighings, using laxatives, diuretics, diet pills, or other over-the-counter medications to lose weight, wishing she was anorexic or bulimic, engaging in some anorexic or bulimic behaviors, although inconsistently, feeling guilty if she allows herself to enjoy food, alternating between periods of excessive control and excessive indulgence with food, cooking for others but not eating, maintaining many rules about good versus bad food, feelings of sinning, being immoral, or being bad when eating a forbidden food, smoking cigarettes, chewing gum, or drinking coffee, soda, or water to avoid eating, obsessively anticipating what food will not be eaten or how calories eaten will be burned up. (pp. 88–89)

These behaviors can easily be overlooked, but major health concerns emerge based on the frequency and intensity of these behaviors (Maine & Kelly, 2005). The fact that these behaviors seem so common and may not rise to a diagnostic level invites inquiry and criticism about societal norms and what is permitted and perpetuated. Root causes of eating disorders frequently look the same as root causes for other manifestations of body image concerns: major life transitions, such as puberty or entering high school or college, are frequently causes. New relationships, family problems, social adjustment issues, teasing and bullying, traumatic events such as sexual abuse, psychiatric illness, and low self-esteem are also frequent culprits that can lead a person toward eating-disordered behavior, and sometimes diagnosis.

Body dysmorphic disorder (BDD) is a diagnosis given when an individual has an ever-present obsession with how she looks or how she perceives she looks. BDD is vastly different from the typical range of discomfort that many people feel regarding their own appearance. People with BDD tend to have a persistent obsession with a particular part or parts of their body (American Psychiatric Association, 2013). Oftentimes they get fixated on this body part. Common fixations are hair, skin, genitalia, breasts, chest, stomach, buttocks, and face, but really any body part could be the object of fixation. To the person with BDD, the feature is experienced as a flaw, regardless of its actual state. In many cases, the feature may be a very slight imperfection or be completely invisible to others; generally, the feature actually goes unnoticed by others. People with BDD frequently have trouble focusing due to their body fixation interfering in events, activities, and, eventually, relationships. In many cases, body image begins to steer behavior and social engagements as it grows to interfere with daily life (American Psychiatric Association, 2013). Many people experience social anxiety and social aversion; they frequently fear ridicule and rejection and seek to avoid the possibility of this. Clients with BDD will go to great lengths to camouflage their flaws; in some cases, they elect to undergo surgery and physical alterations that are medically unnecessary and potentially dangerous. These behaviors usually do not provide lasting relief from the perpetual worry they experience (American Psychiatric Association, 2013).

In a culture now reliant on social media, some argue that body image concerns have increased. Issues of body consciousness do not reside solely in those who have diagnostically significant symptoms. Indeed, many otherwise functional and even healthy adults are burdened by body image concerns. Cutting across this wide swath of the population makes these preoccupations and worries seem normal; they are in fact unhealthy and potentially dangerous. Levine and Murnen (2009) called for research that examines the deleterious effects of poor body image over time, as well as ways to increase media literacy as a form of harm reduction and prevention. Mass media is considered to be a causal risk factor for both poor body image and also disordered eating in women. In addition to cultural influences, personal history may also raise the risk of symptomology.

Post-traumatic stress disorder (PTSD) is a diagnosis that may not appear related to body image; however, people who have sustained significant traumas also commonly develop pervasive body image issues. PTSD is a disorder that arises following a traumatic incident, whereby an individual is plagued with extreme behavioral and psychological dysfunction at a level that is typically life-interrupting. Many people experience agitation, hypervigilance, irritability, social isolation, hostility, self-destructive behaviors, emotional detachment, intrusive thoughts, loss of interest in typical activities of pleasure, and disturbances in eating, sleeping, and other typical daily activities (American Psychiatric Association, 2013). These experiences quickly become life altering and negatively affect the ability to work, play, and socialize. Studies suggest a great correlation between individuals with PTSD and those with eating disorders (Brewerton, 2007; Dansky, Brewerton, O'Neil, & Kilpatrick, 1997; Hudson, Hiripi, Pope, & Kessler, 2007; Mitchell, Mazzeo, Schlesinger, Brewerton, & Smith, 2012). These diagnoses often occur together.

Cohen and Mills (1999) indicated that "for psychotherapy to be complete and successful for individuals with post-traumatic disorders, it is necessary to investigate body image" (p. 204). Cohen and Mills (1999) discussed the obstacles to open discussions related to body image and the support for using art as an effective means of evaluating a distorted body image. The Diagnostic Drawing Series (DDS), an art therapy diagnostic and assessment tool, can be a revelatory tool for better understanding the complications and intricacies of a client's trauma and body image (Cohen & Mills, 1994; Kessler, 1994). The DDS theory, developed by Cohen and Mills (1999), provides an effective metaphoric tool in "skin/paper/bark" that incorporates the reading and assessing of artwork and understanding these as facets of a client's experience that can help explain multiple aspects of their body image issues.

TREATMENT INTERVENTIONS

There are many recommendations for activities to improve body image. Some are quite simple and can be done at home, such as developing a practice of expressing gratitude (Young & Hutchinson, 2012) or trading a negative thought for a positive. While some of these strategies may be successful, some may yield undesirable consequences. For example, signing out of social media may eliminate negative messages from peers and media, but it may also eliminate a means of connection with friends, relatives, and other support systems. Because many of these recommendations work best for individuals within the context of healthy relationships, they may be less effective for some clients. Thus, some clients need a space in therapy to learn and practice techniques both simple and complex.

Intentional Checking

While many resources provide worthwhile ideas like "stop checking" or "accept yourself," they do not always include instructions on what to actually do to achieve this. Specific quantified tasks may raise awareness, or change the frequency, of detrimental behaviors. Asking a client to count and limit the number of times she looks in the mirror, gets on the scale, or berates herself while eating can be a useful strategy. Some may argue that this draws undue attention to behavior or highlights things that need greater avoidance. However, counting can raise awareness about what is already happening and provide baseline data that can be used to help a client measure success.

Body Maps

Another way to raise awareness is through the use of body maps. This idea is related to the concept of cognitive mapping and mind mapping; it is used in cognitive behavioral art therapy (CBAT) toward the goal of changing maladaptive thought patterns by drawing events or situations that are causing problems (Buchalter, 2015; Rosal, 2018). Body mapping challenges an individual to view their body as a landscape of sorts that is evolving; clients can visualize "sites" slated for razing and changing, and others may be identified as sites of preservation (Wallace, 2015). Buchalter (2009) suggested that clients use a predrawn body outline to fill in with human aspects such as hair, clothes, and facial features, and then mark areas where they feel pain in their body. The strength of the exercise comes from consideration, identification, and demarcation, which can then be tools to use in future examining of issues of pain in counseling. The use of art therapy can also be beneficial for clients with body image issues and eating disorders.

Art Therapy

Moschini (2005) offered insight regarding body image in art therapy, looking at how clients might omit, reinforce, exaggerate, distort, or blacken body parts, and possible meanings to be inferred. The use of art in exploration of body image issues where content and origins are often latent can be a useful approach. Rubin (2005) suggested, "What is repressed can be expressed in images more easily than in words," which allows clients to "get in touch with the affects and ideas behind their symptoms" (p. 15). Moreover, using art materials can satisfy the intense need of such patients to be in control. The availability of media can also be experienced as a kind of feeding, with the therapist as provider of something taken in and then used by the patient for herself. Another ongoing tool for clients is a body image journal.

Body Image Journal

A body image journal can provide a tool for a client to confront herself and her self-defeating stereotypes, self-consciousness, and personal critique, so that she looks and feels better in her own skin (Cash, 1995; Mayo Clinic, 2019). There is a tradition of using repetitive journal writing in counseling to better understand an individual's experience and help the client analyze it as a means of moving toward change (Makin, 2000; Rubin, 2005). Journaling has been shown to decrease stress, improve development, enhance cognitive awareness, emotional satisfaction, and self-esteem (Buchalter, 2015; Hieb, 2005; Mercer, Warson, & Zhao, 2010). Journaling has been combined into a number of DBT and CBT therapy models (Clark, 2017; Rosal, 2018) and can help strengthen the resolve of the author, giving them a sense of agency and control (Buchalter, 2015). Journaling can include creative writing, stream-of-conscious writing, and art. Some clients find benefit in noting when certain thoughts appear and then creating art about the experience of those thoughts (Kabat-Zinn, 1994).

ETHICAL CONSIDERATIONS

Considering the high prevalance of body image issues and eating disorders, their high comorbidity, and their high fatality rates, counselors must be knowledgeable and skilled in addressing such issues. First and foremost, clinicians do not practice out of their scope; therefore, seek training and supervision to treat body image issues and related disorders. Second, informed consent and discussion of confidentiality might be a concern for some, especially when treating young adolescent girls. Counselors need to be transparent about limits of confidentiality in their informed consent and openly discuss them. Moreover, they obtain consent from parents and assent from young adolescents in order to engage in counseling. Body image disorders and eating disorders are accompanied by other disorders, such as major depressive disorder. Such comborbidity and severity of symptoms may require inpatient treatment and postdischarge services from various providers. When working with an interdisciplinary team, clinicians should ensure collaboration and share information only after obtaining a release by written consent from the client and her parents if dealing with minors. Despite the fact that body image issues and related disorders might share presentation, clinicians need to be multiculturally competent to adjust assessments and treatments to clients' diverse backgrounds, work with their families, and provide ongoing psychoeducation, support, and resources.

CULTURAL CONSIDERATIONS

Research on prevalence and treatment of body image issues and related disorders in minority populations is lacking. Most studies have been conducted with white adolescents and young women, but attention is needed on these disorders in diverse populations. Some research supports that eating disorders are more common among nonwhite girls and women due to acculturation into mainstream U.S. culture (National Eating Disorder Association, 2019). Acculturative stress may contribute to body image issues and eating disorders. Further, all ethnic groups exhibited dieting that was associated with weight dissatisfaction and low body pride. In terms of gender, 85 percent of people with body image issues and eating disorders are women (National Eating Disorder Association, 2019). Approximately one-third of women diagnosed with body image or eating disorders were thirty years old and older, which may be surprising to some. The percentage of women with body image and eating disorders in midlife continues to climb, confirming lifespan pervasiveness. Clearly, individuals in counseling who are dealing with body image issues are as diverse as all of the clients in counseling. But it behooves the counselor to consider certain issues and ask certain questions in order to provide the best treatment possible.

BEST PRACTICES

In session, intervention ideas may be most valuable to clinicians whose clients have identified body image issues that need the focus of therapeutic attention. Following are several effective practices and considerations that trained counselors should employ in clinical practice:

1. Be knowledgeable about the etiology, prevalence, and presentation of body image issues and eating disorders.
2. Consider the developmental stage of clients since body image concerns and eating disorders are prevalant across the lifespan and may have different etiologies and resolutions.
3. Be familiar with risk factors and their impact on the development of body image issues and eating disorders.
4. Have knowledge of appropriate assessment tools for body image concerns and eating disorders and be skilled in scoring the results and in interpreting and delivering results in the most effective and client-centered manner.
5. Be familiar with and engage in the most effective evidence-based treatments of body image and eating disorders and collaborate ethically when necessary.
6. Seek supervision and consultation, as needed, to maintain therapeutic effectiveness and self-care.
7. Be multiculturally competent and seek further training in order to address the needs of clients with diverse background, especially when addressing symptoms and concerns that are not typically associated with diverse groups.
8. Have plenty of resources available for the client and her family.
9. Incorporate expressive art and creativity when working with women with body image and eating disorders due to the alignment between image and representation.

CASE VIGNETTE WRAP-UP: SADIE

Sadie talked in counseling about the start of her eating-disordered behavior, which seemed to correlate with pubertal changes that caused feelings of shame, as well as some bullying she endured. When male peers in her school ridiculed her nose, her face, and her breasts, she would become visibly flushed and exhibit a reaction that encouraged further bullying. These behaviors went unchecked by adults, as Sadie was told that "boys will be boys" and that this behavior indicated that the bullies liked her. These typical experiences led Sadie to internalize the belief that there was something wrong with her that she needed to "fix" and "control." She accomplished this by binging and purging. This became her primary coping mechanism, and it provided her with a sense of control over her body.

Now, at thirty-four, Sadie has reached out to Jamie, her counselor, in an effort to get past these lingering feelings of self-dislike. Sadie's progress with Jamie is strong, and Sadie remains in therapy for several years, during which time Jamie provides a variety of interventions to help Sadie overcome her self-imposed limitations. Body mapping is integrated into therapy, and this helps Sadie identify sites of specific trauma and evaluate those traumas from an adult perspective. Through body mapping, Sadie was able to visit aspects of her body that she had caused harm to, and she was surprised to discover parts of herself that she valued and respected.

Jamie suggested that Sadie begin a "body image journal" as well. Sadie's body image journal began with short regular entries with two extreme themes; on one extreme, she stated her dislike of her body and challenge getting dressed for work in the morning, and on the other extreme, she logged her daily exercise and her run lengths. These entries provided a representation of her thought processes and helped to build up consistency in Sadie's journaling practice. Over time, Jamie would provide Sadie with short prompts to gently shift her process. For example, on a day when she wore her favorite outfit, Jamie asked her to write about why she liked it and how she felt when she wore it. Each week, Sadie would bring her journal with her to therapy in case there was something she wanted to share. The journal provided a space in which Sadie could continue working at home on her treatment goals. Journaling can underscore and provide a means to assess the significant changes that therapy inspires but which can happen slowly.

After several years, Sadie felt ready to end her counseling work with Jamie. She had ceased all self-injurious and eating-disordered behavior some years earlier but had continued working on issues that arose once her coping mechanisms were revised. Sadie had divorced her abusive husband and, after years of alone time and casual dating, was now in a healthy, mutually supportive relationship with a man who treated her like a partner and an equal. She was still physically active but had gained a new perspective on her body, fitness, and abilities after being sidelined by an injury for over a year. She was repairing her relationship with her mother, had whittled down friends to the most crucial and valuable, and even embraced her few graying hairs. She talked about the likelihood of body image issues resurfacing again in her life, much the way counselors talk with clients about the likelihood of trauma being retriggered or symptoms reerupting. However, Jamie and Sadie spent time developing a relapse plan. Sadie also developed hobbies that were strengths and projects that were reminders of therapeutic successes. While body image concerns may not be completely eradicated, Sadie no longer felt any pressing need for intervention or fear of her safety to self. She took greater joy in identifying her strengths than her weaknesses. She was on a path to loving herself and appreciating her body, and was doing great work.

QUESTIONS FOR REFLECTION

1. What are the crucial components of client history that should be considered when diagnosing a client with body image issues and disordered eating? Regarding the client presented in this chapter, what might be some additional information you would want to know when conducting a thorough assessment?
2. When working from a strengths-based perspective, how would you begin therapeutic work with a client like Sadie? What are some potential risk factors (if any) and protective factors (if any) in Sadie's presentation, and might how they affect Sadie's prognosis?
3. What has worked for this client before when solving problems, either in or out of treatment, and what would you consider as additional effective interventions in treating Sadie?
4. How do you think relationship qualities influence body image issues? What are some ways you might work with families and significant others?

REFERENCES

American Psychiatric Association. (2013). *Diagnostic and statistical manual of mental disorders* (5th ed.). Washington, DC: American Psychiatric Press.

Body Image Therapy Center. (n.d.). Eating disorders facts and statistics. Retrieved from https://thebodyimagecenter.com/education-awareness/eating-disorder-statistics/

Bono, G., & McCullough, M. (2006). Positive responses to benefit and harm: Bringing forgiveness and gratitude into cognitive psychotherapy. *Journal of Cognitive Psychotherapy, 20*, 147–58.

Brandoff, R., & Thompson, A. (2019). *Quick and creative art projects for (very) limited budgets*. London: Jessica Kingsley.

Brewerton, T. D. (2007). Eating disorders, trauma, and comorbidity: Focus on PTSD. *Eating Disorders, 15*(4), 285–304. doi: 10.1080/10640260701454311

Brewerton, T. D., & Dennis, A. B. (2015). Perpetuating factors in severe and enduring anorexia nervosa. In S. Touyz, P. Hay, D. Le Grange, & J. H. Lacey (Eds.), *Managing severe and enduring anorexia nervosa: A clinician's handbook* (pp. 28–63). New York, NY: Routledge.

Buchalter, S. I. (2009). *Art therapy techniques and applications.* London: Jessica Kingsley.

Buchalter, S. I. (2015). *Raising self-esteem in adults: An eclectic approach with art therapy, CBT and DBT based techniques.* London: Jessica Kingsley.

Cash, T. F. (1995). *What do you see when you look in the mirror?* New York, NY: Bantam Books.

Clark, S. M. (2017). *DBT-informed art therapy: Mindfulness, cognitive-behavior therapy, and the creative process.* Philadelphia, PA: Jessica Kingsley Press.

Cohen, B. M., & Mills, A. (1994). An introduction to the Diagnostic Drawing Series: A standardized tool for diagnostic and clinical use. *Art Therapy: Journal of the American Art Therapy Association, 11*(2), 105–10. doi: 10.1080/07421656.1994.10759060

Cohen, B. M., & Mills, A. (1999). Skin/paper/bark: Body image, trauma and the diagnostic drawing series. In J. Goodwin & R. Attias (Eds.), *Splintered reflections: Images of the body in trauma* (pp. 203–21). New York, NY: Basic Books.

Dansky, B. S., Brewerton, T. D., O'Neil, P. M., & Kilpatrick, D. G. (1997). The National Women's Study: Relationship of victimization and posttraumatic stress disorder to bulimia nervosa. *International Journal of Eating Disorders, 21*, 213–28.

Hanna, A. C., & Bond, M. J. (2006). Relationships between family conflict, perceived maternal verbal messages, and daughters' disturbed eating symptomatology. *Appetite, 47*(2), 205–11. doi: 10.1016/j.appet.2006.02.013

Hawkins, N. (2014). Battling our bodies: Understanding and overcoming negative body images. Center for Change. Retrieved from https://centerforchange.com/battling-bodies-understanding-overcoming-negative-body-images/

Hieb, M. (2005). *Inner journeying through art-journaling: Learning to see and record your life as a work of art.* London: Jessica Kingsley.

Hirschmann, J. R., & Munter, C. H. (1995). *When women stop hating their bodies.* New York, NY: Fawcett Columbine.

Hudson, J. I., Hiripi, E., Pope, H. G., Jr., & Kessler, R. C. (2007). The prevalence and correlates of eating disorders in the National Comorbidity Survey Replication. *Biological Psychiatry, 61*(3), 348–58. doi: 10.1016/j.biopsych.2006.03.040

Kabat-Zinn, J. (1994). *Wherever you go, there you are: Mindfulness meditation in everyday life.* New York, NY: Hyperion.

Kater, K. J., Rohwer, J., & Levine, M. P. (2000). An elementary school project for developing healthy body image and reducing risk factors for unhealthy and disordered eating. *Eating Disorders: Journal of Treatment and Prevention, 8*(1), 3–16. doi: 10.1080/10640260008251208

Kessler, K. (1994). A study of the Diagnostic Drawing Series with eating disordered patients. *Art Therapy: Journal of the American Art Therapy Association, 11*(2), 116–18. doi: 10.1080/07421656.1994.10759062

Levens, M. (1995). *Eating disorders and magical control of the body: Treatment through art therapy.* London: Routledge.

Levine, M. P., & Murnen, S. K. (2009). "Everybody knows that mass media are/are not [pick one] a cause of eating disorders": A critical review of evidence for a causal link between media, negative body image, and disordered eating in females. *Journal of Social and Clinical Psychology, 28*, 9–42. doi: 10.1521/jscp.2009.28.1.9

Liebmann, M. (2005). *Art therapy for groups: A handbook of themes and exercises* (2nd ed.). New York, NY: Brunner-Routledge.

Maine, M. (2000). *Body wars: Making peace with women's bodies.* Carlsbad, CA: Gurze Books.

Maine, M., & Kelly, J. (2005). *The body myth: Adult women and the pressure to be perfect.* Hoboken, NJ: John Wiley & Sons.

Makin, S. R. (2000). *Therapeutic art directives and resources: Activities and initiatives for individuals and groups.* London: Jessica Kingsley.

Mayo Clinic. (2019). Body dysmorphic disorder. Retrieved from https://www.mayoclinic.org/diseases-conditions/body-dysmorphic-disorder/diagnosis-treatment/drc-20353944

Mercer, A., Warson, E., & Zhao, J. (2010). Visual journaling: An intervention to influence stress, anxiety and affect levels in medical students. *Arts in Psychotherapy, 37*, 143–48. doi: 10.1016/j.aip.2009.12.003

Mitchell, K. S., Mazzeo, S. E., Schlesinger, M. R., Brewerton, T. D., & Smith, B. N. (2012). Comorbidity of partial and subthreshold ptsd among men and women with eating disorders in the National Comorbidity Survey—replication study. *International Journal of Eating Disorders, 45*(3), 307–15. doi: 10.1002/eat.20965

Moschini, L. B. (2005). *Drawing the line: Art therapy with the difficult client.* Hoboken, NJ: Wiley.

National Eating Disorders Association. (2019). Statistics and research on eating disorders. Retrieved from https://www.nationaleatingdisorders.org/statistics-research-eating-disorders

O'Brien, C., Johnson, J., & Miller, B. (1978). Cartoons in counseling. *Personnel and Guidance Journal, 57*(1), 55–56.

Piran, N. (1994). Prevention: Can early lessons lead to a delineation of an alternative model? A critical look at prevention with schoolchildren. *Eating Disorders, 3*(1), 28–36. doi: 10.1080/10640269508249143

Polivy, J., & Herman, C. P. (1991). Undieting: A program to help people stop dieting. *International Journal of Eating Disorders, 11*(3), 261–68.

Rosal, M. L. (2018). *Cognitive-behavioral art therapy: From behaviorism to the third wave.* New York, NY: Routledge.

Rubin, J. A. (2005). *Artful therapy.* Hoboken, NJ: John Wiley & Sons.

Schneider, S., Ostroff, S., & Legow, N. (1990). Enhancement of body-image: A structured art therapy group with adolescents. *Art Therapy, 7*(3), 134–38. doi: 10.1080/07421656.1990.10758908

Shallcross, L. (2013). Body language. *Counseling Today, 56*(1), 30–40. Retrieved from https://www.counseling.org/resources/library/Counseling%20Today/July2013CTOnline.pdf

Wallace, K. O. (2015). *There is no need to talk about this: Poetic inquiry from the art therapy studio.* Rotterdam, Netherlands: Sense.

Young, M. E., & Hutchinson, T. S. (2012). The rediscovery of gratitude: Implications for counseling practice. *Journal of Humanistic Counseling, 51*, 99–113.

Chapter Fifteen

Counseling Women with Low Self-Esteem

Lucy Parker

CASE VIGNETTE: ROBERTA

Roberta, forty-one, a blond-haired woman, smiling, but initially apologetic, with glasses, comes into your office. From a first impression, Roberta seems to have no obvious or egregious presenting issues. She shares with you that she recently earned her master's in business but feels "like an imposter." She then elaborates that she recently moved to this state from another for a recent career change after graduating. She talks quickly, continues to apologize, and then shares that she feels "not enough" when it comes to her career or "overall in life." Roberta then asks you, "Am I being annoying?" She apologizes more and shares that she realizes she is "weak" and needs to "just suck it up."

During this initial conversation, Roberta continues to avoid eye contact and presents a closed posture and crossed arms. After the bulk of the session, you also notice that Roberta's voice remains very soft and that her apologies continue and seem out of proportion. When asked if she is annoying you, how do you respond to Roberta? What do you believe may be one of Roberta's primary presenting issues? What basic skills would be important to use with Roberta, especially if she continues to self-deprecate and excessively apologize to you?

* * *

When working with women dealing with a poor self-image, it is essential for the counselor to help them gain greater acceptance and appreciation for all that they are. Acceptance and commitment therapy (ACT) is a relatively new therapy approach. Developed in part by Dr. Steven Hayes, ACT focuses on clients gaining self-awareness and psychological flexibility (Hayes, Strosahl, & Wilson, 2012). According to Harris (2009), ACT consists of six core processes: contacting the present moment, defusion, acceptance, self-as-context, values, and committed action. ACT has been shown to be a very effective therapeutic approach for women with intrapersonal and other concerns. ACT helps clients cope by learning about emotions and using mindfulness (Harris, 2009; Hayes, Pistorella, and Levin, 2012). Some of the main principles addressed include self-acceptance, self-soothing, and mindfulness for women with self-esteem concerns. Varying ACT themes, techniques, and ways to help Roberta theoretically and practically will be discussed below.

ACT therapists assert that when clients are rigid psychologically, they may also be separated from their values and life purposes (Chiesa & Serretti, 2014). Helping clients gain acceptance of the present moment, mindfulness, emotional and psychological flexibility, and acceptance of oneself with problems (while not defining oneself from these problems) are ways that ACT therapists facilitate client change (Chiesa & Serretti, 2014; Hayes, Strosahl, & Wilson, 2012). More specifically, ACT-guided helpers may influence client psychological flexibility and change by deconstructing rigid psychological rules that clients present, such as "would haves, could haves, and should haves." Clients are encouraged to embrace the present moment even with negative feelings or discomfort and accept these fallibilities along with their imperfect selves (Chiesa & Serretti, 2014; Hayes, Strosahl, & Wilson, 2012).

When working with Roberta, an ACT-guided helper may informally ask about Roberta's feelings about herself. When asked, Roberta may exhibit self-shame. ACT-guided counselors conceptualize that a client's reported excessive self-shame may be a part of low self-esteem and may be influenced by self-defeating thoughts to which a client is "fused" (Chiesa & Serretti, 2014; Hayes, Strosahl, & Wilson, 2012). A helpful and practical ACT-guided technique for clients like Roberta may include asking questions about who and what clients think "they should be." Similar to other clients with shame or low self-esteem, a counselor would want to ask Roberta who she believes she should be and what she should be doing different in life. After various sessions of processing what Roberta expresses as "her should," it is important for a counselor to help Roberta identify these "shoulds" as thoughts that in excess may be negative. Helping Roberta challenge her negative thoughts, such as "I should be more experienced" or "I am not enough, but I should just suck it up," may help Roberta accept her true self and begin to reduce or abstain from unnecessarily apologizing to others.

ACCEPTANCE AND COMMITMENT THERAPY BEST PRACTICES

Acceptance and commitment theory encourages counselors to collaborate with clients and remind clients of their strengths and their values. Various best practices based in ACT that counselors can use with clients like Roberta facing self-esteem issues include (1) strength bombardment and values finding, (2) the concept of psychological flexibility and the technique of finding exceptions, and (3) facilitating client use of self-affirmation and defusion through ACT metaphors and journaling. The below paragraphs provide an example for each of these best practices as well as descriptions of how these can be most efficaciously used by counselors.

When considering best practices, especially for clients like Roberta, Erford (2015) notes that focus on strengths is often needed. The emphases of strength finding and depathologizing interventions are used less in medicalized models versus humanistic models of counseling (Erford, 2015). Whether using medically emphasized or empirically emphasized models to foster assessment, psychoeducation, and diagnosis, many CBT- and ACT-guided counselors today also incorporate humanistic elements and interventions, such as finding strengths (through the strengths bombardment intervention, for example) (Morton, Roach, Reid, & Stewart, 2012; Roemer & Orsillo, 2002; Waern, 2018). In fact, this author strongly encourages ACT interventions for clients like Roberta because ACT-based interventions often incorporate both CBT (such as behavior change, assessment, and diagnosis) and humanism (Morton et al., 2012; Waern, 2018).

CBT and related models are briefly introduced, as CBT-based models are documented to work well with many clients who engage in self-defeating or self-sabotaging behaviors, which perpetuated low self-esteem (McElhinney, Reid, & Morton, 2016; Morton et al., 2012; Waern, 2018). Given the clinically intuitive and empirically validated connection between self-defeating behaviors and lower self-esteem, it is necessary to preserve the behavioral change emphases that interventions guided through CBT and related models use (Roemer & Orsillo, 2002). As mentioned in the foundational theory section, ACT interventions (including the strength bombardment and values sort interventions) incorporate new behaviors of finding strengths in replacement of only focusing on one's imperfections. Thus, using ACT interventions includes using what has been proven to traditionally help female clients with esteem issues as well as new elements that are now being seen as efficacious as well. With the three main interventions below, clients can explore added insight to find new strengths and learn to challenge self-defeating thoughts and feelings that may catalyze or perpetuate self-esteem issues (McElhinney et al., 2016; Morton et al., 2012; Roemer & Orsillo, 2002; Waern, 2018).

Strength Bombardment

One of the three featured best practices that fosters self-affirmation and esteem building is the strength bombardment and ACT-based values finding intervention (Berman, Morton, & Hegel, 2016; Erford, 2015; Feary, 2018; Luoma, Kohlenberg, Hayes, & Fletcher, 2012; Steele, 1988). As a prerequisite to the ACT intervention of values finding, a counselor may help the client explore what she identifies as her strengths. As the reader can infer from Roberta's case vignette, she and other female clients facing self-esteem issues may not easily generate strengths. To foster self-reflections on strengths, a counselor may use what Erford (2015) and Steele (1988) term a strength bombardment. Erford shares that modeling and generating new, kind dialogue for women facing negative and entirely self-critical dialogue (which manifests in low self-esteem) helps these clients see that "mood, self-perception, and self-image" can improve when they actively take part in saying or finding positive aspects of themselves, even when uncomfortable, new, and seemingly simplistic (Erford, 2015, p. 108). Many counselors use strength bombardment in group counseling for peer clients, not to praise but genuinely to provide realistic reassurance and strengths for their peer group members. Additionally, if we imagine working with Roberta, we could implement strengths bombardment in an individual session as well. Implementing strengths finding and strengths bombardment may be as simple as remind Roberta of all they she has versus has not accomplished in her career. Questioning to help Roberta find strengths can also be used. Examples of dialogued questions include, "Roberta, you share that you feel not enough; however, if I had finished the same degree you did, I would have the same accolades. This standardization shows I do have enough of a skill set to be in this career. Would you think I would be enough? If so, how is this different from you?" Another (more general) example is, "Roberta, though you share you don't feel like 'enough,' what are three strengths that those who care most about you might say you possess?"

Depending on what strengths Roberta can identify and when she begins to find strengths, the counselor can facilitate the ACT-specific technique of value finding. Values finding is an intervention in which clients identify their core values. Waern (2018) shares that "identifying values is finding out what really matters to a person—who they want to be and what they want to do" (p. 18). The counselor may use various mediums to help clients like Roberta explore values. For example, a counselor may provide various cards in a single deck or multiple decks, either blank or preidentified with common human values. Clients are then asked to pick the top ten values they hold, even if they feel they do not possess or show these currently. After selecting various values through either value sort cards or traditional list making or verbal discussion, the client is asked how they might express these values even with their imperfect selves. Clients are also asked questions that help them express times they may have exhibited the current values they hold, even though imperfectly. It is also important for the counselor to continue to help these clients gain new introspection and reflect values as they continue to attend counseling, while also recognizing that values are not goals or various "shoulds" that clients may conflate.

Fostering Psychological Flexibility

Helping clients challenge the view of "who they should be" and thoughts of needing to be "perfect" is another intervention useful especially to female clients coping with shame and low self-esteem. Helping clients defuse from their "shoulds" is related to an additional best practice, which is fostering psychological flexibility. Waern (2018) asserts that psychological flexibility is the ability of people to think in increasingly dialectic and holistic versus rigid or binary ways. Counselors can facilitate psychological flexibility with clients like Roberta through the use of the intervention finding exceptions (Erford, 2015). Finding exceptions for clients means listening for times when the client may not engage in the presenting problem (Erford, 2015).

Finding Exceptions

For Roberta, an example of finding exceptions may be times where she does verbally or nonverbally validate herself. This may include helping Roberta find behaviors or self-talk that she engages in that validate her personal or professional self. A concrete example: "Roberta, you share that you are not enough or that you do not love yourself; however, you seem to love yourself in some ways as you are loving yourself by coming to counseling. What are some other possible times you have loved yourself or simply cared for yourself? How can you increase these behaviors toward self-love?" The purpose of these questions is to facilitate Roberta in sharing about times when she did not present with low self-esteem. Thus, this is called "exceptions," as a counselor would benefit Roberta by helping her find exceptions from her self-doubt or low self-esteem.

Cognitive Defusion

According to Harris (2009) and Hayes, Pistorella, and Levin (2012), cognitive defusion is the process of a person looking at their thoughts separate from themselves versus looking at themselves as dictated by the person's thoughts (Harris, 2009). It is important to use the practice of helping clients create defusion from self-defeating thoughts by modeling and directing clients to use affirming language when speaking about themselves. One example of this technique with Roberta might include helping Roberta defuse from her thought of "I am not enough." A counselor may ask Roberta, "What is enough?" When helping clients defuse thoughts, ACT-guided counselors introduce what it means to "fuse" to and "defuse" from one's thoughts. For example, Berman and colleagues (2016) share that a counselor may state known phrases to clients, such as "Mary had a little . . ." or "Twinkle, twinkle, little . . . ," and then ask the clients to fill in the blank. When clients are able to complete such sentences, a counselor can then metaprocess with their client that these "filling in the blank" examples are products of the client being fused to a thought. Just as these phrases are learned, habituated, and hard to break, so too are negative thoughts that clients may be fused to. After this metaprocessing and psychoeducation is facilitated with the client, a counselor using this ACT best practice may then empathically confront Roberta and encourage her to practice replacing her fused negative thought of "I am not enough" with a more validating thought, such as "I may not feel enough now, but this feeling will change."

"Acting as If"

One specific technique that can help clients to continue self-affirmation even when it feels less natural is called "acting as if" (Sweeney, 2019). Acting as if is a technique where clients are encouraged by the counselor to "act as if you feel like enough, even if you don't always." Clients may be encouraged to "act" as though they are anything that they are "trying to be." Acting as if encourages clients to practice the positive thoughts and behaviors they often mistakenly assume will only come with perfection or unrealistic change.

In other words, the ACT-guided counselor uses techniques such as these above best practices to help clients process and release thoughts and feelings and become further distanced and potentially completely defused from these self-sabotaging or self-deprecating thoughts.

CULTURAL CONSIDERATIONS

Acceptance and commitment therapy is efficacious with many client types because of its focus on strengths and defusion from a common distortion that "there is one way to live life" (Woidneck, Pratt, Gundy, Nelson, & Twohig, 2012). In fact, various counselors have used ACT in working with various clients as ACT, similar to other multiculturally inclusive theories, is categorized in the fourth force of counseling (Woidneck et al., 2012). Theories categorized in the fourth and fifth forces of counseling theory evolvement commonly conceptualize varying intersections of clients. Within the ACT lens, clients are seen as multidimensional beings not to by typecasted nor labeled from one dimension of their identity. Person-first language is also encouraged in these theories. For example, instead of labeling a client "the insecure client," an ACT-guided counselor may restate this as "the client presenting with insecurity."

Though ACT theory does allow for the incorporation of various perspectives, this theory, being relatively new in the helping field, may be less empirically supported for working with all client types (Woidneck et al., 2012). Thus, just as with other theories, it is important for ACT-guided counselors to critically and contextually conceptualize clients in ways beyond theory alone. Clinically, it is also important to remember clients' symptomology may be contextually and culturally relative. ACT-guided counselors and theorists, as well as other postmodern theorists, emphasize that change occurs with a collaborative and egalitarian relationship.

ETHICAL CONSIDERATIONS

Acceptance and commitment therapy techniques are used with Roberta as this theory is highly strength based, inclusive, and congruent for esteem building (Berman et al., 2016; Erford, 2015; Feary, 2018; Luoma et al., 2012; Steele, 1988). When considering ethical bounds, it is most important for counselors working with clients with esteem issues to promote client beneficence through strength-building techniques, empowerment, and advocacy. One ethical consideration for counselors is empowering clients to build autonomy through self-advocacy (American Counseling Association [ACA], 2014). Not only is empowerment from self or others important for clients who have not empowered themselves, potentially due to shame or esteem issues, but also advocacy is included in the ACA Code of Ethics. Promoting client advocacy is specifically stated in the ACA Code of Ethics Standards Section A regarding the Counseling Relationship (ACA, 2014). Additionally, with clients such as Roberta, counselors must remember that client empowerment should not be conflated with imposing one's values or "fixing" a client. In addition to client empowerment, appropriate boundary modeling and setting is another important and foundational ethical consideration (ACA, 2014).

ADVOCACY OPPORTUNITIES

Advocacy for Roberta and other clients with similar presenting esteem issues includes continued assertiveness skills and macroscale advocacy (Enns, 1992; McBride, 1990; Rani, Chandran, & Singal, 2016; Tajabadi et al., 2018). Assertiveness skills training is encouraged by this author, as often clients with self-esteem issues don't feel they have a voice, and this may be reinforced by others in their life or by society (Enns, 1992; McBride, 1990; Rani et al., 2016; Tajabadi et al., 2018). Assertiveness training helps clients gain self-advocacy skills and allows counselors to reinforce social justice efforts to counteract potential oppression these clients may be facing. One way to further demonstrate the ACA Code of Ethics Standard A.7.a., which is advocacy, may be to provide clients like Roberta with the ACT concept of psychological flexibility to remember that some self-advocacy and self-assertiveness is not selfish but healthy. Many women are socialized to internalize all assertiveness as selfishness, and this is a fused idea that promotes a lack of self-assertiveness (Enns, 1992; McBride, 1990; Rani et al., 2016; Tajabadi et al., 2018). Thus, helping clients like Roberta remember that they can be assertive and are not being selfish is important.

CASE VIGNETTE WRAP-UP: ROBERTA

As a holistic review, ACT techniques that a counselor could use with Roberta to cope with low self-esteem issues include (1) strength bombardment and values finding, (2) the ACT concept of psychological flexibility and the technique of finding exceptions, and (3) self-affirmation and defusion through ACT metaphors and journaling. Some guiding questions that could prove efficacious in Roberta's acceptance and commitment therapy guided session include the following: Who do you feel you should be? Who has the power to decide if you are good enough? What are your values? How do you believe "should" language creates a barrier for you? When can you replace the word "can" with the word "should" in your life?

QUESTIONS FOR REFLECTION

1. A person's self-esteem is said to be based on how she feels she is seen through the eyes of others. What are some ways you might integrate this perspective with clients who suffer from low self-esteem?
2. What are some ways you could encourage a client to value herself on internal standards versus external media-driven expectations?
3. What are some ways you find your self-image is influenced by other people or external measures?
4. What are some ways you could encourage a client to advocate against external standards of women's worth?

REFERENCES

American Counseling Association. (2014). *ACA code of ethics*. Alexandria, VA: Author.

Berman, M., Morton, S., & Hegel, M. (2016). Health at every size and acceptance and commitment therapy for obese, depressed women: Treatment development and clinical application. *Clinical Social Work Journal, 44*(3), 265–78.

Chiesa, A., & Serretti, A. (2014). Are mindfulness-based interventions effective for substance use disorders? A systematic review of the evidence. *Substance Use & Misuse, 49*(5), 492–512.

Enns, C. Z. (1992). Self-esteem groups: A synthesis of consciousness-raising and assertiveness training. *Journal of Counseling & Development, 71*(1), 7–13.

Erford, B. T. (2015). *40 techniques every counselor should know.* New York, NY: Pearson Higher Education.

Feary, A. (2018). Case study: Acceptance commitment therapy for a youth athlete: From rumination and guilt to meaning and purpose. *Sport & Exercise Psychology Review, 14*(2), 73–86.

Harris, R. (2009). *ACT made simple: An easy-to-read primer on acceptance and commitment therapy.* Oakland, CA: New Harbinger Publications.

Hayes, S., Pistorella, J., & Levin, M. (2012). Acceptance and commitment therapy as a unified model of behavior change. *Counseling Psychologist, 40*(7), 976–1002.

Hayes, S. C., Strosahl, K. D., & Wilson, K. G. (2012). *Acceptance and commitment therapy: The process and practice of mindful change* (2nd ed.). New York, NY: Guilford Press.

Luoma, J. B., Kohlenberg, B. S., Hayes, S. C., & Fletcher, L. (2012). Slow and steady wins the race: A randomized clinical trial of acceptance and commitment therapy targeting shame in substance use disorders. *Journal of Consulting and Clinical Psychology, 80*(1), 43–53.

McBride, M. C. (1990). Autonomy and the struggle for female identity: Implications for counseling women. *Journal of Counseling & Development, 69*(1), 22–26.

McElhinney, R., Reid, H., & Morton, L. (2016). A controlled trial of a CBT group for women with low self-esteem. *Clinical Psychology Forum, 287*, 21–24.

Morton, L., Roach, L., Reid, H., & Stewart, S. H. (2012). An evaluation of a CBT group for women with low self-esteem. *Behavioural and Cognitive Psychotherapy, 40*(2), 221–25.

Rani, S., Chandran, S., & Singal, A. (2016). A quasi experimental study to assess the effectiveness of assertiveness training on assertive behaviour and self esteem among adolescent girls in selected government schools of Panipat, Haryana, 2015. *International Journal of Psychiatric Nursing, 2*(2), 25–31.

Roemer, L., & Orsillo, S. (2002). Expanding our conceptualization of and treatment for generalized anxiety disorder: Integrating mindfulness/acceptance-based approaches with existing cognitive-behavioral models. *Clinical Psychology: Science & Practice, 9*(1), 54–68.

Steele, C., M. (1988). The psychology of self-affirmation: Sustaining the integrity of the self. In L. Berkowitz (Ed.), *Advances in experimental social psychology: Social psychological studies of the self* (Vol. 2, pp. 261–302). San Diego, CA: Academic Press.

Sweeney, T. J. (2019). *Adlerian counseling and psychotherapy: A practitioner's wellness approach.* New York, NY: Routledge.

Tajabadi, F., Ahmadi, A., Forouzi, M., Ahmadi, Z. S., Jahani, Y., Najafi, K., & Bafghi, M. J. A. (2018). The effect of Adlerian group counseling on the level of assertiveness among midwifery students in clinical setting. *Indian Journal of Forensic Medicine & Toxicology, 12*(2), 216–21.

Waern, S. (2018). Acceptance and commitment therapy versus cognitive behavioural therapy: Supporting people in acute and ongoing trauma. *Clinical Psychology Forum, 306*, 7–10.

Woidneck, M. R., Pratt, K. M., Gundy, J. M., Nelson, C. R., & Twohig, M. P. (2012). Exploring cultural competence in acceptance and commitment therapy outcomes. *Professional Psychology: Research and Practice, 43*(3), 227–33.

Chapter Sixteen

Counseling Women with Depression

Marcela Kepic and Wendy Killam

CASE VIGNETTE: YVONNE

Yvonne is a thirty-eight-year-old Hispanic woman who recently found out that her husband, Paulo, was having an affair. Yvonne and Paulo began to experience increasing conflict approximately two years ago. She wasn't able to identify a particular event, but Yvonne remembered that was when her husband stopped paying for things and told her she had to pay for the utilities and her own things. He refused to pay for their annual family vacation that year, and so they did not go. This was a surprise, and when she brought up the issue, it led to more escalated conflict. She knew that her husband, who was a strong earner, was frugal, but she felt these new behaviors were extreme.

The marital discord led her to feel anxious and withdrawn. She feared that her postpartum depression was returning, and she did not want that to happen as she was in remission for more than six years. Yvonne's son was eight years old and was a happy and healthy child. Yvonne and Paulo stopped having sex over the last two years, and when Yvonne tried to initiate intimacy, Paulo turned her down and claimed to be "too tired." She met with her best friend and shared her concerns about her marital situation and confessed that she feared Paulo was seeing someone else. Her friend wasn't surprised at all and confirmed Yvonne's suspicion by sharing that she had seen her husband twice with a young girl having dinner at a restaurant and kissing. Yvonne was horrified and started to cry. A few weeks later, she began having difficulty sleeping, began overeating, and had difficulty concentrating. She even missed a few days of work due to having too little energy to get herself ready. She confronted Paulo one evening about her suspicions, but he denied having an affair and told Yvonne that her mind was "going crazy" again and playing tricks on her. She asked for a divorce, and Paulo had no hesitation and immediately responded, "Fine!" Stunned by his quick response, Yvonne collapsed into a chair and started to sob.

* * *

The most common psychiatric disorders are depressive disorders (American Psychiatric Association [APA], 2015). Within a recent revision of the *Diagnostic and Statistical Manual of Mental Disorders* (DSM-5), depressive disorders were separated from other mood disorders, such as bipolar I or II, and stand alone in their own chapter. There are eight depressive disorders, each with its own diagnostic criteria: major depressive disorder (including major depressive episode), disruptive mood dysregulation disorder, persistent depressive disorder (dysthymia), premenstrual dysphoric disorder, substance/medication-induced depressive disorder, depressive disorder due to another condition, other specified depressive disorder, and finally unspecified depressive disorder (APA, 2015). It is beyond the purpose of this chapter to specifically name all the criteria of each disorder, but rather some commonalities among such disorders will be highlighted and counseling consideration will be discussed.

Symptoms of depressive disorders typically include sadness, feelings of emptiness, social withdrawal, irritable mood, and somatic or cognitive changes affecting daily functioning. What will vary are duration, frequency, severity, and presumed etiology (APA, 2015). Being affected by a depressive disorder has an impact on the overall function of an individual and can also have an adverse effect on the function or development of others. For example, the children of women who experience depression during pregnancy or after giving birth may suffer a variety of effects due to their mother's condition.

WOMEN AFFECTED BY MAJOR DEPRESSIVE DISORDER

Major depressive disorder (MDD) is one of the leading causes of disability in the United States and is more prevalent in women than men (Kasen, Cohen, Chen, & Castille, 2003; Noble, 2005). Approximately twelve million women in the United States experience depression each year, and about one in every eight women will develop MDD in their lifetime (National Institute of Mental Health [NIMH], 2017). Adolescent girls and young women are twice as likely to develop depression as teenage boys and young men (Pearson, Janz, & Ali, 2013). Later in life, however, the risk prevalence evens out, but women during the onset of reproductive years are at a greatest risk for developing depression. There are some biological factors responsible for women's predisposition to depression and include genetics and hormonal fluctuation that arise from various aspects of reproductive functions (e.g., menses, pregnancy, and menopause) (Noble, 2005). Fluctuating hormones may affect brain functioning, contributing to the onset of premenstrual dysphoric disorder and postpartum depression. There are other psychosocial factors influencing women's mood and coping, including life roles, victimization, gender socialization, and social status in society (Noble, 2005). Further, women tend to be more susceptible to stress-induced depression (e.g., infertility, miscarriage) and to changes in light. Additionally, 80 percent of those suffering from seasonal affective disorder are women (Noble, 2005).

Beyond the typical symptoms of depression, MDD includes a major depressive episode, and symptoms must last for a minimum of two weeks (APA, 2015). Due to the severity and intensity of symptoms, daily functioning is also impacted. Symptoms of major depressive disorder can linger for six months. Even though major depressive disorder may begin with a single depressive episode, 50 percent of clients will experience a recurrent episode within a year, and 85 percent of clients will experience recurrence at some point in their life (APA, 2015). Women who are struggling with depression tend to have more health problems, family challenges, and issues with marriage, work, and social life. Depression touches every aspect of a woman's life. Women carry tremendous responsibilities in their lives for themselves and for others, including partners, children, colleagues, and so on. In addition, their social status and other sociocultural circumstances can generate concerns that contribute to stress and, for many, the development of depression leading to temporary or permanent withdrawal from the workforce. Depression costs an estimated $100 billion for U.S. employers, including $44 billion a year in lost productivity (Beck et al., 2014). Given its prevalence and its impact on the lives of women and others, addressing depression effectively is a primary concern of mental health professionals.

WOMEN AFFECTED BY OTHER FORMS OF DEPRESSIONS

Despite the fact that MDD has a plethora of adverse effects on one's life, other forms of depression may significantly contribute to lesser quality of life and relationship issues. Although not as prevalent as MDD, these include persistent depressive disorder (dysthymia), premenstrual dysphoric disorder, and other specified and unspecified depressive disorder. Other depressive disorders tend to have fewer symptoms and might be less intense and less frequent but can prevail for much longer periods of time. Despite the fact that their symptoms might be of a lesser intensity, they can still cause substantial disruption to daily functioning.

Persistent Depressive Disorder (PDD)

Formerly known as dysthymic disorder, persistent depressive disorder is characterized by chronic low levels of depressive symptoms that usually last for an extensive period of time and in some cases longer than two years. In 2016, it was estimated that approximately 1.5 percent of adults in the United States were diagnosed with persistent depressive disorder (NIMH, 2017). This form of depression is twice as common in women as in men. Midlife women seem to be affected the most by persistent depressive disorder, and as a woman ages, the likelihood of developing this disorder increases (NIMH, 2017). Approximately half of women diagnosed with persistent depressive disorder suffer from the most severe form, meaning that their impairment in their daily functioning is severe, whereas about 30 percent suffer from the moderate form and approximately 20 percent from the mild form (Harvard Medical School, 2007).

Perinatal and Postpartum Depression (PPD)

Depression impacts approximately 25 percent of women during pregnancy (i.e., perinatally) and 10 to 15 percent of women in the first year after giving birth, which is referred to as postpartum depression (Gavin et al., 2005; Priest, Austin, Barnett, & Buist, 2008). As noted earlier, biological factors may contribute to such prevalence. During pregnancy, increased levels of estrogen and progesterone have been linked to decreased levels of norepinephrine (i.e., noradrenaline, a hormone and neurotransmitter responsible for vasoconstriction, the fight-or-flight response, and more). Lower levels of norepinephrine were found to be correlated with increased levels of depression, suggesting lower levels of norepinephrine due to increased levels of estrogen and progesterone might be responsible for depression (Ambade, Arora, Singh, Somani, & Basannar, 2009; Treadway, Kane, Jarrahi-Zadeh, & Lipton, 1975).

Women's psychological adaptation may play an important role in susceptibility to depression. For example, for women concerned about bodily changes and giving birth, or not having a support of her partner, or if the pregnancy was unplanned and rather disrupted the present lifestyle, such factors were associated with more depressive symptoms (Lemme, 2006). Further, women being pregnant for the first time are at a higher risk for depressive symptoms as opposed to those women with subsequent pregnancies because of potential fears of the unknown. Research also has found that women with a history of depression are at a greater risk for perinatal and postpartum depression, as are those from low socioeconomic backgrounds (Sampson, Villarreal, & Rubin, 2016). There are many other sociocultural and psychological factors that contribute to depression during pregnancy, but gender and history of depression seem to be the two significant ones.

Perinatal and postpartum depression (PPD) deserve a lot of attention due to effects on the newborn child as well as the mother. O'Hara and McCabe (2013) indicated women with PPD are at a higher risk for chronic depression, suicidality, marital difficulties, poor self-care and infant care, and poor mother–child interaction. Moreover, children of mothers with PPD tend to have cognitive, emotional, and behavioral challenges, often lasting into adulthood (Dagher, McGovern, Dowd, & Gjerdingen, 2012; Goodman et al., 2011; Josefsson & Sydsjo, 2007). Researchers investigating effective interventions to treat PPD found that with timely interventions, such adverse effects can be alleviated (Posmontier et al., 2019; Sampson et al., 2016).

Premenstrual Dysphoric Disorder and Perimenopausal Depression (PMDD)

Premenstrual dysphoric disorder (PMDD) is a new disorder in DSM-5. It is similar to premenstrual syndrome but has more symptoms, some of which are more severe. Approximately 3 to 8 percent of women in their reproductive years will experience symptoms severe enough to affect their daily functioning. Thus, there was enough clinical evidence for its inclusion in DSM-5. PMDD is composed of psychological, physical, and behavioral symptoms. Psychological symptoms include feeling irritable, moody, sad, teary, overwhelmed, isolated, and sensitive to rejection. Physical symptoms include breast tenderness, headache, muscle ache and joint pain, abdominal bloating, swelling of extremities, and changes in appetite and sleep. Behavioral symptoms include fatigue, poor concentration, and forgetfulness (APA, 2015). Such symptoms typically occur one to two weeks prior to menses and resolve with the onset of menses. Women report worsening of symptoms with age, especially as they approach menopause. Further, due to the severity of symptoms and their interference with daily responsibilities, research found that women untreated for PMDD were likely to experience a loss of three quality-adjusted life years during their lifetime as a result (Yamada & Kamagata, 2017). When looking at etiology, it is still uncertain what is responsible for PMDD, but a biological origin seems plausible. It is proposed that it is not the abnormal levels of hormones, or hormonal dysregulation, but rather a particular sensitivity to normal cyclical hormonal changes (Schmidt et al., 2017). Fluctuating estrogen and progesterone levels may affect levels of norepinephrine and serotonin and cause irritability, depressed mood, and even carbohydrate cravings. Other disorders often occur with depression.

Depression as a Co-occurring Disorder

Depression often coexists with other disorders, both physical and mental. It is highly co-occurring with medical conditions such as heart disease, diabetes, Alzheimer's disease, Parkinson's disease, and hormonal disorders (APA, 2014). Approximately 25 percent of women with cancer and women who have suffered a stroke will experience depression (NIMH, 2017). Of women who survive a heart attack, one in three will experience depression, and those women with further coronary artery disease are 60 percent more likely to have a heart attack or cardiac death. Approximately 30 percent of those women diagnosed with diabetes are also diagnosed with depression (Holt, de Groot, & Golden, 2014). Having polycystic ovary syndrome is also associated with depression (Damone et al., 2018). Lastly, women living with HIV have high rates of depression (Rabkin, 2008).

Depressive disorder frequently exists with a variety of mental health disorders. Research has shown a strong relationship between eating disorders and depression. Approximately 30 to 50 percent of women diagnosed with an eating disorder are also diagnosed with MDD, primarily in young females (Ulfvebrand, Birgegard, Norring, Hogdahl, & von Hausswolff-Juhlin, 2015). Some women who experience anxiety also suffer from depression. Lastly, depressed women are likely to experience substance use issues. Currently, a little over 30 percent of American women suffering from depression have an alcohol or substance use disorder (NIMH, 2017). Since depression is likely to accompany other medical or mental health illnesses, clinicians need to pay attention to detailed assessment of depression, in its many forms, and screen for other conditions as well. Approximately 30 to 50 percent of women are misdiagnosed, and less than half of those who suffer from depression will seek treatment (Centers for Disease Control and Prevention [CDC], 2019). When co-occurring disorders exist, practitioners should collaborate with other medical and mental health professionals to ensure that women receive the best care possible. Involved professionals (e.g., a treatment team) should strive to avoid duplication of services. Left untreated, depression can lead to suicide.

SUICIDALITY ASSESSMENT

Depression is a serious mental health illness often associated with suicide and suicide attempts. According to the CDC (2018), suicide accounted for 36,909 deaths in 2017 and was the second leading cause of death in young adults and fourth leading cause in middle adulthood. Approximately two-thirds of adult suicides are attributed to undiagnosed, misdiagnosed, or untreated depression. Given such statistics, the urgency for screening, proper diagnosis, and treatment is high. During assessment, clinicians pay attention to not only duration, severity, and frequency of depressive symptoms but allow necessary time for suicide risk assessment on an ongoing basis.

Risk Factors and Warning Signs

One of the major risk factors for committing suicide across all populations is mood disorders (e.g., depression and bipolar disorder) and alcohol and drug use (CDC, 2019). Other risk factors include family history of suicide, previous suicidal attempts, alienation, discrimination, isolation and no access to mental health, acculturation, loss, illness, disability, trauma, and access to lethal means. While women attempt suicide more frequently than men, they use less lethal means and are less likely to be successful than men (CDC, 2019). Clinicians pay attention to the warning signs as well, such as bringing up a discussion about death, feeling like being a burden to others, and having no reason to live. Further, women might begin to isolate, withdraw from activities, give their possessions away, drink more, grow aggressive or fatigued, and say good-byes. All of these signs are typically present during the time when women are depressed, anxious, have lost interest, or are humiliated. It is important also to recognize a sudden improvement in such moods because that might be a sign a client has made up her mind and is ready to proceed with suicide plans.

Protective Factors

Clinicians must also assess for protective factors. This can increase the clinician's understanding of the likelihood of suicidal behavior. Some of the most significant protective factors across cultures include access to mental health care, being connected to people (e.g., friends, family, neighbors), ability to solve problems, and having a sense of purpose or meaning in life (CDC, 2019). Additionally, many times religion and spirituality serve as protective factors, but it is the job of a clinician to ask and bring such topic to the surface. The more a woman feels connected to others and identifies social support and purpose in life, the less likely she is to attempt suicide. Clinicians should help the client boost their protective factors and engage in safety planning as well.

TREATMENT FOR DEPRESSION

Addressing depression will look different for each client; however, research has identified effective ways of treating depression and approximately 80 percent of people diagnosed with depression can be treated successfully (CDC, 2019). In fact, the National Institute of Mental Health (2017) reported that approximately 80 percent of those treated for depression show an improvement in their symptoms within the first six weeks of therapy (i.e., medication and psychotherapy). When the combined treatment of medication and psychotherapy is not successful, this likely reflects noncompliance with treatment.

Cognitive behavioral therapy (CBT) approaches (i.e., individual and group) have been found to be successful in treating depression. CBT helps to identify negative thought patterns, challenge them, and replace them with more neutral or positive thoughts. CBT offers strategies for developing effective coping mechanisms and typically is time limited (e.g., eight to sixteen sessions). For example, problem-solving therapy interventions have been found effective with women diagnosed with PPD who received this type of treatment during home visits. After five sessions, they experienced a statistically significant decrease in depressive symptoms (Sampson et al., 2016). Similarly, interpersonal psychotherapy was effective in treating postpartum depression (Posmontier et al., 2019). Interpersonal therapy focuses on improving problems in personal relationships and in other areas of life that might be contributing to depressive symptoms. Interventions are focused on evaluating clients' interactions and improving how they relate to others.

Medication treatment many reduce or control depressive symptoms. Typically it takes somewhere between two to four weeks for antidepressants to begin working and up to twelve weeks to show full effect. Commonly used antidepressants are selective serotonin reuptake inhibitors (e.g., Prozac, Zoloft, Celexa), serotonin and norepinephrine reuptake inhibitors (e.g., Cymbalta, Effexor), tricyclic antidepressant (e.g., Elavil, Sinequan, Vivactil), and, finally, monoamine oxidase inhibitors (e.g., Nardil, Parnate, Emsam). It is imperative that clinicians understand psychopharmacology and at the same time not recommend or make decisions about medications. Their role is to refer clients to agencies and psychiatrists who can handle medication treatment if needed.

For PMDD, a combination with adjusting nutrition, such as avoiding caffeine, sugar, and sodium, might be sufficient for those with rather mild symptoms. In addition, a decrease in alcohol and nicotine intake and adding adequate sleep might help. Further, nutritional supplements and regular aerobic exercise can demonstrate beneficial effects on emotional and physical symptoms of PMDD. For more severe cases of PMDD, pharmacological treatment might be necessary to alleviate symptoms.

PRACTICAL CONSIDERATIONS

Every woman is different and unique, and so will be her presentation of depression. Clinicians need to pay attention to described symptoms and circumstances under which symptoms are presented. It is also important to be knowledgeable about some common attitudes women and society have toward depression. For example, women often believe that it is normal to be depressed during menopause and that treatment is not necessary. This might be the case for some but not for all women. Further, some women tend to believe that depression is a normal part of aging. Next, at least half of women cite denial as a huge barrier to treatment. Many women will also feel embarrassed or ashamed and therefore will not consider mental health counseling (Mental Health America, 2019). There is a lot of stigma (e.g., guilt, shame, judgment) still associated with mental health and asking for help, so appropriate psychoeducation is necessary.

BEST PRACTICES

1. Be knowledgeable about depression, its forms, symptom presentation, and prevalence. Consider cultural factors and their influences on manifestation of depressive symptoms.
2. Understand women's developmental phases and how depression manifests differently during various life stages.
3. Be knowledgeable about depression and suicidality assessments (e.g., Beck Depression Inventory [BDI], Edinburgh Postnatal Depression Scale [EPDS]) and competent in administering, scoring, and interpreting their results.
4. Be thorough with gathering detail biopsychosocial histories when starting to work with women diagnosed with depression, and explore strengths and coping mechanisms used in the past.
5. Be knowledgeable about psychotropic medications and their side effects, but at the same time understand your scope of practice.
6. Empower women to make their own decision about their treatment after consultation with health professionals.
7. Be aware of societal perspective and stereotypes related to depression, and effectively challenge these and psychoeducate about depression.
8. Be knowledgeable and skilled in various effective approaches to treatment of depression and adjust according to clients' cultural backgrounds.
9. Be prepared to share adequate resources when treating women with depression, and collaborate effectively with other professionals who are involved with your client.
10. Encourage social support building and activity engagement.
11. Provide support and psychoeducation to family members of clients suffering from depression.
12. Understand ethical standards pertaining to treating someone with depression, especially confidentiality and its limits (e.g., suicidality).

13. Understand your own biases regarding depression and strive for an unbiased approach when counseling women with depression.
14. Consider further training in depressive disorders and cultural competency in order to use the latest and most effective approaches in treating depression.
15. Despite the fact that depression might look similar, approach each client as a unique individual and unique depression presentation.

CULTURAL CONSIDERATIONS

Treatment for mental health concerns often varies according to an individual's unique culture. In fact, Cheng, Kwan, and Sevig (2013) found that minority women often do not seek psychological or mental health services due to cultural factors as well as stigma. In some cultures, seeking help and sharing familial concerns is viewed in a negative light. Unfortunately, African American women tend not to seek mental health services for depression; financial concerns are often cited. However, even those with financial means and insurance seek services at a much lower rate than white women (Watson & Hunter, 2015). Additionally, some minority women turn to their religious and spiritual leaders for help with depression. This is particularly true for African American women (Wei-Chin Hwang & Myers, 2013). Thus, there are several reasons minority women are less likely to seek treatment, and when they do seek professional care, counselors should be especially attuned to the need to build trust and rapport in order to provide effective services and encourage treatment completion.

ETHICAL CONSIDERATIONS

When working with clients, there are a number of ethical considerations that should be at the forefront of a practitioner's mind. These include avoiding imposing one's own values, beliefs, and biases onto clients. Furthermore, when a client is depressed, assessing for suicidal ideation is essential. In cases where a client is suicidal, appropriate steps should be taken to protect the client from self-harm, and in some cases this requires a mandatory breach of confidentiality. Taking care to provide only the necessary information and only to the necessary individuals is essential.

ADVOCACY

Counselors may need to advocate for their clients and also teach clients to self-advocate. Self-advocacy efforts can be empowering for the client. Within society, there is still considerable stigma (e.g., guilt, shame, judgment) associated with mental health and asking for help, so appropriate psychoeducation is necessary. It is important to educate the client, the client's family, as well as the community about mental health issues as opportunities arise. Some clients might also engage in efforts to educate the community regarding mental health issues. When a person is diagnosed with a major mental illness, there may be a sense of denial and the client might try to minimize the symptoms and the impact of the illness. For the family, it can be challenging to adjust and find ways to be helpful and supportive without the client feeling devalued and useless. Family members may benefit from understanding more about depression and appropriate treatment options. For clients who have no family support or limited family support, it can be beneficial to connect them with support groups and other services in the local area.

RESOURCES FOR COUNSELORS AND CLIENTS

American Counseling Association: https://www.counseling.org
American Psychiatric Association: 703-907-7300; https://www.psychiatry.org
Anxiety and Depression Association of America: 240-485-1001; https://adaa.org
Beck Depression Inventory
Calendar of Premenstrual Experiences (COPE): https://www.ncbi.nlm.nih.gov/pubmed/12012879
Daily Record of Severity Problems (DRSP): https://www.ncbi.nlm.nih.gov/pubmed/17470584
Depression and Bipolar Support Alliance (DBSA): 1-800-826-3632; http://www.dbsalliance.org
International Foundation for Research and Education on Depression: http://www.ifred.org
National Institute of Mental Health: 866-615-6464; https://www.nimh.nih.gov
National Suicide Prevention Lifeline: 1-800-273-TALK (8255); http://www.suicidepreventionlifeline.org
Prospective Record of the Severity of Menstruation (PRISM)
Zero Suicide in Health and Behavioral Health Care: http://zerosuicide.sprc.org

CASE VIGNETTE WRAP-UP: YVONNE

Overwhelmed, sad, and anxious about her future, Yvonne called her old counselor. She was no longer working there, but the receptionist was able to recommend a new clinician, Maudie, and schedule an intake with her. This is Yvonne's second session, and Maudie is completing the biopsychosocial assessment, risk assessment, and mental status assessment. Yvonne denied suicidal and homicidal ideation but reported deep hopelessness and helplessness. She struggles with getting out of bed in the morning and spends hours crying. Paulo occasionally helps with their son, but many times Yvonne's best friend drops off and picks up her son from school. Maudie learned about Yvonne's postpartum depression and asked in detail about the progression and treatment of the illness. Further, she asked about what she learned and took away from that time and what had worked for her. Carefully writing things down, Maudie is learning that Yvonne was on anxiolytics and antidepressants for almost a year, with the conjunction of CBT-oriented therapy. Yvonne stated that her old therapist would use a lot of mindfulness techniques and cognitive behavioral strategies to address her depression and anxiety. She remembered challenging irrational thoughts by finding evidence and counterevidence for automatic or negative thoughts, which was effective. Yvonne also remembered writing in her journal, but she did not like that technique that much.

As Maudie gathered a thorough psychiatric history, she continued with exploration about Yvonne's current relationship struggles since this was a new issue for Yvonne. Yvonne shared that she needs to find a lawyer in order to file for a divorce. Still not believing her circumstances, she shook her head and said, "What a jerk! I can't believe he did that to me. And to our son! Awful, isn't it?" After some silence, she continued, "I don't know what I am going to do! I don't have money. My part-time job doesn't pay much! I will end up on the street because I'm sick and they gonna take my son away." After this outburst, Yvonne started to cry. Maudie can easily pick up on crucial challenges that Yvonne is facing: loss of her marriage, loss of her husband, loss of stability, possible relocation, and financial struggles. All of these factors can significantly either cause the onset of or exacerbate Yvonne's depressive symptoms. Relying on a long remission, coping skills learned in the past, having a friend, and professional support, the counselor is hopeful that with CBT interventions and a relational-cultural approach in therapy Yvonne will be able to overcome challenges she is presently facing. They explore possible treatment goals and prioritize them according to Yvonne's needs.

Treatment Plan

1. *Stabilize overall mood*

    a. *Decrease depressive symptoms by half within the next six weeks*

b. *Improve coping mechanisms by learning two additional strategies in the next six weeks*
c. *Address irrational thoughts and replace them with more neutral or positive thinking patterns*
d. *Explore medication support and if desired refer to a psychiatrist*

2. *Find legal help*

a. *Improve availability of adequate resources in the next two weeks*
b. *Establish legal connection within the next two weeks*

3. *Address loss through counseling*

a. *Improve understanding of losses in her life—ongoing*
b. *Increase a sense of control over some life circumstances*
c. *Increase acceptance of losses in her life*
d. *Explore the meaning of loss and possibly brainstorm new vision for life*

Brief Case Conceptualization

Yvonne as a middle-aged adult, a mother, a wife, and a Hispanic woman who suffered from postpartum depression in the past and is currently facing a plethora of challenges related to marital discord and her husband's extramarital affair. Caring for family and being employed part-time fulfilled her purpose and provided a sense of generativity. Suddenly, some roles have been disrupted, and Yvonne is facing losses associated with roles and responsibilities to which she had grown accustomed. Her identity and responsibility as a wife and partner are altered and may soon be dissolved. This type of loss is affecting her emotional stability and producing anxious and depressed feelings. Yvonne cannot make sense of her circumstances because there are no true answers available. Her unending search for nonexistent answers is emotionally draining and leaving her angry, confused, and depressed. Her counselor needs to carefully explore meanings associated with Yvonne's major identities and roles and help her effectively address them so she can reach a sense of understanding, acceptance, and closure, and, eventually, the development of a new sense of self and associated roles. Her identity as a mother is still present and must be acknowledged and supported because her emotional state can adversely affect the responsibilities associated with such a role. This identity can provide a relatively stable sense of self and needs to be utilized in counseling sessions in order to help transfer skills and coping strategies. Further, her part-time work can be viewed as a positive aspect in her life, serving as a distractor, resource, and stable part of her identity. Lastly, Yvonne's depression history and current depressive symptoms need attention in order to effectively work on loss, meaning, and identities.

Outlook for Yvonne

Yvonne's counselor pays attention to other identities and, through careful identification of strengths and resources from the past, acknowledges Yvonne's ability to overcome tough circumstances. Using CBT-oriented interventions, Maudie also builds on already acquired mindfulness skills, such as grounding and relaxation. She further incorporates more expressive arts-based techniques for emotional and cognitive sharing. As she is working with Yvonne, the counselor not only is mindful of assessing and reassessing Yvonne's goal progress but evaluates her depressive symptoms and suicidality on a regular basis. Learning more about Yvonne's cultural identity and background, Maudie incorporates and build up resources and social connections that will help Yvonne with daily functioning and responsibilities.

QUESTIONS FOR REFLECTION

1. What are some pieces of additional information a counselor would need in order to understand Yvonne's situation more and complete her case conceptualization?
2. What are some other counseling approaches a practitioner might use effectively when working with women who are diagnosed with depression?
3. Are there any ethical concerns when working with Yvonne or other clients who are depressed?
4. What do you think are the major advocacy aspects for clients like Yvonne?
5. What might be your prognosis for Yvonne and why?

REFERENCES

Ambade, V., Arora, M. M., Singh, P., Somani, B. L., & Basannar, D. (2009). Adrenaline, noradrenaline and dopamine level estimation in depression: Does it help? *Medical Journal Armed Forces India, 65*(3), 216–20. doi:10.1016/S0377-1237(09)80006-3

American Psychiatric Association. (2014). *Understanding mental disorders: Your guide to DSM-5.* Washington, DC: American Psychiatric Publishing.

American Psychiatric Association. (2015). *Depressive disorders: DSM-5 selections*. Arlington, VA: Author.

Beck, A., Crain, L. A., Solberg, L. I., Unuetzer, J., Maciosek, M. V., Whitebird, R. R., & Rossom, R. C. (2014). The effect of depression treatment on work productivity. *American Journal of Managed Care, 20*(8), e294–301.

Centers for Disease Control and Prevention. (2013). Suicide among adults aged 35–64 years—United States, 1999–2010. *Morbidity and Mortality Weekly Report 62*(17), 321–25.

Centers for Disease Control and Prevention. (2018). Web-based injury statistics query and reporting system (WISQARS). Retrieved from https://www.cdc.gov/ncipc/wisqars

Centers for Disease Control and Prevention. (2019). Violence prevention: Risks and protective factors. Retrieved from https://www.cdc.gov/violenceprevention/suicide/riskprotective factors.html

Cheng, H.-L., Kwan, K.-L. K., & Sevig, T. (2013). Racial and ethnic minority college students' stigma associated with seeking psychological help: Examining psychocultural correlates. *Journal of Counseling Psychology, 60*, 98–111.

Dagher, R. K., McGovern, P. M., Dowd, B. E., & Gjerdingen, D. K. (2012). Postpartum depression and health services expenditures among employed women. *Journal of Occupational and Environmental Medicine, 54*, 210–15.

Damone, A. L., Joham, A. E., Loxton, D., Earnest, A., Teede, H. J., & Moran, L. J. (2018). Depression, anxiety and perceived and update. *Current HIV/AIDS Reports, 5*(4), 163–71.

Gavin, N., Gaynes, B., Lohr, K., Meltzer-Brody, S., Gartlehner, G., & Swinson, T. (2005). Perinatal depression: A systematic review of prevalence and incidence. *Obstetrics and Gynecology, 106*, 1071–83.

Goodman, S. H., Rouse, M. H., Connell, A. M., Broth, M. R., Hall, C. M., & Heyward, D. (2011). Maternal depression and child psycho-pathology: A meta-analytic review. *Clinical Child Family Psychology Review, 14*, 1–27.

Harvard Medical School. (2017). National Comorbidity Survey (NCS): Data table 2: 12-month prevalence DSM-IV/WMH-CIDI disorders by sex and cohort. Retrieved from https://www.hcp.med.harvard.edu/ncs/index.php

Holt, R. I., de Groot, M., & Golden, S. H. (2014). Diabetes and depression. *Current Diabetic Report, 14*(6): 491–508. doi:10.1007/s11892-014-0491-3

Josefsson, A., & Sydsjo, G. (2007). A follow-up study of postpartum depressed women: Recurrent maternal depressive symptoms and child behavior after four years. *Archives of Women's Mental Health, 10*, 141–45.

Kasen, S., Cohen, P., Chen, H., & Castille, D. (2003). Depression in adult women: Age changes and cohort effects. *American Journal of Public Health, 93*(12), 2061–66.

Lemme, B. H. (2006). *Development in adulthood.* Needham Heights, MA: Allyn and Bacon.

Mental Health America. (2016). *Prevention and early intervention B4Stage4: The state of mental health in America 2016*. Alexandria, VA: Mental Health America.

National Heart, Lung, and Blood Institute. (2017, April 17). Heart disease and depression: A two-way relationship. Retrieved from https://www.nhlbi.nih.gov/news/2017/heart-disease-and-depression-two-way-relationship

National Institute of Mental Health. (2013). U.S. leading categories of diseases/disorders. Retrieved from https://www.nimh.nih.gov/health/statistics/disability/us-leading-categories-of-diseases-disor
ders.shtml

National Institute of Mental Health. (2017). Persistent depressive disorder. Retrieved from https://www.nimh.nih.gov/health/statistics/persistent-depressive-disorder-dysthymic-disorder.shtml

Noble, R. E. (2005). Depression in women. *Metabolism, 54*(5), 49–52.

O'Hara, M. W., & McCabe, J. E. (2013). Postpartum depression: Current status and future directions. *Annual Review of Clinical Psychology, 9*, 379–407.

Pearson, C., Janz, T., & Ali, J. (2013). Mental and substance use disorders in Canada. *Health at a Glance, 82*(624), 1–8.

Posmontier, B., Bina, R., Glasser, S., Cinamon, T., Styr, B., & Sammarco, T. (2019). Incorporating interpersonal psychotherapy for postpartum depression into social work practice in Israel. *Research on Social Work Practice, 29*(1), 61–68.

Priest, S., Austin, M.-P., Barnett, B., & Buist, A. (2008). A psychosocial risk assessment model (PRAM) for use with pregnant and postpartum women in primary care settings. *Archives of Women's Mental Health, 11*, 307–17.

Rabkin, J. G. (2008). HIV and depression: 2008 review and update. *Current HIV/AIDS Report, 5*(4), 163–71.

Sampson, M., Villarreal, Y., & Rubin, A. (2016). A problem-solving therapy intervention for low-income, pregnant women at risk for postpartum depression. *Research on Social Work Practice, 26*(3), 236–42.

Schmidt, P. J., Martinez, P. E., Nieman, L. K., Koziol, D. E., Thompson, K. D., Schenkel, L., . . . Rubinow, D. R. (2017). Premenstrual dysphoric disorder symptoms following ovarian suppression: Triggered by change in ovarian steroid levels but not continuous stable levels. *American Journal of Psychiatry, 174*(10), 980–89.

Treadway, C. R., Kane, J. F., Jr., Jarrahi-Zadeh, A., & Lipton, M. A. (1975). A psychoendocrine study of pregnancy and the puerperium. In R. K. Unger & F. L. Denmark (Eds.), *Women: Dependent or independent variable?* (pp. 591–604). New York, NY: Psychological Dimensions.

Ulfvebrand, S., Birgegard, A., Norring, C., Hogdahl, L., & von Hausswolff-Juhlin, Y. (2015). Psychiatric comorbidity in women and men with eating disorders results from a large clinical database. *Psychiatry Research, 230*(2), 294–99.

Watson, N. N., & Hunter, C. D. (2015). Anxiety and depression among African American women: The costs of strength and negative attitudes toward psychological help-seeking. *Cultural Diversity & Ethnic Minority Psychology, 21*(4), 604–12.

Wei-Chin Hwang & Myers, H. F. (2013). The explanatory model of illness catalogue: Ethnic differences in women's illness beliefs and help-seeking for depression. *Journal of Cultural Diversity, 20*(2), 57–65.

Yamada, K., & Kamagata, E. (2017). Reduction of quality-adjusted life years (QALYs) in patients with premenstrual dysphoric disorder (PMDD). *Quality of Life Research, 26*(11), 3069–73. doi:10.1007/s11136-017-1642-1

Chapter Seventeen

Counseling Women with Anxiety

Lucy Parker and Nina Mendez

CASE VIGNETTE: CHU

Chu is a forty-seven-year-old female. Her real name is Chunhwa, but she goes by "Chu" because most people cannot pronounce her name. Chu attended college in the United States and obtained political asylum when she graduated with her Ph.D. Her parents had been killed for crimes against the government, and she was fearful of returning. She met her husband, Jack, in college. His family immigrated to the United States from South Korea when he was two years old. They have two daughters who are currently in college. They are enjoying the American dream, most of the time. However, Chu often feels very overwhelmed in both her professional and her personal life.

She shares with you in your first session together that she often replays and continues to think about small comments people make to her, for days and days. She also shares that she often immediately wonders "what if?" when something in her life goes as predicted, as if she had no control over how things turn out. After this disclosure, Chu begins to cry, and then she immediately and repetitively apologizes for her tears and self-deprecates as if her feelings were not valid. You also notice that Chu becomes very flushed and speaks very rapidly in the session. Her hands also appear to have many bleeding cuticles. When Chu is preparing to leave your office, she turns to you and asks, "What should I do next?"

* * *

What do you believe are the best ways to help this client obtain and maintain increased wellness? What features of anxiety do Chu present? Are these features only cognitive? Are there other indicators of potential anxiety related to Chu's disposition? How do you think Chu's past life and cultural identity shape her current presenting self? What feelings may she be experiencing, and how can these be processed? How can you, as a dedicated counselor, empower and advocate for Chu? What other considerations may arise from Chu and her story of resilience, but with current marginalization?

ANXIETY DISORDERS

The presence of some anxiety is not in itself typically an issue of significant concern. Almost everyone experiences anxiety in some aspects of their lives, whether in academic settings, professional settings, or social settings. Anxiety can show up as feelings of nervousness, lack of concentration, irritability, and a sense of dread. Anxiety can also produce physical symptoms. These are often felt as palpitations, a racing heart, breathlessness, muscle tension, digestive upset, or skin sensations such as goose bumps. Anxiety that is mild and experienced in ways that don't get in the way of normal activities is not concerning. However, when symptoms increase in frequency and intensity and begin to create barriers that keep a client from enjoying life, assistance from a clinician is encouraged.

There are several different types of anxiety disorders, and each one manifests in its own manner, although there are commonalities in the symptoms they produce. As a disorder, anxiety is extremely prevalent and is the most frequently diagnosed disorder, with approximately 20 percent of adults experiencing an anxiety disorder sometime in their lifetime (Kessler, Chiu, Demler, Merikangas, & Walters, 2005). However, women are approximately twice as likely to experience an anxiety disorder of any type in their lifetime, although social anxiety disorder is more evenly experienced between genders. These are the five most common types:

Generalized Anxiety Disorder. This disorder, abbreviated GAD, is described as a pervasive feeling of anxiety not typically attributable to any specific source. This disorder generates feelings of chronic anxiety, unwarranted worry, and heightened tension that seemingly arise out of nowhere and create discomfort.

Obsessive-Compulsive Disorder. This disorder, abbreviated OCD, is experienced as the constant presence of obsessions, which are recurrent and unwanted thoughts, and compulsions, which are repetitive behaviors that an individual feels compelled to complete, whether they consciously want to or not. The compulsions typically include repeated hand washing, counting (such as steps across a room or to a destination or objects in a room), checking (such as returning to check that a door is locked multiple times even though it was just checked moments before), and cleaning. These ritual behaviors are hoped by the individual to be a source of eliminating their obsessive thoughts, but the completion of the ritual is a temporary solution and the thoughts return, yet if the ritual is not completed, the individual's feelings of anxiety become intensified.

Panic Disorder. This disorder is marked by episodes in which a feeling of panic is experienced in cognitive, emotional, and physical ways. To be considered a panic disorder, there must be repeated episodes of panic marked by a heightened fear response and often symptoms such as chest pain, pounding heart, breathlessness, dizziness, and digestive upset. Panic attacks can come on suddenly and be experienced as seemingly life-threatening events that mimic symptoms of serious physical illness, such as heart attacks and strokes. There can be a sense of doom and dread, and a person often feels paralyzed and terrified.

Post-Traumatic Stress Disorder. This anxiety disorder, commonly termed PTSD, develops after an individual has experienced or witnessed a significantly traumatic event in which grave harm was experienced or the potential for grave harm existed. The event produces a sense of terror and fear in the moment, which is natural, in the face of traumas such as violent assaults, disasters, accidents, combat, or personal violence. When disturbing or intrusive thoughts and feelings continue well after the trauma or threat has ended, a person may be experiencing PTSD. Nightmares, flashbacks, and nonthreatening events that reignite the trauma response can hinder a person's ability to lead a normal life.

Social Phobia/Social Anxiety Disorder. This form of anxiety is marked by significant anxiety and self-consciousness that are experienced in everyday, nonthreatening situations. It may manifest in varying levels of severity and in isolated or more general settings. Fear of public speaking is a frequently acknowledged form of social anxiety. In more severe instances, individuals may suffer severe anxiety in any situation involving social interaction.

Specific Phobias

Phobias are marked by an intense fear of a stimulus that can be an object, animal, sensation, setting, or circumstance. The fear usually begins early in life, although phobias can develop over time in adulthood. The fear produces anxiety that can reach significant levels and prohibit a person's ability to be near the source of the phobia. Some of the more frequently reported phobias include heights, flying, spiders and snakes, hypodermic syringes, and blood.

Regardless of the type of anxiety disorder, the physical and emotional experience of anxiety can be quite similar. While there are medications to treat anxiety disorders, these treat the symptoms; they cannot "cure" the client of the disorder. Therefore, learning how to manage and minimize anxiety symptoms is an important aspect of treatment.

FOUNDATIONAL THEORY OF COGNITIVE BEHAVIORAL THERAPY

Cognitive behavioral therapy (CBT) is one of the most established and empirically validated therapies today (Carter, Sbrocco, Gore, Marin, & Lewis, 2003; Erford, 2015; Gallegos-Guajardo, Ruvalcaba-Romero, Langley, & Villegas-Guinea, 2015; Latif & Khanam, 2017; McElhinney, Reid, & Morton, 2016; Montal, 2010; Roemer & Orsillo, 2002). CBT has empirical support in helping female clients with anxiety. Specifically, CBT is used to help clients gain awareness of cognitions that may escalate other emotions, such as anxiety (Carter et al., 2003; Gallegos-Guajardo et al., 2015; Latif & Khanam, 2017; Montal, 2010; Roemer & Orsillo, 2002). Extended discussion about CBT and ways it is used to help women with anxiety will be presented in this chapter. Additionally, ways to help the featured client, Chu, will be addressed theoretically and practically.

Cognitive behavioral therapy recognizes both a client's cognitive (thinking) processes as well as their emotions and behavior (Erford, 2015; Latif & Khanam, 2017). CBT also recognizes various physiological processes that may influence a client's anxious behaviors. To address various physiological and psychological issues, which may be interrelated for a client such as Chu, and presenting anxiety, CBT therapists use a combination of strategies to teach clients about their (1) thoughts, (2) emotions, and (3) behaviors and the interrelatedness of these concepts (Erford, 2015; Latif & Khanam, 2017). Clients are specifically given psychoeducation about potential cognitive distortions (i.e., faulty thinking patterns) that may reinforce their anxiety (Erford, 2015; Latif & Khanam, 2017; McElhinney et al., 2016). A counselor using CBT best practices may help Chu or a similar client find out more about her "core beliefs," which may be triggering or perpetuating her anxiety. Let's explore a CBT-oriented example with Chu.

When considering Chu, a helper or therapist guided by CBT may provide Chu with psychoeducation about the triad of thoughts, feelings, and behaviors (Erford, 2015; Latif & Khanam, 2017; McElhinney et al., 2016). Chu would be asked about her automatic and current core thoughts about herself and her world. She would then work with the therapist to track thoughts that may trigger or escalate her fears and anxiety. Psychoeducation to help Chu understand that anxiety is a fear-based emotion would also be discussed. For example, a helper may encourage Chu to read about fear and what it means to have a rationale fear versus an exacerbated or irrational fear. Chu may also be encouraged to complete a weekly thought log to investigate which thoughts she experiences when having the most anxiety, such as during a panic attack or saturating worries (Erford, 2015; Latif & Khanam, 2017; McElhinney et al., 2016). Various best practices that may help Chu better understand her anxiety, but not define her through anxiety, include (1) thought stopping and (2) challenging negative thoughts and emotions (Carter et al., 2003; Maruna & Mann, 2006). An introduction to best practices while using CBT is below.

BEST PRACTICES

Various CBT-oriented best practices to help Chu and similar clients include providing her with psychoeducation about anxiety, facilitating the intervention of thought stopping, helping her to challenge negative emotions through learning about and confronting cognitive distortions, and facilitating relaxation techniques. Psychoeducation is often a standard part of most mental health disorder treatment.

Psychoeducation

According to Banks (2017), psychoeducation refers to strategies in therapy that are largely preventative, skill based, and educational in nature. Psychoeducation differs from therapy in that it has an educational focus when compared to standard interventions (Ayres, Bankman, Fried, & Luce, 2017; Banks, 2017). In integrating psychoeducation into therapy for anxiety, the first step is to provide clients with an understanding of the term *anxiety* and how this manifests itself in their everyday life. This can occur in one session or across multiple sessions of therapy. It is critical when working with clients who have anxiety that they understand their condition etiology, symptoms, risks, clinical course, and treatment options (Banks, 2017). By providing education surrounding anxiety, clients will be better able to be actively involved in their treatment and may learn ways they can be an integral component in improving their condition.

Thought Stopping

It is important to facilitate a client's belief in her ability to change the recurring maladaptive behaviors or thoughts that can keep her "stuck" in anxiety. For example, another intervention that could be used with Chu is helping her to challenge negative thoughts. One way to do this is by helping her understand what cognitive distortions are and to identify any that she holds (Carter et al., 2003; Maruna & Mann, 2006). Cognitive distortions were originally defined by Aaron Beck (1963) and David Burns (1989). Beck defined a cognitive distortion as a cognition that refers to "a specific thought, such as an interpretation, a self-command or self-criticism" (1989, p. 326). Other cognitive theorists have shared how cognitive distortions can serve as "an individual's internal processes, including the justifications, perceptions and judgments" for various maladaptive behavior (Abel et al., 1989, p. 137). In other words, cognitive distortions are thinking patterns that are maladaptive for clients.

Helping Chu learn what her cognitive distortions are and how to confront them is the central intervention in deescalating her anxiety. By challenging these distortions, she will be able to decrease some of the anxiety triggered by them. According to Burns (1989), frequently held cognitive distortions include all or nothing thinking (i.e., seeing things in binaries: "If I don't get into medical school, I'll never be happy with my life"), overgeneralization (i.e., using one event to generalize all events: "I didn't have any luck when I posted a profile on Bumble, so I know that trying eHarmony won't work either"), mental filters and disqualifying the positive (i.e., only focusing on negative things that happen: "I always end up screwing up in the final job interview," although the speaker actually has been offered several excellent jobs that she has chose to turn down), jumping to conclusions (also known as mind reading or fortune-telling: "There's no point in applying for that job, because I know I'd never get an interview"), magnification (also known as catastrophizing or unintentionally blowing things out of proportion: "I wasn't able to make it to her party last week, so I doubt she'll ever include me in another event she hosts"), should statements (i.e., telling oneself that you or your life "should" be a certain way: "I'm thirty-two now, so I really should have had my first child before now"), labeling (i.e., drawing conclusions and labels even when labels may be punitive: "I am always a loser; I know that because I haven't been able to lose the weight I gained after I turned forty"), and overpersonalization (i.e., attribute everything to oneself: "It's my fault that his brother didn't want to meet us for dinner; I know he must think I talk too much").

To best help a client challenge the self-limiting cognitive distortions that contribute to anxiety, counselors should encourage clients to identify the cognitive distortions that most often show up in their thoughts. Once a client makes a list of these distorted thought patterns, her awareness is heightened to the frequency with which these thoughts appear. In session, the counselor can work with the client to find ways to challenge these distorted thoughts and to confront them each time they appear. Between sessions, the client is instructed to keep a written record of how she confronts her most frequently experienced distortions. By checking in with the client each week, the counselor can monitor the frequency of the thoughts as well as the client's success in confronting and eliminating the negative thought patterns.

Mindfulness and Relaxation Techniques

Another group of interventions found to help anxious clients includes mindfulness techniques (Cayoun, 2011; Valikhani, Kankat, Hariri, Salehi, & Moustafa, 2019). Mindfulness is found so efficacious that counselors also may use CBT-related mindfulness protocols (Cayoun, 2011). In a metaanalysis that compared the effectiveness of cognitive behavioral interventions and mindfulness interventions, researchers found no significant difference between the two forms of treatment (Singh & Gorey, 2018). In cases where financial ability limits the number of counseling sessions a woman can afford, training and resources for mindfulness activities may be more beneficial over the long term than cognitive behavioral therapy with the clinician. Mindfulness techniques may include self-care activities such as clients engaging in non-task-related activities. Some concrete examples include counselor-facilitated meditation, deep breathing activities, chair yoga, reflective and creative (but nonevaluative) art techniques, sandtray therapy, and music therapies.

Deep Breathing Body Scan

Specifically, one creative technique that helps clients utilize self-care and mindfulness is mindful deep breathing (Cayoun, 2011; Valikhani et al., 2019). In this intervention, a counselor invites the client to participate. Once assent is received, the counselor instructs the client, "I'm going to ask you to get into a comfortable position as you sit here with me. For the next five minutes or so, I am going to ask you to slow down your breathing and to take deep belly breaths. Breathe in slowly through your nose, expanding your abdomen as your breath fills your lungs and chest. Then, after holding your breath for a count of four, slowly release your breath from the belly up through the lungs. Once you've gotten into a rhythm after a few moments, I am going to direct your attention to different parts of your body. Continue breathing deeply and slowly, but direct your mental attention to whatever part of the body that is named. Just let your breathing remain steady as your mind gently scans each part of the body that is named." The counselor will then slowly move through a body scan with the client, starting at the feet (for example, the counselor might say, "Bring your attention to your feet, now. Just be aware of the sensations experienced there, in your feet"), then moving to the legs, the knees, the hips, the abdomen, the chest, the shoulders, the hands, the arms, the elbows, back to the shoulders, the neck, and the head. Invite the client to mentally focus on each area, noticing whatever feelings or sensations arise.

After completing the body scan, the counselor would say to the client, "Take a few more deep breaths as you sit with the feelings and sensations that arose as you traveled around your body." To process the body scan, the client can be asked to describe what came up for her during the exercise, how she felt, and whether she felt a sense of calmness or any change in anxiety levels during and after the body scan.

Anxiety Visualization

In this exercise, the counselor asks the client if she would feel comfortable engaging in a mental visualization exercise. Upon agreement, the counselor invites the client to sit comfortably and to close her eyes. The counselor can play soft, relaxing instrumental music to facilitate relaxation. The counselor invites the client to slow down her breathing rate and to take deep belly breaths, slowly drawing in a breath through her nose that expands her belly and chest as it fills her lungs. During their time listening to instrumental music and deep breathing, the counselor asks the client to picture their anxiety as an object, such as a rolling ball. Instead of forcing the anxiety to be gone, clients are often asked to "observe your anxiety" rather than "force it away." Through observing their feelings, clients are able to recognize that they are "not their anxiety" and that their true identity is more than just their anxiety. Letting their anxiety sit "outside" of themselves, even if only during the meditation in the beginning, helps clients feel empowered to overcome the anxiety that is keeping them from enjoying the life they would like to live. The counselor can encourage the client to continue her slow, deep breathing while imagining her anxiety rolling away from her and leaving her in a state of calmness. After the client has had a few moments to experience this sensation, the counselor should ask the client to slowly open her eyes and share what it feels like to let go of her anxiety. Techniques such as mindfulness will help clients relax not only psychologically but also physically, which may help them be better aware of cognitive distortions and other presenting issues.

Visual Arts Interventions

Studies have found that engaging in visual art making can lower anxiety (Aaron, Rinehart, & Ceballos, 2011; Sandmire, Gorham, Rankin, & Grimm, 2012). In fact, guided art making is actually more effective than free-form, "blank canvas" art making or puzzle solving. It is believed that the process of creating art fosters a meditative state for clients, and they are able to let go of anxiety while engaging with the art medium provided. While art making can be included during counseling sessions, clients can also be encouraged to engage in art-related activities outside of the session during times when they are feeling their anxiety rising. There are multiple sources of adult coloring books and mandala forms that can be easily obtained and that provide the guided activity that research suggests is most effective.

Exercise and Physical Activity Interventions

There has been some support for the introduction of physical exercise as a treatment for anxiety disorders, especially low-impact and mindfulness-based, mind-body-connected activities, including tai chi (Zheng et al., 2018) and yoga (Cramer et al., 2018). Curtiss and Klemanski (2014) found that individuals who suffer from both anxiety and depression also tend to present with low mindfulness, in that they are less aware in the moment of their thoughts, feelings, sensations, or environment. Individuals who experience disordered levels of anxiety are often experiencing reactive responses to the world around them rather than more mindful responses that arise out of deeper awareness of themselves and their circumstances. Thus, engaging in activities that involve mindful awareness in the moment provide clients with anxiety disorders practice in short-circuiting the tendency to react rather than respond.

DIVERSITY CONSIDERATIONS

When working with Chu and other clients who experience anxiety, it is important to consider their phenomenological experience. For example, as shared in the vignette above, Chu identifies as an American resident who was born in South Korea. When considering her contextual background, it is important for a counselor to ask Chu, "How do you think your anxiety is getting in your way?" Open-ended questions such as this are encouraged, rather than a counselor making noncontextual assumptions about Chu. Contextual understanding and cultural considerations are always needed, as perhaps Chu's cultural background affects her anxiety or perhaps her cultural identity is not at all related to her presenting anxiety. Moreover, learning about a client's culture should not be considered as if in a silo in selected sessions. Awareness of the role played by cultural identity should be infused into all sessions with clients.

In other words, when considering clients with anxiety and diversity domains, it is important not to overpathologize clients' experiences, and considering clients within different cultural contexts should always be an ethical duty for counselors (American Counseling Association [ACA], 2014; Carter et al., 2003; Council for Accreditation of Counseling and Related Educational Programs [CACREP], 2016). One concrete way counselors can help clients with anxiety address their presenting issues while also learning about these clients is open-ended assessments such as use of the RESPECTFUL Model (Ivey, D'Andrea, & Ivey, 2011). The RESPECTFUL Model has the client describe various intersections about themselves, specifically the following: **r**eligious and spiritual identity, **e**conomic class background, **s**exual identity, **p**sychological maturity, **e**thnic and racial identities, **c**hronological and developmental challenges, **t**rauma and threats to their well-being, **f**amily background and history, **u**nique physical characteristics, and **l**ocation of residence and language differences (D'Andrea & Daniels, 2001; Ivey et al.,

2011). With open-ended assessments such as the RESPECTFUL Model (i.e., ones that serve as an informal assessment), counselors can gain a fuller and culturally richer picture of a client without overgeneralizing based on their common, but sometimes misunderstood, reports of anxiety.

ETHICAL CONSIDERATIONS

One form of ethical bracketing that clinicians can use particularly when working with clients with anxiety is counselor engagement of self-care. Self-care can involve treating oneself weekly with intrinsically interesting and "grounding" activities or rewards or simply being present for small daily living activities throughout the week (i.e., fitting in routines of cooking our own meals, engaging in daily hygiene, and taking breaks from work). Ethical dilemmas often arise if counselors do not model the same self-care and mindfulness that they facilitate for their clients. Conversely, participation in counselor self-care will promote congruency and avoid countertransferences or even burnout. Furthermore, the Council for Accreditation of Counseling and Related Educational Programs (CACREP) suggested "that counseling education programs integrate a wellness concept in their curriculums" (CACREP, 2016). Incorporation of mindfulness in the curriculum reminds counselor education students and counselors to do self-care and model this same self-care for clients. It is also salient to note that, even if you are a counselor who did not receive self-care strategies in your training, you can still engage in your own self-care. Reminding ourselves, as counselors, to be mindful can combat any countertransference, especially those that may be unintentionally provoked by clients with anxiety. To reinforce this ethical need, the American Counseling Association (ACA) also articulates that counselors and counselor educators engage in and model self-care (ACA, 2014).

ADVOCACY OPPORTUNITIES

Advocacy directly related to clients with anxiety includes counselors confronting clients' shame or internalized stigma about their need to seek mental health, which may be escalated due to cognitive distortions and anxiety (Burns, 1989; Carter et al., 2003; Maruna & Mann, 2006). It is additionally important for counselors to combat societal messages that shame or stigmatize any clients seeking mental health help (Ramlall, 2019; Roemer & Orsillo, 2002). Furthermore, a concrete advocacy strategy includes providing educational seminars, events, or general awareness on why clients with anxiety would benefit from attending counseling. A few of the societal organizations known for destigmatizing mental health related to anxiety include the National Alliance on Mental Illness (NAMI), the Anxiety and Depression Association of America (ADAA), and Minding Your Mind (MYM). On a large scale, teaching young students in schools (and all clients) about what impairing anxiety versus functional, everyday anxiety feels like is a first step to normalizing anxiety disorders as well as encouraging treatment when a client's anxiety becomes "too much."

CASE VIGNETTE WRAP-UP: CHU

As a holistic review, CBT techniques that a counselor could incorporate in sessions to help Chu manage anxiety, include psychoeducation about anxiety, thought stopping, challenging negative emotions, and relaxation techniques (Burns, 1989; Carter et al., 2003; Cayoun, 2011; Maruna & Mann, 2006; Valikhani et al., 2019). In addition to these techniques, it is also important for the counselor to continue to collaborate with Chu on her unique phenomenological experience. Chu may have additional therapeutic needs or presenting concerns. Thus, processing and conceptualizing Chu's anxiety may be a catalyst to learning about other aspects, including trauma, other diagnoses, and environmental influences.

Here are some guiding questions that could prove efficacious in Chu's cognitive behavioral therapy guided session: What are everyday fears that you experience? What are some rational fears you believe you have? What are some irrational fears you believe you have? Other questions that may be used with clients who are anxious include reframing question, exploratory questions, and exploratory reflections. For example, Chu could be asked, "If you could, what parts of your situation would you most like to change? What are some ironic or unforeseen benefits from this situation?"

QUESTIONS FOR REFLECTION

1. Anxiety is on the increase around the globe. What are some ways anxiety might show up in the clients you see?
2. How might you integrate cognitive behavioral mindfulness interventions with women across the lifespan?
3. What are ways that culture influences levels of anxiety and stress?

REFERENCES

Aaron, R. E., Rinehart, K. L., & Ceballos, N. A. (2011) Arts-based interventions to reduce anxiety levels among college students. *Arts & Health, 3*, 27–38. doi: https://doi.org/10.1080/17533015.2010.481290

Abel, G. G., Gore, D. K., Holland, C. L., Camp, N., Becker, J. V., & Rathner, B. A. (1989). The measurement of the cognitive distortions of child molesters. *Annals of Sex Research, 2*, 135–53.

American Counseling Association. (2014). *ACA code of ethics*. Alexandria, VA: Author.

Ayres, I., Bankman, J., Fried, B., & Luce, K. (2017). Anxiety psychoeducation for law students: A pilot program. *Journal of Legal Education, 67*, 118–138.

Banks, T. L. (2017). Psychoeducation. In J. Carlson & S. B. Dermer (Eds.), *The Sage encyclopedia of marriage, family, and couples counseling* (pp. 1339–44). Thousand Oaks, CA: Sage.

Beck, A. T. (1963). Thinking and depression: 1. Idiosyncratic content and cognitive distortions. *Archives of General Psychiatry, 9*, 324–33.

Burns, D. (1989). *The feeling good handbook: Using the new mood therapy in everyday life.* New York, NY: William Morrow.

Carter, M., Sbrocco, T., Gore, K., Marin, N., & Lewis, E. (2003). Cognitive-behavioral group versus a wait-list control in the treatment of African American women with panic disorder. *Cognitive Therapy & Research, 27*(5), 505–18.

Cayoun, B. A. (2011). *Mindfulness-integrated CBT: Principles and practice.* Malden, MA: John Wiley & Sons.

Council for Accreditation of Counseling and Related Educational Programs. (2016). 2016 accreditation standards. Retrieved from: http://www.cacrep.org/for-programs/2016-cacrep-standards

Cramer, H., Lauche, R., Anheyer, D., Pilkington, K., de Manicor, M., Dobos, G., & Ward, L. (2018). Yoga for anxiety: A systematic review and meta-analysis of randomized controlled trials. *Depression and Anxiety, 35*, 830–43. doi: 10.1002/da22762

Curtiss, J., & Klemanski, D. H. (2014). Teasing apart low mindfulness: Differentiating deficits in mindfulness and in psychological flexibility in predicting symptoms of generalized anxiety disorder and depression. *Journal of Affective Disorders, 166*, 41–47. doi: 10.1016/j.jad.2014.04.062

D'Andrea, M., & Daniels, J. (2001). RESPECTFUL counseling: An integrative model for counselors. In D. Pope-Davis & H. Coleman (Eds.), *The interface of class, culture and gender in counseling* (pp. 417–66). Thousand Oaks, CA: Sage.

Erford, B. T. (2015). *40 techniques every counselor should know.* New York, NY: Pearson Higher Education.

Gallegos-Guajardo, J., Ruvalcaba-Romero, N., Langley, A., & Villegas-Guinea, D. (2015). Selective prevention for anxiety and resilience promotion: Outcomes of an anxiety prevention and resilience program with girls at risk. *Pensando Psicologia, 11*(18), 11–23.

Ivey, A. E., D'Andrea, M. J., & Ivey, M. B. (2011). *Theories of counseling and psychotherapy: A multicultural perspective.* Thousand Oaks, CA: Sage.

Kessler, R. C., Chiu, W. T., Demler, O., Merikangas, K. R., & Walters, E. E. (2005). Prevalence, severity, and comorbidity of 12-month DSM-IV disorders in the National Comorbidity Survey Replication. *Archives of General Psychiatry, 62*(6), 617–27. doi: 10.1001/archpsyc.62.6.617

Latif, M., & Khanam, S. J. (2017). Effectiveness of cognitive behaviour therapy in reducing anxiety, depression and violence in women affected by intimate partner violence: A randomized controlled trial from a low-income country. *Journal of Postgraduate Medical Institute (Peshawar-Pakistan), 31*(4), 425–31.

Maruna, S., & Mann, R. E. (2006). A fundamental attribution error? Rethinking cognitive distortions. *Legal and Criminological Psychology, 11*(2), 155–77.

McElhinney, R., Reid, H., & Morton, L. (2016). A controlled trial of a CBT group for women with low self-esteem. *Clinical Psychology Forum, 287*, 21–24.

Montal, S. (2010). Fear of recurrence: A case report of a woman breast cancer survivor with GAD treated successfully by CBT. *Clinical Psychology & Psychotherapy, 17*(1), 346–53.

Ramlall, S. (2019). Advocacy for mental health and mental illness: Silence is complicity. *Mental Health Matters, 6*(2), 1–2.

Roemer, L., & Orsillo, S. (2002). Expanding our conceptualization of and treatment for generalized anxiety disorder: Integrating mindfulness/acceptance-based approaches with existing cognitive-behavioral models. *Clinical Psychology: Science & Practice, 9*(1), 54–68.

Sandmire, D. A., Gorham, S. R., Rankin, N. E., & Grimm, D. R. (2012). The influence of art making on anxiety: A pilot study. *Journal of the American Art Therapy Association, 29*(2), 78–73. doi: 10.1080/07421656.2012.683748

Singh, S. K., & Gorey, K. M. (2018). Relative effectiveness of mindfulness and cognitive behavioral interventions for anxiety disorders: Meta-analytic review. *Social Work in Mental Health, 16*(2), 238–51. doi: 10.1080/15332985.2017.1373266

Valikhani, A., Kankat, L. R., Hariri, P., Salehi, S., & Moustafa, A. A. (2019). Examining the mediating role of stress in the relationship between mindfulness and depression and anxiety: Testing the mindfulness stress-buffering model. *Journal of Rational-Emotive & Cognitive-Behavior Therapy*, forthcoming, 1–12.

Zheng, S., Kim, C., Lal, S., Meier, P., Sibbritt, D., & Zaslawski, C. (2018). The effects of twelve weeks of tai chi practice on anxiety in stressed but healthy people compared to exercise and wait-list groups: A randomized controlled trial. *Journal of Clinical Psychology, 74*, 83–92. doi: https://doi.org/10.1002/jclp.22482

Chapter Eighteen

Counseling Women with Addictions

Suzanne Degges-White

CASE VIGNETTE: SYLVIE

Sylvie, a thirty-four-year-old Caucasian, is a middle school English teacher who lives with her husband, Dane, and their twin eleven-year-old daughters. Sylvie and Dane met in college at a church near campus in a Sunday school class during their freshman year. They were instantly attracted to one another and especially pleased that they shared the same faith and belief practices. Sylvie arrives for counseling at a community mental health center and describes her presenting issue as "confusion about her choices and feeling anxious that she isn't as good a mother or wife as she should be." Tabby, her counselor, sits down with Sylvie for the first session and notices that Sylvie seems a little confused, has bloodshot eyes, and is trembling. Tabby reviews the brief intake information that Sylvie provided and then encourages, "Sylvie, I see what you've written down as your main concerns here, but I'd like to hear you share with me more about what's brought you into counseling at this time in your life?" Sylvie tears up as she shrinks back into her chair and whispers, "I think I have a problem with medicine. . . . Last winter, I slipped on the ice and broke my elbow. I needed the painkillers they prescribed after they set my arm. But it's been a year, now, and I don't need them for my arm anymore, but I'm still taking them." Tabby responds, "So, it sounds like you're concerned that you might be struggling with overuse of the painkiller that your physician prescribed." Sylvie's tears turn into sobs as she states, "I know I have a problem. I'm addicted to the stuff. The bottle says Dilaudid, but on the corner, it's called juice, smack, dust, whatever. It's really just poison. And I can't get away from it no matter how hard I've tried."

* * *

Until the 1960s, alcoholism and addiction were perceived as "men's issues" rather than something that women might experience (Murray, 1962). In fact, even in 1962, a woman's alcohol addiction was described as the "housewife's secret sickness." While men are more likely to use substances that lead to addiction (Center for Behavioral Health Statistics and Quality, 2017), there is no difference between genders in the likelihood that a substance abuse disorder will occur (Anthony, Warner, & Kessler, 1994). In the United States, approximately 30 percent of adults meet the criteria for diagnosis with an alcohol use disorder at some point in their lives (Hasin, Stinson, Ogburn, & Grant, 2007).

The DSM-V (American Psychiatric Association, 2013) outlines eleven areas of assessment for substance use disorders:

- Taking larger amounts of the substance or using it longer than it should be
- Inability to control and lower your intake even when you try to do so
- Spending a significant amount of time planning, acquiring, using, or recovering from use
- Experiencing a craving and strong urge to use the substance of choice
- Substance use keeps you from functioning in the ways that you should or ways that you used to function—missing appointments, work, social commitments, or feeling unable to be fully present for people you care about
- Knowing that your substance use is creating problems in your relationships, but being unable to control your use
- Turning down opportunities to engage in social, work, or leisure activities due to substance use
- Unable to stop using even when substance use is creating problems in your life or leads you to make unsafe choices that put your health or safety at risk (risk of accidents, physical injury, STDs, violence)
- Recognizing that you have a physical or mental health problem related to using, but continuing to use anyway (memory blackouts, depression, suicidal ideations, overdoes history, etc.)
- Realizing that you need more and more of the substance to reach the same level of high or intoxication that lesser levels used to provide
- Experience withdrawal symptoms when you cannot use (restlessness, shakiness, racing heart, etc.) that would subside once you used again ("hair of the dog that bit you")

The DSM-V defined the severity of a person's substance use problem based on the number of these symptoms she exhibits: two to three symptoms means a person has a "mild" substance use disorder (SUD); four to five symptoms means a person has a "moderate" SUD; and six or more means the person suffers from a "severe" SUD.

DOES GENDER MATTER IN ADDICTION ONSET?

Research continues to indicate that women are less likely than men to use most any illicit substance, according to the latest report from the NIH (National Institute on Drug Abuse, 2018). Men are also more likely to end up in the emergency room due to substance-related incidents, and as of now, men are still more likely to overdose than women. The gender difference, however, skews against women in that they are just as likely to develop a substance use disorder and more likely to experience cravings and relapses. Because many addiction studies have used only men as participants, we are still learning about the ways women's physiologies and psychologies are influenced by and influence substance use concerns.

A woman's body changes over time in ways dissimilar to that of men; her reproductive capacity and its related hormonal and physiological demands create a different playing field when assessing the effect of addictive and illicit substances on the body. Body composition, regardless of weight differences, also differs between genders, thus altering the ways illicit substances affect the body and the length of time they remain in the body. Preventing substance use disorders is an ideal goal, just as preventing unwanted pregnancies through sex education in schools is the ideal goal. Unfortunately, the reasons women enter into substance use and abuse are often complex and culturally influenced due to the realities of a gendered society.

COMMON REASONS FOR SUBSTANCE USE IN WOMEN

Today, several reasons women might experiment with illicit substances are due to circumstances inherent to a predominantly patriarchal society. Too often, cultural expectations about a woman's role in society send a message that women should look, behave, and believe in ways that support the men in their lives. Women's roles and presence in the business world may shift, but the cultural norm is for women to continue to hold responsibility for maintaining a "happy home" and oversee the running of the household for her family. The energy required may be more than a woman possesses, so she may look for stimulants to help her keep moving forward. Other women may use stimulants as a weight loss tool to manage their weight and appearance. One study found that individuals who undergo one of the most popular weight loss surgeries, sleeve gastrectomy, are at a higher likelihood of subsequently developing an alcohol use disorder (Ibrahim et al., 2019). The etiology of this is still unclear, but it gives credence to the idea that there are unanticipated risks in efforts to forcibly alter one's body. Further, women who are dealing with domestic violence may turn to illicit substances as numbing agents to cope with the physical and emotional pain they endure.

One of the most frequently explored causes of initiation into substance use is exposure to trauma (Goldstein, Bradley, Ressler, & Powers, 2017). As Goldstein and colleagues (2017) noted, a diagnosis of PTSD is an indicator that a woman is more likely to utilize alcohol when facing emotional or situational challenges. Alcohol and other drugs become the "medication of choice" when trying to cope with situations that exacerbate psychological symptoms. Although many illicit substances work as depressants, the immediate numbing effect that users experience can provide the short-term relief they feel necessary when they are unable to utilize healthier coping methods. Escaping or blacking out become preferred methods of coping with the pain.

Women may look to the illicit substance as a tool that will allow them to escape or to better meet demands they feel are placed on them by others and themselves. However, their experimentation can transform into addictions more rapidly than expected. While women may drink less or use smaller amounts of other illicit substances, they may experience the effects much more strongly than men. Women also become addicted more quickly than men. While most clinical research on substance abuse has focused on men, the government called for increasing research in the area of treatment of women's substance use disorders (Tuchman, 2010). One response to the call for greater research revealed that women are less likely to seek any type of treatment for their substance abuse problem, and the reason that was cited most frequently was that women believed their problems would abate without intervention (Gilbert, Pro, Zemore, Mulia, & Brown, 2019).

ADDICTION AND TREATMENT

The treatment of addiction is often framed within Prochaska and DiClemente's (1984) transtheoretical model of change (TTM). From this model, a process termed motivational interviewing (MI) (Miller & Rollnick, 2002) originated that provides a framework within which counseling for change can occur. After a discussion of TTM, an overview of MI will be presented.

Transtheoretical Model of Change (TTM)

The Transtheoretical Model of Change is a model of care composed of six stages of change that range from the period of time before change has been considered all the way through relapse and back around. Following is a brief description of these stages.

Precontemplation. In this stage, it may be unlikely that the client recognizes an actual problem exists. The most significant sign that something is amiss is likely feedback received from other individuals in the client's life. In this stage, a client may be forced to reckon with undesired consequences of their behavior—work-related problems, relationship struggles, or legal issues such as DUI charges. Clinicians working with clients in this stage focus on helping the client recognize the significance of the problems their behavior is causing, the risks involved in continuing the behavior of concern, and the need to accept that their behavior must change. Consciousness raising is used to facilitate a client's awareness of the presence of a problem.

Contemplation. Clients in this stage exhibit ambivalence and conflicted feelings about the desire to change. Change is never an easy process, but trying to overcome addictions—which are physiological and emotional—can be especially daunting. Counselors can encourage clients to develop "pros and cons" lists regarding recovery. Empathy and support are key at this point in encouraging a client to commit to change. In addition, helping clients recognize the stumbling blocks they foresee along with plans for coping with these barriers can bolster confidence in the ability to beat the addiction. Counselors should recognize that clients often get stuck in this stage due to feelings about readiness, commitment, or ability to give up the behavior.

Preparation. This stage can include gathering resources and information about the change process. Clients can be encouraged to formalize their goals by writing these down. Clients can be encouraged to develop their plans for change by identifying triggers, developing plans for avoiding these, or coping with them when encountered. Some clinicians will ask their clients to write down motivational statements to use as reminders to keep them moving forward toward change. This is when clients seek out information about support groups such as twelve-step groups, group counseling resources, and supportive members in their friendship groups and families. Encouraging clients to build up a "tool kit" for combating their addiction may be helpful. Referring clients to relevant self-help books, films, novels, or documentaries regarding recovery can help them plan for success as well as prepare for potential challenges. Clients may need to assess who in their support networks will be helpful in their change efforts and who may need to be temporarily, or completely, eliminated from their network.

Action. In this stage, clients are actively engaged in avoiding use of the addictive substance. Clients often reach this stage with a high level of commitment to change and may be enthusiastic about the outcome of their behavioral change. Due to the difficulty inherent in lifestyle changes and the power of addictive behaviors, it is important to encourage your client to build in rewards for early successes to encourage continued commitment. Some clients may save the money that would have been spent on the addiction and, after it reaches a certain level, spend it on a tangible reward for their progress to date. Others may reward themselves for the time that is back in their days by consciously engaging in a different, but pleasurable, activity in place of the addiction. Motivation can be found in self-talk, continued with the counselor, or through support groups such as Alcoholics Anonymous or Narcotics Anonymous. These groups are populated with individuals at varying levels of recovery, and their firsthand experience can be especially helpful to clients who do not have intact social support networks nearby.

Maintenance. Many clients new to addiction recovery may arrive with high hopes at this stage after having developed what they hope are new lifelong habits and behaviors. Efforts to maintain changes begun in the action stage must continue, and clients must remain focused on making the right choices when confronted with temptation to use again. Staying involved in self-help groups can be especially supportive, as these programs often build in rewards (such as chips for thirty days, sixty days, and so on) that encourage continued recovery. During this phase, the potential for relapse may appear as clients may give into temptations to return to trigger locations or to spend time with people who trigger the behavior. If clients report having relapsed and using the addictive substance, counselors should remind them that relapses are temporary lapses and do not have to be harbingers of a return to their prior lifestyle.

Relapse. Although most clients who are making their first effort to beat an addiction may have strong expectations of unchallenged success, the vast majority of recovering addicts experience relapse at some point in their full recovery process. Helping clients prepare for a potential relapse may be more helpful in the long run than encouraging the belief that their initial effort at recovery will be completely successful. By devoting time in session with your client to discuss potential relapses and ways to handle them, your client can be primed to recognize the urgency of reentering a prior stage, either preparation, action, or maintenance. Clients may "beat up on themselves" or feel that their prior progress was pointless if they relapse. Help the client recognize that relapses are not uncommon, that they may happen again in the future, but that their response to relapse is more important to their recovery than having experienced a temporary setback. Explore with the client the trigger to which they attributed the relapse and help them develop a plan to avoid or better handle the trigger in the future. Encourage the client to continue to use helpful resources and reach out to supportive others as they continue their efforts toward sobriety.

Motivational Interviewing (MI)

One of the most effective methods of counseling individuals wrestling with addiction is motivational interviewing (Miller & Rollnick, 2002). It has been found to be successful in reducing use of drugs and alcohol (Lundahl, Kunz, Brownell, Tollefson, & Burke, 2010). It has also been found to be an effective intervention to implement in the first session, if it may be your only session, as it provides the platform to build self-efficacy regarding change and to encourage clients to begin to contemplate change (Berman, Forsberg, Durbeej, Källmén, & Hermansson, 2010; Forman & Moyers, 2019).

The four principles of MI (Miller & Rollnick, 2002) emphasize the clinician's acknowledgment of the client's role in therapeutic success. The four basic principles are these:

1. Resist the righting reflex. Clinicians must avoid telling the client what is "right" or "best" for the client. When people are told what they "should" do, it often encourages them to continue doing what is not in their best interest.
2. Understand the client's personal motivation for change. The client's reasons for personal change are the motivating factors that matter most; a clinician should use these reasons as a guide to how to help the client position herself for change. By understanding the client's feelings about change and her reasons for changing and her reasons for maintaining a status quo, the counselor will be better positioned to help facilitate change.
3. Listen with empathy. The better a counselor understands a client, the more effective the helping relationship will become. Counseling sessions should include "give and take" between client and counselor, with the counselor yielding about half of session time to client dialogue.
4. Empower your client. When counselors involve their clients in treatment planning and empower their clients to actively engage in their treatment, there is greater likelihood of client improvement. Instilling hope is also key for successful treatment; if clients are encouraged to believe they can overcome their addictions, they are more likely to be successful.

There is also a set of basic skills that counselors use in the application of MI. These skills include asking open-ended questions; affirming the client's positive steps and strengths; reflecting the client's feelings, statements, and beliefs; and summarizing appropriately throughout the session. By utilizing these behaviors, the counselor's engagement in the therapeutic process is made evident to the client through a focus on the client's experiences, strengths, and challenges. In the following section, two highly prevalent forms of addiction and current best practices for treatment will be presented. These include alcohol addiction and opioid addiction.

ALCOHOL ADDICTION

Relapse poses a formidable challenge, and data indicates that a vast proportion of users will experience relapse at some point in the recovery process. Estimates suggest that between 40 and 75 percent of individuals addicted to alcohol will relapse (National Institute on Drug Abuse [NIDA], 2018) and as many as 90 percent of individuals addicted to opiates will do the same (Smyth, Barry, Keenan, & Ducray, 2010). Researchers in one study found that the primary self-reported cause for relapse is the desire to experience a positive mood (Kadam et al., 2017). Addiction to any substances includes not just the actual introduction of the substance into the body but also the presence of rituals and surroundings, including people and places, that accompanies substance use. Helping a client end an addiction will involve a great deal of attention to relapse concerns. Helping a client identify her personal triggers will allow her to develop personalized plans for avoiding the triggers and develop plans for coping with the craving that relapse triggers can worsen. In one study, researchers found cravings for alcohol can be reduced through the consumption of approximately a quart of water after experiencing a craving for alcohol (Koopmann et al., 2017). While this may be effective for some clients, any client wanting to overcome an addiction must be committed and motivated to overcoming her addiction in order for treatment to be effective. Evidence-based treatments for alcohol addiction include residential treatment, pharmacological treatment, cognitive behavioral therapy, and mutual help groups.

Residential Treatment

Although our culture and media have popularized the concept of the "twenty-eight day" stay at residential treatment centers, this period is seldom adequate on its own to serve as effective long-term treatment for addictions. Recovery is a lifelong process, and some individuals may experience multiple stays at rehabilitation centers before they are able to maintain long-term sobriety. Treatment programs, either in-patient or out-patient, which are shorter than three months are unlikely to result in long-term change for individuals (NIDA, 2018). Residential treatment centers vary greatly in terms of levels of service and care as well as cost. While the majority of residential treatment centers are not gender specific, there are some programs that are for women only (Neale, Tompkins, Marshall, Treloar, & Strang, 2018). However, Neale and colleagues (2018) found women who were placed in gender-specific treatment centers were not necessarily seeking this type of environment, often due to their prior poor experiences in same-gender friendships. Residential treatment that better reflects an individual's typical milieu may be the best option.

Pharmacological Treatment

There are two primary medications used to treat alcohol use disorder; these are naltrexone and acamprosate (Anton et al., 2006; Reus et al., 2018). Naltrexone is helpful in decreasing craving for alcohol, increasing the number of nondrinking days, and avoidance of relapse. Acamprosate also decreases cravings and urges to drink. If neither of these two medications is effective, physicians suggest the use of disulfiram, topiramate, or gabapentin. As is the case with any medication, there are certain side effects, drug interactions, and risks inherent in their use, so medical management is an essential aspect of treatment with any of these medications. In the COMBINE study by Anton and colleagues (2006), it was found that medical management was a positive adjunctive treatment to pharmacological treatment of addiction. In this particular study, medical management included an initial forty-five-minute meeting with a member of the medical team and then follow-up appointments over the course of the treatment. The continuity of care and relationship maintenance that the follow-up meetings allow may play a significant role in providing support and accountability to clients.

Cognitive Behavioral Therapy

Cognitive behavioral therapy (CBT), delivered by a competent clinician, encourages individuals to change their behaviors by changing their thoughts. This form of therapy is highly structured and goal oriented, and this form of intervention aligns with the needs of individuals battling addictions. It can be used as clients take their first steps toward sobriety as well as throughout their lives as they continue to remain in recovery.

The first step in CBT is to have clients identify the triggering events that lead them to drink. This can include activating events, places clients frequent, or specific people. Clients are encouraged to avoid contact with all of the potential triggers, where possible. For those triggers that cannot be avoided, clients are asked to develop coping skills that support them in avoiding alcohol intake. Often, clients have come to rely on alcohol use as a primary coping method; thus, they need to learn new coping methods that will help them resist substance use and replace substance use as a preferred method.

When in the vicinity of a trigger, clients may need to "take five" and leave the trigger area to have space to strengthen their resolve to refrain from drinking. The pairing of the trigger with substance use is often a highly conditioned response, and short-circuiting the prior learned behaviors can be challenging. Clients can be encouraged to develop self-talk that helps them cope internally with unavoidable situational triggers. For instance, a client may need to remind herself that she doesn't "have" to drink to celebrate the end of the workday when she gets in from work. A client may need to learn a new route home from her children's school if she had a routine of stopping at a particular liquor store after dropping off her children in the morning.

Using Prochaska and DiClemente's (1984) TTC framework as a guide, clinicians can help clients build in positive rewards to mark their success in withstanding temptation or getting through a day without using. Celebrating early successes and developing plans for marking longer-term successes can help clients stay on track as they develop new patterns of behavior. The TTC model includes the practice of planning for relapse. Clinicians can help their clients think through potential plans for coping with and returning from a relapse.

Mutual-Help Groups

While many people tend to think first of Alcoholics Anonymous (AA) as the primary group setting for community-based addiction self-help, there are multiple other groups that, combined with AA, make up the population of mutual-help groups. Due to the faith-based nature of AA, there are many individuals who do not feel comfortable joining these meetings. Thus, there are multiple forms of support groups that exist for individuals trying to overcome an addiction. In a study of long-term effectiveness of group programming for sobriety, Zemore, Lui, Mericle, Hemberg, and Kaskutas (2018) found that faith-based twelve-step groups were similar in effectiveness to other groups, such as Women for Sobriety, LifeRing, and SMART Recovery.

Mutual-help groups are designed to offer support to members who are actively working to stay sober. In essence, a mutual-help group is the presence of two or more people who share a common concern and meet to offer support to one another as each person individually faces the shared challenge. Other characteristics common to mutual-help groups include the expectation that members are accountable for their behaviors. The groups also offer understanding from members; there is usually a great deal of flexibility in the scheduling and attendance at meetings. Sponsors can be assigned, and this can provide a strong sense of connection and support to individuals battling addiction. One of the most attractive features of mutual-help groups is that there is seldom a charge for attendance or membership. This can provide women in recovery with accessible support, and the frequency of meeting times offers flexibility in scheduling around other responsibilities; some groups also provide childcare options. Although it is difficult to determine the long-term effectiveness of participation in mutual-help groups, Moos and Moos (2006) conducted a sixteen-year longitudinal study and collected data suggesting that participation in AA, specifically, positively influenced the sobriety of participants over the long term. The key component in recovery is an individual's commitment to sobriety. Attendance at mutual-help group meetings provides consistent support toward that goal, and regardless of the specific programming or focus (faith-based or secular), the social support received can be extremely effective in helping many individuals reach that goal. In fact, research indicates that younger women are as likely as women thirty and over to benefit from participation (Hoeppner, Hoeppner, & Kelly, 2014). In summation, this type of treatment is beneficial and extremely cost-effective, indicating that counselors should recommend this form of substance abuse treatment to clients, and attendance should be encouraged (Kelly & Yeterian, 2011).

OPIOID ADDICTION

The United Nations released a report in June 2019 stating that the opioid crisis had reached epidemic proportions in the country. The rate of opioid overdose is at an all-time high. According to Ait-Dauoud, Blevins, Khanna, Sharma, and Holstege (2017), women are being affected disproportionately by opioid misuse and addiction compared to men. In fact, fatal drug overdoses increased by approximately 260 percent from 1999 to 2017 for U.S. women aged thirty to sixty-four (VanHouten, Rudd, Ballesteros, & Mack, 2019). In addition, the highest percentage rate changes for overdose rates have been among women aged forty-five to sixty-four (Centers for Disease Control, 2013). The average age at death has been increasing over the past few years, suggesting that as women age the occurrence of physical pain may increase and, concomitantly, the frequency of opioid prescriptions likely increases. This may contribute to the epidemic-level rates of opioid addiction and overdose among middle-aged women. While women in midlife pose special concerns due to their vulnerability to overdose, there are also concerns about the use of these types of pain medications with women who are pregnant. Opioid addiction, whether the outcome of prescription misuse or illicit behaviors, can lead to fatal consequences and creates a problem that is far from easy to solve.

Treatment

Opioid addiction is more than a psychological addiction; it is a physiological addiction that can be extremely difficult to combat. Research shows that the most effective treatment involves the inclusion of an opioid replacement medication such as methadone, buprenorphine, and naltrexone (NIDA, 2018). However, women battling addictions may also be facing difficulties in multiple sectors of their lives. In fact, it is often the collateral damage that is being caused by the addiction that is the impetus for the client to seek help. The fallout may be job related, including loss of employment due to habitual absences or poor performance. It may be difficulties in primary relationships, such as marriage or parenting. It could include legal issues related to substance possession or misuse. Criminal behaviors, including identity theft, burglary, and forgery, may result in mandatory treatment and incarceration. Clinicians should be aware that women diagnosed with addictive disorders may need referrals for medical care, parenting classes, career/vocational services, social services, and, potentially, legal services. Clinicians working with these clients beyond specialized treatment centers need to maintain up-to-date resource listings that they can share with their clients. It is also helpful for clinicians working with these individuals to invest in development of collegial relationships with those other professionals who may be called upon to work with their clients.

CULTURAL CONSIDERATIONS

Addiction is a disease that affects women across demographic boundaries. Unfortunately, women run up against a larger number of barriers to substance abuse treatment than men do (Tuchman, 2010). Thus, clinicians should be especially attentive to any reference clients make to substance use or misuse and explore further, as needed. It is important to note that Native Americans and Hispanics report higher rates of high-risk drinking (Chartier & Caetano, 2010), yet ethnic minorities experience disparities in treatment utilization. It is essential that substance abuse treatment for ethnic minorities be culturally sensitive, focus on the development of healthy coping mechanisms, consider spiritual and religious belief systems, and consider the role that family support systems may play in the client's life.

ETHICAL CONSIDERATIONS

Substance use and abuse are often taboo topics that families may grow highly adept at avoiding even when an intimate family member is in the grips of addiction. While the individual battling the addiction may experience shame at their disease, the stigma may also affect the family of the addict. Thus, clinicians must be sensitive in how they work with clients and their families and how they approach family-held beliefs about addiction. In addition, clinicians must be mindful of their own values and perspectives related to substance use and addiction in order to ensure that their services are not unduly influenced by their own personal beliefs. Being able to balance the five core ethical principles of justice, autonomy, beneficence, nonmaleficence, and fidelity is essential. The clients' goals and client welfare, not clinician's personal agendas, should always be the focus of therapeutic work.

ADVOCACY OPPORTUNITIES

As noted, addictions to alcohol and opioids have grown in their prevalence among women and do not discriminate based on age, income, ethnicity, or other demographic status. Thus, advocacy efforts can benefit all women who struggle with or whose lives are affected by addiction. As appalling as it may seem, research shows that people of color continue to experience discrimination in mental health and substance abuse care settings (Mays, Jones, Delany-Brumsey, Coles, & Cochran, 2017). So long as perceptions of discrimination are a factor, these individuals may be more hesitant to seek treatment early and also be held back by the stigma that mental health care often carries. Advocacy efforts for fair treatment of marginalized populations in mental health-care settings may come in the form of grassroots efforts, public campaigns for equity, and encouragement of news outlets to cover this issue. If you are a practitioner, advocacy can be practiced through your work with these clients. Offering limited pro bono service in appropriate locations is one way of helping ensure that needs are being met.

CASE VIGNETTE WRAP-UP: SYLVIE

After learning more about Sylvie's increasing use of Dilaudid, Tabby realizes that she will likely need to refer Sylvie to a clinic where opioid replacement medications are dispensed as part of her treatment. Tabby understands the scope of addiction and has a significant amount of experience working with individuals in recovery; thus she also knows that opioid addiction is seldom treated with talk therapy alone. Informed by her knowledge of the principles of motivational interviewing, Tabby uses open-ended questions to encourage Sylvie to share information about her struggles with opioid use, the ways it has affected her and her family, and her hopes about the future. Tabby affirms her client's desire to overcome her addiction and helps Sylvie recognize that the perceived benefits of ending the addiction, regardless of how difficult the task, outweigh any reasons for not changing. Tabby recognizes that Sylvie might be ambivalent about actually engaging in the work that recovery requires. However, because family and faith are of great importance to Sylvie, Tabby believes these two structures could provide motivation for Sylvie to begin and continue the work. Tabby affirms her commitment to Sylvie's well-being, but notes that they are partners in this challenge and Sylvie had to be as committed as Tabby for Sylvie to succeed. Tabby's presence is empathic and supportive, but also intentional and directive, as Tabby knows that this is necessary to keep Sylvie on the path to recovery.

At the end of their first session, Tabby summarizes the content and emotions that Sylvie has shared and exhibited, expresses empathy with Sylvie's struggles, and affirms her client's strength for taking the first steps toward change. Tabby also provides referrals to a medical clinic as well as a family counselor. Addiction disorders negatively affect the user, their families, and their relationships. Tabby can continue working with Sylvie, but she believes that the family would benefit from family counseling to heal from the damage the addiction has generated. Tabby continues to work with Sylvie individually over the next four months, and this provides Sylvie the support she needs to reach "day one hundred" of abstinence from opiates. Sylvie's husband attends a mutual-help group for family members of individuals dealing with substance abuse, which helps him to understand his and their children's experiences better. Sylvie is likely to need methadone for a year or more, but her active engagement in her own treatment and her motivation to be a better partner and parent appear strong enough to keep her committed to sober living.

QUESTIONS FOR REFLECTION

1. Addiction and drug overdoses have grown into epidemics in this country. What are some ways that prevention might be accomplished by counselors working with children in schools? With at-risk teenagers?
2. What resources are available in your area that would be helpful to you if you suspected that a minor client was using illegal substances?
3. Addictions affect millions of families in a multitude of ways. If you have addiction in your family history, what are some of the preconceived notions or beliefs that may have been shaped by this? What will you need to do to ensure that you are the most effective counselor you can be for a client suffering from an addiction disorder?

REFERENCES

Ait-Doaud, N., Blevins, D., Khanna, S., Sharma, S., & Holstege, C. P. (2017). Women and addiction. *Psychiatric Clinics of North America, 40*, 285–97.

American Psychiatric Association. (2013). *Diagnostic and statistical manual of mental disorders* (5th ed.). Washington, DC: Author.

Anthony, J. C., Warner, L. A., & Kessler, R. C. (1994). Comparative epidemiology of dependence on tobacco, alcohol, controlled substances, and inhalants: Basic findings from the National Comorbidity Survey. *Experimental and Clinical Psychopharmacology, 2*(3), 244–68.

Anton, R. F., O'Malley, S. S., Ciraulo, D. A., Cissler, R. A., Couper, D., Donovan, D. M., . . . Zweben, A. (2006). Combined pharmacotherapies and behavioral interventions for alcohol dependence: The COMBINE study: A randomized controlled trial. *Journal of the American Medical Association, 295*, 2003–17.

Berman, A. H., Forsberg, L., Durbeej, N., Källmén, H., & Hermansson, U. (2010). Single-session motivational interviewing for drug detoxification inpatients: Effects on self-efficacy, stages of change and substance use. *Substance Use and Misuse, 45*(3), 384–402.

Center for Behavioral Health Statistics and Quality. (2017). *Results from the 2016 National Survey on Drug Use and Health: Detailed tables.* Rockville, MD: Substance Abuse and Mental Health Services Administration. Retrieved from https://www.samhsa.gov/data/sites/default/files/NSDUH-DetTabs-2016/NSDUH-DetTabs-2016.pdf. doi:10.1080/10550881003684582

Centers for Disease Control. (2013). Vital signs: Overdoses of prescription opioid pain relievers and other drugs among women—United States, 1999–2010. *MMWR Morbidity and Mortality Weekly Report, 62*, 537–42.

Chartier, K. G., & Caetano, R. (2010). Ethnicity and health disparities in alcohol research. *Alcohol Research and Health, 33*, 152–60. PMCID: PMC3887493

Forman, D. P., & Moyers, T. B. (2019). With odds of a single session, motivational interviewing is a good bet. *Psychotherapy, 56*(1), 62–66.

Gilbert, P. A., Pro, G., Zemore, S. E., Mulia, N., & Brown, G. (2019). Gender differences in use of alcohol treatment services and reasons for nonuse in a national sample. *Alcoholism: Clinical and Experimental Research, 43*, 722–31.

Goldstein, B., Bradley, B., Ressler, K. J., & Powers, A. (2017). Associations between posttraumatic stress disorder, emotion dysregulation, and alcohol dependence symptoms among inner city females. *Journal of Clinical Psychology, 73*(3), 319–30. doi:10.1002/jclp.22332

Hasin, D. S., Stinson, F. S., Ogburn, E., & Grant, B. F. (2007). Prevalence, correlates, disability, and comorbidity of DSM-IV alcohol abuse and dependence in the United States: Results from the National Epidemiologic Survey on Alcohol and Related Conditions. *Archives of General Psychiatry, 64*(7), 830–42.

Hoeppner, B. B., Hoeppner, S. S., & Kelly, J. F. (2014). Do young people benefit from AA as much, and in the same ways, as adults aged 30+? A moderated multiple mediation analysis. *Drug and Alcohol Dependency, 143*, 181–88.

Ibrahim, N., Alameddine, M., Brennan, J., Sessine, M., Holliday, C., & Ghaferi, A. A. (2019). New onset alcohol use disorder following bariatric surgery. *Surgical Endoscopy, 33*(8), 2521–30.

Kadam, M., Sinha, A., Nimkar, S., Matcheswalla, Y., & De Sousa, A. (2017). A comparative study of factors associated with relapse in alcohol dependence and opioid dependence. *Indian Journal of Psychological Medicine, 39*(5), 627–33.

Kelly, J. F., & Yeterian, J. D. (2011). The role of mutual-help groups in extending the framework of treatment. *Alcohol Research & Health, 33*, 350–55.

Koopmann, A., Lippmann, K., Schuster, R., Reinhard, I., Bach, P., Weil, G., . . . Kiefer, F. (2017). Drinking water to reduce alcohol craving? A randomized controlled study on the impact of ghrelin in mediating the effects of forced water intake in alcohol addiction. *Psychoneuroendocrinology, 85*, 56–62. doi:10.1016/j.psyneuen.2017.08.005

Lundahl, B. W., Kunz, C., Brownell, C., Tollefson, D., & Burke, B. L. (2010). A meta-analysis of motivational interviewing: Twenty-five years of empirical studies. *Research in Social Work Practice, 20*, 137–60.

Mays, V. M., Jones, A., Delany-Brumsey, A., Coles, C., & Cochran, S. D. (2017). Perceived discrimination in healthcare and mental health/substance abuse treatment among blacks, Latinos, and whites. *Medical Care, 55*, 173–81.

Miller, W. R., & Rollnick, S. (2002). *Motivational interviewing. Preparing people for change* (2nd ed.). New York, NY: Guilford Press.

Moos, R. H., & Moos, B. S. (2006). Participation in treatment and Alcoholics Anonymous: A 16-year follow-up of initially untreated individuals. *Journal of Clinical Psychology, 62*, 735–50.

Murray, D. (1962, January 27). The housewife's secret sickness. *Saturday Evening Post, 253*(4), 80–83.

National Institute on Drug Abuse. (2018). *Principles of drug addiction treatment: A research-based guide* (3rd ed.). Washington, DC: Author.

Neale, J., Tompkins, C. N. E., Marshall, A. D., Treloar, C., & Strang, J. (2018). Do women with complex alcohol and other drug use histories want women-only residential treatment? *Addiction, 113*, 989–97.

Prochaska, J. O., & DiClemente, C. C. (1984). *The transtheoretical approach: Crossing traditional boundaries of therapy.* Homewood, IL: Dow Jones-Irwin.

Reus, V. I., Fochtmann, L. J., Bukstein, O., Eyler, A. E., Hilty, D. M., Horvitz-Lennon, M., . . . Hong, S.-H. (2018). The American Psychiatric Association practice guideline for the pharmacological treatment of patients with alcohol use disorder. *American Journal of Psychiatry, 175*(1), 86–90.

Smyth, B. P., Barry, J., Keenan, E., & Ducray, K. (2010). Lapse and relapse following inpatient treatment of opiate dependence. *Irish Medical Journal, 103*, 176–79.

Tuchman, E. (2010). Women and addiction: The importance of gender issues in substance abuse research. *Journal of Addictive Diseases, 29*, 127–38.

VanHouten, J. P., Rudd, R. A., Ballesteros, M. F., & Mack, K. A. (2019). Drug overdose deaths among women aged 30–64 Years—United States, 1999–2017. *Morbidity Mortality Weekly Report, 68*, 1–5.

Zemore, S. E., Lui, C., Mericle, A., Hemberg, J., & Kaskutas, L. A. (2018). A longitudinal study of the comparative efficacy of Women for Sobriety, LifeRing, SMART Recovery, and 12-step groups for those with AUD. *Journal of Substance Abuse Treatment, 88*, 18–26.

Part VI

Caring for Self and Caring for Others

Chapter Nineteen

Women with Chronic Illness and Disabilities

Yuleinys A. Castillo

CASE VIGNETTE: ZAHRA

Zahra, a thirty-two-year-old African American female, was recently diagnosed with diabetes. She lives in an affluent mostly Caucasian neighborhood with her African American husband and their two dogs. She has a medium frame but reports some weight gain after turning thirty. She considers herself a healthy person, but she explains that she desires to improve her eating habits and exercise routine. She is concerned that family and friends may misjudge her because of her "condition." Thus, she has decided that she is going to wait to disclose to her loved ones and employer that she has diabetes because it is "nobody's business!" She shares that she would like to focus on having a child, finishing up her online certificate, and starting a small business. She is taking no prescription medication and complains of "some" sleep disturbance.

* * *

When working with women and girls with disabilities and chronic illnesses, mental health providers need to recognize the influence of personal, social, and cultural forces on clients' perceptions and reactions to life situations. Women with disabilities, such as Zahra, have wide-ranging roles and responsibilities that interact with environmental factors affecting decision making, values, and views of self. Because of their complex situations, counselors need to address social, emotional, and behavioral issues in sessions when working with women with disabilities in a respectful and genuine way.

Women and girls with disabilities and chronic illnesses belong to a large and diverse group of individuals whose needs are sometimes neglected in their families and by community-based services. They also possess valuable experience and self-knowledge that may be disregarded and ignored in decision making, social participation, and treatment. Women and girls with disabilities are also subjected to double discrimination: sexism and ableism. Double discrimination and cultural biases, due to gender and disability, create barriers that devalue their participation in society and access to services (Rousso, 2003). They encounter social and environmental barriers to their independence and opportunities in the community. Furthermore, low socioeconomic status, ethnic/racial backgrounds, gender identification, and sexual orientation integrate layers of identity and social group membership that also face social bias and discrimination. Due to prejudice and discrimination, these women experience low employment rates, low educational attainment, limited access to health services, and, potentially, violence. Double, and sometimes multiple, discrimination translates to social and cultural challenges influencing treatment and social participation for these women.

Women and girls with disabilities belong to a heterogeneous group. Because this is a very large, diverse female group, it can be challenging to determine its size and issues. In this chapter, women with disabilities include female clients with varied physical, sensory, emotional, intellectual, mental, and neurodiverse abilities as well as visible or invisible, stable, progressive medical conditions or chronic illnesses. Each woman and girl has a unique experience that influences her self-worth, social participation, and opportunities. Consequently, having a disability is a uniquely personal experience for each female client.

DISABILITY PERSPECTIVE

Disability is exceptionally diverse, and many definitions have been used to improve its understanding around the world. According to the International Classification of Functioning, Disability, and Health (ICF), disability is an umbrella term for impairments, activity limitations, and participation restrictions (WHO, 2011). Disability is the interaction between a health condition and personal and environmental factors that affect the individual and is different for every woman. Thus, when working with individuals with disabilities, it is important to consider the usage of the term *disability*. Davis (1995) explained that *disability* is a sweeping term that spans a very broad group of individuals. Subsequently, Davis urged the use of the word as a "descriptive term and not as an absolute category" (1995, p. 8). By seeking to learn about the client's experience of disability, the counseling process is enriched through recognition of the presence of the condition and its impact on the person's life. In some cases, clients may struggle with addressing their disabilities because of negative social and personal definitions. Counselors can explore their clients' perspectives on living with a disability or chronic illness and how this condition shapes their lives.

From a social constructivist perspective, disability represents the "other" opposite from the definition of normal. Disability is constructed using able-bodied norms and standards that promote differential or unequal treatment of people with disabilities (Campbell, 2009). These social norms utilize a health normative perspective that marginalizes the experience of chronic illness and disabilities. From a disability perspective, the normal binary shapes the existing social power and privilege (Mohamed & Shefer, 2015). The experience of having a disability is a complex issue that involves the lived realities of individuals that interact with influential physical, social, and cultural forces (Wendell, 1996). These personal, cultural, and environmental forces directly affect the experience of having a disability or chronic illness for women.

GENDERED DISABILITY EXPERIENCE

The experiences of women and girls with disabilities and chronic illness have gained a stronger voice in society in the last few decades. Disability as a possible component of female identity and the awareness of the different experiences of men and women with disabilities have become relevant issues for disability advocates (Sumskiene, Grigaite, & Jankauskaite, 2016). Swain and French (2000) described disability as a positive social identity in contrast to a personal tragedy as part of an affirmation model. Gender differences, in power and life experiences, have been recognized as influences on understandings of the self and social relationships (Dohrenwend & Dohrenwend, 1976; Elliott, 2013). Gender, as a social ideology, determines power relations, with social hierarchies of attitudes that affect access to and control of resources as well as the experiences of individuals (Maruzani & Mapuranga, 2016).

Females with disabilities have a unique experience different from that of males, which needs recognition and understanding. Feminist disability studies argue that cultural expectations, perceived attitudes, social institutions, and conditions for persons who are categorized as both "female" and "disabled" result in double marginalization (Garland-Thomson, 2001, p. 4). Social interactions are shaped by dominant cultural values and expectations that continuously influence identity and view of self (Castillo, 2017). Women with disabilities navigate cultural demands and perceived attributes that shape their own experience with their medical conditions and impairments. Similarly, these social and cultural forces create expectations and challenges for these women with disabilities and chronic illnesses.

Women with disabilities may encounter more negative social narratives than women without disabilities. Women are often judged as weak and dependent (Koening, 2018); however, social expectations for women with disabilities add layers to their social and cultural experiences. These expectations exclude sexuality, employment, and motherhood. Women with disabilities also struggle with violence and accessibility barriers more frequently than women without medical impairments. In this chapter, some challenges for women with disabilities in the form of health issues, access to services, sexual health, social participation, and violence are discussed to increase understanding of the experience of women with disabilities.

Health and Disability

When working with women with disabilities and chronic illnesses, counselors need to consider gender relations and gendered experiences of clients. Considering the intersection of gender and disability, counselors should assess the reaction of clients to socially produced and self-constructed identities (Thomas, 1999). Women with disabilities, in some instances, face different challenges and have limited resources that affect their general well-being. The experience of having a disability can affect the ability to fulfill gender-based roles, social expectations, and gender-normative participation, supporting feelings of devaluation and self-stigma (Nosek, 2010). Therefore, female clients with disabilities may struggle with perceptions of unfulfilled social roles, dissatisfaction with self, and disability adjustment issues.

The experience of having a disability for a woman can also affect her ability to cope with life events, manage stress, and function. Women are disproportionately affected by mental health concerns in comparison to men, and they may be more susceptible to mental illness due to biological factors, marital status, education, employment, and roles in society (Miller, 2019). People with disabilities, who perceive discrimination, are less likely to seek health-care services (Moscoso-Porras & Alvarado, 2018), experience a lower level of life satisfaction (Daley, Phipps, & Branscombe, 2018), and deal with threats to psychological well-being (Schmitt, Branscombe, Postmes, & Garcia, 2014). The gendered role of women also creates a high level of stress that affects well-being and social participation (Gajendragad, 2015). Due to social biases and expectations, women with disabilities must work hard to overcome the invalidation, discrimination, and oppression that is found in the sociocultural milieu but also ingrained within the health-care professions, such as psychiatry (Pilgrim and Rogers, 2009).

The gendered experience of women from ethnic and racial minority groups underscores the gender disparities in health-care services and treatment. Black and Hispanic women exhibit a higher prevalence of several chronic conditions than Caucasian ones, with black women being the most disadvantaged (Hayward, Crimmins, Miles, & Yu, 2000). Additionally, women who identify as members of a racial or ethnic minority exhibit higher levels of functional limitations compared to white women (Chinn & Hummer, 2016). Minority women may receive poor services or choose to avoid treatment because of previous negative experiences, perceived discrimination, and prior insensitive interactions with providers (Aguerrevere, Castillo, Nicks, Juan, & Curtis, 2016). To diminish health disparities and to achieve health equity, counselors must effectively utilize multicultural competencies when working with minority women with disabilities to diminish health disparities.

Access to Health-Care Services

Women with disabilities and chronic illness face barriers to adequate access to health-care services, which negatively affects their treatment and general well-being. Women are more likely to experience rejection, stigmatization, denial of care, and poor access to appropriate health-care facilities (Moorkath, Vranda, & Naveenjumar, 2018). These barriers derive from multiple sources, including inadequate legislation, policies, and strategies; problems with service delivery; negative attitudes and discrimination; and lack of participatory services (WHO, 2015). They also experience lack of consultation and involvement in service delivery, issues with accessibility to buildings and information, and issues with reliable transportation. Finally, they may not understand recommended services, forms, prescriptions, resources, and recommendations due to scant access to information and communication barriers. Women with disabilities may, for instance, struggle with limited or absent interpreting services, poorly trained staff, and disability misconceptions during treatment, affecting access to services. The structure and services of the health system can also affect how women with disabilities perceive and access services (Nanjappan & Nakkeeran, 2018). Employees' attitudes and behaviors can unfortunately shape clients' perception of treatment, affect self-esteem, and create feelings of stigma (WHO, 2015). Negative attitudes and discriminatory behaviors such as violation of privacy, negligence, sexual exploitation, rude behavior, and delay in treatment are part of the experience in the health system for women with disabilities. These negative behaviors can limit the opportunity for female clients with disabilities to receive information, work in collaboration with providers, and receive preventive services.

Sexual and Reproductive Health

Women who have disabilities are often perceived as helpless, asexual, and unsuitable for maternity; they are then pushed away from traditional female roles as wives, housewives, or mothers, in the predominant social discourse (McDonald, Keys, & Balcazar, 2007). Because of social assumptions of sexual inactivity, women with disabilities often lack proper information regarding contraception, safe sex, counseling, and testing for sexually transmitted diseases (WHO, 2015). In fact, women with disabilities may not be screened for sexually transmitted diseases, informed about safe sex practices, prepared for healthy pregnancies, and scheduled for regular gynecological exams due to medical professionals' asexual attributions to women with disabilities (HHS, 2011). Therefore, social assumptions about women with disabilities reduce access to women's health services and increase the risk of risky sexual practices. Whether it is an unplanned or planned pregnancy, women who become pregnant experience additional barriers to care.

As with the issues of reproductive health, women with disabilities and chronic illnesses struggle with proper prenatal services and expectations about motherhood. Because of the potential adverse effect of pregnancy on disease and its outcomes, women with disabilities can usually benefit from neonatal medicine to manage a high-risk pregnancy. Women with chronic illness need a planned and well-managed pregnancy in order to minimize risks during pregnancy (Galappatthy, Jayasinghe, Paththinige, Sheriff, & Wijayaratne, 2017). Society often questions and doubts that women with a disabilities can mother effectively (Prilleltensky, 2004); this generates negative attitudes, skepticism, and prejudicial assumptions about their ability to be mothers (Redshaw, Malou, Gao, & Gray, 2013). Women may refuse to seek proper prenatal or postnatal care to avoid negative interactions with rude or judgmental medical providers. Undeniably, women with disabilities can have a more pleasant pregnancy by receiving proper prenatal monitoring by medical professionals who understand their condition.

Motherhood is a complex socially mediated state that involves biological, psychological, social, environmental, and political factors that can create equilibrium or disequilibrium in a woman's life (Burley, 2003). Transitioning to motherhood represents a potential change to a person's development due to personal and social responsibilities, expectations, and perceptions. There are specific socially constructed benchmarks that define an ideal mother; however, mothers who are unable to fit this definition may be perceived as irresponsible mothers (Malacrida, 2009). Women with disabilities may be misjudged as unfit mothers because of a perceived limited ability to meet socially agreed standards for mothers. Moreover, these social expectations combined with their own personal aspirations may give rise to unexpected distress in mothers with disabilities.

Social Participation

Women with disabilities are vulnerable and disadvantaged individuals who face barriers to social participation and healthy development (HHS, 2011). These women struggle with denial of economic resources, lack of education, poor legal and health services, poor physical and mental nurturance, exhaustion from overwork, and abuse across their lifespan (WHO, 2015). Additionally, they are more likely to live in poverty, which can exacerbate disabilities and complicate improving a challenging financial situation (Trani & Loeb, 2012). Women with disabilities also tend to exhibit lower educational achievement and less economic participation than women without disabilities (WHO, 2015). These characteristics create barriers for these women to fully participate in educational and employment opportunities that others might access.

Educational Outcomes

Women and girls with disabilities struggle in education more than males with disabilities or female without disabilities (WHO, 2015). Both attitudinal and environmental barriers block female students with disabilities from reaping the potential benefits of education. This can have a lifelong effect, as education supports informed decision making, especially valuable for marginalized communities, to counter sociocultural constraints (Green, 2007). Girls with disabilities are seen as helpless and powerless, leading to exclusion from educational opportunities, with limited educational programs made available (UNICEF, 2017). For instance, under current disability diagnostic methods in the educational system, boys are more likely to be diagnosed than female students (Hibel, Farkas, & Morgan, 2010). A significant number of women who received dependent-child services from the government do not have high school diplomas, due in large part to undiagnosed learning disabilities that went without appropriate treatment (National Center for Family Literacy, 2000). Not only are educational needs not being met, girls with disabilities may miss out on opportunities to enhance freedoms and develop human agency (Walker & Zhu, 2006). Education represents an opportunity for girls with disabilities to improve their quality of life by acquiring long-lasting skills, developing a sense of connectedness to their communities, and weakening the impact of social and cultural barriers.

Employment Outcomes

Although employment represents a viable solution to improve financial worries, women with disabilities represent a very small portion of the workforce. Employees with disabilities encounter barriers such as inaccessible work spaces or equipment, lack of transportation, limited personal assistance services, misconceptions about hiring and accommodating disabilities, and social biases (Anand & Sevak, 2017). Participation barriers in education and vocational training set people with disabilities at a disadvantage in the job market (Morgon Banks & Polack, 2014). Beyond attitudinal barriers and stigma, inaccessible work environments and unfavorable policies are barriers to employment for women with disabilities (Rohwerder, 2015). In addition to facing persistently low employment, women with disabilities often face difficulties accessing adequate housing, health care, and education; equal hiring and promotion standards; and equal pay (WHO, 2015). Women with disabilities have many social obstacles to overcome to secure and retain employment in societies that underestimate their potential and talent. In some cases, they are not only underestimated but also victimized.

Violence

Another challenge facing women and girls with disabilities is abuse. They are at high risk for physical, sexual, and emotional abuse by loved ones, care providers, and strangers. The Convention of the Rights of Persons with Disabilities reports that women and girls with disabilities experience greater risk of violence, injury or abuse, neglect, maltreatment, or exploitation (United Nations, 2012). Unfortunately, women with disabilities can be more vulnerable to intimate partner violence and, as a group, are often ignored by society. Research indicates that they are at least twice as likely to experience domestic violence and other forms of gender-based and sexual violence as nondisabled women; they are also likely to experience abuse over a longer period of time and to suffer more severe injuries as a result of the violence (Ortoleva & Lewis, 2012). Some women with disabilities experience violence or abuse by partners (Breiding & Armour, 2015). They may also experience intimate partner violence, including rape, sexual violence, physical violence, stalking, psychological aggression, and control of sexual health, more than women without disabilities (Breiding & Armour, 2015). Caregivers and personal assistants may also prey on women with disabilities (Plummer & Findley, 2012). These women may feel isolated and less supported to report the abuse, and in many cases, they may be dependent on the abuser for care (Ortoleva & Lewis, 2012). They may be less likely to acknowledge or discuss their abuse due to a lack of understanding of what healthy relationships look like and concern over the possibility of losing a significant person in their lives. Therefore, counselors need to properly screen women with disabilities for domestic violence and learn about available inclusive resources for victims of violence.

CULTURAL CONSIDERATIONS AND INCLUSIVE IMPLICATIONS FOR COUNSELORS

Even though the perception and experiences of having a disability have changed in recent decades, remnants of past beliefs still influence prejudicial and attitudinal practices toward people with disabilities (Munyi, 2012).

These remnants contribute to continued discriminatory behaviors, inaccessibility, and social practices that create challenges for women with disabilities. By increasing understanding of disability, mental health practitioners will be in a better position to recognize the perceptions and effects of power and oppression on social interactions as well as the influence of cultural narratives on the experiences of individuals with disabilities (McDonald et al., 2007). Social biases and discriminatory practices are a reality for women with disabilities and can be discussed in a safe counseling environment.

Women with disabilities struggle with cultural biases based on gender and disability that can potentially limit access to services, educational opportunities, employment options, and social relationships. Disability should not be treated simply as the result of a medical condition as it requires interventions to remove environmental and social barriers, combined with a change in societal attitude (Yee et al., 2018). A disability or chronic illness is just one aspect of the female client's experience and identity; therefore, counselors should incorporate clients' views and assessment of their disability in treatment as well as recognition of the ways social and cultural forces affect the client.

Proper access to health-care services can improve preventive services, reduce hospitalization, and enhance the quality of life of women with disabilities. Monitoring and enforcing mandated accessibility requirements, as established by the Americans with Disabilities Act (ADA) (Frieden, 2015), can increase accessibility as well as educate providers on appropriate informed treatment for women with disabilities. Counselors should learn about services available in their communities to share with their clients, and they should encourage their clients to report any interference to proper services. Clients may not realize that they have the right to informed treatment, information, and advocacy. Moreover, women with disabilities may lack knowledge and tools to promote wellness and prevent illness, reducing opportunities for being healthy.

Counselors also need to understand how health-related factors affect the treatment and experience of women with disabilities. Previous research has shown that the prevalence of certain health conditions, such as obesity, smoking, hypertension, and diabetes, is higher among persons with disabilities (Yee et al., 2016). While women on average live longer than men, they are more likely than men to experience nonfatal chronic conditions, functional impairments, and multiple comorbidities (Gorman & Read, 2006). Even the severity of an ailment or disease has been found to be relatively greater among women with disabilities. Women with disabilities are more prone to injuries and accidents, less able to engage in regular physical activity; less likely to receive preventive care, and suffer from poorer treatment outcomes and disease management (Wheeler, Foreman, & Rueschhoff, 2013). Counselors should educate women with disabilities about preventive services as well as health management practices to address potential disability complications and to potentially improve their quality of life.

In order to improve the social participation of women with disabilities, counselors need to assess educational and employment opportunities and their related challenges in session. Even though legislative interventions have mitigated the impact of social attitudes, there is still a need to address negative attitudes that interfere with equity in education. People with physical disabilities or health concerns reported facing the greatest number of accessibility barriers and were also least likely to receive accommodations at work (Anand & Sevak, 2017). Counselors can utilize resources in their communities to inform clients about employment services to secure work, obtain accommodations, and educate employers. Beyond the educational and professional realms, there are other areas in which women with disabilities or chronic illnesses may face significant obstacles.

Gender- and disability-sensitive training and services can enhance gender equity in education, employment, and service delivery for women with disabilities (UNICEF, 2017). When working with women with disabilities who have experienced interpersonal trauma and abuse, counselors need to assess the treatment process from a woman's perspective, provide informed services, and evaluate the impact of trauma on the person's life (Center for Substance Abuse Treatment, 2014). Promoting policies that recognize community expectations may help to reduce biases toward pregnancy and increase access to reproductive health services among women with disabilities (Redshaw et al., 2013). Although people with disabilities experience a disproportionate impact, they are usually excluded from emergency preparation and readiness activities. This can lead to an exacerbation of preexisting conditions after disasters (Twigg, Kett, & Lovell, 2018). Creating a counseling environment that promotes gender inclusion, fosters a collaborative relationship, and identifies specific issues for women with disabilities can improve the quality of services.

Disability, mental health, sexual orientation, and gender identity are all dimensions that can lead to health inequities, stigma, and discrimination for women (Nanjappan & Nakkeeran, 2018). The intersections of identity components combine with attitudinal and environmental barriers that shape the experience of having a disability. Counselors should consider and incorporate all aspects of identity when working with women with disabilities. Moreover, counselors can explore the factors affecting daily interactions with others while considering the oppressive nature of some of these factors as part of a larger system. Finally, counselors must recognize any practices that can create an ablest environment for their clients—including attitudinal, societal, and environmental forces. Counselors should also recognize that each woman with a disability is bringing a unique experience to counseling. A number of statutory and regulatory protections have helped mitigate social bias and discrimination, with improvements in inclusion, opportunity, and accessibility for individuals with disabilities. Evaluating clients' previous experiences can help properly identify interventions and tools to help them meet their individual needs. Supporting clients in their efforts to advocate for themselves is essential as this enables them to recognize that they can make a difference in their own lives and grow from their experiences.

CASE VIGNETTE WRAP-UP: ZAHRA

Although Zahra refuses to acknowledge her new disability diagnosis outside the counseling office, she struggles with self-stigma, gendered disability biases, and identity changes. She may not experience issues related to low socioeconomic status, but her employment and relationships may be affected by her diabetes. She will need to integrate this new aspect of her identity into her day-to-day routines to effectively practice health management and prevent further health complications from diabetes. Because she is currently ignoring her medical condition, Zahra may feel isolated if she continues to avoid some social settings, restricted due to the need to change her diet, and somewhat lost without proper medical treatment. In Zahra's case, she can manage her diabetes to live a long, healthy life by intentionally following a self-care plan. The counselor should encourage Zahra to find ways to improve her well-being through such steps as building a support team, collaborating with health-care professionals, following a healthy food plan, developing an exercise routine, and managing her stress levels.

QUESTIONS FOR REFLECTION

1. What are your experiences engaging with women with disabilities? Have you ever been challenged to determine the "right thing" to say or do?
2. What are some ways that disabilities or chronic illnesses are portrayed in the media, and how might "heroic portrayals" contribute to an individual's healthy development? How might these portrayals negatively affect self-esteem or self-image?
3. Are there any "hidden disabilities" about which counselors should especially be aware?
4. What are some ways that you might engage in advocacy for women with disabilities or debilitating conditions?

REFERENCES

Aguerrevere, L. E., Castillo, Y. A., Nicks, R., Juan, R., & Curtis, K. (2016). Pain-related symptom reporting among Hispanics: Implications for forensic psychological evaluations. *Psychological Injury and Law, 9*(4), 341–59. doi: 10.1007/s12207-016-9271-5

Anand, P., & Sevak, P. (2017). The role of workplace accommodations in the employment of people with disabilities. *IZA Journal of Labor Policy, 6*(12): 1–20.

Breiding, M. J., & Armour, B. S. (2015). The association between disability and intimate partner violence in the United States. *Annals of Epidemiology, 25*(6), 455–57.

Burley, E. S. (2003). *Antenatal education in the transition to motherhood.* Plymouth, UK: Faculty of Social Science and Business, University of Plymouth.

Campbell, F. K. (2009). *Contours of ableism: The production of disability and abledness.* Basingstoke, UK: Palgrave Macmillan.

Castillo, Y.A. (2017). Disability and identity development. In W. Killam & S. Degges-White (Eds.), *College student development: Applying theory to practice on diverse campus* (159–71). New York, NY: Springer.

Center for Substance Abuse Treatment. (2014). Understanding the impact of trauma. In *Trauma-informed care in behavioral health services* (chap. 3). Treatment Improvement Protocol (TIP) Series. Rockville, MD: Substance Abuse and Mental Health Services Administration. Retrieved from https://www.ncbi.nlm.nih.gov/books/NBK207191/

Chinn, J. J., & Hummer, R. A. (2016). Racial disparities in functional limitations among Hispanic women in the United States. *Research on Aging, 38*(3), 399–423. doi: 10.1177/0164027515620244

Daley, A., Phipps, S., & Branscombe, N. R. (2018). The social complexities of disability: Discrimination, belonging and life satisfaction among Canadian youth. *Population Health, 5*, 55–63.

Davis, L. J. (1995). *Enforcing normalcy: Disability, deafness, and the body.* London: Verso.

Dohrenwend, B. P., & Dohrenwend, B. (1976). Sex differences in psychiatric disorders. *American Journal of Sociology, 81*, 1447–54.

Elliott, M. (2013). Gender differences in the determinants of distress, alcohol misuse, and related psychiatric disorders. *Society and Mental Health, 3*, 96–113. doi: 10.1177/2156869312474828

Frieden, L. (2015, July 23). The impact of the ADA in American communities: Celebration of the 25th anniversary of the Americans with Disabilities Act. University of Texas Health Science Center.

Gajendragad, J. M. (2015). Struggles of women with mental illness. *Journal of Humanity Social Science, 20*, 37–41.

Galappatthy, P., Jayasinghe, J. D., Paththinige, S. C., Sheriff, R. M., & Wijayaratne, L. S. (2017). Pregnancy outcomes and contraceptive use in patients with systemic lupus Erythematosus, rheumatoid arthritis and women without a chronic illness: A comparative study. *International Journal of Rheumatic Diseases, 20*(6), 746–54. doi: 10.1111/1756-185X.12996

Garland-Thomson, Rosemarie. (2001). *Reshaping, re-thinking, re-defining: Feminist disability studies.* Washington, DC: Center for Women Policy Studies.

Gorman, B., & Read, J. (2006). Gender disparities in adult health: An examination of three measures of morbidity. *Journal of Health and Social Behavior, 47*(June), 95–110.

Green, S. (2007). Components of perceived stigma and perceptions of well-being among university students with and without disability experience. *Health Sociology Review, 16*(3–4), 328–40.

Hayward, M. D., Crimmins, E. M., Miles, T. P., & Yu, Y. (2000). The significance of socioeconomic status in explaining the racial gap in chronic health conditions. *American Sociological Review, 65*, 910–30.

HHS (U.S. Department of Health and Human Services). (October 2015). Lesbian, gay, bisexual, and transgender health, 2011. https://www.healthypeople.gov/2020/topics-objectives/topic/lesbian-gay-bisexual-and-transgender-health?topicid=25.

Hibel, J., Farkas, G., & Morgan, P. L. (2010). Who is placed into special education? *Sociology of education, 83*(4), 312–32. doi: 10.1177/0038040710383518

Koening, A. (2018). Comparing prescriptive and descriptive gender stereotypes about children, adults and the elderly. *Frontiers in Psychology, 9*, doi: 10.3389/fpsyg.2018.01086

Malacrida, C. (2009) Performing motherhood in a disablist world: Dilemmas of motherhood, femininity and disability. *International Journal of Qualitative Studies in Education, 22*(1), 99–117.

Maruzani, N., & Mapuranga, B. (2016). Gender and disability: A review of available literature. *Research on Humanities and Social Sciences, 6*(6), 74–86.

McDonald, K., Keys, & C., Balcazar, F. (2007). Youth with disabilities. In D. DuBois & M. Karcher (Eds.) *Handbook of Youth Mentoring*. Thousand Oaks, CA: Sage.

Miller, J. (2019). A perfect storm: Biological, behavioral, social, and environmental factors affecting women's mental health. American Mental Health Counselors Association. Retrieved from https://www.amhca.org/blogs/joel-miller/2019/04/29/a-perfect-storm-biological-behavioral-social-and-e

Mohamed, K., & Shefer, T. (2015). Gendering disability and disabling gender: Critical reflections of gender and disability. *Agenda, 29*(2), 2–13.

Moorkath, F., Vranda, M. N., & Naveenjumar, C. (2018). Lives without roots: Institutionalized homeless women with chronic mental illness. *Indian Journal Psychological Medicine, 40*, 476–81.

Morgon Banks, L., & Polack, S. (2014). *The economic costs of exclusion and gains of inclusion of people with disabilities: Evidence from low and middle income countries*. CBM, International Centre for Evidence in Disability, and London School of Hygiene and Tropical Medicine. Retrieved from https://www.cbm.org/fileadmin/user_upload/Publications/Costs-of-Exclusion-and-Gains-of-Inclusion-Report.pdf

Moscoso-Porras, M. G., & Alvarado, G. F. (2018). Association between perceived discrimination and healthcare-seeking behavior in people with a disability. *Disability and Health Journal, 11*(1), 93–98.

Munyi, C. W. (2012). Past and present perceptions towards disability: A historical perspective. *Disability Studies Quarterly, 32*(2), 1–7.

Nanjappan, N., & Nakkeeran, N. (2018). Disability, mental health, sexual orientation and gender identity: Understanding health inequity through experience and difference. *Health Research Policy and Systems, 16*(S1), 9–19.

National Center for Family Literacy. (2000). Learning disabilities and gender bias in an employment context. *Momentum*, 3–5.

Nosek, M. (2010). Feminism and disability: Synchronous agendas in conflict. In H. Landrine & N. Russo (Eds.), *Handbook of diversity in feminist psychology* (pp. 501–33). New York, NY: Springer.

Ortoleva, S., & Lewis, H. (2012). Forgotten sisters: A report on violence against women with disabilities: An overview of its nature, scope, causes and consequences. Northeastern University School of Law Research Paper 104-2012. Retrieved from https://ssrn.com/abstract=2133332

Pilgrim, D., & Rogers, A. (2009). Survival and its discontents: The case of British psychiatry. *Sociology of Health and Illness, 31*(7), 947–61. doi: 10.1111/j.1467-9566.2009.01166.x

Plummer, S. B., & Findley, P. A. (2012). Women with disabilities' experience with physical and sexual abuse: Review of the literature and implications for the field. *Trauma and Violence Abuse, 13*(1), 15–29.

Prilleltensky, O. (2004). *Motherhood and disability: Children and choices*. Basingstoke, UK: Palgrave Macmillan.

Redshaw, M., Malouf, R., Gao, H., & Gray, R. (2013). Women with disability: The experience of maternity care during pregnancy, labour and birth and the postnatal period. *BMC Pregnancy and Childbirth, 13*(1), 174.

Rohwerder, B. (2015). *Disability inclusion: Topic guide*. Birmingham, UK: GSDRC, University of Birmingham.

Rousso, H. (2003). Education for all: A gender and disability perspective. World Bank.

Schmitt, M., Branscombe, N., Postmes, T., & Garcia, A. (2014). The consequences of perceived discrimination for psychological well-being: A meta-analytic review. *Psychological Bulletin, 140*(4), 921–48. doi: 10.1037/a0035754

Sumskiene, E., Grigaite, U., & Jankauskaite, M. (2016). Intersection between a social gender and disability: A self-concept of women with disabilities in the post-feminist context. *Considering Disability CIC, 1*(3–4), 1–35, doi: 10.17774/CDJ1.32016.1.20575874

Swain, J., & French, S. (2000). Towards an affirmative model of disability. *Disability and Society, 15*, 569–82.

Thomas, C. (1999). *Female forms: Experiencing and understanding disability.* Buckingham, UK: Open University Press.

Trani, J. F., & Loeb, M. (2012). Poverty and disability: A vicious circle? Evidence from Afghanistan and Zambia. *Journal of International Development, 24*, S19–S52. doi: 10.1002/jid.1709

Twigg, J., Kett, M., & Lovell, E. (2018). *Disability inclusion and disaster risk reduction: Overcoming barriers to progress.* London: Overseas Development Institute.

UNICEF. (2017, June). Still left behind: Pathways to inclusive education for girls with disabilities. UNIGEI United Nations Girls Education Initiative, Leonard Cheshire Disability. Retrieved from http://www.ungei.org/Still_Left_Behind_Full_Report.PDF

United Nations. (2012, March 30). Thematic study on the issues of violence against women and girls and disability. General Assembly. Retrieved from https://www2.ohchr.org/english/issues/women/docs/A.HRC.20.5.pdf

Walker, I., & Zhu, Y. (2006). Child support and partnership dissolution. *Economic Journal, 116* (510), C93–C109.

Wendell, S. (1996). *The rejected body.* Abingdon, UK: Routledge.

Wheeler, J. B., Foreman, M., & Rueschhoff, A. (2013). Improving women's health: Challenges, access, and prevention. National Conference of State Legislatures. Retrieved from http://www.ncsl.org/research/health/improving-womens-health-2013.aspx

World Health Organization (WHO). (2011). *World health statistics 2011.* Geneva, Switzerland: WHO.

World Health Organization (WHO). (2015). *World health statistics 2015 indicator compendium.* Geneva, Switzerland: WHO.

Yee, S., Breslin, M. L., Goode, T., Havercamp, S. M., Horner-Johnson, W., Iezzoni, L. I., & Krahn, G. (June 2016). Compounded disparities: Health equity at the intersection of disability, race and ethnicity. Paper commissioned by the National Academies of Science, Engineering and Medicine, Washington, D.C. Available at http://nationalacademies.org/hmd/Activities/SelectPops/HealthDisparities/Comm issioned-Papers/Compounded-Disparities.aspx

Yee, S., Breslin, M. L., Goode, T. D., Havercamp, S. M., Horner-Johnson, W., Iezzoni, L. I., & Krahn, G. L. (2018). Compounded disparities: Health equity at the intersection of disability, race, and ethnicity. Retrieved from http://nationalacademies.org/hmd/Activities/SelectPops/HealthDisparities/Commissioned -Papers/Compounded-Disparities.aspx

Chapter Twenty

Counseling Women Who Caregive

Marcela Kepic and Kim M. Tassinari

CASE VIGNETTE: SONYA

Sonya is a fifty-four-year-old married white woman who lives with her husband and three teenaged children, ages thirteen, fifteen, and seventeen, in a suburban town in the northeast region of the United States. Her oldest son is about to finish high school, and her youngest son is starting high school. Sonya and her husband have started college planning for their oldest son. While on her way to a doctor's appointment with her husband, who suffers from some health issues, Sonya received a call from her seventy-eight-year-old father that her seventy-seven-year-old mother had been diagnosed with stage four lung cancer.

Sonya is of second-generation Italian descent and the youngest of three siblings and the only daughter in the family. Sonya's parents hold strong Italian cultural values, and Sonya's birth order and gender lead her parents to rely heavily on her for pretty much everything. After speaking with her parents, and knowing how little help her brothers have ever provided, Sonya recognizes that she will be assuming the role of primary caregiver for her mother. Also, as a devout Catholic, Sonya has always relied on her faith to get her through adversity. Presented with this new role, Sonya went to her church to pray for her mother's recovery and for guidance on how to proceed in caring for her terminally ill mother.

Shortly after this devastating news, Sonya decided to reach out to her two older brothers to ask for their assistance. Much to her surprise, both brothers were in denial of the seriousness of their mother's condition. Sonya knew that she should probably consult with her mother's doctor soon to see how serious her condition was. After learning that her mother had three to six months to live, Sonya sat with her mother to learn more about her wishes. As

Sonya took on this new responsibility of caregiver, her stress levels increased and she began having difficulty sleeping at night. Sonya's husband had to step up and take their oldest son on college visits, and all of the boys had to participate in household chores. Life became out of balance for Sonya, and caregiver distress set in. Sonya's caregiving duties continued to increase, and she started providing medical interventions that would normally be performed by nurses. In consultation with her mother's medical team, Sonya learned that her mother likely had only weeks to live. At this point, Sonya made the decision to transition her mother from curative care to palliative care. When Sonya discussed this decision with her father and brothers, she was met with resistance from all parties. Sonya felt that her stress and anxiety levels were through the roof, and she realized she needed to seek counseling in order to care for herself.

* * *

The population of older adults is increasing as baby boomers cross into older adulthood. In fact, the number of older adults in the United States will reach an estimated eighty million by 2040 (Administration on Aging, 2010). While older adults are living longer (Aldwin & Gilmer, 2013), they frequently live with disabilities and chronic diseases requiring management and assistance. Approximately 19 percent of the U.S. adult population is currently providing caregiving or some assistance to an adult age fifty or older (National Alliance for Caregiving [NAC], 2015), and much of this caregiving is happening in the home (Gomes, Calanzani, Gysels, Hall, & Higginson, 2013). The majority (57 percent) of these caregivers also work full-time and are responsible for their own family's needs (NAC, 2015). Women tend to assume the role of primary caregiver for family members, and it has been found that female caregivers tend to report higher levels of depression, anxiety, and general psychiatric symptomatology and lower levels of life satisfaction than male caregivers (Pinquart & Sörensen, 2006; Yee & Schulz, 2000). It is important, therefore, for counselors to understand the stresses that primary caregivers endure, the issues and challenges they face, and the complexities that arise during the caregiving journey.

TYPES OF CAREGIVERS AND THEIR IDENTITIES

There are two main categories of caregiving, formal caregiving and informal caregiving. Older adults might rely on formal caregiving and pay for these services. Others may call on family members, extended family members, or friends to provide informal caregiving, which is unpaid (Gallagher-Thomson & Coon, 2007). Family caregivers may be spouses, partners, adult children, relatives, or friends (Knussen, Tolson, Swan, Stott, & Brogan, 2005; Mehta, 2005). About a third of individuals receiving care reside in the same home with their caregiver (NAC, 2015), which can make caregiving easier in many ways but creates additional stressors in others. Women caregivers tend to spend more time providing care for a loved one and attending to more difficult caregiving tasks such as bathing, toileting, and dressing (NAC, 2016). While differences exist in terms of age, gender, and relationship diversity within the caregiver population, there are commonalities that caregivers share, including caregiver stress, uncertainty, life imbalance, shifts in identity, and unexpected rewards.

Caregiver Identity

When a person takes on the role of primary caregiver for a family member, they develop a new, emergent identity (Montgomery & Kosloski, 2009). This shift in identity can influence the caregiver's self-understanding, self-concept, self-efficacy, relational shift, and use of external resources (Kepic, Randolph, & Hermann-Turner, 2019). Montgomery and Kosloski (2009) proposed five phases corresponding to caregivers' identity development. First, the initial phase is characterized by the onset of caregiving activities that previously were not part of the familial role. Caregivers face challenges and adjustments as they realize that their original role has been "engulfed" by this emerging identity (Eifert, Adams, Dudley, & Perko, 2015, p. 360). The second phase is marked by an understanding that her responsibilities now extend beyond her original familial role, and she begins to view herself as a caregiver as a result of the cocreated identity built with the care recipient. This shift is a product of frequent interactions between caregiver and care recipient, learning about the care recipient's needs, and alterations to original patterns of social and familial interactions. As the care recipient's needs increase and the caregiver assumes many more responsibilities, including decision making, she enters the third phase of identity development. Responsibilities can include upkeep of personal hygiene, dressing, and medical (nursing) activities. Such activities extend greatly beyond the original role in familial relationships, and this shift might be very challenging and uncomfortable to both the caregiver and the care recipient. The fourth phase requires even further changes in caregiver identity, as she assumes a dominant role in the dyad. It is often during this fourth phase that options for nursing homes or hospice are considered or reconsidered. The fifth and final phase of caregiver identity development occurs when the care recipient is moved to a different setting or dies. The caregiver turns over her responsibilities to another or, alternatively, the caregiver responsibilities end due to death. In this phase, the caregiver recovers some of the original role identity (Montgomery & Kosloski, 2009). These phases are not rigid, and not every caregiver will experience every phase in a linear manner, if at all. Caregiver identity development is a dynamic process that shifts between periods of significant change, through the acceptance of new norms, and into the stability that sets in after necessary behavioral or perceptual adjustment (Montgomery & Kosloski, 2009).

In a metaanalysis of articles exploring caregiver identity, Eifert and colleagues (2015) identified five themes: loss of self, loss of cocreated identity established with the care recipient, shifts in familial obligation and gender-based stereotypes, emergence of an obligatory responsibility, and finally, the full caregiver identity that overtakes all original roles. There are variations in development, of course, as each experience is unique and case specific, and much will depend on the illness trajectory as well. For instance, in the case of spousal care, one partner cares for another, and the level of care and caregiver responsibility will shift and change as the needs of the care recipient will change (Kepic et al., 2019). Thus, because illness and disability trajectories are unpredictable, caregivers travel an unpredictable path that, in and of itself, can contribute to elevated stress levels, challenges, and caregiver burden.

ISSUES WOMEN CAREGIVERS FACE

Regardless of whether care is provided in the home or in a facility, many caregivers will experience a variety of burdens and stressors, including unmet needs, changes in illness trajectory, and learning additional skills to facilitate home-based care (Waldrop & Meeker, 2011). Caregivers often are required to make important medical decisions regarding treatment and financial administration, in addition to providing physical and emotional support (Hudson, Remedios, & Thomas, 2010). The cumulative effect can be compromised physical and psychological well-being. Caregivers report being more stressed, depressed, and having lower levels of subjective well-being, physical health, and self-efficacy than noncaregivers (Pinquart and Sörensen, 2006). Female caregivers tend to report higher levels of depression, anxiety, and general psychiatric symptomatology and lower levels of life satisfaction than male caregivers (Pinquart & Sörensen, 2006; Yee & Schulz, 2000).

Primary caregivers, in particular, are the voice for their loved ones. Not only do they care for, support, and comfort their care recipients, they also work closely with medical professionals to learn new skills, advocate for quality of care, and communicate the needs of their loved ones to ensure they are met (Adams, 2006; Dhar, 2012). These tasks can be more than equivalent to a full-time job. In addition, caregivers have their original roles to fulfill, such as partner, parent, sibling, and coworker. Pulled in many directions, such circumstances will often leave caregivers feeling overwhelmed and with elevated stress levels.

Stress and Burden

Taking on the role of caregiver for a loved one can feel burdensome for many (Grunfeld et al., 2004). For example, it can be stressful to manage an ever-changing role that requires adjustments along the way (Kepic et al., 2019). Other stressors include the uncertainty felt throughout the caregiving trajectory (Tassinari, 2017), financial burdens and feelings of being relatively unskilled when it comes to the care recipient's medical needs, feeling like life is out of balance, and the frequent family relational tension from oppositional family members (Ahmad, 2012; Segerstrom & Miller, 2004; Shaffer, Kim, Carver, & Cannady, 2017; Taylor & Field, 2003). Typically, caregivers who feel overwhelmed tend to neglect their own needs and forgo self-care, which exacerbates their stress levels (Pinquart & Sörensen, 2006; Yee & Schulz, 2000). Caregivers often have higher prevalence of elevated blood pressure, anxiety, depression, and emotional distress (Cameron, Franche, Cheung, & Stewart, 2002; Givens, Mezzacappa, Heeren, Yaffe, & Fredman, 2014; Joling et al., 2012; Rhee et al., 2008). They can experience other challenges when they lack necessary resources, training, and support, such as for respite services. Not every caregiver is prepared to handle the administration of medications and medical technologies or physical or occupational therapy, which can also increase stress and burden (Kepic et al., 2019; Tassinari, 2017). Family caregivers may also be confronted with the loss of a loved one's abilities, such as independence, health, or ability to communicate effectively, which many times leads to confrontation with grief (Humphrey, 2009). Continuous stress associated with caregiving demands may lead to physical and emotional exhaustion, decreased productivity, isolation, lack of motivation, changes in appetite, and therefore abandonment of a healthy lifestyle or balance (Givens et al., 2014; Shaffer et al., 2017). Some authors found that at least a third of caregivers suffer from clinical depression (Schoenmakers, Buntinx, & DeLepeleire, 2010; Schreiner, Morimoto, Arai, & Zarit, 2006), and others report that such a diagnosis is more severe for those who care for loved ones with dementia, schizophrenia, and bipolar disorder (Mohamed, Rosenheck, Lyketsos, & Schneider, 2010; Schulz & Martire, 2004). Another line of research, focused on an examination of psychosocial risk factors longitudinally related to caregivers' physical health changes, showed that continuous stress adversely impacts the immune system. Caregivers exposed to chronic stress are more susceptible to chronic illnesses and infectious diseases (Segerstrom & Miller, 2004; Shaffer et al., 2017; Swore-Fletcher, Miaskowski, Given, & Schumacher, 2012). In a similar vein, caregivers who care for their loved ones with cancer for five or more years developed physical morbid conditions in addition to depressive symptoms (Shaffer et al., 2017).

Unknown Territory

Caregivers can minimize some of the challenges associated with caregiving by learning as much as possible about their care recipient's illness trajectory and prognosis. While there are typical paths for illness and protocols for care, each patient is unique and will respond differently to treatment. Navigating illness trajectory is likened to chart unknown territory. It can be daunting for families and more so for the primary caregiver, who has to make many decisions along the way. Caregivers and families must therefore prepare for rapid changes that can potentially occur (Blum & Sherman, 2010; Northfield & Nebauer, 2010). Caregivers have reported having to "learn on the job" during their caregiving endeavors and in doing so to consistently inform family members who disapproved of certain decisions based on lack of knowledge (Tassinari, 2017). Counselors who work with caregivers can help by providing psychoeducation for caregivers and families to inform and encourage collaboration during caregiving, which can reduce some of the stress and improve communication that is needed during the process.

Roles and Relationships

Once catapulted into the caregiving role, primary caregivers might notice a shift in relationships, whether that be the parent–child relationship, relationships with siblings, or those with extended family members. These relationships may strengthen or become impaired, depending on the circumstances presented. One of the most important relationships that take shape is the parent–child relationship where the child, now an adult, cares for their parent, experiencing a role reversal. During this important transition, the primary caregiver negotiates her new role with her ailing parent while preparing for the caregiving endeavor (Gill & Morgan, 2012; Tassinari, 2017), and at times it does not come without a cost. Women who become primary caregivers become responsible and in charge of care; therefore, it is important that counselors encourage caregivers to establish clear boundaries at the onset of the caregiving journey and to anticipate the potentiality of disagreeable family members. Family discord is common and should be anticipated, especially if relationships are strained prior to the onset of caregiving (Tassinari, 2017).

Family Discord

Family dynamics may create unexpected challenges as the caregiving role is assumed. Whether these are disagreements between siblings or difficulty with other family members during the caregiving journey, relational tension is common during caregiving, especially during the end stages of life. As a loved one's health declines rapidly, primary caregivers are required to make important medical decisions—especially when cure is no longer an option.

Transitioning a loved one from curative care to palliative care is one of the most difficult decisions a primary caregiver must make. At this point, anxiety levels and anticipatory grief are at their highest. Caregivers have reported at least one or more encounters with a family member who has either protested or opposed a decision that was made in the interest of the care recipient (Tassinari, 2017). Feeling exhausted and overwhelmed, primary caregivers experience additional stress from family members who were not supportive of their decision making as well as physical ailments and physical exhaustion from increased stress levels associated with family discord (Tassinari, 2017).

Anticipatory Grief

Key findings in caregiver research have indicated that caregivers struggle with intense emotions such as anxiety, sadness, anger, and hostility due to the impending death of a loved one (Holley & Mast, 2009; Waldrop, 2007), in addition to anticipatory grief. Caregivers have reported that endings can be unexpectedly intense and somewhat traumatic, as they watch their loved ones suffer (Tassinari, 2017). Clinicians must encourage caregivers to seek support such as hospice care or palliative care services, as well as physicians who can provide psychoeducation to help family members prepare for the end (Hudson, 2004; Tassinari, 2017; Ward-Griffin, McWilliam, & Oudshoorn, 2012).

Bereaved Caregivers

While most bereaved caregivers and family members are able to adjust to life after caregiving, some bereaved caregivers have difficulty adapting to loss. For example, caregivers who were in poor physical and psychological health prior to caregiving tend to be at risk for more depressive symptoms during (Allen, Haley, Small, Schonwetter, & McMillan, 2013; Ling et al., 2013) and after their loved one's death (Hudson, Thomas, Trauer, Remedios, & Clarke, 2011; Schulz et al., 2003). Additionally, for caregivers who have held the caregiving role for a number of years, there is often a "void" felt as their role of caregiver ends (Tassinari, 2017). Some caregivers feel haunted by the images of the suffering loved ones endured and may ruminate about the experience. Others may feel resentful toward family members for their lack of caregiving participation and the related stress this created, in addition to stress experienced from relational tension (Tassinari, 2017). During postloss adjustment, caregivers often seek counseling to process painful feelings of sadness, guilt, and emptiness. Despite the negative impacts of caregiving, most caregivers appear to be resilient and typically report positive outcomes from their caregiving journey, such as personal and spiritual growth (Bonanno, 2009; Stroebe & Schut, 1999), and ascribe meaning to their experiences (Tassinari, 2017), later discussed in the section "Unexpected Gifts."

Complex Emotional Responses after Loss

While most caregivers experience relief as their role ends, they also feel guilt. Many complex and overlapping emotional responses occur, which can be difficult for caregivers to comprehend, but quite common. As Tassinari (2017) noted, caregivers may make statements such as, "I miss my parents, but I don't miss being a caregiver," or "I feel guilty for feeling relieved." Caregivers might also feel guilt over other things that may have occurred during their caregiving experience. These may include questioning whether they could have done more for their loved one or done something differently. Some caregivers have also reported feeling guilty for spending too much time providing care but not enough quality time with their loved ones. In some cases, they may experience angst over their decisions for utilizing extensive measures to keep their loved ones alive and now wonder whether they prolonged their loved one's suffering. It is important that counselors understand that caregivers frequently engage in rumination and self-assessment after loss, so counselors should work to normalize these feelings in counseling.

Unexpected Gifts

While most caregivers experience caregiver burden and distress during caregiving, some have identified positive aspects of their caregiving journey. For example, caregivers have reported that caregiving was a "mixed blessing," on the one hand, but it had been burdensome, on the other. Some describe it as the opportunity to "give back" to their loved ones a "gift," even when it was incredibly stressful (Tassinari, 2017). Many view their caregiving as meaningful and purposeful and feel that it is a special privilege to be present as their loved one is approaching death (Tassinari, 2017). All of these feelings are congruent with meaning reconstruction in the context of sense making and benefit finding in loss, according to meaning-reconstruction theory of bereavement (Neimeyer, 2001), which is addressed further in the section "Addressing Grief."

In some cultures, caregiving carries special value. Recent research shows that Hispanics and African Americans experience more positive aspects of caregiving than white caregivers (Roth, Dilworth-Anderson, Huang, Gross, & Gitlin, 2015). Caregivers feel that their efforts are appreciated, needed, and useful. They also may feel a sense of confidence as they learn effective communication skills, among other new skills (Haley et al., 2009). Perceived positive aspects of caregiving therefore may depend largely on culture, demographic factors, perceptions of the caregiver role, spirituality, religiosity, and socioeconomic status.

PRACTICAL CONSIDERATIONS IN COUNSELING

Regardless of how long the caregiver's role lasts, there may be multiple shifts in identity that can lead to unexpected stress and compromised well-being. The trajectory of the care recipient's illness is an important consideration (Tassinari, 2017) as this marks the beginning and the end of the caregiver's responsibilities. Throughout this trajectory, caregivers face various challenges and experience different needs. Practitioners should know the best practices in providing support for these individuals.

Self-Care

Caregivers, overwhelmed with responsibilities, multiple roles, and uncertainty, have minimal or no time for self-care, an area that is imperative for healthy functioning and overall well-being. Clinicians are in an excellent position to enhance caregivers' coping mechanisms and accentuate the need for self-care (Kepic et al., 2019). Utilization of formal or informal caregivers' burden and stress assessments is an important part of clinical work that may provide a valuable starting point for the work with caregivers. Even more important is the assessment of caregivers' strengths, talents, and hobbies because these can be key to building and expanding on resources and self-care. Clinicians may psychoeducate caregivers about the importance of self-care and help clients take responsibility for implementing self-care strategies. Self-care will look different for each client, but some self-care strategies might include taking a break from caregiving responsibilities for a few hours or a day, going out with friends one evening, spending quality time with a partner, attending yoga, practicing yoga and meditation, or taking part in any recreational activities that a caregiver might find relaxing and pleasurable. When caregivers are unable to take off time from their responsibilities, they can engage in simple breathing exercises that will promote calm or make a quick phone call to a member of their support system. Clinicians are encouraged to be creative in exploration of self-care interventions with clients as well as to ensure that self-care activities do not create burdens but are designed to relieve distress.

Addressing Grief

Each caregiver's grief and experience of loss will be unique. Certain grief tasks have been observed, however, among the majority of those who grieve (Bonanno, 2009; Stroebe, Schut, & Stroebe, 2005; Worden, 2009). Grief tasks, grief process, and the counselor's approach are described in greater detail in chapter 21; however, following is a brief overview.

In recent years, grief research has launched from the groundbreaking work of Elisabeth Kübler-Ross (1969) and her prescribed stages of grief (i.e., denial, anger, bargaining, depression, and acceptance) to contemporary grief models such as Stroebe and Schut's (1999) dual process model of grief and Neimeyer's (2001) meaning reconstruction theory of bereavement. The dual process model of grief views grief as a dynamic process that oscillates between focusing on the loss (i.e., loss orientation) and reengaging with restorative activities to cope and work through loss (i.e., restoration orientation). Bereaved caregivers will typically confront loss (e.g., missing and longing for the lost family member) and at the same time deal with the harsh reality of adjusting to changes associated with the loss.

J. William Worden (2009) determined that there are four common tasks of grief that serve to help us understand the needs of the bereaved: acceptance of the loss, experiencing the pain of a permanent loss, adjustment to a new environment without the presence of the loved one, and reinvestment of energy into the life ahead. Furthering grief research and through a constructivist framework, Robert Neimeyer (1999) presents the meaning reconstruction theory of bereavement as a different perspective on how we address grief through three interactive processes: sense making, benefit finding, and identity reconstruction. Counselors who work through this lens believe that human beings are inveterate meaning makers and can process grief through the telling and retelling of their loss story with a goal of re-creating a new narrative (Neimeyer, 1999, 2001). Other researchers (Brandstätter et al., 2014) suggest that specific interventions such as applied techniques using meaning reconstruction during palliative care and bereavement are important in helping individuals strengthen and regain a sense of meaning and purpose. Counselors who work with caregivers and bereaved caregivers can help process caregiver grief through examining meaning structures and through the facilitation of meaning making throughout the caregiving journey. Additionally, counselors can provide other support, such as identifying resources and support services for caregivers as well as other information to assist the needs of caregivers.

Support and Resources

Throughout the caregiving process, caregivers need multiple forms of support. While family members are often a source of support, family dynamics are often altered as a result of taking on the new roles of caregiver and care recipient (Qualls, 2016). As family members take on new roles, this can contribute to disequilibrium and stress due to varying opinions, values, and experiences. Counselors can help navigate difficult conversations and provide models of effective communication among the family members (Kepic et al., 2019). Ideally, once roles and responsibilities are clearer, family members can provide a respite for the primary caregiver by helping with demanding responsibilities or stepping in fully as a respite caregiver for a few hours or few days.

Caregiver support groups are another valuable resource. In such groups, a caregiver might be grateful to meet other caregivers who are coping with similar challenges. This can provide a sense of acknowledgment, understanding, commonality, and possibly sense of relief as her experiences are normalized. Support groups can provide suggestions for navigating specific issues related to caregiving. Caregivers can learn about additional resources while providing and receiving emotional support. Psychoeducational skill-based groups help members improve coping strategies and reduce stress (Pepin, Williams, Anderson, & Qualls, 2013). Topics such as transitions, effective communication, decision making, emotional regulation, and self-care are key. In rural or more isolated areas where support groups might not be an option, individual counseling, in person or via technology, can be effective. Counselors might provide resources and links for ancillary services, such as care management, volunteer home visits, or respite care, to help alleviate the stress caregivers experience (Chen, 2016; Qualls, 2016). Web-based programs and telephonic services can provide information, support, and socialization for caregivers who feel isolated and overwhelmed. Various organizations (listed in the "Advocacy Opportunities and Resources" section) offer specific psychoeducational programs for caregivers and are easily accessible online. Day program services for care recipients are another resource that can be utilized by caregivers, allowing them to have time for other responsibilities or self-care. Finally, religious personnel and other professionals, such as primary care physicians, might assist initially with referrals and links to resources. As an increasing number of individuals are moving into caregiving roles, clinicians will play a crucial role in caregivers' services, and this calls for competencies in counseling those who care for loved ones.

BEST PRACTICES

Clinical professionals must prepare themselves to work with caregivers, particularly women caregivers, as formal caregiving is most often provided by women. Caretakers' multiple responsibilities often lead to chronic stress, so it is advantageous for clinicians to develop a working knowledge and a skill set to address caregiver stress and burden. The following are helpful guidelines for this practice area:

1. Be knowledgeable about relevant issues for caregivers, including the challenges and benefits that caregivers experience in this role.
2. Understand the trajectory of caregiver identity development, and recognize that women may follow a nonlinear path in their experiences as caregivers.
3. Consider cultural backgrounds and their influence on each caregiver and the ways culture influences the expectations surrounding the caregiving role. Religion and spirituality might be a key component to one's coping.
4. Recognize that women caregivers typically experience an initial rejection of or resistance to counseling services, and acknowledge their courage when they do seek support.
5. With empathy, sensitivity, and validation, acknowledge caregivers' feelings, thoughts, and behaviors without judgment.
6. Be aware of societal stereotypes and your own biases toward caregivers, older adults, and the terminally ill population, and address these during supervision and further diversity training.
7. Acquire knowledge about appropriate caregiver assessments, administration, scoring, and interpretation of results; incorporate these in your counseling practice. Assessments might pick up on issues that are not obvious, and assessment data can guide the conversation and clinical practice.
8. During the counseling process, bear in mind that caregivers will appreciate the opportunity to be heard and to have their concerns taken seriously. Acknowledgment and validation are important as caregivers often feel they are underappreciated.
9. Incorporate creativity in work with caregivers to maximize the limited resources they have or that you can offer.
10. Have knowledge about ethical and legal issues pertaining to caregivers, and keep up with the new legal developments and advocacy related to caregiving.
11. Be prepared to share a variety of resources with caregivers, and link them with necessary support groups as appropriate.
12. Recognize that grief and loss are often intertwined with caregiving, so be prepared to address any real or perceived loss.
13. Be flexible and explore options for technology-assisted counseling to serve clients who may experience significant claims on their time.
14. Establish and maintain sporadic check-ins via technology to provide necessary support if weekly counseling sessions are difficult for a caregiver to manage.

CULTURAL CONSIDERATIONS

Cultural background frequently influences the ways provision of care is experienced by women. As examples, Middle Easterners and South Asian caregivers are less likely to use formal services, which leads them predominantly to utilize family members as caretakers. Some common reasons for not utilizing formal services include lack of trust, restricted access, and cultural traditions or a family orientation to care for their own (Ahmad, 2012).

Half of the caregivers in such regions are daughters-in-law due to the cultural traditions (Ahmad, 2012). Even though caregiving in Middle Eastern and South Asian cultures is a given responsibility and is viewed more positively, the majority of women caregivers reported multiple stressors leading to poor sleep, fatigue, and exhaustion. Some challenges that are frequently documented by women caregivers are difficulty administering medications, difficulty caring for wounds, and mainly challenges associated with noncooperation on the part of the care recipient (Hooyman & Kiyak, 2011; Sanders, 2005). Hispanic and African American populations also tend to rely on informal services, not only due to mistrust but due to such services being restricted to them (Collins & Hawkins, 2016). Hispanic caregivers tend to utilize pastoral services for emotional support and comfort. African American caregivers utilize their congregations for support and engage them in navigating formal support. Besides racial and ethnical diversity, individuals whose sexual orientation differs from heterosexual orientation experience multiple challenges when it comes to caregiving.

Even though the LGBTQ population has becomes more visible, enormous caregiving challenges remain. Due to experienced discrimination, victimization, and previous marginalization, LGBTQ adults may not seek out or use formal services (Fredriksen-Goldsen & Emlet, 2012), and those who need assistance prefer to live independently. Thus, they will rely on help and support from partners and friends. Informal care will provide some safety from real or perceived discrimination (Fredriksen-Goldsen & Emlet, 2012), with intimate partners most likely to assume a role as caregiver (Cahill, Ellen, & Tobias, 2002). Lesbian caregivers are even more likely than other populations to experience negative effects of caregiving, such as isolation, depression, and anxiety (Fredriksen-Goldsen & Emlet, 2012). As documented by Meyer and Northridge (2007), a lack of access to health services and discrimination accelerate chronic illness and a decline in mental health for both the caregiver and the care recipient. Overall, many minority caregivers find it difficult to use formal services due to either restriction or unavailability of services, lack of trust from previous experiences of discrimination, or lack of sensitivity and respect for minorities.

For some bereaved caregivers, spirituality and religious practices will play a role in coping with the loss. Many may draw on their beliefs about

God, religious practices, and more importantly, connection to a religious community. Research supports the positive effects of some religious coping with loss on mental, physical, and spiritual well-being (Kelley & Chan, 2012; Pargament & Abu Raiya, 2007). Clinicians need to be sensitive to clients' views of religion and spirituality and respect their preferences. Further, an understanding of historical and current sociopolitical issues pertaining to minorities, awareness of one's own biases, and understanding of the possible challenges and emotional benefits associated with caregiving are paramount in providing culturally sensitive and effective counseling services.

ETHICAL CONSIDERATION

When counseling caregivers, confidentiality and informed consent may present an important concern, especially when more than one family member is involved in caretaking, due to the potential need to share information. When a caregiver and other family members seek counseling services, the clinician needs to clearly spell out the limits of confidentiality and clarify the identity of the primary client, whether it is an individual or the family. Clinicians are obligated to report any signs of elder abuse and neglect; therefore, they need to be knowledgeable about what pertains to active and passive neglect and what constitutes elder abuse. Multiple relationships can be of concern, especially in isolated areas, where counselors might serve in roles beyond that of counselor. Due to lack of time, transportation, or other factors, caregivers might utilize long-distance or technology-assisted counseling. In such cases, clinicians might want to check state regulations for such services and, moreover, need to ensure each client's security, privacy, and confidentiality.

Palliative care and hospice situations might present end-of-life concerns, especially when a care recipient is very ill. Concerns about how much and what kind of care should be provided to a loved one with limited life expectancy may be shared with a counselor; therefore, clinicians do not shy away from conversations about such topics. Clinicians must approach these discussions with knowledge, sensitivity, and cultural competence. Because ethical and legal issues are part of the caregiving role, clinicians may need to provide resources that will facilitate a client's assumption of legal rights, in the case of the care recipient's incapacity. Conversations about advanced directives are quite common, and clinicians should encourage caregivers to have such conversions with care recipients and physicians early enough to avoid unexpected or last-minute decision making. When uncertain or in doubt, clinicians always seek consultation with their supervisors and clinical directors.

ADVOCACY OPPORTUNITIES AND RESOURCES

Despite the fact that services and resources for caregivers have improved, they remain insufficient to effectively address caregivers' burdens and needs. There are ongoing challenges associated with locating appropriate services, respite, and consultation. Caregivers know the challenges best and might be the best advocates for their own needs and their family's needs. Moreover, they might also be the most effective in influencing and changing public policy. Clinicians work on empowering caregivers in their immediate needs, but can guide them and join them in advocacy work. Providing education to those with legislative power to develop public policy that would maximize the effectiveness of services and minimize the burden and stress of caregivers is one avenue that counselors can take. This might involve contacting legislative representatives and asking them to support bills that provide resources for the elderly, the sick, and their caregivers, such as HR1; the Long-Term Care Act; the Older American Care Act Title III Programs; and the Recognize, Assist, Include, Support, and Engage Family Caregivers Act.

When working with caregivers, clinicians can help through sound counseling incorporating appropriate assessment, culturally sensitive counseling strategies, and plenty of resources. Listed below are some crucial assessments, organizations, and further online resources from which caregivers might benefit.

Caregivers Assessments

Caregiver Strain Index (Robinson, 1983): http://www.npcrc.org/files/news/caregiver_strain_index.pdf

Zarit Burden Scale (Zarit, Reever, & Bach-Peterson, 1980): http://dementiapathways.ie/_filecache/edd/c3c/89-zarit_burden_interview.pdf

Caregiver Reaction Assessment Scale (CRA) (Given et al., 1992): https://nadrc.acl.gov/sites/default/files/uploads/docs/Caregiver%20Reaction%20Scale.pdf

CAREQOL-MS: Caregiver Quality of Life (Benito-Leon et al., 2011): https://www.sciencedirect.com/science/article/abs/pii/S0895435610002866

Organizations for Caregivers

AARP
Alzheimer's Association
Caregiver Action Network
Caregiver Support Services

Family Caregiver Alliance
Home Alone Alliance (part of AARP)
National Adult Day Services Association
National Alliance for Caregivers
VA Caregiver Support
Well Spouse Association

Online Resources

America Red Cross Family Caregiving Program
Caregiver Health Education Program
Caring for You, Caring for Me: Education and Support for Family and Professional Caregivers
Coping with Caregiving
Powerful Tools for Caregivers

CASE VIGNETTE WRAP-UP: SONYA

Sonya contacted Thomasina, a counselor who specializes in caregiver care, after she began experiencing anxiety, depression, and difficulty sleeping. Sonya had never taken any medication and wanted to stay the path and work through her situation with a counselor. Feeling extremely sad over her mother's condition, Sonya also shared that her anxiety was "through the roof" and she felt helpless in trying to do anything more for her mother. Thomasina empathized with Sonya as she took an in-depth history of Sonya's presenting issues. She asked Sonya to share more about her relationships with her husband, children, siblings, and parents. Thomasina also wanted to learn more about Sonya's social support system (i.e., friends, coworkers) and her faith. Sonya explained that she had a good marriage and her husband had been a tremendous support. She described her kids as somewhat helpful but noted they were busy with school and sports. Sonya also has a close group of girlfriends but explained that she doesn't really like to share her problems with them. Sonya described herself as a devout Catholic who attends church regularly. She stated that her faith has helped her get through other adversities in life. For example, Sonya shared that she recently lost a close friend, and she had gotten through her grief with exercise and attending church. Thomasina determined that Sonya was still grieving the loss of her friend and asked Sonya to talk more about the incident.

Interventions: Grief Counseling Using Both a Meaning-Reconstruction Lens and a Strengths-Based Approach

Thomasina begins the therapeutic process by first focusing on establishing trust with Sonya. Sonya appreciates Thomasina's warm and caring approach and readily begins goal setting with Thomasina. During their first session, Thomasina explores Sonya's developmental history, cultural background, social supports, and relevant values. In addition, Thomasina taps into some of Sonya's hobbies and self-care practices. She also learns how important Sonya's family is to her and the cultural practices that she and her family value and share. For example, because she is the only female of three siblings, Sonya readily agreed to take on primary caregiving responsibility for her ailing mother. Sonya shares, however, that she has anger and resentment toward her brothers for their lack of support or interest in helping her with the caregiving. Thomasina validates Sonya's feelings, and together they process some of the anger and resentment Sonya carries. The cocreated goals for Sonya were as follows:

1. *Decrease Sonya's anxiety through relaxation techniques*

    a. *Identify triggers for anxiety*
    b. *Learn relaxation techniques*
    c. *Enhance current coping strategies*

2. *Increase Sonya's sense of control and emotional preparedness for the impending loss of her mother*

    a. *Differentiate between what is in her control and what is not and cognitively restructure her thoughts accordingly*
    b. *Increase understanding of anticipatory grief and process emotional responses*

3. *Increase Sonya's sense making*

    a. *Explore meaning-reconstruction processes such as benefit finding*
    b. *Explore and assist with identity reconstruction in postloss adjustment*

Brief Conceptualization

From a developmental perspective, Sonya is a member of the sandwich generation. She is caring for her own teenage children and now serving as primary caregiver to her mother. Women in the sandwich generation experi-

ence higher levels of stress and anxiety due to the multidirectional caregiving they provide. While she is in the generativity phase of her life, she has taken on a new role that serves as a means to further her generativity. However, this new role can be stressful and a burden that adversely affects her functioning. As the Thomasina learns about Sonya's cultural background, the related gender expectations placed on Sonya, and the value Sonya's familial role holds for her, Thomasina recognizes that Sonya might self-impose additional pressures that might be detrimental to her well-being. Sonya highly values her roles of wife and mother and may overreach her capacities if she tries to keep up with all of the responsibilities she has at home and as a new caregiver. Balancing home and caregiving, therefore, will be a challenge for Sonya; as a result, she might sacrifice her own self-care to manage it all. Further complications arise for Sonya as a result of sibling relational tension, including her anger and resentment toward her brothers. These emotions must be addressed and normalized through work with Thomasina. Additionally, Sonya is still grieving the loss of her close friend while concurrently experiencing anticipatory grief over the loss of her mother. Considering relevant supportive factors, Sonya may have a good group of friends, but she acknowledges that she seldom calls upon them for support. Sonya also has a strong, Catholic faith and attends church regularly; this is a protective factor that may warrant further exploration in future sessions.

Final Wrap-Up

While working with Sonya, Thomasina needs to establish a supportive atmosphere where Sonya can come into the session and decompress from her increased stress levels. Thomasina might begin each session with some breathing exercises or other strategies such as thought-stopping techniques (Meichenbaum, 1994) to address Sonya's increased anxiety levels and negative thought patterns. While respecting and acknowledging Sonya's cultural heritage, Thomasina can help Sonya explore cultural values, expectations, and assumptions that Sonya carries as a result of prior experiences so that she can examine how these might conflict with her current situation. Helping Sonya see that her situation is temporary, Thomasina can support Sonya's capacity for reevaluation and exploration of other possibilities while she maintains her role as caregiver. Thomasina would employ meaning-making strategies to address Sonya's current grief and explore the meaning and significance of the loss of her friend as well as the impending loss of her mother. Regarding Sonya's current sibling relationships, Thomasina might help Sonya process painful feelings of anger, sadness, and grief while also helping Sonya establish and maintain boundaries during caregiving. Thomasina might also assist Sonya in developing more effective communication skills for dealing with difficult family members. As some women thrive through connections with others, some focus might be given to Sonya's current relationships to determine what, if any, adjustments should be made. Together, Sonya and Thomasina can continue to address painful feelings through emotional expression in the sessions, continue to focus on strengthening self-care behaviors as well as self-preservation, and maintain the therapeutic alliance throughout the caregiving process and in preparation for postloss adjustment.

QUESTIONS FOR REFLECTION

1. What is your experience with caregiving with family members or others?
2. What are some of the issues related to end-of-life decision making that might be challenging for you to address as a counselor?
3. What might be an additional helpful theoretical lens to incorporate in counseling sessions with Sonya or similar clients?
4. When working with women who are taking on too many responsibilities, what interventions might you use to help them manage care of others and care of self?
5. What are some steps you might take to learn more about cultural perspectives on caregiving for elders and end-of-life considerations?

REFERENCES

Adams, K. (2006). The transition to caregiving: The experience of family members embarking on the dementia caregiving career. *Journal of Gerontological Social Work, 47*(3–4), 3–29.

Administration on Aging. (2010). *A profile of older adults: 2010*. Retrieved from http://www.aoa.gov/AoARoot/Aging_Statistics/Profile/2010/docs/2010profile.pdf

Ahmad, K. (2012). Informal caregiving to chronically ill older family members: Caregivers' experiences and problems. *South Asian Studies, 27*, 101–20.

Aldwin, C. M., & Gilmer, D. F. (2013). *Health, illness, and optimal aging: Biological and psychological perspectives*. New York, NY: Springer.

Allen, J. Y., Haley, W. E., Small, B. J., Schonwetter, R. S., & McMillan, S. C. (2013). Bereavement among hospice caregivers of cancer patients one year following loss: Predictors of grief, complicated grief, and symptoms of depression. *Journal of Palliative Medicine, 16*(7), 745–51. doi:10.1089/jpm.2012.0450

Benito-León, J., Rivera-Navarro, J., Guerrero, A. L., Heras, V., Balseiro, J., Rodríguez, E., . . . Martínez-Martín, P. (2011). The CAREQOL-MS was a useful instrument to measure caregiver quality of life in multiple sclerosis. *Journal of Clinical Epidemiology, 64*(6), 675–86. https://doi.org/10.1016/j.jclinepi.2010.08.003

Blum, K., & Sherman, D. (2010). Understanding the experience of caregivers: A focus on transitions. *Seminars in Oncology Nursing, 26*(4), 243–58. doi:10.1016/j.soncn.2010.08.005

Bonanno, G. A. (2009). *The other side of sadness: What the new science of bereavement tells us about life after loss*. New York, NY: Basic Books.

Brandstätter, M., Kögler, M., Baumann, U., Fensterer, V., Küchenhoff, H., Borasio, G., & Fegg, M. (2014). Experience of meaning in life in bereaved informal caregivers of palliative care patients. *Supportive Care in Cancer, 22*(5), 1391–99. doi:10.1007/s00520-013-2099-6

Cahill, S., Ellen, M., & Tobias, S. (2002). *Family policy: Issues affecting gay, lesbian, bisexual and transgender families.* New York, NY: National Gay and Lesbian Task Force Policy Institute.

Cameron, J. I., Franche, R. L., Cheung, A. M., & Stewart, D. E. (2002). Lifestyle interference and emotional distress in family caregivers of advanced cancer patients. *Cancer, 94*(2), 521–27. doi:10.1002/cncr.10212

Chen, C. K. (2016). Defiance, denial, and defining limits: Helping family caregivers of individuals with dementia distinguish the tap-out from the cop-out. *Journal of Psychotherapy Integration, 26*, 353–65. doi:10.1037/int0000017

Collins, W. L., & Hawkins, A. D. (2016). Supporting caregivers who care for African American elders: A pastoral perspective. *Social Work and Christianity, 43*, 85–103.

Dhar, R. (2012). Caregiving for elderly parents: A study from the Indian perspective. *Home Health Care Management & Practice, 24*(5), 242–54. doi:10.1177/1084822312439466

Eifert, E. K., Adams, R., Dudley, W., & Perko, M. (2015). Family caregiver identity: A literature review. *American Journal of Health Education, 46*(6), 357–67. doi:10.1080/19325037.2015.1099482

Fredriksen-Goldsen, K. I., & Emlet, C. A. (2012). Research note: Health disparities among LGBT older adults living with HIV. *Aging Today Online*. https://www.asaging.org/blog/research-note-health-disparities-among-lgbt-older-adults-living-hiv

Gallagher-Thompson, D., & Coon, D. W. (2007). Evidence-based psychological treatments for distress in family caregivers of older adult. *Psychology & Aging, 22*(1), 37–51. doi:10.1037/0882-7974.22.1.37

Gill, E. A., & Morgan, M. (2012). Older parents and adult daughters: A comparison of communication and coping during the decision to move to a care facility. *Research on Aging, 34*(6), 714–37. doi:10.1177/0164027512447821

Given, C. W., Given, B., Stommel, M., Collins, C., King, S., & Franklin, S. (1992). The caregiver reaction assessment (CRA) for caregivers to persons with chronic physical and mental impairments. *Research in Nursing & Health, 15*, 271–83. doi:10.1002/nur.4770150406

Givens, J. L., Mezzacappa, C., Heeren, T., Yaffe, K., & Fredman, L. (2014). Depressive symptoms among dementia caregivers: Role of mediating factors. *American Journal of Geriatric Psychiatry, 22*(5), 481–88. doi:10.1016/j.jagp.2012.08.010

Gomes, B., Calanzani, N., Gysels, M., Hall, S., & Higginson, I. J. (2013). Heterogeneity and changes in preferences for dying at home: A systematic review. *BMC Palliative Care, 12*(1), 7–19. doi:10.1186/1472-684X-12-7

Grunfeld, E., Coyle, D., Whelan, T., Clinch, J., Reyno, L., Earle, C. C., . . . Glossop, R. (2004). Family caregiver burden: Results of a longitudinal study of breast cancer patients and their principal caregivers. *Canadian Medical Association Journal, 170*, 1795–1801. doi:10.1503/cmaj.1031205

Haley, W. E., Allen, J. Y., Grant, J. S., Clay, O. J., Perkins, M., & Roth, D. L. (2009). Problems and benefits reported by stroke family caregivers. *Stroke, 40*, 2129–33. doi:10.1161/STROKEAHA.108.545269

Hammer, L. B., & Neal, M. B. (2008). Working sandwiched-generation caregivers: Prevalence, characteristics, and outcomes. *Psychologist-Manager Journal, 11*(1), 93–112. doi:10.1080/10887150801967324

Holley, C. K., & Mast, B. T. (2009). The impact of anticipatory grief on caregiver burden in dementia caregivers. *Gerontologist, 49*(3), 388–96. doi:10.1093/geront/gnp061

Hooyman, N. R., & Kiyak, H. A. (2011). *Social gerontology: A multidisciplinary perspective.* Boston, MA: Allyn & Bacon.

Hudson, P. (2004). Positive aspects and challenges associated with caring for a dying relative at home. *International Journal of Palliative Nursing, 10*(2), 58–65.

Hudson, P. L., Remedios, C., & Thomas, K. (2010). A systematic review of psychosocial interventions for family carers of palliative care patients. *BMC Palliative Care, 9*, 17–22. doi:10.1186/1472-684X-9-17

Hudson, P. L., Thomas, K., Trauer, T., Remedios, C., & Clarke, D. (2011). Psychological and social profile of family caregivers on commencement of palliative care. *Journal of Pain & Symptom Management, 41*(3), 522–34. doi:10.1016/j.jpainsymman.2010.05.006

Humphrey, K. M. (2009). *Counseling strategies for loss and grief.* Alexandria, VA: American Counseling Association.

Joling, K., Smit, F., van Marwijk, H., van der Horst, H., Scheltens, P., Schulz, R., & van Hout, H. (2012). Identifying target groups for the prevention of depression among caregivers of dementia patients. *International Psychogeriatrics, 24*(2), 298–306. doi:10.1017/S1041610211001633

Kelley, M. M., & Chan, K. T. (2012). Assessing the role of attachment to god, meaning, and religious coping as mediators in the grief experience. *Death Studies, 36*(3), 199–227. doi:10.1080/07481187.2011.553317

Kepic, M., Randolph, A., & Hermann-Turner, K. M. (2019). Care for caregivers: Understanding the need for caregiver support. *Adultspan Journal, 18*, 40–51.

Knussen, C., Tolson, D., Swan, I. C., Stott, D. J., & Brogan, C. A. (2005). Stress proliferation in caregivers: The relationships between caregiving stressors and deterioration in family relationships. *Psychology & Health, 20*(2), 207–21. doi:10.1080/08870440512331334013

Kübler-Ross, E. (1969). *On death and dying.* New York, NY: Macmillan.

Ling, S., Chen, M., Li, C., Chang, W., Shen, W., & Tang, S. (2013). Trajectory and influencing factors of depressive symptoms in family caregivers before and after the death of terminally ill patients with cancer. *Oncology Nursing Forum, 40*(1), E32–E40.

Liu, W., & Gallagher-Thomson, D. (2009). Impact of dementia caregiving: Risks, strains and growth. In S. Qualls & S. Zarit (Eds.), *Aging families and caregiving* (pp. 85–103). Hoboken, NJ: John Wiley & Sons.

Mehta, K. (2005). Stress among family caregivers of older persons in Singapore. *Journal of Cross-Cultural Gerontology, 20*, 319–34. doi:10.1007/s10823-006-9009-z

Meichenbaum, D. (1994). *Assessing and treating adults with posttraumatic stress disorder.* Waterloo, ON: Institute Press.

Meyer, I., & Northridge, M. (2007). *The health of sexual minorities: Public health perspectives on lesbian, gay, bisexual, and transgender populations.* New York, NY: Springer.

Mohamed, S., Rosenheck, R., Lyketsos, C. G., & Schneider, L. S. (2010). Caregiver burnout in Alzheimer disease: Cross-sectional and longitudinal patient correlates. *American Journal of Geriatric Psychiatry, 18*, 917–27. doi:10.1097/JGP.0b013e3181d5745d

Montgomery, R., & Kosloski, K. (2009). Caregiving as a process of changing identity: Implications for caregiver support. *Generations, 33*(1), 47–52.

National Alliance for Caregiving. (2015). *Caregiving in the U.S. 2015 report.* Retrieved from https://www.caregiving.org

National Alliance for Caregiving. (2016). *Caregiving in the U.S. 2016 report.* Retrieved from https://www.caregiving.org

Neimeyer, R. A. (1999). Narrative strategies in grief therapy. *Journal of Constructivist Psychology, 12*(1), 65–85. doi:10.1080/107205399266226

Neimeyer, R. A. (2001). Meaning reconstruction and loss. In R. A. Neimeyer, *Meaning reconstruction and the experience of loss* (pp. 1–9). Washington, DC: American Psychological Association.

Northfield, S., & Nebauer, M. (2010). The caregiving journey for family members of relatives with cancer. *Clinical Journal of Oncology Nursing, 14*(5), 567–77.

Pargament, K. I., & Abu Raiya, H. (2007). A decade of research on the psychology of religion and coping: Things we assumed and lessons we learned. *Psyke & Logos, 28*, 742–66.

Pepin, R., Williams, A. A., Anderson, L. N., & Qualls, S. H. (2013). A preliminary typology of caregivers and effects on service utilization of caregiver counseling. *Aging & Mental Health,* 17, 495–507. doi:10.1080/13607863.2012.758232

Pinquart, M., & Sörensen, S. (2006). Gender differences in caregiver stressors, social resources, and health: An updated meta-analysis. *Journals of Gerontology Series B: Psychological Sciences & Social Sciences, 61*(1), 33–45.

Pope, N. D. (2013). Female caregivers' plans for late life. *Qualitative Social Work, 12*(4), 507–22. doi:10.1177/1473325012442439

Qualls, S. H. (2016). Caregiving families within the long-term services and support system for older adults. *American Psychologist, 71*, 283–93. doi:10.1037/a0040252

Rhee, Y. S., Yun, Y. H., Park, S., Shin, D. O., Lee, K. M., Yoo, H. J., . . . Kim, N. S. (2008). Depression in family caregivers of cancer patients: The feeling of burden as a predictor of depression. *Journal of Clinical Oncology, 26*(36), 5890–95. doi:10.1200/JCO.2007.15.3957

Robinson, B. C. (1983). Validation of a caregiver strain index. *Journal of Gerontology, 38*(3), 344–48. https://doi.org/10.1093/geronj/38.3.344

Roth, D. L., Dilworth-Anderson, P., Huang, J., Gross, A. L., & Gitlin, L. N. (2015). Positive aspects of family caregiving for dementia: Differential item functioning by race. *Journals of Gerontology Series B: Psychological Sciences and Social Sciences, 70*, 813–19. doi:10.1093/geronb/gbv034

Sanders, S. (2005). Is the glass half empty or half full? Reflections on strain and gain in caregivers of individuals with Alzheimer's disease. *Social Work in Health Care, 40*, 57–73. doi:10.1300/J010v40n03_04

Schoenmakers, B., Buntinx, F., & DeLepeleire, J. (2010). Factors determining the impact of care-giving on caregivers of elderly patients with dementia: A systematic literature review. *Maturitas, 66*, 91–200. doi:10.1016/j.maturitas.2010.02.009

Schreiner, A. S., Morimoto, T., Arai, Y., & Zarit, S. (2006). Assessing family caregiver's mental health using a statistically derived cut-off score for the Zarit Burden Interview. *Aging & Mental Health, 10*, 107–11. doi:10.1080/13607860500312142

Schulz, R., & Martire, L. M. (2004). Family caregiving of persons with dementia: Prevalence, health effects, and support strategies. *American Journal of Geriatric Psychiatry, 12*, 240–49. https://doi.org/10.1097/00019442-200405000-00002

Schulz, R., Mendelsohn, A., Haley, W., Mahoney, D., Allen, R., Zhang, S., & Belle, S. (2003). End-of-life care and the effects of bereavement on family caregivers of persons with dementia. *New England Journal of Medicine, 349*(20), 1936–42.

Segerstrom, S. C., & Miller, G. E. (2004). Psychological stress and the human immune system: A meta analytic study of 30-years of inquiry. *Psychological Bulletin, 130*, 601–30 doi:10.1037/0033-2909.130.4.601

Shaffer, K. M., Kim, Y., Carver, C. S., & Cannady, R. S. (2017). Effects of caregiving status and changes in depressive symptoms on development of physical morbidity among long-term cancer caregivers. *Health Psychology, 36*, 770–78. doi:10.1037/hea0000528

Stroebe, M. S., & Schut, H. (1999). The dual process model of coping with bereavement: Rationale and description. *Death Studies, 23*, 197–224.

Stroebe, W., Schut, H., & Stroebe, M. S. (2005). Grief work, disclosure and counseling: Do they help the bereaved? *Clinical Psychology Review, 25*(4), 395–414.

Swore-Fletcher, B., Miaskowski, C., Given, B., & Schumacher, K. (2012). The cancer family caregiving experience: An update and expanded conceptual model. *European Journal of Oncology Nursing, 16*, 387–98. doi:10.1016/j.ejon.2011.09.001

Tassinari, K. M. (2017). *End-of life caregiving and meaning reconstruction: Experiences of adult children providing home-based end-of-life care for a parent* (Doctoral dissertation). Retrieved from ProQuest Dissertations & Theses Global (1867767625).

Taylor, S., & Field, D. (2003). *Sociology of health and health care.* Malden, MA: Blackwell.

Waldrop, D. P. (2007). Caregiver grief in terminal illness and bereavement: A mixed-methods study. *Health & Social Work, 32*(3), 197–206.

Waldrop, D. P., & Meeker, M. A. (2011). Crisis in caregiving: When home-based end-of-life care is no longer possible. *Journal of Palliative Care, 27*(2), 117–125. https://doi.org/10.1177/082585971102700207

Ward-Griffin, C., McWilliam, C., & Oudshoorn, A. (2012). Relational experiences of family caregivers providing home-based end-of-life care. *Journal of Family Nursing, 18*(4), 491–516. doi:10.1177/1074840712462134

Worden, J. W. (2009). *Grief counseling and grief therapy* (4th ed.). New York, NY: Springer.

World Health Organization. (2012). Interesting facts about ageing. Retrieved from https://www.who.int/ageing/about/facts/en/index.html

Yee, J. L., & Schulz, R. (2000). Gender differences in psychiatric morbidity among family caregivers: A review and analysis. *Gerontologist, 40*(2), 147–64.

Zarit, S. H., Reever, K. E., & Bach-Peterson, J. (1980). Relatives of the impaired elderly: Correlates of feelings of burden. *Gerontologist, 20*(6), 649–55. https://doi.org/10.1093/geront/20.6.649

Part VII

Coping with Grief and Loss over the Lifespan

Chapter Twenty-One

Counseling Women Who Have Lost Their Mothers

Suzanna Wise and Elisa M. Woodruff

CASE VIGNETTE: CAMILLE

Camille, twenty-four, is a cisgender, heterosexual woman who presents to a university clinic at the behest of her advisor. She is the first generation born in the United States to parents who are both from China, she is an only child, and she is the first in her family to pursue higher education. Camille is a full-time research assistant in a public policy laboratory on the same campus where she is now pursuing a law degree. She and her partner of three years graduated from undergrad two years ago, and they became engaged just before he enlisted in the U.S. Navy and left for basic training. That same summer, Camille's mother was diagnosed with stage three breast cancer during a routine mammogram. With her partner away, Camille moved home to help her father care for her mother. Camille's parents encouraged her to continue pursuing her dream of law school, despite the financial hardship it would create for the whole family. Camille's mother died three months ago at the age of forty-six, just weeks before the first semester began. Now nearing the end of the fall semester, Camille has lost her motivation to pursue her degree and has fallen behind on schoolwork and job responsibilities. Her wedding is planned for the spring, and when the intake counselor asked her how she feels about it, she changed the subject. Specific symptoms noted on her intake forms include exhaustion, social withdrawal, difficulty focusing, and somatization in the form of headaches and body pains. She told the intake counselor she no longer knows who she is or what she wants. Camille has no prior history of mental health treatment or diagnosis.

* * *

This chapter focuses on women whose mothers have died, for which there is ultimately little counseling and psychotherapeutic research, especially for adult losses. Comparatively more has been written about the experience of grievers in childhood and adolescence, given their vulnerability to trauma and potential for interruption of developmental processes. Literature presented here includes longitudinal and reflectively oriented studies on long-lasting effects of a mother's death throughout the lifespan, as well as qualitative data in exploring what grief is like for clients who go through it. Like counseling in general, there is not one true, empirically prescribed path through grief. As we will expand upon later, grief is a complex process, but it is also a necessary one that individuals *grow through*, as illustrated by Clayton (1996): "Grief is a spiritual journey, transformative and profound" (p. 39). Succinctly, Doka (2016) described grief as "the price we pay for love" (p. 4). Ultimately, grief is what *our clients* say it is because it is their process and should be honored as such.

Many of us, including the authors of this chapter, share the experience of losing our mothers. This type of loss requires the often painful reorganization of one's personal worldview, recognition of the psychological and physical spaces where one's mother should be, and the spiritual and emotional spaces where one's mother now is. Parental bereavement is significant, and through this chapter, the authors hope readers will be able to connect with their own past, current, and anticipatory losses and find some virtual companions on their journey.

Lastly, we discuss the unique bonds of mother–daughter relationships, and we represent the work of several bereavement scholars to provide best practices, models, and ideas for counselors who work with clients experiencing losses and grief. For illustration, we present a case study on which to reflect over the course of the chapter and conclude with our suggestions toward interventions in this scenario.

FOUNDATIONS OF GRIEF WORK

Before we delve into the chapter, we should examine the construct of gender when thinking about grief. We choose to decouple *male* from *masculine* and *female* from *feminine* because we do not subscribe to binary notions of gender, nor do we wish to reinforce traditional and historical gender role stereotypes. Grief does not essentialize along gender lines; it particularizes to individual experiences. Humans cannot force an exact way that grief will express itself and still move through the process with authenticity. We assert that feminine, masculine, and nonbinary energies exist in the same being, where there are no true absolutes or stereotypical themes and behaviors by gender. This position is supported by practitioners and researchers, who have evolved in their thinking about the *feminization* of grief, where only tears, evocative expressions of emotion, verbal processing, and gathering together are the "right" ways to move through grief, and that the realm of grief men often find themselves in is somehow ineffectual and stunted if they do not perform the above behaviors (Doka, 2016; Golden, 2014; Martin & Doka, 2011).

Most people experiencing the death or loss of a loved one will persist through grief with the help of friends, family, spiritual communities, other existing support systems, and internal resolve (Corr, Corr, & Doka, 2019; DeSpelder & Strickland, 2005; Neimeyer, Harris, Winokuer, & Thornton, 2011). These individuals may never seek counseling through their grieving process unless well-meaning others encourage it when they see maladaptive behaviors emerge or there is an inability to participate in the activities of daily living for a prolonged and worrisome period. Grievers who do recognize these personal needs for additional support may resist seeking counseling due to a variety of reasons, which may include the societal stigma against asking for professional help, the potential shame of not being able to get through it on their own, or the pressing need to return to a stable sense of normalcy in externally imposed time frames. Still others may not have tangible access to mental health professionals. In families where external help was not the norm, counseling and therapeutic services may be completely uncharted territory. For those relative few who do seek the support of professional counselors, we meet them where they are.

Types of Grief

For additional context, it is important to explore a few of the types of grief clients may experience. There are several others, such as traumatic grief, complicated grief, or abbreviated grief, which may be a subject of interested for further study by the reader. Prior to marriage equality and shifts toward more progressive national, state, and local policies, those in nonheterosexual relationships faced additional challenges in grieving the deaths of spouses, partners, and significant others. During the AIDS crisis, Doka (1989) coined the term *disenfranchised grief*, which reflects the grief we are not allowed by society and our families to express openly. When someone loses a loved one who is not an accepted part of the griever's life, the griever is on her own in her mourning experience. She is not permitted to express her grief without risking argument or abandonment. Clayton (1996) characterized this as "we pay a lonely price for loving outside the lines drawn by our cultures" (p. 31).

In addition to marginalized relationships, disenfranchised grief can also present where the mother was no longer recognized as a contributing member of the family at the time of death or where fracture of the family occurred. Children may not find solace in a collective grief process with their siblings or the surviving parent (Worden, 2018). Each member may be expected to *not* grieve the loss due to the cause or history of the estrangement. Boss (1999) identified a phenomenon she called *ambiguous loss*, grieving someone who was physically present but psychologically and emotionally absent, as in the case of a mother in a coma or late-stage dementia who cannot respond to their daughter's need to communicate and share remaining time together. Conversely, Boss (1999) also included those who were physically absent but emotionally and psychologically present, such as a mother who was imprisoned, deployed, or otherwise removed from daily life. If the mother should die while away, the news of her death may take time to reach loved ones and come as quite a shock when it does.

The final type of loss discussed here is connected to an individual's *anticipatory grief* (Lindemann, 1944) in knowing that death will come but not the exact when or how of it. This type of grief is contended with most often in chronic illness and a prolonged death process. Daughters who expect their mother's death may do some preliminary work in the grieving process and begin reorganizing their new roles and responsibilities in the family (Rastogi & Bhatia, 2016), but even though their mother's death is foreseen, it can still be incredibly painful and feel sudden.

Grief Models and Best Practices

A myriad of grief models exists for those who appreciate the boundaries of patterns, stages, levels, tasks, and checklists. These were developed by mental health practitioners, medical professionals, scholars and researchers in thanatology (the study of death and dying), and others. Perhaps the most well-known is that of Elisabeth Kübler-Ross, a Swiss psychiatrist whose 1969 stage model of denial, anger, bargaining, depression, and acceptance quickly permeated culture. Ultimately, her model was oriented toward experiences of the dying, different from those left behind. So instead, we begin with a process model devised by a female counselor focused on bereaved female clients. We then provide a spectrum model on styles of grieving, and finally, we highlight a longstanding task model. All the models were created with the premise that grief takes as long as it takes, and it travels no prescribed steps, stages, or time.

Despite taking as generalist an approach as we can toward grief, this chapter does focus on maternal bereavement for women. To that end, we provide research supporting the unique relationships between mothers and daughters and the implications of this important loss when the mother dies. The literature represented here includes the work of attachment and object relations theorists, as well as the first grief process model from Clayton (1996).

Mother–Daughter Relationships and Implications of Loss

The affective bonds that exist between mothers and daughters are powerful and transcend time (Bowlby, 1988), geography (O'Connor, 1990), and death (Shmotkin, 1999). Reasons for this strength have been discussed by feminist, psychodynamic, and systems theorists. Object relations theorist Chodorow (1978) pointed out that while young males in binary gender societies must symbolically reject their primary female caretakers in order to socialize with men and transition to adulthood, young females stay attached to their mothers by virtue of needing to replicate that process with women. By never really rejecting their initial object of attachment, women maintain looser emotional and identity boundaries. According to Chodorow (1978), these bonds serve young women by teaching them to be more sensitive to others' needs, but they also perpetuate generational cycles of dependence when they later project their unmet needs onto their own daughters.

Anxiety as a reaction to the loss of primary caretaking figures has been proposed by attachment theory researcher Bowlby (1988) as a reason why connections to primary mothering figures endure into adulthood. While mothers may no longer serve as the primary attachment relationship when daughters become independent, they serve as the ones to which all others are compared. Sometimes this anxiety manifests as chronic dependency, inability to express emotions, chronic low self-esteem, indecisiveness, or other dysfunction, and clinicians may find themselves conceptualizing the causes as "enmeshment, undifferentiation, pattern of covert loyalties, unmourned grief" (Williamson, 1981, p. 441).

Our growing continued dependence on parents has been described as the process of *differentiation* by Bowen (1972). In this process, healthy mother–daughter relationships involve transmission of family boundary patterns, as daughters move toward autonomously enacting those family values in their own lives and with their own families. Williamson (1981) described these processes more violently, calling them "termination of the hierarchical boundary" between generations and describing them as based on "intergenerational intimidation" and a type of "outright revolution" (p. 441). The range of ways to describe these processes demonstrates the multitude of perspectives and experiences clients may have, and clinicians may use this diversity to conceptualize the nature of these relationships both in life and in death. As one such example, Clayton (1996) offers a wide variety of grief vignettes as presented by her clients, and they cover all types of losses under all types of circumstances and with all types of bereavement processes.

Clayton's Phases of Grief

Jean Clayton was a practicing psychotherapist who worked with grief and bereavement with many women over the course of her career. Though she counseled both men and women, she focused her writing about grief on the feminine perspective, explaining her rationale as follows:

> Men have their own struggle, but their personal and social context is different, and their ways of coping are also often different. Men are more likely to replace a lost partner within a year or two and have more social and financial freedom. They are more likely to distract themselves from their pain by over-work or addictive substances. They also tend to receive more support from those around them (usually women) because women have tended to more easily extend nurturing. Sometimes, we do this to outrun our own pain by focusing on the needs of others. Sometimes we do it because it brings us comfort. Sometimes we do it because we care. (p. 5)

Clayton shared her own desires in a grieving time. "What I really needed was someone to sit with me, hold me, be with me, listening, until I had worked through my feelings" (p. 8). Clayton provided a variety of vignettes and interweaved reflections of her own. She proposed a process model in three phases: *not true*, *the great angry sadness*, and *moving on*—not linear steps, but "intertwined" throughout the grieving process (1996, p. 11).

Not True. "Not true is like an anesthetic our body provides to prevent pain from destroying us. It is meant to wear off gradually. It takes a long time to wear off completely" (Clayton, 1996, p. 16). Not true feels like struggling to acknowledge the reality of the loss, feeling "crazy" and disoriented, like the mind is playing tricks while seeking to protect itself from believing the loss really happened. Clients may experience cognitive dissonance, derealization, extrasensory experiences of their loved one, a powerful longing, separation anxiety, and specific reactions associated with the type of loss. They may describe feeling dazed and confused, numb, forgetful, or like on autopilot.

The Great Angry Sadness. This phase is the messiest of the three. Clayton (1996) characterized it as "a long, slow crisis" (p. 38). The client may feel they are getting worse, not better. There may be distinct feelings of aloneness, guilt, neglect, anger at being "robbed, betrayed, violated" (p. 17), and feeling left behind. Despite often conflated terms, Clayton described *loneliness* as a feeling and *isolation* as a place (p. 28). One of her clients illustrated this isolation as if they were in a parallel dimension after the death of a loved one, where they could see and hear everyone living their lives as if nothing had happened while their world had shattered. In this phase, clients may fuel their isolation through avoidance of people, places, and events that can be triggers or catalysts for deep sadness or anger, in a desire to escape the penetrating gazes and clichéd well-wishes of social or family situations.

Adult daughters whose mothers die, especially after a long illness, may feel very little space to grieve this loss among family and friends, because, after all, older adults are *supposed* to die, and clients may receive messages that they should be grateful for their mothers' having lived a long life (Kerr, 1994). At times, clients may feel like their sadness is a burden to others, so they wear a mask to overcompensate in social performance, which can cause internal stress. If the loss was traumatic, clients may be the subject of fascination for others, asked to tell and retell the story of the loss, risking continuing traumatic reactions or retraumatization. Alternatively, clients may fear that healing from the loss will mean forgetting, so they unendingly ruminate about the details of the loss and readily share the story. The great angry sadness can drive risky behavior, further cognitive disturbances, depression, resentment, regret, despair, and sometimes self-harm, especially among marginalized groups (Denckla et al., 2019). Seeking and maintaining routine medical attention is crucial in this phase as clients may experience somatic stress, which can affect the immune system and manifest infection, illness, digestive disruptions, sleep issues, eating problems, headaches, body aches, and more serious stress-related vascular conditions (Kerr, 1994).

Clients are shouldering the burden of grief along with the personal and social expectation of "getting over it," possibly feeling a lack of compassionate validation from others as they go back to work, back to school, back to parenthood, back to relationship, back to self-care, back to "normal," at the same time as they feel a loss of the future, a loss of the hope things will truly be good again, a loss of the ability to even form possibilities.

Move On. This is the phase of re-creation and access to new beginnings. Clayton (1996) offered a distinction between *sorting through* rather than *letting go* of the grief (p. 43) to illustrate how clients can retain aspects of grieving that are transformative and bring change, rather than try to put the past behind them. In this phase, they may begin to make new friends, visit new places, and try new external images of themselves like clothing, hairstyles, and presenting themselves differently. They might be able to explore photo albums again without crushing pain and sadness. Ultimately, they may alter the way they perceive the world, their friendships, intimate relationships, spiritual beliefs, and capabilities in many areas of life. The death or loss of someone close often motivates a reorganization of previously held beliefs about self and others and the formation of a legacy. In maternal bereavement, clients may need to assume a new role in the family or develop a new confidence in their ability to be their best support and resource. This phase is characterized by the return or uncovering of courage and hope, to move forward through the pain of grief into a new future.

Doka's Styles of Grief

Martin and Doka (2011) and Doka (2016) found that we most frequently model the affective and behavioral schema of those whom we grow up around at home and at school, inside the scripted patterns of the society in which we live. Therefore, based on generational templates, it can appear that women grieve a certain way and men grieve a certain way. However, especially in contemporary life, individuals are not as well defined as Clayton (1996) briefly described. Martin and Doka (2011) cite that gender "influences but does not determine" grief styles (p. 70). Researchers in the field of thanatology agree that we have a vast combination of styles of grief within us (Doka, 2016; Golden, 2014; Neimeyer et al., 2011) and that men and women do not grieve all that differently; in fact, there are many shared characteristics. From this evolution in research findings, Martin and Doka (2011) discerned that humans tend to experience grief processes along a spectrum, bookended by two style labels, guided by affect and behavior more than by gender role.

The first style is that of the *intuitive griever*, someone who expresses emotional reactions to loss. They will be more likely to actively feel their feelings, experience palpable waves of grief, feel emotionally exhausted, and cry often. Intuitive grievers may be more likely to process their feelings in the company of others, especially ones connected to their specific loss or similar experience, such as a formal support group, or a group known colloquially as "the dead mothers club" (Green & Rubin, 2014), composed of other maternally bereaved friends who share a unique understanding.

The second style is that of the *instrumental griever*. This process may look more physical, cognitive, and action oriented. This type of griever often falls victim to *affective bias*, the belief that the only true way to process loss and grief is through tears and evocative emotion (Doka, 2016). If an instrumental griever is expected to perform as an intuitive griever when it is unnatural to them, they may feel like they are not "doing grief correctly," and this lack of understanding can create a sense of isolation when they need support and connection. Like Clayton's *not true* phase, these grievers will experience confusion, cognitive disturbances, disorientation, and forgetfulness and may have more difficulty with these until they can regain some sense of personal stability and control.

Worden's Tasks of Mourning

As grief often feels amorphous and unending, many clients may seek to put a framework around their grief and utilize language that might describe what they are going through. One of J. William Worden's long-lasting contributions to the study of bereavement and working with clients suffering a loss lives in his broad four-task model, with a handbook for helping professionals now in its fifth edition (2018). These four steps are (1) to accept the reality of the loss, (2) to process the pain of grief, (3) to adjust to a world without the deceased, and (4) to find an enduring connection with the deceased in the midst of embarking on a new life.

This set of tasks asserts that clients must begin with an awareness that the death or loss has taken place before movement to subsequent tasks will make sense. The activities that ground this task are funeral rites, holding visitations, sitting shiva, burials and cremations, interment, celebrations of remembrance, and time spent with the deceased in a culturally responsive way. In the second task, clients must contend with the messiness of the grief process and face their difficult thoughts, feelings, and behaviors in conjunction with those around them. The third task requires significant internal, external, and spiritual adaptation on the part of the bereaved. It is in this task that the activities of daily living must be attended to, such as the often complicated processes of bill paying, reconciling large debts, locating insurance policies and wills and trusts, sorting through contents of the house, and negotiating among surviving family members who might want mementos and keepsakes. For some families, this process can be a time of comforting nostalgia and remembrance; for others, it is full of contention and difficulty. Worden's fourth task involves adjusting and adapting to a life without the loved one's physical presence. This may involve building daily time to connect to feelings of grief, perhaps creating a physical space dedicated to the deceased or intentionally scheduling time to visit the deceased's grave or interment site. This may also be a time of incorporating the activities, objects, or artistic elements that the deceased loved into the bereaved's life in some way. This period of adjustment and adaptation will be wholly individual to the bereaved. Worden's only anchored task is the first, and he strongly acknowledges that clients will traverse the subsequent three tasks repeatedly, outside a linear fashion, and for an undetermined amount of time.

GRIEF IMPLICATIONS IN IDENTITY DEVELOPMENT

The loss of a mother can propel a daughter into an unintended exploration of her identity and a reassessment of her place in the world, different than any other loss might. The mother–daughter connection, whether the relationship was healthy or toxic, close or distanced, or some mix of those, has a tremendous impact on the client's life trajectory. In a large-scale study on parental bereavement, Umberson (2003) found that a ubiquitous theme for the surviving child(ren) was the impact on the client's identity development, even far into adulthood. Umberson stated that, "A parent's death propels the social and psychological transition from childhood to adulthood. . . . Even adults who did not rely regularly on their parent may experience the feeling of being on their own for the first time" (2003, p. 80).

Janoff-Bulman (1992) as cited in Tedeschi and Calhoun (2004, p. 1) describes these highly stressful loss events as "sets of circumstances that represent significant challenges to the adaptive resources of the individual, and that represent significant challenges to individuals' ways of understanding the world and their place in it." This understanding clients have of the world and their place in it is formed over time with repetition of activities and events, the closeness they form in relationships with others, the safety they establish, and the freedom they feel to explore the world around them. In Edelman's (2014) vignettes, bereaved daughters write about how essential mothers are to the process of growth and development because they represent the presence of a roadmap through life; a companion for, and witness to, major life events and milestones; the go-to phone call with a quick question, funny story, or life crisis for which they need support.

Bowlby and Ainsworth's work in attachment theory (Bretherton, 1992) can give counselors a helpful perspective in discerning the client's bereavement process from an attachment standpoint. A psychologically healthy mother will be more likely to create and maintain a *secure* base for her child(ren), and this may forge a stronger and long-lasting connection between mother and daughter such that the bereaved daughter will experience what scholars call *normal* grief, which is much of what this chapter describes. If mothers are psychologically unhealthy, they may be unable to provide this secure base, and instead their child(ren) may develop an *anxious*, *ambivalent*, or *disorganized* attachment style that will potentially engender a *complicated* grief or bereavement process that is more difficult to process (Connors, 2011).

For those clients whose expectations are particularly strong and who have rigid plans and ideas about the events of their lives, parental bereavement may engender a more significant short-term impact as the individual is faced with rewriting their life plan and removing the daily benefit of the deceased parent. Without intervention, this can be a daunting process for an individual to encounter, and there is potential for lengthier recovery and complicated grief reactions (Kerr, 1994). Tedeschi and Calhoun (2004) described how losses that still seem unbelievable long after they have occurred are challenges to the assumptive world. These clients will require additional work around creating new meaning in their lives and learning to be more flexible and adaptable.

The Bereavement of Adult Children

Reevaluating and restructuring are natural parts of mother–daughter relationships. Fischer (1981) studied shifts that happened in mother–daughter relationships when daughters chose a partner and then became mothers themselves. Respondents in this mixed-method study described a symbolic evaluation that occurred as daughters demonstrated and proved their adulthood skills to their mother, mothers' needs to respect boundaries in daughters' new primary relationship (their partners), and newfound bidirectional respect that resulted from these processes. Following these stages, mother–daughter bonds became more involved.

The work of Shmotkin (1999) underlined the care clinicians must take to see that these restructuring processes continue when mothers die. Shmotkin (1999) tested qualities contributing to intensity of affective bonds in adult children (bond intensity) in whom one or both parents were deceased while independently ranking children's positive or negative perceptions of the relationships (bond evaluation). For both sons and daughters, bond intensity was not lower when parents were deceased, and for daughters, two of three bond intensity factors (perceived closeness in the relationship and influence the relationship had on daughters) was higher for mothers when they were deceased. Shmotkin asserted that parents' "imaginary presence and emotional impact" continue and may even increase when they are gone (1999, p. 478). For some clients, negative coping mechanisms may begin to develop, both due to the need to emotionally regulate and from the absence of elders after whom to model behavior. Shmotkin (1999) concluded that daughters' increase in intensity of relationship with their mothers underlined the need to not see stages and end goals in "grief work" and to instead focus on how relationships might evolve and become restructured beyond death.

In both Umberson's (2003) and Edelman's (2014) studies, many accounts of women after the death of their mother included the realization that a generational buffer between them and their own mortality was now removed, engendering existential questions and deeper explorations of life meaning. When bereaved daughters encountered important milestones, when they achieved goals and overcame challenges, they reported wishing to tell their mothers and then feeling the pain of the loss anew.

Developmental Approaches and Influencing Factors

The identity development process is ever more impactful when mothers die before daughters have grown up. When working with clients, counselors should consider the client's age at the time of the loss and their cognitive and developmental milestones. Counselors may be helpful to surviving parents or caregivers in crafting conversations appropriate for the young client's developmental stage. Counselors should be aware of the role of mothers in young clients' lives and what their relationships were like, to help clients process their now unmet needs and unrealized expectations as they face life without their mother. Helping clients adapt to a relationship with their mother that moves from the practical to the emotional, spiritual, and symbolic will be helpful in maintaining the client's sense of self and remembering their mother in ways that help them move forward (Worden, 2018). Counselors should also be attuned to the nature of the loss, especially as a trauma-informed approach may be the most helpful. No matter how a client's parent died, clients will need considerable support to process their loss, especially if surviving parents or caregivers cannot be emotionally present to provide that support. Clients need the opportunity to grieve. In addition to helping them find the grief style that works for them, this process may include being given clarity of information about the death in a developmentally appropriate way and being encouraged to participate in rituals of remembrance. Worden (2018) calls the above considerations "mediators of mourning" (p. 57) as each will affect the griever in unique ways.

Cait (2006) echoed the idea that continued evolution of mother–daughter relationships was important. For younger clients whose initial identity development may be in more tender stages, this may mean direct work integrating relationships with deceased mothers with a daughter's evolving sense of self, whereas older clients may need to revisit previous developmental stages or see how their own sense of self reconciles with other adult relationships. For both groups, activities allowing exploration of historical information about the deceased and their process of illness and death was reported as being both an instinct upon death and beneficial to processing the loss.

In cases where there is a longer span of time since the death, different interventions may be indicated. When Greene and McGovern (2017) studied adult children whose parents died, they found that dispositional gratitude (a tendency to seek positive in the world) was positively correlated with psychological well-being and posttraumatic growth (Tedeschi & Calhoun, 2004). It was also negatively correlated with depression. Gratitude grew naturally from the experience of the death of these participants' parent (likely due to scarcity heuristics) but could be inhibited by additional traumatic experiences, anxiety, fearfulness, mistrust of others, and resentment. Thus, clinicians may want to encourage clients to engage in activities known to increase gratitude (e.g., gratitude journals, meditation, or spiritual/religious activity), while also working to identify and address inhibiting factors through cognitive or behavioral interventions.

Cultural Factors in Bereavement

Western (and more specifically, American) society has long been said to be death denying, as demonstrated by removing death processes from public view, placing dying people far away from living people, and encouraging fantasy depictions in the media of cartoon and live-action characters coming back to life (Corr, 2015). This can obfuscate the realization that everyone dies and there is no getting out of life alive (Lutovich, 2002), a realization that may, in fact, help us live more meaningful and fulfilling lives. Due to this discomfort with death and dying, most of the grief experience is felt on an individual basis; rarely is it a collective process beyond the funeral service and the initial weeks following the death.

Given the individualistic nature of work in Western society, this death-denying feature of Western culture has similarly influenced how grief is treated in the workplace. The typical Western work setting offers bereavement leave based on the relationship of the bereaved to the person who has died. This allotted paid time off does not generally exceed a few days, at which time the worker is expected to return and resume established levels of productivity (Rastogi & Bhatia, 2016). Paid time off usually only applies to salaried workers, whereas hourly workers are on their own to determine if they can afford to take time off. Undocumented workers with no workplace protections may forfeit their job altogether if they take any time off to mourn their loss.

Religious and spiritual beliefs also strongly factor into the bereavement process and often guide how the client will move through their grief. Clinicians should develop a keen awareness of, and knowledge about, different religious belief systems that were historically, or are currently, important to their clients. There are clear differences between the afterlife beliefs of Christianity, Islam, Judaism, Buddhism, and other Eastern practices that will influence dialogue in counseling. Key tenets of these faith practices may provide some necessary insight into healing as well as provide context into the client's family traditions (Rastogi & Bhatia, 2016). Bereavement may also spark a transformation process in the client's spiritual belief system (Cait, 2004), a process that may not be easily facilitated by clergy but is better aided by the more objective stance of a professional counselor. In Cait's (2004) study of eighteen female college students, *struggle* and *connection* emerged as the key factors in the bereavement process as the students reconciled their grief and their spiritual foundations. Specifically, the participants in the study comprised a diverse illustration of this struggle:

> Of the women interviewed, four women both pushed religion away while simultaneously pulling it towards themselves. Five women attempted to detach themselves from religion and belief in God after the death; two women's religious beliefs were strengthened; five women were never religious before or after the death; one woman's core belief in God remained the same. The final subject started thinking more seriously about God's existence, though she connects this more to her development than to the death of her parent. (Cait, 2004, p. 170)

Both key factors reflected the difficulty in relocating the deceased to a spiritual realm while yearning for a physical connection to them.

Cultural Difference in Mother–Daughter Relationships

Rastogi and Wampler (1999) were critical of how conceptualization of grief recovery might pathologize cultures that were less individualistic in nature, so they studied three cultures (European American, Asian Indian American, and Mexican American) regarding mother–daughter relationships. Later, Rastogi (2002) validated an instrument based on the findings. Three aspects that added strength to mother–daughter relationships in all three cultures were connectedness (not only geographic), interdependence, and trust in the hierarchy of the relationship.

ETHICAL CONSIDERATIONS

Prior to working with daughters who have lost their mothers, clinicians should study the foundational ethical codes for their respective professions. In doing so, attention may be paid to issues of veracity and fidelity, as clients with a history of loss may struggle with issues of attachment (Bowlby, 1988). As with any client presentation, it is also important that clinicians seek knowledge, awareness, and skills and engage in advocacy surrounding issues that will be addressed (Ratts, Singh, Nassar-McMillan, Butler, & McCullough, 2015). Knowledge may include learning about client belief systems, the manner of the mother's death, and any medical, legal, or other social issues impacting grieving daughters. An example of pursuing awareness and skill may include study of the Association for Spiritual, Ethical and Religious Values in Counseling (2009) competencies or similar sources. These documents serve to better understand how client worldviews may impact grief counseling as well as ways for clinicians to avoid cultural encapsulation when discussing values surrounding death, family, and other interrelated topics.

ADVOCACY CONSIDERATIONS

Grieving women may face pressure to conform to culture-bound beliefs of what is "normal" on individual, systemic, and institutional levels, and clinicians must be prepared to advocate as a way to support specific clients and also engage in preventative psychoeducation and political activism to shift societal attitudes. For instance, in the model put forth by Toporek and Daniels (2018) for counseling advocacy, clinicians may work for or with clients in individual, organizational, and public arenas. Counselors advocating with grieving clients in individual arenas may help grieving clients to discuss their experiences with a partner or other family member, but counselors advocating on behalf of clients in public arenas may push to implement statewide curriculums in schools where students learn about grief, or in workplace advocacy to encourage more paid leave for bereavement. Clinicians working with young clients may need to advocate in schools to encourage gentle accommodations in the grief process and to normalize difficult and complex feelings at younger developmental stages. Finally, all clients may find need for additional community resources, connections to complementary or adjunct therapies, referrals to external practitioners, and encouragement toward sustaining spiritual or religious belief systems for clients who participate, and other sources of strength for clients who do not.

COUNSELOR INTERVENTIONS

Our broad responsibilities as counselors include being present to our clients' loss experiences, companioning them in their grief process, and helping them shore up their natural and new support systems. Counselors must be able to discern normal grief, complicated grief, traumatic grief, self-harm risk, and comorbidities with other existing, or potential, diagnoses that would call for greater clinical support and attention. We need to be aware of and recognize losses when we see them in the client's life, as these may be more impactful than the client is aware. As counselors, we also must be cognizant of our own loss experiences and know how they have affected our lives, how we have coped with them, how we have spent our time grieving, and how we have recovered (Worden, 2018).

In a practical sense, using the models previously presented, there are distinct ways clients may be helped through the process of grief. In Clayton's (1996) not true phase, interventions are best focused on being with the griever, giving them time and space to vent and tell stories, empowering their process, and when they are ready, helping them put together the puzzle of what has just occurred in their lives. In the great angry sadness, it may seem daunting for clients to cultivate self-compassion for wherever they are in the process, so counselors can provide this compassion and reminders that the client is where they are meant to be. This phase can also be incredibly creative as clients find outlets for their rage and sadness. Sometimes without realizing it, their grief may fuel poetry, music, journaling, dance, or other artistic expression that helps them process pieces of their grief. Locating a support group while in this phase may help them connect to others who may understand their loss experience, and it can also be beneficial to learn self-care strategies from others who have been through it, especially the first time an anniversaries occur—a loved one's birthday, special holidays, and the "deathiversary." Rituals may be helpful in this phase, especially around the anniversaries, to reestablish traditional practices or create new ones with family, friends, and self. The move on phase may call for counselors to take a more existential or postmodern approach in helping the client develop a new sense of self and find ways to reshape long-lasting attachments to their loved one.

Doka's (2016) intuitive grievers may also turn to creative means to express what they are feeling. Counseling may be helpful for intuitive grievers to explore life changes and transitions as a result of their loss and feelings that may be difficult to process in other ways. Instrumental grievers are more likely to process their difficult feelings by thinking about their loss, by making plans to honor their loved one, and through physical activity, such as building something, destroying something, performing athletic feats, or returning more quickly to work and productivity. Instrumental grievers may not find much benefit in support groups or individual therapy, though cognitive behavioral approaches can offer a helpful structure to the grief process. These grievers may rely on their existing support systems and may also engage in creative pursuits to remember their loved one, which can certainly involve their communities and groups connected with their specific type of loss.

CASE VIGNETTE WRAP-UP: CAMILLE

Camille's case serves to underline several considerations put forth previously in this chapter. Because grief is such an individual process, we choose to address the case by suggesting factors counselors might consider and ways of assessing, with less attention paid to prescription of interventions. For instance, a multiculturally competent counselor will immediately note a constellation of overlapping identities. Camille is an only child, first to pursue higher education, a child of immigrants from a collectivist culture, soon to be a member of a military family, and a cisgender heterosexual woman. Counselors will want to assess how these identities might provide strength but also how they might cause inner conflict—particularly as they relate to acculturation between Chinese and U.S. culture; loyalty to her family of origin and fiancé; and how circumscription, compromise, and cultural roles may play out when it comes to career choices (Gottfredson, 2005).

At the age of twenty-four, Camille has entered adulthood and is contending with the death of her mother, which may force her to revisit earlier developmental processes. Bowen (1972) described that she may be trying to reconcile patterns from her family of origin and what she wants to bring forward as she starts her own family, and Williamson (1981) characterized this task more violently, as a form of symbolic revolution. Fischer (1981) also noted a symbolic change in the mother–daughter relationship when daughters choose a mate and start their own families. Counselors may want to assess how Camille viewed these processes both before her mother's death and now that the death has occurred. It sounds like her desire to pursue both her education and the wedding have changed in intensity or quality, and it may be important to note where the original motivations came from and where they stand now. She may feel that she is doing it in order to honor her mother—not for her own reasons. Due to the anticipatory nature of her mother's death, some of these processes may have begun, but that does not take away from their intensity and impact.

An important piece of assessment will be where Camille is in her grief. It sounds like pressure from her parents to continue with school and the upcoming wedding may be prematurely pushing her into Clayton's (1996) move on phase before she is ready, and her body is revolting in the form of exhaustion, somatic symptoms, and lack of focus. As stated earlier in this chapter, many will not seek grief counseling until significant functional problems present or become too difficult to deny. In Camille's case, her advisor recommended she seek counseling support at a crucial point in her graduate work; thus, she may benefit from structured assistance in processing her great angry sadness before she can effectively begin moving on.

Another way to determine how to proceed will be to assess how Camille processes her grief using Doka's (2016) spectrum model of the instrumental and intuitive grievers. It sounds like the time helping her parents and then being suddenly thrust into school may have put her in a position to be an instrumental griever—prioritizing actions over feelings—but that may not be her natural style. Now that the shock has waned, there may be time to reassess. This may be achieved by asking Camille what kind of activities she is finding herself drawn toward, activities that bring relief versus more distress. Clients many need to push through distress, so the quality of the distress should be discussed as well as what value it serves in her process. Counselors may also ask how Camille has dealt with past losses or other difficulties in her life. As with all assessments, the intent here is not to prescribe a specific path forward but to help create the best conditions to identify patterns, add them to larger schemas along with other data provided, and open authentic and healthy lines of communication with Camille that she can use with her loved ones. Camille may be struggling particularly with Worden's (2018) third and fourth tasks of adapting to a world without her mother, taking significant next steps in her life, and figuring out how to bring her mother along with her in some way. Much care and compassion should be given to Camille during this time as she begins to reorganize her life amid myriad changes. Grief processes are not time bound.

From an advocacy perspective, counselors may be able to help Camille in a few ways. Between school, work, her family responsibilities, and the upcoming wedding, she is pulled in several directions during a time when she may need some space and flexibility. Counselors may help by facilitating conversations with her surviving parent or fiancé to help establish new boun-

daries and manage expectations. She may need assistance in employment and educational arenas, learning how to communicate with human resources personnel, advisers, or other people who are in a place to help with accommodations so she can continue to work toward her goals.

CONCLUSION

In this chapter, we covered a lot of ground in exploring the uniqueness of mother–daughter bonds; described some grief models and best practices; outlined ethical, advocacy, and cultural implications in the grief process; and provided directions for counselor intervention with women whose mother is deceased. We hope we carried forward the idea that while loss is universal, grief is individual. No one's process is going to look exactly like someone else's. We can educate our clients about frameworks they might use to find their way through grief, what their grief "may" look like, and the paths they "might" take, but it is more important that we sit in empathy with them. Grief is muddy. It is unpredictable, incredibly painful, and troubling, but it can also be a meaningful gift. There are a multitude of grief-related resources for clients to find what works for them, healthfully supports them, and connects them with kindred others on their grief journey.

REFERENCES

Association for Spiritual, Ethical and Religious Values in Counseling. (2009). *Spiritual and religious competencies: Competencies for addressing spiritual and religious issues in counseling* (Organizational document)]. Arlington, VA: American Counseling Association.

Boss, P. (1999). *Ambiguous loss: Learning to live with unresolved grief.* Cambridge, MA: Harvard University Press.

Bowen, M. (1972). Toward the differentiation of a self in one's own family. In J. L. Framo (Ed.), *Family interaction: A dialogue between family researchers and family therapists* (pp. 111–73). New York, NY: Springer.

Bowlby, J. (1988). *A secure base: Parent–child attachment and healthy human development.* New York, NY: Basic Books.

Bretherton, I. (1992). The origins of attachment theory: John Bowlby and Mary Ainsworth. *Developmental Psychology, 28*(5), 759–75.

Cait, C. (2004). Spiritual and religious transformation in women who were parentally bereaved as adolescents. *OMEGA, 49*(2), 163–81.

Cait, C. (2006). Identity development and grieving: The evolving processes for parentally bereaved women. *British Journal of Social Work, 38*(2), 322–39. doi:10.1093/bjsw/bcl347

Chodorow, N. (1978). Mothering, object-relations, and the female Oedipal configuration. *Feminist Studies, 4*(1), 137–58. doi:10.2307/3177630

Clayton, J. (1996). *Women in mourning: Stories of grieving women.* Omaha, NE: Centering Corporation.

Connors, M. E. (2011). Attachment theory: A "secure base" for psychotherapy integration. *Journal of Psychotherapy Integration, 21*(3), 348–62.

Corr, C. A. (2015). The death system according to Robert Kastenbaum. *OMEGA, 70*(1), 13–25.

Corr, C. A., Corr, D. M., & Doka, K. J. (2019). *Death and dying, life and living* (8th ed.). Belmont, CA: Wadsworth, Cengage Learning

Denckla, C. A., Ongeri, L., Ouma, L., Singa, B., Maingi, C., Bosire, R., . . . Manduku, V. (2019). Prevalence of parental bereavement among female sex workers (FSW) in Kibra, Kenya. *Journal of Loss and Trauma, 24*(2), 129–42.

DeSpelder, L. A., & Strickland, A. L. (2005). *The last dance: Encountering death and dying* (7th ed.). New York, NY: McGraw-Hill.

Doka, K. J. (Ed.). (1989). *Disenfranchised grief: Recognizing hidden sorrow.* Lexington, MA: Lexington Books.

Doka, K. J. (2016). *Grief is a journey: Finding your path through loss.* New York, NY: Atria Books.

Edelman, H. (2014). *Letters from motherless daughters: Words of courage, grief, and healing.* Boston, MA: Da Capo Press.

Fischer, L. R. (1981). Transitions in the mother–daughter relationship. *Journal of Marriage and the Family, 43*(3), 613–22. doi:10.2307/351762

Golden, T. R. (2014). *The way men heal.* Gaithersburg, MD: G. H. Publishing.

Gottfredson, L. S. (2005). Applying Gottfredson's theory of circumscription and compromise in career guidance and counseling. In S. D. Brown & R. W. Lent (Eds.), *Career development and counseling: Putting theory and research to work* (pp. 71–100). Hoboken, NJ: John Wiley & Sons.

Green, K., & Rubin, C. (Directors). (2014). *The (dead mothers) club* [Video file]. United States of America: Passion River Films. Retrieved from https://www.amazon.com/Dead-Mothers-Club-Rosie-ODonnell/dp/B06ZXSLS2K

Greene, N., & McGovern, K. (2017). Gratitude, psychological well-being, and perceptions of posttraumatic growth in adults who lost a parent in childhood. *Death Studies, 41*(7), 436–46. doi:10.1080/07481187.2017.1296505

Janoff-Bulman, R. (1992). *Shattered assumptions: Towards a new psychology of trauma.* New York, NY: Free Press.

Kerr, R. B. (1994). Meanings adult daughters attach to a parent's death. *Western Journal of Nursing Research, 16*(4), 347–65.

Kübler-Ross, E. (1969). *On death and dying.* New York, NY: Collier Books/Macmillan.

Lindemann, E. (1944). Symptomatology and management of acute grief. *American Journal of Psychiatry, 101*(2), 141–48.

Lutovich, D. (2002). *Nobody's child: How older women say goodbye to their mothers.* New York, NY: Routledge.

Martin, T. L., & Doka, K. J. (2011). The influence of gender and socialization on grieving styles. In. R. A. Neimeyer, D. L. Harris, H. R. Winokuer, & G. F. Thornton (Eds.), *Grief and bereavement in contemporary society: Bridging research and practice* (pp. 69–77). New York, NY: Routledge.

Neimeyer, R. A., Harris, D. L., Winokuer, H. R., & Thornton, G. F. (Eds.). (2011). *Grief and bereavement in contemporary society: Bridging research and practice.* New York, NY: Routledge.

O'Connor, P. (1990). The adult mother/daughter relationship: A uniquely and universally close relationship? *Sociological Review, 38*(2), 293–323. doi:10.1111/j.1467-954x.1990.tb00913.x

Rastogi, M. (2002). The Mother–Adult Daughter Questionnaire (MAD): Developing a culturally sensitive instrument. *Family Journal, 10*(2), 145–55. doi:10.1177/1066480702102004

Rastogi, M., & Bhatia, T. K. (2016). Young adult daughters' experience of maternal loss: Self, relationships, and culture. *Journal of Systemic Therapies, 35*(4), 23–40.

Rastogi, M., & Wampler, K. S. (1999). Adult daughters' perceptions of the mother–daughter relationship: A cross-cultural comparison. *Family Relations, 48*(3), 327–36. doi:10.2307/585643

Ratts, M. J., Singh, A. A., Nassar-McMillan, S., Butler, S. K., & McCullough, J. R. (2015, July 20). *Multicultural and social justice counseling competencies* (Organizational document). Alexandria, VA: American Counseling Association.

Shmotkin, D. (1999). Affective bonds of adult children with living versus deceased parents. *Psychology and Aging, 14*(3), 473–82. doi:10.1037/0882-7974.14.3.473

Tedeschi, R. G., & Calhoun, L. G. (2004). Posttraumatic growth: Conceptual foundations and empirical evidence. *Psychological Inquiry, 15*(1), 1–18.

Toporek, R. L., & Daniels, J. A. (2018). *Advocacy Competencies* (Organizational document). Alexandria, VA: American Counseling Association.

Umberson, D. (2003). *Death of a parent: Transition to a new adult identity*. Cambridge, UK: Cambridge University Press.

Williamson, D. S. (1981). Personal authority via termination of the intergenerational hierarchical boundary: A "new" stage in the family life cycle. *Journal of Marital and Family Therapy, 7*(4), 441–52. doi:10.1111/j.1752-0606.1981.tb01398.x

Worden, J. W. (2018). *Grief counseling and grief therapy: A handbook for the mental health practitioner* (5th ed.). New York, NY: Springer.

Chapter Twenty-Two

Counseling Women Who Have Lost a Partner

Marcela Kepic

CASE VIGNETTE: CYNTHIA

Cynthia is a forty-eight-year-old Asian American female who lost her husband, Danny, approximately six months ago. Danny was on his bike when a young driver under the influence of alcohol struck him. Danny died shortly after being transported to a trauma hospital. Cynthia was left with two children, a fourteen-year-old boy and a sixteen-year-old girl. Cynthia and Danny had been married twenty years and had considered themselves happily married and blessed with the arrival of their two healthy children. Cynthia has no siblings, and her parents live in China, where they returned after having lived in the United States for a number of years. She has only two relatives, both cousins, here in the United States. She is a college graduate and had been employed in a career in finance until her children were born. Their financial situation had allowed her to be a stay-at-home mother since their son was born. She and Danny had traveled frequently and were active in sports, recreational activities, and their community. Danny's survivors include a younger brother and mother; Danny and his brother grew up without a father in the home. Although Danny was brought up in the Christian faith, Cynthia had no religion affiliation. After they got married, they agreed to bring up their children in the Christian faith. The family attended church sporadically, predominantly on the major holidays. Cynthia is a reserved woman, and it surprises her when she breaks down and shares her feelings of grief when a neighbor drops by to bring some fresh produce from her garden.

At the urging of the neighbor, with whom she is closest, she schedules an intake session with a counselor. At their first session, Katja, the counselor, invites Cynthia to share with her what has brought her to counseling. Cynthia shares the basic facts about her loss and then begins to slowly open up further in the safety of Katja's supportive presence. Cynthia states that her husband was an excellent and involved father to their children, which she attributes to Danny having grown up fatherless. Cynthia has maintained a few close friends from college and notes that she has some neighborhood moms with whom she is somewhat close, but that they had been much closer friends when her children were younger. In the weeks immediately following the death of Danny, Cynthia's friends were very supportive. However, six months later, everyone has returned to their routines, and she feels like she is expected to do the same.

Cynthia affirms that she was "there for the children," and she states that she continues to drive them to and from school, after-school activities, Saturday soccer, and track practices. She relates that she is doing the bare minimum in terms of housekeeping tasks, such as cleaning, cooking, and shopping. She repeats several times that her life is "not the same without Danny." She relates that she is missing him more and more as time goes by. She reports that she is suffering from insomnia most nights, has lost fifteen pounds in the last two months, and is crying increasingly often, which she notes her children witness. She states that she has flashbacks of her the last time she saw her husband's face after the accident, just a few minutes after he was declared dead. In addition to behaviors indicating being withdrawn, Cynthia affirms that she feels alone and without support. She states that she needs to return to work as finances are getting very tight, but she has been unable to secure a job yet. At her age and being out of the workforce for fifteen years, she is struggling with trying to put together a résumé.

* * *

Aging and death are not the most popular of topics for many to discuss. In many families, the loss of a loved one is an event that should be "gotten over" as quickly as possible so that everything can return to normal. People may have expectations that shortly after a death they must put away their feelings and avoid any intense emotional expression of their grief. Subsequently, the grief that is experienced after losing someone close is viewed as a pathological state that needs to be addressed by mental health professionals (Johnson, 2004). Even when a person loses a spouse, they may feel that explicit expression of grief or mourning-related behaviors are not "socially acceptable." Almost fourteen million people in the United States are widowed, and women account for approximately eleven million of them (Administration on Aging [AOA], 2010). Due to the rapid increase of our older population and the fact that women are surviving their partners, it is estimated that about seven hundred thousand women become widowed every year (AOA, 2010). Women are less likely than men to remarry; two out of three women remain widowed after losing their partners. In 2010, among adults sixty-five and older, there were seventy-two men to every one hundred women (AOA, 2010). This number changes for ages eighty-five and older, averaging forty-nine men to every one hundred women (AOA, 2010).

Holmes and Rahe (1967) noted widowhood is one of the most stressful life events in adulthood. Such loss may affect women in a variety of unfortunate ways. Widowhood puts individuals at a greater risk for declining health (Johnson, Backlund, Sorlie, & Loveless, 2000; Williams, 2004), depression (Lee & DeMaris, 2007), despair and distress (Onrust & Cuijpers, 2006), alcohol abuse (Harwood, 2005), institutionalization (Elwert & Christakis, 2008), and decreased income (American Association of Retired Persons [AARP], 2012; Gass, 1989). The latter is especially true for women, as their financial security is often connected to the presence of a spouse (Kepic, 2019). Despite the presence of some commonalities, factors such as personal attributes, inner resources, cultural background, values, and societal place will determine exactly how grief is expressed and bereavement experienced.

GRIEF AND BEREAVEMENT

Grief refers to the response or emotional reaction to the death of a loved one (Lemme, 2006). Humphrey (2009) stated that "grief refers to (a) an emotion, generated by the experience of loss and characterized by sorrow and/or distress, and (b) the personal and interpersonal experience of loss" (p. 5). It comes with emotional, physical, cognitive, and behavioral challenges and can be experienced as deep distress, lack of sleep, loss of appetite, and so on (Kübler-Ross, 2009). Bereavement is defined as the period of mourning after the death of a loved one (Stroebe, Hansson, Stroebe, & Schut, 2001). There is no single model or time line for grief that can be applied universally; however, some general phases of grief have been identified (Kübler-Ross, 2009; Stroebe, Stroebe, & Hansson, 1993).

Grief Phases

The first phase typically begins with the death of the loved one and lasts about three to four weeks. This phase is characterized by shock and denial, and a person may feel disoriented, numb, or empty. It's been suggested that these reactions are forms of protection against the pain of the loss. As they subside, they are replaced with periods of crying, fear, and anxiety. While the intensity varies for each individual, the initial phase resembles a crisis state. The bereaved may break down, feel unable to continue living, lose her sense of purpose in life, and experience physical symptoms of panic. After a few weeks, these symptoms typically subside, and this may signal the onset of the second phase of grief, the intermediate phase (Stroebe et al., 1993). In this phase, the bereaved is slowly done with the business details of the death, including processing the will, dealing with insurance companies, and transferring titles. As these responsibilities come to an end, the reality of the death begins to set in, and the bereaved may experience a variety of emotions, such as anger, sadness, guilt, and most importantly loneliness. The bereaved often replays the details of the death and wonders how it might have been prevented (e.g., "What if . . . ," and "If only . . ."). Further, the bereaved tries to make sense of the death and may even search for the deceased. Finally, the survivor may feel the presence of the deceased and even have conversations with him (i.e., visual or auditory hallucinations). Most people who experience hallucinations have lost their loved one unexpectedly. As these behaviors decrease with time, the bereaved experiences increasing periods of peace and quietness and the "emotional roller coaster" grows less intense and less frequent. A sense of hope starts setting in, and the survivor slowly enters the recovery phase, in which her overall functioning starts improving. The majority of people begin to recover within a year of the loss (Bonanno et al., 2002). The recovery phase is the final phase, beginning around the start of the second year (Stroebe et al., 1993), and people slowly return to their preloss functioning. Energy, sleep, and appetite return to normal, and social interactions improve. People may make new friendships and try new or forgotten activities. Despite the fact that functioning is back to normal, mourning might still continue, but with less frequency and intensity. Anniversaries and holidays can be especially difficult for many years after the loss. It is crucial to remember that grieving phases do not necessarily occur in a linear progression and will not all manifest for each person. Phases do not have strict boundaries, but they may rather overlap with each other, and the process may resemble a zig-zag pattern. More importantly, grief phases are proposed as general guidelines, not as a set rigid pattern, and may vary between individuals based on the bereaved person's cultural background.

Grief Tasks

Worden (2009) identified four tasks of grief that can help clinicians understand the needs of the bereaved. The first is the acceptance of the loss. This happens as the bereaved realizes that the loved one is not physically present. The second task is to experience the pain of such a permanent departure. This task is difficult yet unavoidable. The third task requires adjustment to a new environment without the presence of the loved one and learning to depend on oneself. The final task is for the bereaved to reinvest her energy into moving forward. The time it takes each person to complete these tasks can vary significantly, from less than a year to many, many years when grief is complicated (Lucas, Clark, Georgellis, & Diener, 2003; van Baarsen & van Groenou, 2001).

Complicated Grief

Some people may experience more intense, severe, and prolonged grief. Researchers have not reached consensus on the best term to use for these experiences. The *Diagnostic and Statistical Manual of Mental Disorders* (5th ed.) has proposed "persistent complex bereavement disorder" and its conditions for further field studies. Shear (2013) suggested the term *prolonged grief disorder* due to the presence of prolonged, intense, and acute symptoms of grief manifesting in emotions, cognitions, physiology, and behavior of a survivor, affecting their daily functioning. The Inventory of Complicated Grief (Shear, 2015) might be helpful to identify these forms of grief. Approximately 10 percent of bereaved people will experience prolonged or complicated grief (Cicchetti, McArthur, Szirony, & Blum, 2016). Complicated grief may be associated with issues pertaining to unresolved grief. Researchers agree that one of the crucial grief tasks is acceptance (Humphrey, 2009; Kübler-Ross, 2009; Worden, 2009). If unable to achieve acceptance of the loss, necessary transition, adjustment, and moving on are difficult to do, and impaired functioning may result. Worden (2009) also proposed four types of complicated grief. *Delayed grief* is typically put off at the time of the loss and resurfaces much later. This can occur if a person is overwhelmed with responsibilities after the death of a loved one and is unable to find time to grieve. *Masked grief* not only may resurface later but may appear with symptoms that are not typical or easily identifiable as grief symptoms. For example, a widow does not fully recognize the impact of the loss at first, but later she may experience intense physical pain (e.g., chest pain, anxiety attacks) and anger outbursts; therefore, it is difficult to identify such as grieving symptoms. *Chronic grief* is present for a prolonged time, such as many years after the death of a loved one. In these cases, a widow is unable to transition and adapt to a new life without her deceased partner and has a hard time accepting her new identity. *Exaggerated grief* presents with symptoms of common or "uncomplicated" grief that are amplified to severe levels. For instance, anger is presented as rage, sadness evolves into a depressive episode, or loneliness evolves into withdrawal (Worden, 2009).

Disenfranchised Grief

Disenfranchised grief, a term coined by Doka (1989), is another type of grief resembling complicated grief. Such grief is present when a loss of a loved one is not socially recognized, supported, or validated. For instance, death by suicide may come with stigma; therefore, family members will not share with others the nature of this type of death due to fear of judgment. Another example would be when a lesbian loses her partner but had not acknowledged their relationship or experienced a lack of acceptance by her family because of their disapproval. The impact of the loss on the survivor may not be recognized or not supported at all. A woman experiencing stillbirth, miscarriages, or abortions may lack support and understanding because such losses are not typically recognized or socially acknowledged; this topic is explored more fully in chapter 23. Secretive or extramarital relationships often belong to this category as well. The death of a significant other that has not been known to others (i.e., kept in secrecy) for various reasons will affect a surviving partner or lover, but they cannot grieve publicly, share, or acknowledge the impact of the loss on their lives (Humphrey, 2009). Doka (2002) further explained that grief symptoms may not only be intensified but may be governed by resentment, guilt, isolation, and self-condemnation.

Again, the types of grief, grief phases, and grief tasks serve as general guidelines for clinicians and others to understand the experiences of the bereaved, but all professionals need to consider diversity as the driving force behind the expression of grief and bereavement. Moreover, not only diversity will determine how one is experiencing and dealing with the death of a loved one, but also personal characteristics, values, developmental stage, the relationship between the bereaved and the deceased, and finally the type of death will contribute to such unique experiences.

Types of Death

The experience of grief and bereavement is mostly influenced by the cultural background of the surviving person and by the circumstances surrounding the death (Lemme, 2006). The cultural backgrounds and diversity consideration will be discussed later below, but right now we turn our attention to the nature of the death (i.e., surrounding circumstances). Literature stresses the importance of whether a death is anticipated (e.g., a partner diagnosed with a terminal illness) or unanticipated (e.g., a partner dies due to an accident). The nature of the loss will affect the way a surviving woman is experiencing and dealing with the death of her loved one.

Anticipated Death

An anticipated death is also called a natural death and is often the result of terminal illness (e.g., cancer, Alzheimer's disease). Because the loss is expected, women may experience anticipatory grief surrounding the inevitable and expected death of a partner. An anticipated death allows for gradual acceptance of the reality of the loss (Worden, 2009). Surviving women can plan ahead, assist their partners, tie up loose ends, complete unfinished business, and prepare for the death of their partner. In some instances, especially when caretaking has been a great long burden, a surviving partner may experience relief once death occurs (Lemme, 2006). When anticipating death, partners may have more time to discuss how the process will look, and therefore they exercise some control over aspects of death. Despite the fact that there might be a bit more control or predictability, anticipated death will still leave a surviving partner in pain; often, however, their reactions may appear less severe (Huber & Gibson, 1990). Some researchers argue that an unpredictable or accidental partner death may increase the severity of the grief response (Fulton, 1987).

Unanticipated Death

Unexpected death or accidental death happens suddenly with no time for anticipation, and its arrival comes as shocking news. Due to its unexpectedness, grief reactions tend to be more intense and severe (Fulton, 1987). The loss may be perceived as traumatizing to a surviving spouse. For example, if a wife wakes up to find that her partner has died in their bed in the night, she may be traumatized by the event and experience severe grief symptoms. The loss of loved ones to such incidents as random violence, natural disasters, and accidents can leave survivors frightened and terrified due to the unpredictable nature of the loss. When an unexpected death occurs, traumatized surviving partners may fear that the event could happen again at any time; therefore, the road to recovery from such a grief experience might be challenging and complex.

BEREAVEMENT AS A RISK FACTOR

Research has thoroughly documented the adverse health effects of grief. When a partner is lost, grief and bereavement have been associated with a decline in well-being (Hagedoorn et al., 2006; Wilcox et al., 2003). Widows tend to experience greater declines in physical health, mental health, and social functioning (Wilcox et al., 2003; Williams, 2004). Further, grief contributes to depression (Lee & DeMaris, 2007), alcohol abuse (Harwood, 2005), and decreased income (AARP, 2012; Gass, 1989). Moreover, the stress of loss raises the risk of infectious disease due to the compromised immunosuppressive response of the body (Lemme, 2006). Prolonged and intense grief increases the risk of accidental injuries, depression, and suicide. Grief may have negative effects on the physical, mental, and psychological well-being of a surviving partner. However, as noted, grief responses can vary greatly between women, and some are much more able to exhibit resilience than others.

RESILIENCE IN LOSS

Some widows may experience less intense symptoms and for a shorter period of time. It is estimated that more than 50 percent of survivors exhibit *resilience* (Bonanno, 2009); this refers to the ability to maintain relatively stable and healthy levels of psychological and physical functioning during highly disruptive life events (Bonanno, 2009). Bonano and Diminich (2013) proposed two types of resilience, emergent resilience and minimal-impact resilience. Emergent resilience can be understood as the gradual emergence of favorable adjustment after long-term negative life circumstances, such as civil war, poverty, and natural disasters (Bonanno & Diminich, 2013). Minimal-impact resilience is referred to as the favorable adjustment after isolated, acute, stressful life events, such as trauma or loss of a loved one. In the latter, Bonanno and Diminich (2013) reported that most research on life adjustment concludes that minimal-impact resilient trajectory is the most common outcome observed following a highly distressing and demanding event, including the loss of a significant other.

When considering predictors of favorable adjustment, or minimal-impact resilience outcomes, there is not one specific single predictor involved. Because of the diversity of those individuals who exhibit the minimal-impact trajectory, researchers conclude that there are multiple predictors (Bonanno & Diminich, 2013). Multiple independent predictors (e.g., socioeconomic status, social support, personality) contribute to favorable outcomes in small percentages (Bonanno, Pat-Horenczyk, & Noll, 2011), but each predictor still might be modified by another factor (e.g., gender, age, race). Bonanno (2009) asserted that one of the important predictors of resilience is the personality trait of hardiness with the following dimensions: being committed to finding purpose and meaning in life, believing that one has some control over life circumstances, and the belief that a person can grow after both positive and negative life circumstances. Women with traits and beliefs such as these tend to adjust favorably to their losses with time. Such findings may indicate that women in postloss and grief counseling might benefit from exploring and strengthening their sense of purpose and meaning in life, finding ways to gain control in some aspects of life, and exploring ways they might find postloss growth.

Another crucial and consistent predictor of resilience following an unexpected acute life event is gender. Gender influences resilience, according to research, because women experience greater objective exposure to trauma than men (Kimerling, Mack, & Alvarez, 2009). These experiences and subjective perception of imminent threats place women at greater risk than men and negatively affect resilience. This is important for clinicians to keep in mind when working with women who have experienced loss. Despite the fact that most people show minimal-impact resilience after losing a partner, women's subjective experience of this type of loss may significantly put them at greater risk for maladaptive adjustment after trauma. Clinicians need to consider each client's unique needs and experiences as they choose interventions to address postloss circumstances.

TRANSITIONING FROM WIDOWHOOD TO SINGLE LIFE

Adjustment to widowhood might be a long and complex process, and the development of a new identity is one of the major roles in the bereavement process (Neimeyer, 2005). After the initial phase of grief, a widow might find herself isolated, often confused about her new status, but still maintaining the *I* of "I am okay" in order to care for children or others. The task of coming to terms with the death of her partner typically presents itself after the initial bereavement phase and before she is able to begin to make meaning of the loss and invest in the construction of her new identity (Haase & Johnston, 2012). Meaning making, or making sense of one's life, is a fundamental human motivation (Frankl, 1959). People imbue life events and circumstances with meaning in order to understand themselves and life, to find purpose, and to establish goals and expectations for the future. As a couple grows into a shared identity, partners form meaning through a concrete vision for their relationship, with dreams and goals for the future. Loss of a significant other abruptly disrupts these goals, purpose, and meaning. Widowed women face a great challenge of making meaning of such loss, finding new purpose in life, and forming a new identity without her partner. The grief process and identity-formation process are interconnected and do not follow any set time line or predictable trajectory due to the individual shape of each woman's bereavement journey. It is probably more understandable that younger widows may have a harder time in their bereavement, especially if the death of the partner was unexpected and inconsistent with their chronological age or developmental stage. Younger widows are typically faced with significant identity shifts that happen in a highly compressed amount of time; they transition from single to married, to widowed, and back to single. Once loss occurs and widowed women slowly come to terms with the death of their partners, they begin the process of relearning the self, the world, and their place in it (Neimeyer, 2005). Some younger widows are more easily able to cope with loss and embrace the emergence of a new identity (Haase and Johnston, 2012); others may experience greater struggles as they try to untangle their own individual identity from the shared identity they had with their partner. There was a time when widowhood stripped away a woman's sense of identity, as they lost the role of wife or partner. Some felt that once their partner died, the major component of their identity had died as well. Transitioning to a newly "single" identity can be difficult, although many do aspire to accept their new reality, being able to form new relationships, begin new careers, and find a way to make a better life for themselves or make a difference in the world. Creating meaning is an important component of moving on, and counselors may integrate meaning-making activities into their work with widows. Examples of appropriate interventions include expressive activities such as journaling, writing letters (some to be sent and some to be kept private), and creating an online blog. The use of the expressive arts, such as poetry, visual art, photography, and music therapy, is also a recommended intervention. Loss and grief can be experienced at multiple levels of awareness, and the use of the arts allows for the expression of feelings and making of meaning at levels that talk therapy might not allow. Haase and Johnston (2012) noted that some widows were able to reconstruct meaning through the reconfiguration of the symbols that represented the couple (e.g., rings, possessions, special memories, gifts, etc.). Another helpful intervention is the encouragement of social interactions and connections, whether face-to-face or via technology, that will help your client remain connected to the present rather than feeling stuck in the past. Relationships are a source of meaning, and it can be healing for clients to connect with those who knew her as part of a couple as well as to create new relationships with individuals who will know her as she is now.

Those who have persisted and found a way to cope with their loss often feel a sense of accomplishment in surviving the terrible pain posed by the death of a loved one (Lemme, 2006). Many women come out of adverse experiences, such as being widowed, stronger and more prepared to overcome other challenges in life (Bonanno, 2009). Many women grieve alone, others seek social support, and some seek professional support. There is no single "right" strategy for helping women respond to such a significant loss, as everyone's experience of loss is unique. However, providing interventions that help them focus on finding meaning and moving forward are supported.

PRACTICAL CONSIDERATIONS

In recent years, there has been a shift away from a staunch belief that grief follows an ordered pattern of stages, such as that of Kübler-Ross (2009), to a dual model of grief processing, that of Stroebe (2005). There is no evidence-based support for the construct of an orderly stage model, and the model has been found to be inadequate to describe the grieving process for all individuals (Silverman, 2004). Postmodernists argue that there are many ways to grieve, and the way one grieves is determined by a variety of factors, such as family relationships and support, culture and values, the circumstances surrounding the death. The dual process model of grief (Stroebe, 2005) conceives of grief as a dynamic process that vacillates between a focus on the loss (i.e., loss orientation) and a focus on avoiding the loss (i.e., restoration orientation). A loss orientation refers to a process of confronting the loss and experiencing the associated pain, such as a widow being preoccupied with missing and longing for her partner. The restoration orientation typically involves the confrontation of daily struggles and the necessary adjustment to changes associated with the loss, such as a widow taking on household tasks that have now fallen on her shoulders with the loss of her partner. It is normal for the bereaved to vacillate between these two poles. However, if the pattern of oscillation generates distress, the clinician may need to help the client identify healthy ways of coping with the distress and support the client in the process of moving forward (Stroebe 2005; Stroebe et al., 2001).

Also, in addition to necessary knowledge and counseling skills (i.e., intellectual competence) (Pope & Vasquez, 2007), clinicians need to be aware of their own emotional strengths and weaknesses related to the provision of grief counseling (i.e., emotional competence) (Pope & Vasquez, 2007). Clinicians must be able to withstand emotional stress arising from intense grief work with clients and competently handle challenging emotions in order to avoid potential compromises in their therapeutic performance. Considering the unique way grief manifests in every individual, clinicians might consider starting in the role of "witness" and observe as their clients share their stories, pain, and challenges. It is imperative that clinicians take a back seat and consider the client as the expert (Humphrey, 2009).

Due to societal messages promoting quick recovery from loss and the reaching of closure, some clients might feel guilty when experiencing grief, especially when it continues for what they feel is longer than it should. Clinicians should normalize their clients' experiences, acknowledge the extent of the loss, and assist in connecting to their feelings. Grief counseling strategies should be process focused and *not* stage focused. Clinicians should support women in their need to grieve in their own way, as opposed to prescribing something that might feel unnatural or forced (Doka, 2002). If needed, provide psychoeducation to gently expand a client's grieving repertoire. Encouraging clients to recognize their own strengths and ways they have overcome difficult situations in the past is recommended. For many, trying to envision days ahead without their partner can be frightening. Clinicians can help clients prepare for the future by inviting them to create a postloss story. As they create their story, they will need to face the disruption of their prior plans and expectations and to revise these in a supportive setting. Therapeutic writing (e.g., acquired wisdom letter, vision plan, new roles, and a decision-making practice sheet) is a frequently integrated component grief work.

BEST PRACTICES

Grief can affect quality of life and potentially generate emotional, cognitive, physical, and behavioral symptoms. Clinicians should always bear in mind the role that cultural identity plays in the ways loss is experienced and bereavement expressed. Below are important guidelines and strategies to implement when working with bereaved females:

1. Be knowledgeable about the ways the type of death may influence the bereavement process. Be familiar with the common tasks associated with grief.
2. Assess for complicated grief, trauma, and symptoms of PTSD. Assess for suicidality, especially when women experience intense grief and depression. When a client communicates feelings of hopelessness, helplessness, and loss of meaning in life, assess.
3. Provide validation, support, and psychoeducation. It is imperative to normalize clients' experiences and feelings of ups and downs, which can be described as roller-coaster-like feelings. Use the terms *common* and *uncommon grief* rather than *normal* or *abnormal grief* when providing psychoeducation on bereavement. Describe the grieving process as *fluid*, oscillating *back and forth*, or *up and down* as opposed to having a linear progression.
4. Invite the client to share her beliefs associated with death, and encourage her to share related rituals.
5. Encourage your clients to tell their stories. Invite them to share memories, both the joyful and the painful, and the ways these have shaped her life and the lives of others.
6. Encourage the writing down of memories (e.g., letter writing), and then process feelings associated with them in session. Allow for the expression of unfinished business and questions that went unanswered before death, especially if the death happened unexpectedly.
7. Encourage your client to sit with negative feelings and tough emotional pain and be present with them in that moment.
8. Incorporate creative arts in expressing thoughts and feelings.
9. Encourage your client to create memorials of some sort for her deceased partner. Explore the possible reconfiguration of symbols pertaining to her deceased partner and the symbols of her "couple" identity.
10. Encourage her to envision her new identity and how she would like this to take shape. Discuss with her what such transition might look like.
11. Encourage the reestablishment or creation of social connections.
12. Provide resources and connect her with appropriate support groups.

13. Pay attention to transference issues, especially when discussing the end of the therapeutic relationship with her. Such endings might bring up sensitive material expressed through heightened intensity of emotions; therefore, work through these themes with your client.
14. Watch out for countertransference that can arise around some topics of death. Your own biases associated with end-of-life issues and death may surface. It is imperative to honestly acknowledge personal issues through participation in supervision or in your own counseling in order to be fully present for your client.
15. Acknowledge the role of resilience and previously obtained coping mechanisms. These may contribute to her adjustment to daily challenges and the transition to her new roles and identity.
16. Always consider diversity factors and intersectionality affecting grief and expression of grief when working with bereaved women.

CULTURAL CONSIDERATIONS

Culture, race, ethnicity, and developmental stage all play a role in the expression of grief. Some cultures experience grief somatically while others might be more externally expressive of their feelings. Some individuals will disconnect and refrain from talking about the deceased to conform to cultural beliefs; some cultural beliefs propose that contact with a dead person is polluting (e.g., the Hopi of Arizona). Some clients may never ask "Why did this happen?" because their culture accepts that death is a normal part of life. In some cultures, such as the Lakota Sioux, mourners are encouraged to be on their best behavior, be role models, and avoid anger, jealousy, and conflict. In other cultures, mourners create altars in their homes and practice rituals that encourage contact with the deceased and the maintenance of ties. Placing food at the altar of a dead relative is a normal practice in some cultures, whereas others might view it as a form of denial or refusal to face reality (Lemme, 2006).

Besides racial and cultural influences on how we grieve, religion and spirituality are often cited as means of coping with loss. In times of grief, many people turn to religious practices as a resource and support in finding meaning in the time of crisis when purpose and meaning may evaporate (Pargament & Abu Raiya, 2007). Not only do belief systems provide support, active engagement with their religious community can offer widows emotional and instrumental support. While counselors should not "prescribe" religion for clients, they can validate the positive benefits that their clients find in their faith practices. Research supports the positive effects of religious coping on mental, physical, and spiritual well-being. For example, Pargament and Abu Raiya (2007) found that a secure relationship with God, spiritual connectedness with others, and a belief that there is a greater meaning in loss was linked with less depression, less anxiety, and greater postloss growth. For some individuals, attachment to God is an important construct in the experience of making meaning following the loss of a significant other (Kelley & Chan, 2012). Further, positive religious coping, and meaning making had significant direct and indirect positive effects on grief and post-loss growth (Kelley & Chan, 2012). When working with women who have lost a partner, it can be helpful to explore their spiritual and religious beliefs and, if relevant, to include these in treatment planning. However, clinicians should be sensitive to clients' views and respect their preferences and presence or absence of beliefs.

Despite some federal legislation in place (e.g., the Fair Housing Act, the Civil Rights Act, the Age Discrimination in Employment Act, the Americans with Disability Act), discrimination and oppression continue to occur. Many minorities experience microaggressions on a daily basis; thus it is not surprising that some individuals will do what they can to avoid exposing themselves to potential discriminatory practices. When loss happens, minority widowed women (e.g., lesbians, transgender, bisexual, disabled, older women) are at greater risk for lack of support, lack of acknowledgment, and isolation when facing bereavement. The practitioner's responsibility is not only to counsel effectively but also to empower such individuals, give them voice, help them act on their behalf, and join them in daily advocacy at any possible level.

ETHICAL CONSIDERATIONS

Death and dying are often difficult topics to address, and there are strong cultural expectations related to how they are approached. Clinicians who provide bereavement counseling must be knowledgeable about best practices when counseling bereaved women. First, clinicians are aware of their own views and beliefs, assumptions and practices, surrounding death. They do not impose their own values and practices on their clients. Second, they do not practice out of their scope of expertise. They should seek training and supervision when working with widows and are encouraged to receive additional training in grief and trauma work to be able to meet the needs of clients who have lost a partner through an unexpected and traumatic manner. Next, considering diversity, clinician approach every client with cultural humbleness, understanding that each woman may experience the loss of a loved one differently; therefore, avoiding stereotyping and prejudice. Clinicians must emphasize the limits to confidentiality, such as self-harm. Some women, especially in the early weeks of bereavement, may lose their sense of meaning or purpose in life and, potentially, express suicidal thoughts. Practitioners should be competent in crisis work and risk and suicide assessment. Clinicians must ensure the safety of their suicidal clients even though it means breaking confidentiality. Lastly, oftentimes, family want to be involved in the bereavement counseling process. Clinicians honor confidentiality and attend closely to their client, the widow, to work out family involvement that is ethical and professional, always keeping advocacy for the client in the forefront of their work.

ADVOCACY OPPORTUNITIES

At a local level, clinicians might share information through in-service trainings or presentations at senior citizen facilities, municipalities, wellness centers, hospitals, and various support groups. There is a good deal of misinformation about loss and grief disseminated by the media that is accompanied by outdated research. Clinicians should keep themselves up to date with current developments in loss and grief issues in order to provide the best care and education for their clients, communities, and the larger society.

Some helping disciplines have developed ethical guidelines related to death as well as grief and death competencies, such as thanatology (i.e., the science of death and losses associated with death) and the Association for Death Education and Counseling (ADEC). Professional counselors have begun the task of developing counseling-based grief competencies. The American Counseling Association's Grief Counseling Interest Network, in collaboration with the Association for Adult Development and Aging, created a task force, the Grief Counseling Competencies Task Force (GCCTF), which is developing such a document. The following are the nationwide resources that focus on loss and grief work:

Mental Health America—Coping with Loss: https://www.mentalhealthamerica.net/conditions/coping-loss-bereavement-and-grief

Family Caregiver Alliance: https://www.caregiver.org/grief-and-loss

Adversity 2 Advocacy (advocacy resource center for grief and loss): http://a2aalliance.org/arc/griefloss/

Resources for a surviving parent and children: https://www.aap.org/en-us/advocacy-and-policy/aap-health-initiatives/Children-and-Disasters/Documents/After-a-Loved-One-Dies-English.pdf

National Center for Victims of Crime: https://victimsofcrime.org/help-for-crime-victims/get-help-bulletins-for-crime-victims/grief-coping-with-the-death-of-a-loved-one

CASE VIGNETTE WRAP-UP: CYNTHIA

Cynthia's counselor, Katja, is seeing her for the third time. In prior sessions, Katja gathered history, administered the Cross-Cutting Level I and Level II assessments (e.g., depression, anxiety, and PTSD subscale), and did a risk assessment and suicidality assessment. Katja also left plenty of room for Cynthia to talk and share her struggles. Arriving to her third session several minutes late, Cynthia sits down and tears begin streaming down her face. Today, Katja plans to administer the Inventory of Complicated Grief (ICG); however, seeing Cynthia crying, she puts the assessment on hold and works with her in the present moment. She allows Cynthia to cry, sitting quietly while Cynthia tries to stop her crying and wipe the tears. They both sit in silence for some time. When crying becomes less intense and Cynthia is able to breathe more calmly, Katja asks, "If your tears could talk, what would they say?" Cynthia takes a deep breath and through a few remaining tears says, "They would say that . . . that . . . I miss him so much . . . miss his presence, his touch, his laugh. . . . It's painful, . . . it hurts." After a few more moments of silence, she continues, "I don't know who I am anymore. It's like I'm lost . . . lost in the thick dark woods. . . everywhere around me are bushes with thorns that stab me when I stretch my arms in front of me. Complete darkness . . . pain. I don't know which way to go. . . . I'm worried that I will lose my kids."

Katja waits a bit, and when Cynthia has nothing to add, Katja responds, "Your tears tell me that you feel pain, you feel abandoned, and you feel lost with no sense of direction. It must be extremely tough." Cynthia nods with her eyes still glued to the floor, wiping away her last few tears. Katja gently says, "Feeling lost, pain, and darkness . . . and you still dropped your kids at school and made your way here." Cynthia looks up and briefly smiles, "Yeah . . . I did and I need to pick them up and feed them." The counselor continues, "So what does that say about you?"

Interventions: Strengths-Based Approach

Katja, after sitting with Cynthia in silence and acknowledging her pain, validates her feelings of being lost, in pain, and in the dark. Katja sought to find evidence of Cynthia's strengths even though she is in such a dark place. Slowly, Katja continues to acknowledge the heaviness of Cynthia's situation, and at the same time she explores her strengths and coping mechanisms she might have used in previous tough moments in life. Cynthia shares that when Danny's mother was visiting, she would go to church frequently and was quick in making new friends. Cynthia got to know these friends because many times she accompanied her mother-in-law to church. Katja notes that Cynthia might use these resources in her daily struggles. Cynthia agrees to make the time to go to church and speak with some of her old friends there. Katja also revisits the feelings of abandonment, and she provides some normalization for Cynthia's situation. She gently explains that being married for twenty years, having a family, making future plans, and, most importantly, having a partner with whom she shared the ups and downs of life, and then suddenly having that person taken, certainly throws your life upside down. Katja assures Cynthia that it is common to feel lost, to feel alone and abandoned, or to feel like there is no way out. At times, such feelings might be stronger; at times, they will be weaker. It is common to feel shifts in the intensity of your feelings. There is no right or wrong way to feel them. It is only your way to experience them.

The counselor gives Cynthia some space to comment and to express her thoughts and feelings. Before Katja focuses on Cynthia's statement, "I don't know who I am anymore," she wants to assess risk factors for suicidality. Cynthia denies any thoughts or plans for hurting herself. Katja also explores other resources for Cynthia to use during the week when she is feeling down (e.g., calling a friend or her mother-in-law or the pastor). After completing the ICG assessment, she provides referrals for a grief support group for widows and hotline numbers in case Cynthia feels that she needs to reach out for additional support. Before they conclude the session, they both agree on the tentative treatment plan for the next few weeks, and Cynthia expresses her openness to incorporating some arts and writing in their work together. Her first home assignment is to write down all the things that her husband meant to her. Cynthia would like to focus on the following goals:

1. *Improve daily functioning*
    a. *Stabilize her mood by decreasing her depressive symptoms and anxiety*
    b. *Expand existing circle of support*
    c. *Engage in utilization of resources*
2. *Make meaning out of the loss*
    a. *Coming to terms with the death of her partner*
    b. *Exploring and defining new perspective on the loss experience*
3. *Improve sense of self—find her new identity*
    a. *Reconstruct her self-perceptions*
    b. *Identify her new purpose*

Brief Conceptualization

Cynthia is a forty-eight-year-old Asian American widowed stay-at-home mother who lost her husband six months ago. Her husband died due to fatal injuries after being struck on his bike by a drunk driver. Cynthia is left with two teenage children and is experiencing great difficulties with moving on. She cries a lot, isolates, has difficulty sleeping, and has lost fifteen pounds in the last two months. She feels abandoned, lost, anxious, and depressed. She expressed that she does not know who she is anymore. She has minimal social support. Her parents are in China, and her mother-in-law lives a thousand miles away. She denies suicidal and homicidal ideation, and she expresses the need to be there for her children. Other potential strengths include that Cynthia is still caring well for her children and household, she might have some connections to her church, she has attempted to look for a job, and she is aware of her responsibilities for her children.

Considering her developmental stage, she is in middle age and the generativity stage of her psychosocial development. In order to experience or regain generativity, she needs to feel she makes an impact and can give and share with children and her community. Due to the loss of her husband, who was a significant component of her identity as a partner and wife, all of the tasks associated with these identities and her developmental stage have been challenged. Her loss of identity and loss of vision for her present and future life are in the forefront of her inner struggles. Further, her career is affected as well. Without her husband, she cannot help with clients she was assisting. Cynthia was a stay-at-home mom, but now with no husband and financial difficulties, she needs to find a job; she faces a significant challenge because she has been out of the job market for the past fifteen years. Although she is facing significant challenges, she does exhibit strengths and resources that can be utilized to help her regain stability, a sense of self, and a transformed meaning for her life.

Final Wrap-Up

Working with Cynthia might present some challenges due to the tough circumstances she is presently experiencing. She exhibits healthy development and enjoyed a balanced life before the loss; therefore, she is likely to overcome these challenges with some professional support. Moreover, recognizing her strengths and utilizing present resources and expanding her resources, she might find herself more stable in the near future. Important areas for clinical consideration include Cynthia's cultural background, her developmental stage, and the roles she had, the roles she still has, and others that she will develop. So long as Cynthia stays motivated, she should be able to make progress, especially if she is allowed to move at her own pace within a supportive and strengths-based counseling environment.

QUESTIONS FOR REFLECTION

1. What are some of your own perceptions and feelings about death? How might these feelings affect your work with a client like Cynthia?
2. What are some other important issues to explore with Cynthia?
3. What strengths do you see in Cynthia, and what strengths do you feel are essential to coping with the loss of a partner?
4. What are some interventions that you would use to help a client such as Cynthia reconstruct her self-perception and find new meaning?
5. What might be some potential challenges in her grief progress?
6. What are some diversity issues that you feel you would need to be sensitive to, accommodate, or address with clients who are different from you?
7. What are some advocacy components that you would engage in when counseling clients like Cynthia?

REFERENCES

Administration on Aging. (2010). *A profile of older adults: 2010*. Retrieved from http://www.aoa.gov/AoARoot/Aging_Statistics/Profile/2010/docs/2010profile.pdf

American Association of Retired Persons. (2012). *Source of income of older Americans*. Retrieved from http://www.aarp.org/content/dam/aarp/research/public_policy_ institute/econ_sec/2013/sources-of-income-for-older-americans-2012-fs-AARP-ppi-econ-sec.pdf

Bonanno, G. A. (2009). *The other side of sadness: What the new science of bereavement tells us about life after loss*. New York, NY: Basic Books.

Bonanno, G. A., & Diminich, E. D. (2013). Annual research review: Positive adjustment to adversity—trajectories of minimal-impact resilience and emergent resilience. *Journal of Child Psychology and Psychiatry, 54*(4), 378–401.

Bonanno, G. A., Pat-Horenczyk, R., & Noll, J. (2011). Coping flexibility and trauma: The perceived ability to cope with trauma (PACT) scale. *Psychological Trauma: Theory, Research, Practice, and Policy, 3*, 117–29.

Bonanno, G., Wortman, C., Lehman, D., Tweed, R., Haring, M., Sonnega, J., . . . Nesse, R. M. (2002). Resilience to loss and chronic grief: A prospective study from preloss to 18-months postloss. *Journal of Personality and Social Psychology, 83*, 1150–64.

Cicchetti, R., McArthur, L., Szirony, G. M., & Blum, C. (2016). Perceived competency in grief counseling: Implications for counselor education. *Journal of Social, Behavioral, and Health Science, 10*(1), 3–17.

Doka, K. (1989). *Disenfranchised grief: Recognizing hidden sorrow*. Lexington, MA: Lexington.

Doka, K. J. (2002). Disenfranchised grief: New directions, challenges, and strategies for practice. Champaign, IL: Research Press.

Elwert, F., & Christakis, N. A. (2008). The effect of widowhood on mortality by the causes of death of both spouses. *American Journal of Public Health, 98*(11), 2092–98.

Frankl, V. (1959). Man's search for meaning. NY: Simon & Schuster.

Fulton, R. (1987). Death, grief, and social recuperation. *Omega: Journal of Death and Dying, 1*, 23–28.

Gass, K. A. (1989). Appraisal, coping, and resources: Markers associated with the health of aged widows and widower. In D. A. Lund (Ed.), *Older bereaved spouses: Research with practical applications. Series in death education, aging, and health care* (pp. 79–94). Washington, DC: Hemisphere.

Haase, T. J., & Johnston, N. (2012). Making meaning out of loss: A story and study of young widowhood. *Journal of Creativity in Mental Health, 7*(3), 204–21.

Hagedoorn, M., Van Yperen, N. W., Coyne, J. C., van Jaarsveld, C. H., Ranchor, A. V., van Sonderen, E., & Sanderman, R. (2006). Does marriage protect older people from distress? The role of equity and recency of bereavement. *Psychology and Aging, 21*(3), 611.

Harwood, D. (2005). Grief in old age. *Reviews in Clinical Gerontology, 15*, 281–87.

Holmes, T. H., & Rahe, R. H. (1967). The social readjustment rating scale. *Journal of Psychosomatic Research, 11*, 213–18.

Huber, R., & Gibson, J. W. (1990). New evidence for anticipated grief. *Hospice Journal, 6*(1), 49–67.

Humphrey, K. M. (2009). *Counseling strategies for loss and grief.* Alexandria, VA: American Counseling Association.

Johnson, K. (2004). Grief in North America, a death-denying society. *International Journal of Palliative Nursing, 10*(9), 435–435.

Johnson, N. J., Backlund, E., Sorlie, P. D., & Loveless, C. A. (2000). Marital status and mortality: The National Longitudinal Mortality Study. *Annals of Epidemiology, 10*, 224–38.

Kelley, M. M., & Chan, K. T. (2012). Assessing the role of attachment to god, meaning, and religious coping as mediators in the grief experience. *Death Studies, 36*(3), 199–227.

Kepic, M. (2019). Life satisfaction after spousal loss: The potential influence of age, gender, and leisure. *Adultspan Journal, 18*, p. 85–98.

Kimerling, R., Mack, K. P., & Alvarez, J. (2009). Women and disasters. In F. H. Neria, Y. Galea, & S. Norris (Eds.), *Mental health and disasters* (pp. 203–17). New York, NY: Cambridge University Press.

Kübler-Ross, E. (2009). *On death and dying: What the dying have to teach doctors, nurses, clergy and their own families.* New York, NY: Routledge.

Lee, G. R., & DeMaris, A. (2007). Widowhood, gender, and depression. *Research on Aging, 29*, 66–72.

Lemme, B. H. (2006). *Development in adulthood.* Needham Heights, MA: Allyn and Bacon.

Lucas, R., Clark, A., Georgellis, Y., & Diener, E. (2003). Reexamining adaptation and the set point model of happiness: Reactions to changes in marital status. *Journal of Personality and Social Psychology, 84*, 527–39.

Neimeyer, R. A. (2005). Widowhood, grief, and the quest for meaning: A narrative perspective on resilience. In D. Carr, R. M. Nesse, & C. B. Wortman (Eds.), *Late-life widowhood in the United States* (pp. 227–52). New York, NY: Springer.

Onrust, S. A., & Cuijpers, P. (2006). Mood and anxiety disorders in widowhood: A systematic review. *Aging & Mental Health, 10*(4), 327–34.

Pargament, K. I., & Abu Raiya, H. (2007). A decade of research on the psychology of religion and coping: Things we assumed and lessons we learned. *Psyke & Logos, 28*, 742–66.

Pope, K., & Vasquez, M. J. T. (2007). *Ethics in psychotherapy and counseling: A practical guide* (3rd ed.). San Francisco, CA: Wiley.

Shear, M. K. (2013). Grief and mourning gone awry: Pathway and course of complicated grief. *Dialogues in Clinical Neuroscience, 14*, 119–28.

Shear, M. K. (2015). Complicated grief. *New England Journal of Medicine, 372*, 153–60.

Silverman, P. R. (2004). *Widow to widow: How the bereaved help one another*. Routledge.

Stroebe, M. (2005). To continue or relinquish bonds: A review of consequences for the bereaved. *Death Studies, 29*(6), 477–494.

Stroebe, M. S., Hansson, R. O., Stroebe, W., & Schut, H. (Eds.). (2001). *Handbook of bereavement research: Consequences, coping, and care.* Washington, DC: American Psychological Association.

Stroebe, M. S., Stroebe, W., & Hansson, R. O. (1993). *Handbook of bereavement.* New York: NY: Cambridge University Press.

van Baarsen, B., & van Groenou, M. I. B. (2001). Partner loss in later life: Gender differences in coping shortly after bereavement. *Journal of Loss and Trauma, 6*, 243–62.
Wilcox, S., Evenson, K. R., Aragaki, A., Wassertheil-Smoller, S., Mouton, C. P., & Loevinger, B. L. (2003). The effects of widowhood on physical and mental health, health behaviors, and health outcomes: The women's health initiative. *Health Psychology, 22*, 513–22.
Williams, K. (2004). The transition to widowhood and the social regulation of health: Consequences for health and health risk behavior. *Journals of Gerontology Series B: Psychological Sciences and Social Sciences, 59*(6), S343–S349.
Worden, J. W. (2009). *Grief counseling and grief therapy* (4th ed.). New York, NY: Springer.

Chapter Twenty-Three

Counseling Women Experiencing Fetal and Perinatal Loss

Donna M. Gibson

CASE VIGNETTE: KHLOE

The pregnancy had felt off the entire time. Khloe, thirty-eight years old, knew her body and had known exactly the timing of the pregnancy, yet the baby was not measuring correctly. Her physician's office had assured her that pregnancies were not an exact science, but this was not Khloe's first pregnancy. She had experienced two early miscarriages and had one live birth prior to this pregnancy. This one felt different, and it was different. At eleven weeks, Khloe started spotting and went for a checkup. Baby's heartbeat was still there, and the spotting stopped. Two weeks later, the spotting returned and the physician asked Khloe to come in for an ultrasound. Khloe and her partner went in and saw that the baby's heartbeat had stopped. They opted to complete the miscarriage through a D&C procedure at the hospital the same day. The next day, life continued in a routine way. But it was not routine for Khloe. This loss was different than the other miscarriages because she had seen this formed baby on ultrasound and had to have it surgically removed from her body. The sadness and feelings of being not in control were related to loss and difficulty in carrying a pregnancy to have a second live child.

Two months after the miscarriage, Khloe received a call from the genetic counselor's office to ask if she wanted to come in to review the lab results from the fetus that was miscarried. Khloe agreed to the appointment, and she was informed that chromosomal abnormalities contributed to the fetus's death. Cognitively, Khloe understood this was an answer to a sometimes unexplainable situation. When asked by the counselor if she wanted to know the sex of the baby, she was surprised that she wanted to know. The counse-

lor told Khloe that it was a boy, and Khloe found herself crying. Up until that moment, she had not allowed herself to think of the baby as a he or she. Finding out that her baby was a boy made the loss more real than before. The sense of loss was overwhelming, and she decided she needed to talk through this more with a counselor.

In her first meeting with the counselor, Khloe disclosed that she was there due to the sadness she felt after the recent miscarriage. When the counselor inquired about other aspects of her life, Khloe began to realize the pressure she had put on herself to have this "second" child for her and her partner. These feelings added to Khloe's feeling out of control, not only physically but with work-related issues. Unresolved grief over her father's death a few years earlier and feeling like she was running out of time to have the second child had her experiencing both sadness and anger with limited coping skills.

* * *

According to the National Center for Health Statistics (MacDorman & Gregory, 2015), the term *perinatal mortality* encompasses two specific definitions of fetal and infant death. Included in definition one are "infant deaths under age seven days and fetal deaths at twenty-eight weeks of gestation or more. Definition two includes infant deaths under age twenty-eight days and fetal deaths at twenty weeks or more (MacDorman & Gregory, 2015, p. 2). Fetal deaths at twenty weeks or more are also known as stillbirths. Intrauterine death of a fetus prior to delivery is considered a fetal death. Fetal deaths that occur prior to twenty weeks are often named a miscarriage in the literature and clinical settings and account for the majority of fetal deaths. Although they occur more frequently than stillbirths and other types of perinatal mortality, most states in the United States only report fetal deaths at twenty weeks or more unless they are recorded as abortions. Therefore, incidence rates are not as reliable for miscarriages but are estimated to occur for 25 percent of the women who become pregnant (Carolan & Wright, 2017). Additionally, national reports on fetal and infant mortality rates are sporadic, with the most recent NCHS report based on 2013 data. At that time, the U.S. fetal mortality rate was 5.96 fetal deaths at twenty weeks of gestation or more per one thousand live births and fetal deaths.

Causes for perinatal mortality and miscarriage can often be unexplained due to the majority of fetal deaths occurring in early pregnancy (MacDorman & Gregory, 2015). For both types of losses, problems with chromosomes, the uterus or cervix, infections, advanced maternal age, and preexisting health conditions can be explanations. In terms of population, the NCHS reported that non-Hispanic black women and Hispanic-origin groups experienced perinatal mortality more than twice the rate for non-Hispanic white women. Due to the unexplained or known reasons for these losses, there is much variability and unpredictability in how women experience fetal deaths. In this chapter, more focus will be given to losses experienced spontaneously than abortions. However, it is noted that women experiencing abortions can have similar experiences.

THE EXPERIENCE OF FETAL LOSS AND PERINATAL DEATH

There may be an assumption that the immediate emotional consequence of fetal death is sadness and possible depression. Although this may be true of some experiences, the feeling of no control over the loss leads many women to have an ambiguous loss experience (Carolan & Wright, 2017). This ambiguity makes it difficult for women to make sense of the experience and leads to stress in tolerating or coping with the loss. In essence, this type of loss is not a normative type of loss, and coping mechanisms and supports used with normal forms of loss are either not applied or not applied effectively (Boss, 2007). Expelling a fetus, having it removed, or laboring to have the baby can add a physical aspect to an emotionally traumatizing life event. With all of these different aspects of the actual loss event, the grief process can be frozen.

To put this experience in a social context, women are raised frequently to integrate the role of "mother" into their identities (Gibson & Myers, 2000). For the majority of women who identify this way, pregnancy and subsequently giving birth to the baby are part of an expected or normal life experience. When a fetal or perinatal death occurs, women may feel excluded from this social role and from their cohort of peers who may be pregnant (Layne, 2003). For women who have integrated the role of both mother and a healthy reproductive person, the loss of a baby during pregnancy or shortly after birth makes them question their identities. When this is questioned, how to make meaning out of the event is confusing. Since meaning making is essential to the grieving process, the process can be disrupted (Worden, 2002). Finally, grieving in this experience is connected to the potential loss of fertility or the fear that carrying full-term or to a live birth will not happen. Grief is connected to the dream of what that baby represented and who she or he would have been like or become when alive. It can be connected to the demise of a relationship between partners or other family members, such as the women feeling like she has disappointed the partner in not becoming a parent or the extended family members in not becoming aunts, uncles, grandparents.

In addition to the individual, unique experience of fetal or perinatal death, there is a social silencing that occurs at the public or societal levels that results in a total lack of an adequate response to individuals in this experience. People in society, including medical professionals, do not know how to discuss or support those who have fetal or perinatal losses (Layne, 2003). In the medical community, this is evident in the lack of statistics reported for miscarriages. Only estimates are provided in research because miscarriages are perceived as normal and inconsequential in the medical community (Carolan & Wright, 2017); hence, many states do not keep records of these events. In the workplace, fetal or perinatal death and the grief that often accompanies it is often ignored to the point that women feel disenfranchised and stifled (Hazen, 2006). These silences do not allow for the acknowledgment that the once celebrated birth of a child is now gone but that the expecting mother is attempting to cope with the experience of loss in a variety of different ways. Ignoring these experiences can lead to more emotional trauma in addition to the trauma of the loss and the grieving process (Pullen, Golden, & Cacciatore, 2012). With the lack of attention, and many times ignoring these events, in society, resources to support women who are coping with these losses are either not known or shared.

COUNSELING WOMEN COPING WITH FETAL OR PERINATAL LOSS

One of the first things to acknowledge is that each person in a partner system copes with fetal or perinatal loss differently. There are coping responses unique to each person in the system, and the partners will need to come together to figure out what this means for their dyad. This chapter will focus more on what counselors may do with the woman who carried the pregnancy. In some cases, this may be the only individual who is coping, but some attention will be given to counseling interventions specific to the partner system.

As outlined earlier, many women are facing a sense of ambiguous loss that has them grappling with many discordant feelings and existential questions. There is a sense of guilt, anger, sadness, and failure that leads to diminished self-esteem. Questions and thoughts, such as the following may be asked: Why did this happen to me? Will I ever become a mother? If I am not a mother, what am I? I did everything right in my pregnancy, and she did not; why was she able to have a baby? What will my partner think of me? Will he or she leave me? Is there a physical problem with me? I am older and my time is running out; what if I cannot give my child a sibling? Will I want to be with my friends who are pregnant? Not surprisingly, these feelings, thoughts, and questions are wrapped up in the woman's identity, which is linked closely to her self-esteem. Since this identity includes a social construction of motherhood that society reinforces, feelings of self-worth and sexual identity are often confirmed when women become mothers (Gibson, 2007). When motherhood does not occur in what is perceived as a normal process (i.e., healthy pregnancy, birth of live and healthy baby), there may be a loss of self, and a reconstruction of identity may be initiated abruptly and can add to the emotional trauma already experienced with the fetal or perinatal death (Hill, Cacciatore, Shreffler, & Pritchard, 2017).

You Are Not Alone

Due to feelings of self-blame and sadness associated with fetal or perinatal loss, women may isolate themselves in this experience. Self-esteem and identity has been altered, and grief looks and feels different than at other times of what is considered normal loss. What complicates this isolation is when the loss is ignored with societal or relational silence. This type of loss is often devalued, so opportunities to validate the woman as a parent will help the process of constructing meaning and, if necessary, reconstructing her identity to manage her feelings and thoughts (Costin & McMurrich, 2013).

Using a relational-cultural theory (RCT) is considered a humanistic approach to counseling, with the main tenets of the theory built on a strong therapeutic relationship (Headley & Sangganjanavanich, 2014). For women coping with fetal or perinatal loss, RCT may be most effective since it "places a special emphasis on assessing resilience, support systems in which clients participate, a sense of belonging or mattering, and authenticity in clients' primary relationships" (Headley & Sangganjanavanich, 2014, p. 249). Hence, if women are feeling isolated and losing connection to others during this time of processing their fetal or perinatal loss, then there is a need to establish a connection between counselors and clients. Using RCT, the counselor will demonstrate mutual respect and openness by using active listening to help the client understand that the relationship between counselor and client is designed to help her and provide her with a sense of psychological well-being, which also helps to ameliorate any power differential that the client may perceive in counseling (Gibson & Myers, 2000). In establishing the connection, counselors need to be aware of the importance of vocabulary around fetal or perinatal death. Clients will come to counseling hearing from the medical community the words *fetus*, *the stillborn*, or *the miscarriage*. Use of these terms invalidates the woman's identity as a parent and possibly the actual birth of the baby, if that occurred (Costin & McMurrich, 2013; Froen, Cacciatore, McClure, Kuti, & Jokhio, 2011). The ability of the counselor to share experiences regarding fetal or perinatal death (e.g., knowledge about women's experiences, work with other clients or support groups) and an openness to learning and being affected emotionally by their client's experiences is part of the mutual empathy process of relational-culture theory. When counselors demonstrate this knowledge and respect for their clients' feelings and thoughts, women are validated and feel less alone in this experience. In growing in the relationship with the counselor, women become more open and empowered to explore what has happened and what it does or will mean for them.

The Story of Us

In individual counseling, using an RCT framework, the primary goal is to provide an opportunity to build a relationship and acknowledge the client's experience as well as the counselor's experience so that the client begins to develop a new integration of self–other experience (Gibson & Myers, 2000). This begins with the counselor modeling empathy and acknowledging the client's feelings in an effort to normalize them. When the woman begins to feel "heard" and understood by the counselor, she can begin to understand her experience and move to a place of self-validation (of her experience).

Because fetal or perinatal loss is riddled with different forms of trauma, there is a place and sometimes a strong need from women to tell their story of the pregnancy, birth, and loss. One postmodern approach to this is to use narrative therapy that incorporates storytelling. When using narrative therapies, there is an assumption that individuals' lives are woven by the stories they share, and the stories are socially constructed and culturally mediated (Akinyela, 2014). With women experiencing fetal or perinatal loss, they will take their own personal and cultural points of view when retelling their stories around these losses (West-Olatunji & Rush-Ossenbeck, 2016).

Counselors using a narrative storytelling technique will need to be prepared with reflexive questions that help counselors understand the meaning that women are assigning to their experiences being told in the story. One way to do this is to help clients identify their internal discourses about the behaviors or thoughts being told in the story. For example, a woman may say that she and her partner came home from the hospital after delivering a stillborn daughter, and she noticed that the door to the nursery was closed. A reflexive question could be, "What did you think when you saw this?" She could respond that she felt anger "because no one was acknowledging that her little girl would not ever be in that room and grow up in that house." This type of response gives the counselor an idea of how her client views not only the loss but also how others are responding, her perception that has become her reality, and how she is making meaning out of this experience. In response, the counselor empathizes with the feelings that the client is expressing and validates her experience, as she is the expert in her own life. Areas that may be covered in this storytelling process may include finding out who her baby is or was, asking about the pregnancy and hopes and dreams she had for the child, finding out names that were considered and if and why the baby's name was chosen (note: not every woman will have named the baby), finding out whether there was a nursery or plans for one, finding out about the actual medical complications and procedures associated with the loss, and finding out about the partner's involvement in the experience. After processing more of the client's experience, storytelling can be used to "restory" her life as she looks at how this may change what she will do in the future.

Rebooting the Self

In the process of storytelling, the experience of fetal or perinatal death is deconstructed to some extent. Reflexive questioning may get at the more socially constructed aspects of the experience, specifically those that influence the woman's identity. Women may have more questions about who they are in relation to others in their lives. Because of the socially isolating phenomena that go with fetal or perinatal death, women may find themselves confused as to their role in society and how to cope with that role (Gibson & Myers, 2000). Using an RCT approach, the counselor can help the client review relationships in her life that represent incongruencies in having a mutually supportive relationship. Who has been supportive? Who has reached out? Who acknowledged the loss and in a sensitive manner? Feelings, thoughts, and beliefs that the client may think she cannot verbalize are encouraged and recognized. The counselor's role is to "objectify these aspects of self and make affective connections with them" (Gibson & Myers, 2000, p. 406). For example, a client may describe several people who are supportive as those who "do not judge her," and that has made her feel less guilty about the loss. When the counselor connects these aspects, she begins to have an image of herself as someone who is not to blame for the loss and can still be supported by certain people in her life even through difficult circumstances.

The process of rebooting self does not begin in counseling in this situation. It begins when the loss occurs, which may come days, months, or years before counseling. Counselors should be aware that how a woman thinks about herself and her role in society after a loss continues to evolve through her lifetime. Identity is developmental, and there are many factors that influence that development. Many women who experience a fetal or perinatal death go on to have live births and healthy babies, and this will impact her identity in a different way than a loss. However, subsequent children do not negate the influence of a fetal or perinatal death on a woman's identity and how the grieving process is a product of meaning making in the experience of this type of loss.

The Process of Grieving

It is difficult to summarize women's experiences with fetal or perinatal death as they are all unique. Depending on the timing of the loss (i.e., first trimester, late pregnancy, at birth, a few days after birth), women assign different meanings to being pregnant, being a mother-to-be, being the mom of a deceased child. Counselors will need to approach each client as someone with a unique experience with unique feelings, thoughts, and coping techniques. As noted previously, society's response is usually quiet but can vary in its silence. For example, the majority of miscarriages occur in the first trimester and go unrecognized by many women's support systems, making it a hidden loss (Sell-Smith & Lax, 2013). Often with a hidden loss, there is a lack of rituals to mark its passage, and this results in what is referred to as disenfranchised grief. Some women may also experience traumatic grief that is considered a sudden, prolonged, disturbed, or extreme form of sorrow (Jacobs, 1999). Because fetal or perinatal death is unexpected, it can bring about feelings of grief but also a trauma-like reaction where the brain and body are overwhelmed and need time to process what has happened.

In counseling, validating the client's experience with the loss, helping her tell her story, and acknowledging her reality, thoughts, and feelings help her process her grief. Rituals and observances of the baby should be offered but not forced. For example, the client may want to create a keepsake or plant a flower, shrub, or tree to remember her child. Partners, extended family members, and older siblings may be suggested as assistants in creating these remembrances, when appropriate. Clients may create a tradition to be carried out in the following years. The main caveat is that the rituals and observances are to bring comfort and acknowledge that the child was a part of the woman's identity as a parent.

Finally, many women may find support groups helpful in their grieving process. Groups can offer relational movement toward awareness of self and others, especially of those who are experiencing a similar form of loss. Counselors can assist a woman in identifying groups that are appropriate for her needs and determining whether she is appropriate for the group's needs. For example, the counselor needs to consider if the woman is emotionally ready to connect with other women who have experienced fetal or perinatal death. Can she empathize with self and others in a group setting? Some women may not want to be in a group because it could be emotionally overwhelming, or they may want to experience this with a partner or close friend.

ETHICAL CONSIDERATIONS

When life events occur without much explanation, there is sometimes an innate need to explain it, investigate it, and apply the explanation to similar occurrences. Counseling women experiencing fetal or perinatal death may often fall in this category, which warrants the reminder that counselors must meet their clients where they are and respect their rights for privacy and confidentiality (American Counseling Association, 2014). Specific details of the actual loss are not warranted unless the woman wants to disclose them, and encouraging the client to reiterate her experience without a helpful intention may be harmful.

Counselors need to evaluate their personal values on a regular basis, especially if fetal or perinatal loss is an experience or an issue that provokes strong emotions and thoughts. As previously noted, fetal deaths include abortions. Women who present in counseling due to feelings, thoughts, and beliefs around having an abortion may present differently than those experiencing fetal or perinatal deaths due to a spontaneous miscarriage, stillbirth, or death of a baby shortly after birth. Professional development, clinical supervision, or personal counseling may be appropriate methods to address the counselor's conflictual values or beliefs in order for them not to impact the counseling relationship negatively.

CULTURAL CONSIDERATIONS AND EMPOWERMENT OPPORTUNITIES

Based on the statistics presented by NCHS (MacDorman & Gregory, 2015), there are higher rates of perinatal death at twenty weeks or more for women identifying as non-Hispanic black and Hispanic compared to non-Hispanic white women. There are also differences based on education levels for white women, with those with less than twelve years of education experiencing stillbirth 30 percent more compared to women with twelve years or more of education (Willinger, Ko, & Reddy, 2009). Although there may be no definitive causal factors for these differences, there may be issues related to economic disadvantage for all of these groups based on systemic oppression issues in the United States. These same issues may prevent women from presenting in private counseling due to the inability to pay or have insurance for these services.

Culture is a part of an individual's reality and is considered a major determinant for the actions, thoughts, and behaviors of the individual (Silman, 2014). Hence, cultural is a factor is how women experiencing a fetal or perinatal death will process and express her grief, make meaning of the experience, and determine how the loss affects her role and identity. Using RCT in counseling is an appropriate approach for women of various cultures as the counselor attempts to establish a mutual and empathic relationship with the client with a priority on lessening any hierarchy in the relationship. In this relationship, the client is the expert, and the counselor will work with her to provide counseling in a culturally responsive manner. This will mean that counselors should continue to ask clients questions and not make assumptions about what is an aspect of her coping versus what may be acceptable culturally. For example, a client may want to talk about the loss and name the baby, but this may not be acceptable in her culture. In the counselor–client relationship, empathizing with her and explaining that women who have similar experiences may feel comfortable doing this only in counseling and may gain confidence to communicate to their family that they need to talk with them about this in the future. This may expand the need for family members to come to counseling and express their own thoughts and feelings as well.

In order to prepare clients to verbalize their needs outside of the counseling environment, counselors have to empower them. In counseling women experiencing fetal or perinatal loss, counselors gain knowledge of their experiences, attitudes, feelings, beliefs, and how they think about themselves based on their experiences. This is all needed to employ an empowering model of clinical intervention (Dass-Brailsford, 2007) and includes gathering additional information about the cultural, historical, and ecological factors that affect women's experience and coping with fetal or perinatal loss. There are three phases of the empowering model, including the initial cognitive phase, an affective phase, and a final cognitive phase. "This process is not to teach clients to adapt to their situations but to reflect on how they manage anxiety, depression, stress, and/or poor self-concept through their strength, courage, and determination" (Gibson, 2019, p. 210). This is a way to assess the client's coping and use of coping resources and leads the counselor and client to plan and coconstruct ways for the client to communicate her needs with others. Once she begins to do this, new internal cognitions will assist in the process of making meaning of the loss and her revised sense of self.

CASE VIGNETTE WRAP-UP: KHLOE

It was apparent that Khloe had been holding back her feelings about a lot of loss and life events until this moment, so Savannah (the counselor) began by using active listening skills of reflection of feeling and empathy: "It sounds like you are feeling overwhelmed with work and your father's death, but miscarriages have you feeling immense amounts of sadness and maybe like you have no control? You must be recognizing this, too, since you are now here for counseling."

Khloe agreed. "It's taking up too much room in my head and my heart. I can't concentrate at work, I don't feel like I'm being a good wife or mother. . . . I feel like I'm dragging myself through the motions of life. But no one wants to talk about the miscarriages, especially the last one."

Savannah answered, "It sounds like you are feeling alone in this, right? Is it okay to talk more about that feeling?"

Khloe agrees to this topic.

Intervention Strategy: Connecting with Client, Showing Respect, and Sharing Knowledge

When Savannah heard her client talk about feeling alone, she was reminded of her own personal and professional experiences with fetal loss. Savannah reflected to Khloe, "I have heard many of my clients echo that same thought about feeling alone after their miscarriages. When I discussed it with them, there were many reasons for this feeling. What do you think may contribute to you feeling this way?"

Khloe was silent for a little while and then responded, "It's not something that is natural to come up in conversation. My miscarriage and D&C happened on a weekend, so no one knew that anything unusual happened since I went back to work on Monday. My son doesn't know that it happened and he is only five years old, and my mom hasn't said anything to me since she dropped my son back at our house the day after the procedure."

Savannah affirmed Khloe by saying, "What you are identifying is what my other clients identified about how our society doesn't know how to respond to this appropriately. Some people don't know how to respond or offer comfort. Many people, including family, don't check in because they fear they will prolong the sadness they are assuming you feel initially."

Khloe nods her head affirmatively. "Yes, exactly. Even my doctor said that I can still get pregnant when I'm ready. I wasn't even ready to hear that . . . and no resources were provided for women who were going through this. I had to find you on my own."

Savannah replied, "I'm glad you did, and it shows that you are resilient in finding support when you need it. There are several resources for women experiencing miscarriage, but many are not widely publicized due to this silence around it. I'll give you some to look at if you would like before you go today."

Telling Her Story and Examining Identity

In the following sessions, Khloe was encouraged to tell her story about the miscarriages. She focused more on the third one that ended in the D&C procedure. There were some signs of trauma related to physical aspects of the miscarriage, such as experiencing spotting, seeing the baby without the heartbeat on the ultrasound, and seeing blood on the sheets in the hospital after she woke up from the procedure. She remembered that her throat was sore from receiving anesthesia, so the physical reminders of the miscarriage were vivid in her memory. However, the event that made it a reality for her was hearing from the genetics counselor that the baby was a boy. Using reflexive questioning during Khloe's story, Savannah discovered that before that Khloe was able to keep the grief on hold or interrupted. Finding out the baby was a boy made her feel sad and guilty for not giving her son a younger brother. Not having a second child also disrupted her dream of an ideal family of a husband and two children. In her mind, Khloe had always thought she would be a mother of two children, and now that part of her identity was shaken because it might not happen. Savannah and Khloe discussed where the idea of two children came from, which involved an examination of Khloe's cultural values, family messages, and ecological considerations that influenced these ideas. Khloe eventually felt more in control after learning more about herself and what this loss meant for her. She felt empowered to talk to her husband more about any future attempts to get pregnant, that this last miscarriage helped her take the pressure off of trying to have two children, and that she felt confident in sharing her story with others so they would not feel alone.

QUESTIONS FOR REFLECTION

1. What messages are sent culturally about fetal and perinatal loss? What messages about fetal and perinatal loss do you know about in your own culture?
2. What are the social constructions around motherhood? What are the social constructions around being child-free for a woman?
3. How does the social construction of women's various roles (i.e., worker, partner, helper, mother, sister, daughter, etc.) impact the overall health and wellness of women?
4. How might you bring more awareness to this experience and the needs of women coping with it? Are there areas for advocacy in the medical community?

REFERENCES

Akinyela, M. M. (2014). Narrative therapy and cultural democracy: A testimony view. *Australian and New Zealand Journal of Family Therapy, 35*, 46–49. doi:10.1002/anzf.1041

American Counseling Association. (2014). *ACA code of ethics*. Retrieved from https://www.counseling.org/resources/aca-code-of-ethics.pdf

Boss, P. (2007). Ambiguous loss theory: Challenges for scholars and practitioners. *Family Relations, 56*, 105–10. doi:10.1111/j.1741-3729.2007.00444.x

Carolan, M., & Wright, R. J. (2017). Miscarriage at advanced maternal age and the search for meaning. *Death Studies, 41*, 144–53.

Costin, A., & McMurrich, C. A. (2013). A discussion of parental validation following stillbirth: Using transforming counseling and education. *International Journal of Childbirth Education, 28*, 71–74.

Dass-Brailsford, P. (2007). *A practical approach to trauma: Empowering interventions*. Thousand Oaks, CA: Sage.

Froen, F. J., Cacciatore, J., McClure, E. M., Kuti, O., & Jokhio, A. H. (2011). Stillbirths I: Why they matter. *Lancet, 377* (9774), 1353–66.

Gibson, D. M. (2007). The relationship of infertility and death: Using the relational/cultural model of counseling in making meaning. *Humanistic Psychologist, 35*(3), 1–15.

Gibson, D. M. (2019). Counseling and the culture of economic disadvantage. In C. L. Lee (Ed.), *Multicultural issues in counseling: New approaches to diversity* (5th ed., pp. 199–214). Alexandria, VA: American Counseling Association.

Gibson, D. M., & Myers, J. E. (2000). Gender and infertility: A relational approach to counseling women. *Journal of Counseling & Development, 78*, 400–410.

Hazen, M. A. (2006). Silences, perinatal loss, and polyphony: A post-modern perspective. *Journal of Organizational Change Management, 19*(2), 237–49.

Headley, J. A., & Sangganjanavanich, V. R. (2014). Creating space for connection: A column for creative practice. *Journal of Creativity in Mental Health, 9*, 245–61. doi:10.1080/15401383.2013.879756

Hill, P. W., Cacciatore, J., Shreffler, K. M., & Pritchard, K. M. (2017). The loss of self: The effect of miscarriage, stillbirth, and child death on maternal self-esteem. *Death Studies, 41*(4), 226–35. doi:10.1080/07481187.2016.1261204

Jacobs, S. (1999). *Traumatic grief: Diagnosis, treatment, and prevention*. Castleton, NY: Psychology Press.

Layne, L. (2003). Unhappy endings: A feminist reappraisal of the women's health movement from the vantage of pregnancy loss. *Social Science & Medicine, 56*, 1881–91. doi:10.1016/s0277-9536(02)00211-3

MacDorman, M. R., & Gregory, E. C. W. (2015). Fetal and perinatal mortality: United States, 2013. *National Vital Statistics Report, 64*(8). Retrieved from https://www.cdc.gov/nchs/data/nvsr/nvsr64/nvsr64_08.pdf

Pullen, S., Golden, M. I., & Cacciatore, J. (2012). "I'll never forget those cold words as long as I live": Parent perceptions of death notification for stillbirth. *Journal of Social Work in End-of-Life & Palliative Care, 8*(4), 339–55.

Sell-Smith, J., & Lax, W. D. (2013). A journey of pregnancy loss: From positivism to autoethnography. *Qualitative Report, 18*(46), 1–17.

Silman, M. (2014). Loss of a baby in a cultural context (Master's thesis). Retrieved from https://pdfs.semanticscholar.org/1220/480defea115467fbea25db731ffd817f556f.pdf

West-Olatunji, C. A., & Rush-Ossenbeck, M. (2016). Constructivist theories: Solution-focused and narrative therapies. In D. Capuzzi & M. D. Stauffer (Eds.), *Counseling and psychotherapy: Theories and interventions* (6th ed., pp. 419–44). Alexandria, VA: American Counseling Association.

Willinger, M., Ko, C.-W., & Reddy, U. M. (2009). Racial disparities in stillbirth risk across gestation in the United States. *American Journal of Obstetrics & Gynecology, 201*(5), 469–77. doi:10.1016/j.ajog.2009.06.057

Worden, J. W. (2002). *Grief counseling and grief therapy: A handbook for the mental health practitioner* (3rd ed.). New York, NY: Springer.

Chapter Twenty-Four

Counseling Women Who Have Lost a Child

Suzanne Degges-White

CASE VIGNETTE: KARLA

Karla, a woman in her midfifties, lost her son, Max, in a car accident over eighteen months ago. Max was a day into a cross-country journey, just two weeks after his graduation from college, heading to California to start his dream job. Although her son was twenty-two when he died, and the accident happened almost two years ago, Karla is still seeking help in lifting herself out of what she calls her "grief bunker." She was referred to Juanita, a counselor in private practice, by Thalia, the leader of a grieving parents' support group sponsored by a local medical center. Thalia felt that Karla's grief was so entrenched that individual counseling might be more effective than the support group had been. Thalia also felt that Karla's lack of responsiveness to the group's potential for healing was possibly having a detrimental effect on other members of the group. Thalia felt that the group's membership, composed primarily of parents who had lost younger children who had been patients at the medical center, was not optimal for the support Karla needs.

At their first meeting, Juanita notes Karla's professional appearance, fashionable clothing, and hairstyle. As they enter the counseling office, both Karla's facial expression and emotional demeanor begin crumbling, and her capable and strong façade fade as she takes a seat while Juanita closes the office door. Before she can ask Karla if she'd like hot tea or some water, Karla has picked up the tissue box, hugged it to her chest, and begun sobbing. Juanita puts a bottle of water on the coaster beside Karla and sits down quietly, giving Karla space to let her tears flow.

A few minutes later, as Karla's sobbing begins to subside, she smiles at Juanita and jokes, "I guess you must be an ace counselor if your clients dissolve into tears before you even ask them what's wrong."

Juanita responds, "I've learned that a quiet room and a closed door are often all we need to feel safe to let out what we're 'really' feeling. And it appears that you are carrying around quite a sizable load of grief."

Karla acknowledges, "Yes, for almost two years now I've been just 'this close' to breaking down, no matter where I am or what I'm doing or who's around. It's like I'm in some kind of fourth dimension or something. It's what I call my 'grief bunker.' I mean, I keep living and working and showing up in life, but there's that other part of me that never leaves the grief bunker. I don't even know if I really want to leave it, sometimes, to be honest. It's like it lets me feel safe in my sadness, and it keeps me connected to Max."

Juanita affirms, "It sounds like you've been using your grief as armor to protect you from having to face life without your son. It's like being hidden in your grief bunker lets you experience your pain, but in a protected, protective way. Does that sound close to what you're feeling?"

Karla nods and says, "I feel like if I step outside the bunker, and see what's going on around me, and begin to let myself feel human again, I'll either fall apart or feel disloyal to Max."

* * *

The death of a child is considered the most painful that a woman can experience. Chapter 23 explored counseling women who have lost a fetal or neonatal child. In this chapter, the focus is on the loss of older offspring through adulthood. When a child enters a family, parents may not even be aware of the expectations and hopes they are forming for the life of the child. While childhood mortality rates have dropped significantly in the past three decades (Centers for Disease Control and Prevention, 2018), the grief experienced after such a loss does not diminish. The period of grieving has no set end point, and prolonged grief can take a continued psychological toll on parents years and decades after a child has died (Pohlkamp, Kreicbergs, & Sveen, 2019). Depression, posttraumatic stress symptoms, and difficulty sleeping are just a few of the more common ways maternal grief manifests. Just as the arrival of a child into a mother's life irrevocably alters her identity, so too does the death of a child. When a mother loses a child, she is thrust into a transition in which she must reconstruct her history, her identity, and her future (Dahdah, Rego, Joaquim, Bombarda, & Nunes, 2019), regardless of the child's age or the mother's age.

POTENTIAL GRIEF RESPONSES TO LOSS OF A CHILD

Losing a child leaves behind a grief more intense than the loss of parents or partners generates (Sanders, 1980). In fact, as Bonanno and colleagues (2002) noted, the loss of a child, by any means or method, will yield traumatic stress symptoms and emotional upset at greater levels than the loss of a partner. There are no standard, "one size fits all" grief responses; however, a mother's age, her self-perceived health, and the age of the child who has died are associated with the grief reactions reported (Raitio, Kaunonen, & Aho, 2015). Older mothers may have stronger grief reactions than younger mothers do at the loss of a child, just as the loss of older children was found to increase the level of depression experienced by the mother (Wijingaards-de Meij et al., 2008). When a mother is already experiencing health deficits, the additional burden of a child's death only exacerbates her condition, and this type of grief can contribute to worsening of symptoms, decreased cardiovascular health, and compromised immune system functioning. Parents are also more likely to rely on psychotropic medications after the death of a child (Rostila, Maki, & Martikainen, 2018). Sadly, research indicates that the mortality rate for parents increases after the death of a child as well. Rostila, Saarela, and Kawachi (2012) found that the mortality risk for mothers was especially high after the loss of a child through an unnatural death, typically accidents or suicide. Mothers of children up to age twenty-five were found to be at increased risk for death after the child's death.

Normal and Complicated Grief

There are generally considered to be two types of grief, normal grief and complicated grief. Although the DSM-V does not include an entry for complicated grief, professionals are strongly supportive of its addition to the manual (Dodd, Guerin, Delaney, & Dodd, 2019). Six months is commonly perceived as the boundary between normal grief and complicated grief. Healing occurs at different paces, and the effect of the loss is never erased for any parent, but it is believed that progress toward a return to emotional stability and to a "new normal" level of functioning should be experienced during the first half year following the loss. Unfortunately, there has been little evidence found to support the effectiveness of trying to prevent complicated grief from developing (Wittouck, Autreve, Jaegere, Portzky, & van Herringen, 2011). However, these researchers did discover that symptoms could be effectively addressed through appropriate treatment. They also affirmed that, by and large, grief work can be accomplished successfully without the intervention of a professional. There are also some individuals who become "stuck" in their grief and who benefit from work with professional clinicians.

Type of Death: Natural or Unnatural Causes

In cases in which a child's death comes at the end of a prolonged illness, there are often opportunities for mothers and other family members to prepare for the loss. Anticipatory grief is often experienced in these cases as well. As the realization that a child's life is nearing its end sinks in, the period of grieving often begins and potentially ushers in responses that include depression, anxiety, increased irritability, and mental rehearsals of how the impending loss will be experienced. This can be a painful period for a mother, which is made even more difficult by the desire to keep up the spirits of the ill child. In fact, encouraging engagement with one's child and focusing on making the most of the time remaining is one suggestion for helping mitigate the grief. Finding support from family members or connecting with close friends or other mothers experiencing similar events can also minimize the negative symptoms of grief.

In cases of violent or otherwise traumatic death, parents tend to have a more challenging time making sense of the loss. Parents may blame themselves for being unable to protect their child or to prevent the death from occurring. While meaning making is considered an integral component of grieving and moving forward after loss (Flesner, 2013), it can be especially challenging for parents who have lost a child through an unnatural manner. In fact, there are indications that focusing first on managing trauma-related symptoms (such as reducing terror, fear, and anxiety) of bereaved family members rather than typical grief work may be appropriate (Asukai, Tsuruta, & Saito, 2011). These researchers found that their pilot program was effective in helping mothers manage traumatic grief. Thus, when working with women whose children died unexpectedly, focusing first on the trauma-related aspects of their emotional response may open the door to more effective grief-related therapy.

BEST PRACTICES FOR MOTHERS SUFFERING GRIEF AFTER THE LOSS OF A CHILD

Grief is a completely normal response to loss of a loved one, and it is not something that always needs to be treated by professional clinicians. However, if a client seeks out counseling to help her manage her response to the loss, the following interventions may be helpful in the case of an expected or natural death of her child:

1. Listen to your client and encourage her to tell the story of her child's life and death. Encourage her to tell the story in such a way that meaning is ascribed to her child's life and allows her to make sense of

her child's death. Help her note the meaning that her child's life had in others' lives beyond the family circle.

2. Invite your client to share her beliefs about death and mourning with you from her cultural perspective so that you can best provide appropriate care. Remind her that others may hold different views and mourning practices, including other members of the family and extended family, which may be difficult for her to accept.
3. Invite her to write down a biographical account of her child's life to allow her to reflect on the ways her child shaped others' lives and the meaning her child's life had for her, as a mother, and for others. The creation of a tangible account of her child's life provides a sense of comfort or substance when a child's absence is so present.
4. Suggest the integration of creative outlets as a way to channel her grief, such as journaling, visual art, dance, music, or gardening.
5. Encourage your client to create a memorial of some sort for her child. This may include the planting of a tree or dedication of a park bench or creation of a labyrinth. By creating a tangible memorial, the client is able to mark her child's life in a way that endures and where she can visit and others can appreciate her child's life.
6. Help your client maintain a connection with social support sources that were present before and during the illness and loss of her child. Remind her that even though her family structure has changed, that doesn't mean that she must re-create her social network.
7. Connect the client with appropriate support groups, if she has not already been referred to one by the medical practitioners who cared for her child. When children are victims of violence or traumatic accidents, it can be especially helpful for mothers to connect with others who have experienced the same type of unexpected loss.
8. Similarly, in the absence of specific grief support groups, help your client connect to other women who have experienced the loss of a child. Parents indicate that conversations with those who have experienced the loss of a child are among the most helpful in their grief work.
9. Help the client prepare and practice responses to questions or comments that they will hear in the coming years. These include questions about how many kids they have, old friends asking about what their child is up to these days, what their plans for Mother's Day will be, and so on. While a person's first response may be indignation or anger at being asked these types of questions, by being prepared for them and being able to remind themselves of the once innocuous nature of them, they will be better able to handle these exchanges.
10. Remind clients that grief does not have a "beginning and an end"; it can ebb and flow over time, and be mindful of using words that imply

that grief is something "to be gotten over" or to imply that "everything will work out okay." Solution-focused responses to parental grief are not appropriate.

Making Meaning from Memories

One method of helping clients integrate the loss of a child into their larger life story is through the use of relational memories (Puigarnau & Morales, 2019). These are memories that tie the bereaved to their deceased loved one, and it is through these memories that a bereaved mother can maintain a bond to the child who has died. Puigarnau and Morales (2019) noted that memories can relate to a variety of things. These might include anything from everyday activities to special rituals or significant events; possessions such as photographs, notes, and items of clothing; or memories of the child's effect on others, such as the child's smile, sense of humor, and so on. Because these memories are related, typically, to positive states, they are not as likely to cause the distress or trauma-related response that death- or illness-related memories may cause.

Some grieving mothers may seem "stuck" on a memory, and this, according to Puigarnau and Morales (2019), may signal the need to complete an unresolved memory. Much like the Gestalt concept of unfinished business, these unresolved memories may be presenting obstacles to moving forward. Through exploration and imagery in session, the client can be guided in using the memory as an impetus for finding resolution related to one aspect of their distress. Clinicians can invite their clients to share a memory in session and then help the client explore it fully by inviting the client to mentally "drop back into the moment." Encourage the client to talk about what being "in the memory" is like, including what is going on in the memory and what it feels like for them physically, emotionally, and cognitively. Encourage the client to explore any unmet or unfinished business that is stirred by the memory. Was something said that should have gone unsaid? Did something interrupt an exchange between the mother and her child? Does the memory focus on a positive exchange that exemplified the positive bond between mother and child? By helping the client explore the memory more fully, the meaning of the memory and any related insights can come to the surface.

Once the client has connected the memory to any feelings of unresolved or not-yet-completed relational exchange between her and her deceased child, encourage her to use mental imagery to fulfill the unmet need for resolution of the memory. While closure over the loss of a child is not the goal, helping the client work through unresolved feelings can be attempted. Invite her to imagine that her child is present and to share with the child what she feels needs to be said. Puigarnau and Morales (2019) used examples such as acknowledging how much a person missed the hugs from her deceased loved one. This led to the client recognizing that the hugs were assurances that the client was safe and loved. By revealing the underlying meaning of the memory, and engaging in an imaginal conversation with the deceased child, a mother can integrate this new information into her awareness. This new awareness can spur growth and sense making after the loss.

Counselors should be careful not to push the client into this intervention if the client seems unready, unwilling, or resistant. If a client begins the exercise and is unable to continue, acknowledge the client's courage for having the willingness to attempt the process and empathize with their struggle to manage the difficult emotional challenge the exercise presents. Remind the client that grief is a process that does not follow a predictable time line and that just because they were not ready for the intervention at this point does not mean that they won't be ready in the near future.

Traumatic or Unnatural Deaths

Mothers are likely in need of counseling that addresses symptoms of traumatic stress exposure as well as grief over the loss of their children. Using the work of Asukai and colleagues (2011) as a guide, counseling sessions may be framed in the following way:

- In the first session, the counselor discusses the planned treatment protocol; invites exploration of the client's loss, including circumstances surrounding the loss and their experience of the death of their child; and educates the client on breathing exercises that encourage present-centered focus and calm.
- In the second session, the counselor provides information and education on the common parental responses to a violent or unexpected death of a child.
- In the third session, in vivo exposure is introduced. This includes encouraging the client to approach safe situations that she has previously avoided due to their connection to trauma-related fear or grief-related bitterness.
- During the fourth and fifth sessions, intensity increases as imaginal exposure is brought into the therapy. This involves the client being asked to recount memories of the time when she was exposed to the death of her child as well as the replaying of times in the session in which she was asked to recount the event. The counselor and client debrief and discuss the client's thoughts and feelings about the experience.
- In the following five sessions, six through ten, the counselor continues to use imaginal exposure but also asks the client to share memories of their child. The client may bring in photographs of their child or use some other tangible prompt or item that belonged to the child.

- In sessions eleven and twelve, in vivo exposure is incorporated, but the client is also asked to take a bit more risk. The counselor asks the client to engage in imaginal conversations with their deceased child. The client is asked to converse from their own standpoint as mother, but also to respond in session as their child.
- The final three sessions, thirteen to fifteen, address the therapeutic process, the content and experiences of the client, and preparation for termination of the therapy.

CULTURAL CONSIDERATIONS

Mourning and bereavement are often culturally bound experiences that can be governed by factors such as family traditions, faith practices, or geographical customs. When working with individuals dealing with grief, be sure to explore their own beliefs about the process along with any cultural influences that surround their beliefs. It is important that the clinician explore these practices and beliefs openly with a client rather than making assumptions based on the clinician's own experiences or identity.

ETHICAL CONSIDERATIONS

While there are specific ethical codes for the various helping professions, there are specific concerns related to counseling the bereaved that may arise. For mothers whose children are suffering from a terminal disease or life-threatening injury, they may wrestle with end-of-life decisions related to their child's death. For example, guilt about weighing a child's suffering against letting a child go may be expressed during therapy, and this may create obstacles in the grieving process for a client. It is essential that clinicians provide nonjudgmental care when working with grieving clients as this is a period of vulnerability for a mother, and survivor guilt may be a significant factor in her grief. Being aware of your own beliefs and being able to keep them outside of the counseling office are essential.

ADVOCACY OPPORTUNITIES

There are many ways that individuals can advocate in the area of loss, including participation in advocate training programs, such as the one sponsored by Healgrief.org. These provide education and experiential learning opportunities to be better prepared to engage with grieving individuals. Another national organization is the MISS Foundation (https://missfoundation.org/); this organization provides resources for the public as well as professional helpers. They offer programming to train to be an advocate and leader as well as information regarding advocacy at the legislative level.

At a more local level, counselors can look for opportunities to give presentations and be featured speakers at community support groups and health and wellness events. Counselors can volunteer to serve as hospice workers and provide emotional support to patients and their families. There are also volunteer opportunities to work with children's grief groups to provide them with age-appropriate psychoeducation and feeling exploration.

CASE VIGNETTE WRAP-UP: KARLA

After the first session with Karla, Juanita believed that the unexpected nature of the loss of her son generated traumatic stress that was hindering Karla from crawling out of her "grief bunker." She felt that Karla might especially benefit from treatment that followed the protocol developed by of Asukai, Tsuruta, and Saito (2011) for resolving complicated, trauma-permeated grief.

At their second session, Juanita opens with a summary of the prior session and invites collaboration on goal setting and treatment planning for Karla. Karla shares that her main goal is getting out of the grief bunker in which she is hiding. She also wants to understand why she is so angry at Max for dying, but she knows she needs to figure out what is keeping her fearful of leaving the safe space of her grief.

Juanita suggests, "Karla, there are some indications that the unexpected and untimely loss of your son has actually traumatized you, and this trauma may be the strongest force that is keeping you from escaping your 'grief bunker.' Because of that, I would like to get your thoughts on incorporating trauma work into the grief work that you shared you wanted to begin. What do you think?"

Karla nods and agrees. "I do feel traumatized, and I agree that that's probably why I feel so stuck. I don't know how to begin to deal with the loss."

During this session, Juanita introduces a breath-work exercise that she explains to Karla might be effective in helping her stay present and calm when thoughts of her son's accident overtake her. Juanita shares the following instructions for breathing retraining (Back et al., 2014).

"First, get into a comfortable position and let your eyes close.

"Now, breathe in through your nose the way you always do, but this time, hold the breath for three seconds.

"Now, after you count to three, slowly exhale through your mouth. Let the air move slowly out of your lungs. As you exhale slowly, you might want to

say a mantra to yourself. What do you need to remind yourself? Maybe say, 'calm,' or 'present,' or even 'breathe.'"

As Karla begins to practice the exercise in session, she shares that she is feeling much more focused and actually beginning to feel that there is some hope she could control her mind enough to keep it centered on the present, not jumping around without focus. Juanita shares that by practicing this breathing exercise a few times a week, for five to ten minutes at a time, Karla will likely begin to utilize this method of coping naturally.

Juanita continues to follow the protocol outline and, over the course of the next few weeks, helps Karla work through painful, trauma-related memories of her son's death as well as venture into other trauma-related spaces emotionally and physically. In vivo exposure prepares Karla to pick up, hold, and open the envelope containing her son's college diploma that had arrived in the mail two weeks after Max died. Karla associates her son's college education with the job that Max lost his life pursuing. By working through this traumatic association, Karla becomes increasingly able to let in happy memories of Max's experiences at his college.

Juanita encourages Karla to choose a memory of an exchange between Max and herself as a focal point for an imaginal conversation. Karla describes the night that Max practically glowed as he told Karla and his father about the job offer in California. Karla shares that she had been unable to share his joy and had tried to talk him out of accepting the job because it was a thousand miles away. Karla weeps as she recounts this memory.

Juanita gently prompts, "Describe where you are, who is there, and what you see."

After Karla describes the room, and where she and her husband and son were sitting, she remembers, "And Max was fiddling with his car keys, tossing them between his hands. It annoys me and his dad does it too. I am trying to convince him to stay close to home. I laid out my own fears and put them all on him. I'm doing what I promised I would never do—try to make him feel guilty about his choices, growing up, whatever. And he worked so hard for his degree and the job was amazing. I'm being selfish and I even realize that as I'm trying to convince him to do what I want him to do."

"You're conflicted and that can be unsettling and upsetting. You are proud of Max and his success, but you worry about him too. I want to invite you to share this, here and now, out loud. Imagine that Max is here beside you. What do you need to share with Max?"

Karla takes a couple of deep breaths and begins. "Max, you are a shining star for me and so many others. You light up the room and others' hearts when you show up in our lives. I treasure you and celebrate you like the gift to life that you really are. I am always amazed that your dad and I could create a creature as special as you are to so many. So smart, so funny, so eager to jump into life head-on. When you were just three years old, you scared us all to death when you jumped into the swimming pool at your uncle's house. You popped right up before anyone could even jump in to rescue you, and you dog-paddled to the ladder giggling all the way. Nothing's ever been too scary or too risky for you!"

"Karla, you're showing such courage . . ."

"And, Max, you're just sitting there, smiling at us, and tossing your keys back and forth. You've always just jumped into things, and I worry that this new job and the move so far away might be the first time that my worries are warranted. I want to grab those keys out of your hands and ground you right now. I was terrified that day when you were three, and I feel that same fear now. I'm scared for you, Max, and even though I know I can't keep you a child forever, I just don't feel ready to let you go yet either."

"Karla, what might Max say in response to your sharing?"

"He'd probably say something like, 'Mom, don't you know it's hard on me too? You and dad have always been my home team, and it's because of how safe you make me feel that I feel I can take risks. You're always there for me, and I know that. But I can't hide from life, and you raised me to follow my dreams. I'm not leaving to get away from home, or you or Dad. I'm not 'leaving.' I'm 'heading' someplace. That's a big difference, Mom."

Karla is choking up, and Juanita supports her by saying, "Juanita, you're so strong. Just take your time, catch your breath. There's no hurry."

"Max was our go-getter, and we encouraged him to set high goals and follow his dreams. That's what he was doing when he died. He was so strong, and nothing I could have said or done was going to keep him from 'heading into life.' Even though his life ended so unfairly, so much sooner than it should have, Max knew where he was heading and his dad and I loved his spirit and were always there for him. I couldn't keep Max from living his life, and I couldn't keep him protected from life either."

Juanita responds, "It sounds like you're able to appreciate the wonderful relationship that you and your son shared. You're acknowledging the courage that he had and the role that you played in making it safe for him to be bold and set high goals for himself."

Karla continues to process the memories, her loss, and the experience of therapy throughout the final sessions. Juanita notes, "You've been brave, Karla, here with me over the past few months. I can see how you would have inspired your son in so many different ways. Your relationship was special."

"Yes," Karla agrees, "he was such a special person, and I am so proud to have raised a man like he had become. I wonder if there's a way that I could somehow honor the memory of him that would help others reach their own goals. Maybe a scholarship? Or a grant program for college students for books or transportation or something like that?"

Juanita and Karla discuss possibilities for a memorial to honor Max, and as they wind down the session, Karla shares, "Juanita, I was afraid at first that your office was going to become a physical 'grief bunker' for me where I would get stuck in my grief because it would be a place where I was expected to focus on it. Yet what we really did was focus on the relationship and my experiences with Max, not just his death, but his life and his continued influence on others. If it weren't such a bad play on words, I'd say this place was a 'grief buster,' not a 'grief bunker.' Well, I said it anyway, and I can just imagine Max hearing me and pulling a silly face and saying, 'Mommmmm!'"

QUESTIONS FOR REFLECTION

1. What are your personal experiences with loss? How might these influence your counseling work with bereaved clients?
2. What are your own cultural beliefs about death and dying? Where did you learn them? Have any of them ever been challenged by your experiences?
3. What are your positions on issues such as palliative care? Living wills? Assisted suicide? What are some of the issues that clients may need to address related to these issues?

REFERENCES

Asukai, N., Tsuruta, N., & Saito, A. (2011). Pilot study on traumatic grief treatment program for Japanese women bereaved by violent death. *Journal of Traumatic Stress, 24*, 470–73. doi:10.1002/jts.20662

Back, S. E., Foa, E. B., Killeen, T. K., Mills, K. L., Teesson, M., Cotton, B. D., . . . Brady, K. T. (2014). *Concurrent treatment of PTSD and substance use disorders using prolonged exposure (COPE): Patient workbook*. New York, NY: Oxford University Press.

Bonanno, G. A., Wortman, C. B., Lehman, D. R., Tweed, R. G., Haring, M., Sonnega, J., . . . Nesse, R. M. (2002). Resilience to loss and chronic grief: A prospective study from preloss to 18-months postloss. *Journal of Personality and Social Psychology, 83*(5), 1150–64.

Centers for Disease Control and Prevention. (2018). CDC WONDER: About natality, 2007–2018. Retrieved from http://wonder.cdc.gov/natality-current.html

Dahdah, D. F., Rego, F., Joaquim, R. H. V. T., Bombarda, T. B., & Nunes, R. (2019). Daily life and maternal mourning: A pilot study. *Death Studies, 43*(5), 292–300. doi:10.1080/07481187.2018.1458762

Dodd, A., Guerin, S., Delaney, S., & Dodd, P. (2019). Psychiatrists', psychologists' and counselors' attitudes regarding complicated grief. *Journal of Affective Disorders, 256*, 358–63.

Flesner, J. M. (2013). A shift in the conceptual understanding of grief: Using meaning oriented therapies with bereaved clients. *Ideas and Research You Can Use: VISTAS, 2013*, article 25. Retrieved from https://www.counseling.org/docs/default-source/vistas/a-shift-in-the-conceptual-understanding-of-grief---using-meaning-oriented-therapies-with-bereaved-clients
.pdf?sfvrsn=4acab18c_12

Pohlkamp, L., Kreicbergs, U., & Sveen, J. (2019). Bereaved mothers' and fathers' prolonged grief and psychological health 1 to 5 years after loss: A nationwide study. *Psycho-Oncology, 28*(7), 1530–36. doi:10.1002/pon.5112

Puigarnau, A. P., & Morales, A. C. (2019). Unfolding meaning from memories: An integrative meaning reconstruction method for counseling the bereaved. *Illness, Crisis, & Loss, 27*(3), 209–25.

Raitio, K., Kaunonen, M., & Aho, A. L. (2015). Evaluating a bereavement follow-up intervention for grieving mothers after the death of a child. *Scandinavian Journal of Caring Sciences, 29*(3), 510–20. doi:10.1111/scs.12183

Rostila, M., Maki, N., & Martikainen, P. (2018). Does the death of a child influence parental use of psychotropic medication? A follow-up register study from Finland. *PLOS ONE 13*(5), e0195500. doi:10.1371/journal.pone.0195500

Rostila, M., Saarela, J., & Kawachi, I. (2012). Mortality in parents following the death of a child: A nationwide follow-up study from Sweden. *Journal of Epidemiology & Community Health, 66*(10), 927–33. doi:10.1136/jech-2011-200339

Sanders, C., (1980). A comparison of adult bereavement in the death of a spouse, child, and parent. *Omega, 10*, 303–22.

Wijngaards-de Meij, L., Stroebe, M., Stroebe, W., Schut, H., Van de Bout, J., Van der Heijden, P., & Dijkstra, I. (2008). The impact of circumstances surrounding the death of a child on parents' grief. *Death Studies, 21*, 237–52.

Wittouck, C., Autreve, S. F., Jaegere, E. D., Portzky, G., & van Herringen, K. (2011). The prevention and treatment of complicated grief: A meta-analysis. *Clinical Psychology Review, 31*, 68–78.

Index

About the Editors

Suzanne Degges-White, PhD, is a professor and chair of the Department of Counseling and Higher Education at Northern Illinois University. She is also a licensed counselor with expertise in counseling adults over the lifespan, especially women in transitions. She has written multiple books on relationships, including friendships and family relationships. Dr. Degges-White is an invited blogger for *Psychology Today* and is a nationally consulted expert on women's friendships and relationships.

Marcela Kepic, PhD, is an associate professor in the Department of Disability and Psychological Studies at the University of Arizona. She is also a licensed professional counselor with expertise in counseling couples and adults over the lifespan. As an approved clinical supervisor, she mentors and supervises students, counselors, and future professionals. Dr. Kepic contributes to peer-reviewed publications and books and presents at national, regional, and state conferences.

Wendy Killam, PhD, is a professor and coordinator of the Counseling and Student Affairs in Higher Education Program in the Department of Human Services at Stephen F. Austin State University in Nacogdoches, Texas. She is also a licensed counselor with experience in counseling adults across the lifespan. She is a certified rehabilitation counselor and enjoys working with college students. Dr. Killam has written peer-reviewed publications and books in the field of counseling and student affairs.

List of Contributors

Rachel Brandoff, PhD, ATR-BC, ATCS, LCAT, is an assistant professor in the Community and Trauma Counseling Program and coordinator of the art therapy specialization at Thomas Jefferson University in Philadelphia, PA.

Bonnie Cardillo, BS, is a master's student in the Department of Counseling and Marital Family Therapy at the University of San Diego in San Diego, CA.

Yuleinys A. Castillo, PhD, LPC, CRC, is an assistant professor in the Department of Counselor Education and Rehabilitation at California State University in Fresno, CA.

Adrienne N. Erby, PhD, LPC, NCC, is an assistant professor in the Department of Counseling and Higher Education at Ohio University in Athens, OH.

Ana Ulloa Estrada, PhD, is an associate professor in the Department of Counseling and Marital and Family Therapy at the University of San Diego in San Diego, CA.

Katherine M. Hermann-Turner, PhD, PLPC, NCC, is an associate professor in the Department of Counselor Education at the University of Louisiana at Lafayette in Lafayette, LA.

Donna M. Gibson, PhD, NCC, LPC, is a professor of counselor education in the Department of Counseling and Special Education at Virginia Commonwealth University in Richmond, VA.

Dana T. Isawi, PhD, LPC, NCC, is an assistant professor in the Department of Counseling and Higher Education at Northern Illinois University in DeKalb, IL.

Rebecca Meeks is a master's student in the Department of Counseling and Marital and Family Therapy at the University of San Diego in San Diego, CA.

Nina Mendez, PhD, is an assistant professor in the Department of Psychology at LaSalle University in Pittsburgh, PA.

Elizabeth R. O'Brien, PhD, LPC-MHSP, is a UC Foundation Professor and codirector of the School of Professional Studies in the College of Health, Education and Professional Studies at the University of Tennessee at Chattanooga in Chattanooga, TN.

Lucy Parker, PhD, is an assistant professor in the Department of Psychology at LaSalle University in Pittsburgh, PA.

Anne Shragal, MA, LCPC, PEL:SC, is a doctoral student in the Department of Counseling and Higher Education at Northern Illinois University in DeKalb, IL.

Jessica Shull is a master's student in the Department of Counseling and Marital and Family Therapy at the University of San Diego in San Diego, CA.

Kim M. Tassinari, PhD, LPC, NCC, is an assistant professor of counselor education at Western Connecticut State University in Danbury, CT.

Suzanna Wise, EdS, LPC(IL), NCC, is a full-time faculty member in the Clinical Mental Health Counseling Program at Valparaiso University in Valparaiso, IN.

Elisa M. Woodruff, ABD, MS Ed, LPC, NCC, is an assistant professor in the Clinical Mental Health Counseling Program at Buena Vista University in Storm Lake, IA.

www.ingramcontent.com/pod-product-compliance
Ingram Content Group UK Ltd.
Pitfield, Milton Keynes, MK11 3LW, UK
UKHW021905150926
475560UK00003B/195